Mimi Sheraton's

Favorite New York Restaurants

by Mimi Sheraton

A Fireside Book
Published by
SIMON & SCHUSTER, Inc. • NEW YORK

Copyright © 1986 by Mimi Sheraton
All rights reserved
including the right of reproduction
in whole or in part in any form
A Fireside Book
Published by Simon & Schuster, Inc.
Simon & Schuster Building
Rockefeller Center
1230 Avenue of the Americas
New York, New York 10020

Fireside and colophon are registered trademarks of
Simon & Schuster, Inc.
Designed by Irving Perkins Associates, Inc.
Manufactured in the United States of America
10 9 8 7 6 5 4 3 2 1
Library of Congress Cataloging in Publication Data
Sheraton, Mimi.
    Mimi Sheraton's favorite New York restaurants.

    Includes index.
    1. Restaurants, lunch rooms, etc.—New York (N.Y.)—
Directories.   I. Title.   II. Title: Favorite New York restaurants.
TX907.S457   1986   647'.95747'025   86–17798
ISBN: 0-671-53202-2

Contents

Acknowledgments

Although I do all the eating and all the writing, I have not done this book alone, and there are a number of people who deserve heartfelt thanks. First, there is my husband, Richard Falcone, who is the loyalest of eaters, even when he would rather be home with a bowl of pasta in front of the television set. Our son, Marc, is another Green Beret among eaters. But there are also many others, good and loyal friends who went with me to any restaurants I chose and ordered the food I wanted to try, all way above and beyond the call of friendship.

I also owe thanks to Monika Pichler, who typed this manuscript, making sense out of my errors and scrawled corrections. Susan Victor, my editor, has my gratitude for her careful attention to details and for her patience. Patience is also what everyone at Simon & Schuster exercised as I missed one deadline and then another. I hope all feel the effort was worth it, and to all I wish a never-ending bon appétit.

Introduction

"What is your favorite New York restaurant?" Not too surprisingly, that is the question I am most often asked. It is also one I find difficult to answer, because a single restaurant name is expected, and I find it almost impossible to make that choice. "Favorite restaurant for what?" is all I can counter with. For though I think the food prepared by André Soltner and his staff at Lutèce makes his the best French restaurant in the city, and I feel that French food is the world's best, there are many instances when Lutèce would not be my first choice for dinner.

Being a restaurant buff and living in New York, I favor different eating places for different moods, dishes, styles and even prices. If I feel like eating linguine with white clam sauce, or a lusty, fragrant pizza, or a red-hot Korean fish soup, or do not want to get dressed up or spend $100 a person for dinner, none of André Soltner's delectables will suffice.

And so this book is a collection of personal favorites in various categories. That the number totals 154 is a tribute to New York's culinary diversity and my own reluctance to exclude any place I really like, if only for a single dish. This book is, in fact, a strategy for eating in New York, knowing where to eat what, in which neighborhood and at what price. To make comparisons easy for the reader, I have grouped restaurants by the type of food they serve—American, French, steak and so on. That way it is easy to tell, for example, the basic differences between Lutèce, La Grenouille, Le Cygne and Le Cirque. All are top French restaurants, but they provide quite different dining experiences. If I were entertaining someone who loved glamorous, gorgeous settings, I would choose La Grenouille or Le Cygne. If it were someone who wanted to dine midst a mad social whirl, it would be Le Cirque. And if it were someone who preferred simple, countrified settings in which to appreciate magnificent food, it would be Lutèce.

Although some might expect that a book of best and favorite restaurants will include only those that are French, Italian and perhaps Chinese and Japanese, this collection ranges over a much wider variety because I find almost all cuisines enticing, and I would rather have a first-rate Korean meal than a third-rate French alternative. That is why, for example, the Tibetan Kitchen is in this book and La Côte Basque is not. The Tibetan Kitchen does what it promises to do better than La Côte Basque does, especially when one considers the telephone rudeness of the latter toward unknowns making reservations. Not every cuisine available in New York is included here because some are so badly represented, Russian and Czechoslovakian being cases in point. Several years back that would not have been true. And even with the spurt of Mexican restaurants we have had in recent years, the cooking of that country barely squeaks through to be included.

Not all favorites are equally favored, of course, hence the rating system in the book. There are even a few I like to go to for the view, the setting or the scene, and they are reviewed for that reason, along with suggestions as to the best food to eat in such surroundings, another kind of strategy. I love to sit in the grill room of "21," for example, and watch the movers and shakers, but there are only a few good dishes there and so I stick to those.

Listing favorites may seem to imply that I go to all of them all the time. Given the choice in New York, that would not be possible, and so even favorites have to be checked to see if they are still performing as I remember them. Therefore I revisited every restaurant at least once specifically for this book, more often two or three times, and in no instance was a free meal accepted. All were paid for. Obviously nothing too new can be a favorite, for consistency has to be part of the evaluation.

I am now recognized in about half the restaurants I visit. To minimize the effect of recognition I almost never make reservations in my own name. The few exceptions occur in four or five restaurants in which I might interview someone, or where my family likes to go for celebrations and we want a special table. At other times reservations are made in the names of friends we dine with, and those friends usually arrive first to see what sort of table and attention they will receive. At times friends even order appetizers before I arrive, so some food will be served before the management sees me.

"Don't you ever just have fun?" someone asked me recently, meaning didn't I ever just go announced to have a great meal. The answer to that is simple: For me the fun is in seeing what a restaurant does for unknown customers. That is the real measure of its dedication.

To anyone who is not a restaurant nut, I would suggest limiting the repertory of restaurants to about six. By becoming a regular at a few places, you will get better food, service and all-around satisfaction. Although in the best of all worlds restaurateurs would be equally nice to everyone, it is understandable that a frequent customer who spends a great deal of money will be given the preferred table and more special treatment. However, rude service and bad food for anyone are never excusable.

Anyone interested enough to buy this book must be aware

of the new restaurant fever that has gripped New York in the past two or three years. On the surface it might seem to be a boon. Actually, I regard very few of the new restaurants as being in any way serious, and very few are good. Nor is the subject food. Rather it is the scene, the living theater that is a restaurant and food is merely a prop. What too many critics regard as "interesting" or "brave" is merely the immaturity of chefs who feel that anything they do should be taken seriously. I find it impossible to admire a bad dish simply because it is a brave effort. If a chef served garlic-flavored ice cream topped with ketchup, chocolate and capers, would that be brave or disgusting? Or, God forbid, "interesting"? Food writers who award premature kudos to chefs-in-training have a lot to answer for in the decline of cooking all over the country. It's too bad they cannot declare a young talent as promising, without having to state that he or she has arrived. Perhaps the hunger for superstars is greater than that for good food.

Despite such depressing recent developments, New York remains the best and most exciting city for food in this country. We have heard much about California of late as usurping this culinary honor, but New Yorkers can rest easy. True, there is a lot of good food in Los Angeles and San Francisco, but if one goes only to the "in" places, there is bound to be an overwhelming sense of déjà vu, for all are virtually alike in menu and execution of dishes. What is lacking there that New York has in abundance is a treasury of older chefs experienced in many ethnic cuisines so we can eat the new or old at will and retain gastronomic perspective. I hope this book does the city justice and is a dependable guide through the maze of temptations it offers.

A Guide to This Guide

Although each review in this book is self-explanatory, some elaboration is necessary on the symbols used for ratings and for the precise meaning of price ranges. Knowing what to expect about a few other details on dining out should also help make those experiences more rewarding.

Ratings

Most restaurants in this book are at the very least good, meaning they have good food. Even so, I have degrees of preferences among them. Another important consideration in arriving at these ratings is price; I expect more and give less margin for error in an expensive restaurant than in one that is moderately or low priced. Food counts for about 75 percent of my ratings, with atmosphere and service making up the rest. But at times even the most exquisite food can be overshadowed by downright rude and inept service. And as much as I like a beautiful setting, it matters least to me, as long as the dining room is clean and pleasant. Dirty restaurants are not reviewed *if* I know they are dirty.

What the stars say:

★★★★ The Best of the Best
★★★ Consistently Excellent
★★Very Good
★ Good

Money Matters, and How

Because prices change (rise) so rapidly, it seemed best to indicate a relative range with the following meanings. Prices are food for one person at dinner, before tax, tip, and wine or liquor are added.

> EXPENSIVE— More than $50
> MODERATELY EXPENSIVE— $35 to $49
> MODERATE— $20 to $34
> INEXPENSIVE— Less than $20

Tipping is, of course, optional, and if more people would leave nothing when service is poor, there would be marked improvement rapidly. In general, tips should run between 15 and 20 percent of the check, before the tax. The higher amount is in order when everything has been perfect and you're feeling generous and in expensive, formal restaurants where there are both a captain and a waiter. The division there is roughly one-third of the check to the captain, two-thirds to the waiter. It is necessary to tip the maitre d' only if he has done something extraordinary or if you are a regular. An easy rule of thumb for most tipping is to double the city sales tax—8¼ percent—meaning that you leave 16½ percent, enough in most cases.

Always scrutinize your check to be sure you are not being overcharged in one way or another—by paying more for something than its menu price, by being charged for something you did not have, or by incorrect addition. To avoid unpleasant surprises, always ask the prices of dishes that are not on the menu but that the captain or waiter describes. Such specials usually cost more than most things on the menu. Restaurants should be required by law to have printed (if only typed or handwritten) lists of specials with prices. Customers have only themselves to blame for this annoying practice, because most are too embarrassed to ask.

Credit Cards

Do not assume all restaurants take all credit cards. Even the information on those cards that is printed in this book can change. Unless you have all cards or enough cash to pay the check, call and ask what cards are accepted. Restaurants should say which, if any, credit cards they accept when customers call for reservations, but few do.

The key to credit card initials in this book is as follows: AE—American Express; CB—Carte Blanche; D—Diners Club; MC—Master Card; V—Visa.

Dress Codes

As with credit cards, when in doubt, call and ask about any required dress. A restaurateur has the right to set any policy he or she wants to as long as it is applied to everyone. You have the right to go elsewhere. If a restaurant has a dress code, it is noted in these reviews.

Smoking

If cigars, pipes or any smoking bother you, inquire before you go if there is any restriction on such practices. It is still too soon to assume every restaurant bars cigars and pipe smoking or restricts smokers to a particular area. Special smoking regulations are noted in those reviews.

Favorite Meals and Favorite Dishes

Knowing which dishes a restaurant does well is one thing. Knowing how to combine them into a harmonious meal is quite another, especially when one is in an unfamiliar restaurant and feels pressured by an impatient captain or waiter. It seemed helpful, therefore, to include my favorite meals in the various restaurants reviewed.

Because menus change, recommended dishes may not always be available. Obviously, I can report only on those I have tried, but even if some are unavailable, the reader will have a hint as to what sort of things the kitchen does best.

Wine and Liquor

Unless otherwise stated, assume that full liquor service is available. Wine and beer only or bring-your-own-bottle policies are indicated in individual reviews. Remember that you usually cannot take your own wine to a place with a liquor license.

Reservations

Except where they are not accepted reservations should be made. Where it is stated that they are needed well in advance, make them two to four weeks ahead.

Complaints

Food that is not what you want it to be should be quietly, politely but firmly returned. If service is poor, a manager or owner should be told. And if food or service is not as described in this book, please let me know for future editions. Address such complaints, or any comments, to me in care of Simon & Schuster.

Restaurant Index

★★★★

Ratings

Four Stars
Arcadia, 38
Kitcho, 232
Lutèce, 145

Three Stars
The Captain's Table, 277
Carnegie Delicatessen &
   Restaurant, 245
Carolina, 45
Cent' Anni, 188
Chanterelle, 130
Le Cirque, 132
The Coach House, 48
Le Cygne, 136
La Gauloise, 139
Georgine Carmella, 198
La Grenouille, 142
Hatsuhana, 240
Huberts, 53
Lusardi's, 203
Il Nido, 209
Palm, 295
Pamir, 35
Pesca, 284
Petrossian, 85
Rao's, 217
Sammy's Famous Roumanian
   Restaurant, 248
Siu Lam Kung, 106
Tanjore, 182
Trastevere Ristorante, 223
La Tulipe, 157

Two Stars
The Ballroom, 288
The Beach House, 261

Le Bistro, 124
Cabana Carioca, 76
Café des Artistes, 317
Café de Bruxelles, 71
Café Luxembourg, 43
Chalet Suisse, 299
Chikubu, 228
Christ Cella, 293
Csárda, 165
Darbar, 174
Dardanelles East Ararat, 268
Da Silvano, 191
Ennio & Michael, 193
Felidia, 195
The Four Seasons, 320
Grove Street Café, 51
Hwa Yuan Szechuan Inn, 94
Jane Street Seafood Café, 279
Lattanzi, 200
Odeon, 58
Omen, 234
Oyster Bar & Restaurant, 282
Positano, 214
Quatorze, 151
Raga, 179
La Ripaille, 153
The Ritz Café, 61
Roxanne's, 325
Saigon Restaurant, 312
Say Eng Look, 98
Seryna, 236
Shun Lee Palace, 100
Shun Lee (West), 103
Siam Grill, 303
Siam Inn, 305
Sistina, 221
Takesushi, 242

17

Type of Food

20

Location

23

Open Late
(after theater)

25

Open Twenty-Four Hours

Carnegie Delicatessen &
  Restaurant (Well,
  practically. It closes only
  from 4:00 to 6:30 A.M.),
  245

Gray's Papaya, 90
Kiev Luncheonette, 83

Open Sunday

Outdoor Dining

Breakfast and Brunch

Facilities for Private Parties

Restaurant
Reviews

★★★★

Afghan

PAMIR

1437 Second Avenue, between 74th and 75th Streets.
Telephone: 734-3791.

Favorite meal:
SHARED BY TWO
Scallion dumplings (aushak) and meat-filled crisp pastry (sambosa goushti)
Grilled ground beef on skewers (kofta kebob)
Spiced spinach (sabsi chalawt)
Pumpkin with yogurt (burancee kady)
Afgan bread (naan)
Baklava (baghlawa)
Afghan tea

OTHER FAVORITE DISHES: All appetizers; all palaws, lamb in spinach sauce (sabsichalaw); chicken, lamb and ground spiced lamb kebobs (shish kebob), eggplant, spinach and pumpkin side dishes.

SETTING: Intimate, exotic and informal; seating is cramped in some areas.

SERVICE: Generally considerate and efficient but can be perfunctory at busiest times.

DRESS CODE: None.

SMOKING REGULATIONS: No special policy.

FACILITIES FOR PRIVATE PARTIES: None.

HOURS: Dinner, Tuesday through Sunday, 5:30 to 11 P.M. Closed Monday.

RESERVATIONS: Recommended.

PRICES: Moderate.

CREDIT CARDS: MC, V.

If I were to become a secret agent, Pamir would surely be one of my favorite meeting places. Everything about this small, dimly lit and exotic spot suggests romance and international intrigue. Oriental rugs on the wall, strange musical instruments, glints of copper in the bar area and the wildly handsome, swarthy staff members add to the effect. If the somewhat cramped quarters makes it difficult to hold a truly secret conversation, at least I would eat well while conspiring.

Although somewhat lustier and more rustic, the food of Afghanistan resembles that of the Middle East, modified by Indo-Persian spicing. In fact, because it was on the path of Mogul warriors who swept down into India, Afghanistan's cooking, it is believed, found its way into the Indian cuisine, most especially with the tandoor-oven method of roasting.

When Pamir opened five years ago, a block south of its present site, the staff was naively gracious and genuinely concerned that customers understand and like their food. Success (even with reservations there can be a line at the door) has brought more self-assurance and professionalism, a trade-off perhaps for the sometimes pushy and distracted service when there is a lineup for tables.

What customers gladly wait for is moderately priced food that is deeply satisfying, with its savory meat and yogurt sauces, its grilled meats and seductive palaw stews on rice, and palate-tingling combinations of mint and chili peppers, cinnamon and pepper, scallions and coriander. Also beguiling is the flat, crisp yeast bread, Afghan naan, flecked with toasted black onion seeds, although on a recent visit those seeds were too sparsely distributed. Soup is the only course to skip, not because the two noodle, meat and vegetable combinations are not well prepared, but because they are served tepid and so become greasy.

Better to start with an assortment of appetizers, sharing them among two to four diners. Included in such are the sambosa goushti, pastry half circles crisply fried and filled with mashed chick-peas and ground beef; bulanee gandana, scallion-stuffed crisp pancakes with a cloudlet of yogurt on top; bulanee kachalou, turnovers with an aromatic beef and potato filling; and aushak, flat dumplings also with scallions, enriched by a minty meat and yogurt dressing.

All kebobs have improved since the early days of Pamir and are now properly juicy and tender. This includes the chunks of chicken (kebob-e-murgh), the nuggets of lamb (shish kebob) and the ground, spiced lamb and beef kofta kebobs. It is a good idea to combine these simple unsauced kebobs with one of the palaws, such as the quabilli, with its gilding of saffron, carrot and orange-rind slivers, or the sabsi chalaw, lamb swathed in a garlic- and onion-accented spinach sauce. The vegetable side

36

dishes of spinach, eggplant and pumpkin can also be ordered in large portions for a completely vegetarian meal.

Baghlawa is the only acceptable dessert and here comes as a big, chunky wedge, heavy with walnuts and a clear syrup. Spiced Afghan tea is a soothing windup. There is full bar service, but beer is the drink best suited to the food.

American–New, Traditional and Regional

Trying to separate the new from the traditional and the regional in American cooking is one of the more difficult and futile tasks facing the writer of a restaurant guidebook. The true name for most of this food should be "new Continental" anyway, for almost all the menus in these so-called new American restaurants owe much to French or Italian kitchens, and increasingly to those of China, Japan and Southeast Asia. That kind of mix, leading to a whole new style, is uniquely American, for combining diverse influences has always marked the development of this country's cooking, thus enriching it.

America, *see* The View, the Setting and the Scene

ARCADIA

21 East 62nd Street, between Fifth and Madison Avenues.
Telephone: 223-2900

Favorite meals:
LUNCH
Country green salad
Grilled duck sausages with pumpkin gratin and black pepper sauce
Chocolate bread pudding with brandy custard sauce
OR
DINNER
Corn cakes with crème fraîche and caviars
Quail with beet sauce, kale and fresh orange
Chestnut ice cream with brandy pecan brittle and chocolate sauce
OR

DINNER
Warm loin of rabbit salad with coriander vinaigrette
Chimney-smoked lobster with tarragon butter and celery root cakes
Lemon curd mousse with fresh fruit

OTHER FAVORITE DISHES: Buckwheat pasta with goat cheese and prosciutto; fusilli with salmon and dill cream; wild mushroom tart with endive and greens; pumpkin pasta with country ham; smoked fish salad with watercress and clementine vinaigrette; lobster bisque; leeks in puff pastry with onion marmalade and chive butter; roast salmon stuffed with onions, Jerusalem artichokes and dill; soft-shell crabs; grilled duck breast with sweet potato and apple gratin; roast lamb with tomato-zucchini casserole and garlic potatoes; roast quail with kasha and savoy cabbage; warm pear charlotte with black currant sauce; warm pecan tart with praline whipped cream; apple timbale with caramel sauce.

SETTING: Sylvan, seasonal mural creates a peaceful and graceful backdrop for this small, posh dining room; peacefulness is badly compromised by tables too closely set and madhouse bar scene.

SERVICE: Attentive, polite and efficient if a bit self-consciously preppie.

DRESS CODE: Jacket and tie required for men.

SMOKING REGULATIONS: No cigars or pipes are permitted.

FACILITIES FOR PRIVATE PARTIES: None.

HOURS: Lunch, Monday through Friday, noon to 2:30 P.M.; dinner, Monday through Saturday, 6 to 10:30 P.M. Closed Sunday and major holidays.

RESERVATIONS: Necessary well in advance, but unknowns have slim chance of getting 1 o'clock lunch or 7 to 8:30 dinner reservations.

PRICES: Expensive.

CREDIT CARDS: AE, MC, V.

For my money, the two best practitioners of new American cooking in the country are John Sedlar of St. Estèphe in Manhattan Beach, California, and Anne Rosenzweig of Arcadia in New York. Both inventive yet solidly grounded in traditional cooking techniques, they do the very best kind of innovations by developing dishes that at once surprise and impart a sense of comfortable recognition in flavor combinations. Some chefs apparently think surprise is enough and that "Wow, how did he ever think of this?" is the prize. Rather, the surprise should be expressed more as "Of course! How come no one has ever done this before?" Cooking is, after all, different from painting or composing. A nice try that is an artistic failure is one thing if you are looking at or listening to a brave effort, but food has to be swallowed and shock beyond a frame of reference had better be extraordinary. That is true of the work of both these young chefs, and in New York that makes Arcadia the mecca for anyone who loves good food, never mind the labels.

What it is not a mecca for is peacefulness and comfort, about which more later, but no cooking less exceptional could draw me to such a hectic scene. I first became a Rosenzweig fan unknowingly, when she was the anonymous brunch and pastry chef at Vanessa in Greenwich Village. Now in partnership with Ken Aretsky, who formerly operated Oren & Aretsky, Anne Rosenzweig has developed a repertory of brilliant and refined creations using American ingredients and regional expressions in a very European way.

The setting for this gastronomic triumph is as engaging as the food, a small, slim supper club of a room, with mauves and beiges set against an around-the-room mural by Paul Davis, which has the four seasons evolving in a sort of stylized impressionist shimmer. Although closely set, banquette tables are comfortable, much more so than the line of deuces that runs down the center of the room. The noise level is high except for larger corner banquettes, but it is still possible to have a conversation without emerging hoarse.

There is a stylish bar at the entrance, somewhat in the Parisian-bistro mode in decor, but what could be a pleasant place for an aperitif is turned into a nightmare every evening from about 8 on as the crowd stands three to four deep so that the entrance becomes impassable, and at the same time people eat, or try to, at the few tables also in that room. Aretsky claims there is nothing he can do about that situation, but of course there is, and someone as experienced as he should know how to handle it. Why anyone would accept a table in that area is beyond me.

The saving grace is that there seems to be no spillover of the bar madness into the dining room. Once you have run the gauntlet and are seated, the sylvan aura of the dining room takes over; hence Arcadia deserves top rating for both the friendly, accommodating and efficient service and wonderful food. It would be only a slight exaggeration to say that I never met a Rosenzweig dish I didn't like. Her appetizers manage to combine solidity of flavor and intriguing ingredients without being overpowering, and the selection is so well balanced that those who want to eat lightly but enjoy variety can order two or three to make a complete meal. From the verdant simplicity of her impeccable country salad of mixed greens to the lusty pastas (buckwheat with country ham, sweet potato, kale and onion marmalade or the corkscrew fusilli with salmon and dill

40

cream), and including such subtle delicacies as the wild mushroom tart with endive and greens, Anne Rosenzweig maintains the balance of flavors and textures and manages to juxtapose mutually enhancing ingredients. Perhaps the true appetizer triumph is the combination of small, slim corn pancakes mellowed with crème fraîche and a combination of caviars, one being the so-called golden whitefish, which reads better than it tastes, and the richer, more authoritative osetra. Duck sausage, if the least bit dry, has nevertheless an engaging, lightly spiced flavor, and the traditional accompaniment of chestnuts and apples, or the more innovative gratin of pumpkin and a black pepper sauce, adds the right moist counterpoints. Smoked fish salad on greens glossed with clementine vinaigrette, and herbed goat cheese served warm are gently satisfying, and her now classic poached leeks packeted in high and handsome puff pastry set on a bittersweet onion marmalade and further accented by chive butter is a lesson in the variations on the onion family and how neatly a knowing hand can contrast them.

Very few soups have been offered here, which I consider a minor shortcoming, but awhile back there was a lovely lobster bisque strewn with wisps of carrot and snappy with the true deep-sea lobster essence.

Some of the appetizers occasionally appear as main courses, among them the pastas and the duck sausage. Add to that such elegant treatments as succulent quail improbably but delectably sauced with a cream-enhanced beet dressing, all complemented by lightly cooked kale and fresh orange to clean and separate the otherwise heavy flavors. Miraculously, the delicate quality of the quail comes through the other ingredients. Another masterpiece is the chimney-smoked lobster that gets a sprightly touch of tarragon butter and is well contrasted with fried celery root cakes.

This dedication to humbler ingredients—celery root, parsnip, rutabaga, kale and the buckwheat kasha that is another foil for quail—typifies Rosenzweig's knowing eclecticism. Roasting salmon is tricky business, that heating method being so potentially drying, but the salmon done that way here, after being stuffed with a sensuous mix of onions, Jerusalem artichokes and dill, remains fresh and moist. Grilled duck breast with a sweet potato and apple gratin, roast lamb with garlic potatoes and a tomato-zucchini casserole, and medallions of venison with wild rice blinis are just a few of the other culinary wonders I have enjoyed at Arcadia. Add the pretty peach-colored pumpkin pasta that is the perfect mild foil for the salty tang of the country ham, a salad of warm rabbit tossed with greens and brightened by a coriander vinaigrette dressing, and several delicious chicken dishes, and you have all the reasons why I love this restaurant.

And then of course there are the desserts, the chef-owner's real calling since that is where she began. Chocolate bread pudding is little short of a miracle, the dense, intense chocolate-sauced brioche with a brandy custard sauce. Warm pecan tart with praline-flecked whipped cream and an apple timbale swimming in a lagoon of burnished caramel sauce are close runners-up. Lemon curd mousse is gently soft yet sharply pungent, and the chestnut ice cream with brandy pecan brittle and warm chocolate sauce is the kind of dessert men leave home for. Or should. I prefer the black currant sauce on the warm pear charlotte to the chocolate that sometimes appears, and the fruit tarts, most especially the raspberry and the apple and quince, could not be improved upon.

In fact, I have had only one dish at Arcadia that I think is basically ill conceived, and it is a best-selling luncheon choice, the lobster club sandwich. As appetizing as the combination of lobster, tomato, bacon and lettuce may sound, layering it all between three pieces of toast makes it, first of all, impossible to pick up and eat as a sandwich. The toast breaks and one struggles through, biting now, cutting with a knife and fork then, and finally winding up with what looks like a messy leftover salad. But even if the sandwich works, the flavors of all that toast, bacon and other ingredients muffle the delicacy of the lobster.

Ken Aretsky should solve that barroom crush, and it could be done by restricting use of the bar to those eating at the restaurant, and then by more carefully timing the booking. Another improvement would be in the manner of the telephone voice-without-a-smile that takes reservations. It tends to be snippy and impatient, and there is an annoying reluctance to give peak-hours to unknowns. Arcadia seems to be heading toward the seatings schedule known as too early or too late.

There is an excellent, careful selection of California and French wines in a good range of prices, which is perhaps why members of the city's wine trade congregate here. Just a few prices seem out of line, most especially a half bottle of California Chardonnay Far Niente. At $14, it is hardly far niente.

Café des Artistes, *see* The View, the Setting and the Scene

CAFÉ LUXEMBOURG

200 West 70th Street, between West End and Amsterdam
Avenues.
Telephone: 873-7411.

Favorite meals:
Cream of mussel soup with saffron
Crisp roasted duck with ginger baked pear
Lemon tart
OR
Country salad with chicory, Roquefort cheese, garlic crou-
tons and bacon
Medallions of lotte with green peppercorn sauce and grilled
leeks
Crème brûlée

OTHER FAVORITE DISHES: Pasta of the day, such as fettuccine
or tortellini with cream and sausage or ham, or with mushrooms and leeks; chicken liver terrine; grilled shrimp with
mustard herb butter or seafood sauce; baked oysters; duck
salad on greens; grilled fillet of salmon; cassoulet of pork,
duck confit, garlic sausage and white beans (winter); roast
leg of lamb; calves' liver with shallots or nuts (but not with
Madeira and currants); roast chicken; maple pecan tart.

SETTING: Casual, crowded and noisy café, with white tile walls
that suggest a 1920s public bath, but nonetheless pleasant.

SERVICE: Fast-then-slow pace is distracting; so is habit of asking guests to wait at bar even when tables are empty; otherwise staff is good natured and friendly.

DRESS CODE: None.

SMOKING REGULATIONS: No cigars or pipes are permitted.

FACILITIES FOR PRIVATE PARTIES: None.

HOURS: Dinner, Monday through Thursday, 5:30 P.M. to 12:30
A.M.; Friday, 5:30 P.M. to 1:30 A.M.; Saturday, 6 P.M. to 1:30
A.M.; Sunday, 6 P.M. to 12:30 A.M.; brunch, Saturday, noon to
3 P.M.; Sunday, 11 A.M. to 3 P.M.

RESERVATIONS: Necessary, especially before and after Lincoln
Center events.

PRICES: Moderate.

CREDIT CARDS: AE, MC, V.

"So how come you sent me to a public bath for dinner?"
my friend and recent co-author Alan King asked after I recommended Café Luxembourg for a pre-Lincoln Center meal.

Certainly the white tile walls might suggest that setting, but I see the convivial young-spirited café-dining room more as a 1920s-inspired stylization and find it all attractive. Less attractive and off-putting is the house habit of asking all customers to wait at the bar even when empty tables are in view. Say "No, I'll wait right here [at the doorway]," and you are almost always seated immediately. If by choice, the bar is a pleasant place to wait, given the hard-boiled eggs on wire stands and the stylish, casual crowd.

Noisy and lively, the dining room does have a certain French-La Coupole kind of activity, but this kitchen, like that of the Odeon, which is under the same management, is directed by Patrick Clark, who gives a new American freshness and engaging simplicity to French, Italian and regional American fare. The staff is totally unpretentious and efficient, but apparently the kitchen cannot quite cope with peak hours, and so the service occasionally slows.

As direct as the heavy, handsome water bottles and big silver sugar bowls on the tables are the dishes featured here. Just the right amount of Roquefort cheese gentled with garlic croutons and warm bacon, all tossed with spiky chicory, make up an engaging country salad appetizer. Pastas only vaguely Italian in taste, but wholly pleasing, include a variety of fettuccine, ravioli and tortellini, forms best sauced with cream and accented by sausage, ham, mushrooms and leeks. Firm fresh shrimp lightly grilled and offset with mustard herb butter and a smooth chicken liver terrine are satisfying starters. House classics are the oysters baked with champagne cream and a coarse seafood sausage, with beurre blanc sauce on lettuce, which, like so many other dishes, reappear on the menu from time to time. I have also enjoyed a warm duck salad, which, with an appetizer pasta following it, would make a fine pre-theater meal. Saffron gilds a tantalizing cream of mussel soup, but a vegetable puree soup lacked zip.

Early on, a main course of lotte medallions sautéed in butter, then finished with leeks and a green peppercorn sauce tasted of overheated fat and was unpleasant. Now that firm, white-fleshed fish emerges more carefully executed. So does grilled fillet of salmon, its butter sauce mildly spiced with ginger. Simple main courses such as herbed roast chicken with french fries and steak frites are pleasantly in keeping with the restaurant's spirit, as is sliced leg of lamb with lentils and gratinée potatoes. Softly braised shallots are what I prefer with the fresh, pink calves' liver; the newer Madeira and currant sauce is only passable, and if the cassoulet has not been overcooked, its garlic-scented white beans and the duck confit and garlic sausage add up to sustaining winter eating. Duck, either with green peppercorns or in a slightly sweeter sauce offset by a ginger

baked pear, is always delicious. But other specials on the menu are less dependable, with creeping sweetness and undersalting being the most common flaws.

Another shortcoming is the absence of a vegetable with some dishes so that one has to order those, especially potatoes, à la carte, thereby increasing what seems like moderate main course prices.

Good desserts at Luxembourg include the fruit sherbets, the crème brûlée, the lemon tart and the flourless chocolate cake (but not the cloying ganache cake). Apple tart lacks sufficient apples, and while the dark chocolate mousse is fine, the white that goes with it was as characterless as usual.

There is an enticing brunch menu at Café Luxembourg and a prix-fixe pre-theater dinner at $19.75, which is an excellent option before attending Lincoln Center. The place is also open late enough to provide a felicitous if noisy after-theater alternative.

CAROLINA

355 West 46th Street, between Eighth and Ninth Avenues.
Telephone: 245-0058.

Favorite meals:
LUNCH
Hot smoked sweet sausage with roasted peppers, SHARED
   BY TWO
Crab cakes
Fruit crisp
OR
DINNER
Corn chowder
Brisket of beef or assorted barbecue platter
Carolina slaw
Pecan fingers dipped in chocolate sauce
OR
DINNER
Barbecue on lettuce
Red pepper shrimp
Corn pudding
Carolina mudd cake
OTHER FAVORITE DISHES: Penthouse chili, green chili soufflé,
   salmon or swordfish steak, barbecued ribs, smoked breast

45

of chicken, filet of beef with caper mayonnaise, barbecued lamb, bourbon baked ham, duck with green peppercorns, barbecue sandwich, gazpacho salad, ice cream with walnuts in maple syrup or with black currant sauce, strawberry short-cake in season.

SETTING: Urbane modern but plush bar area with comfortable seating for meals; back dining room is romantically lit and sparkling mirrors reflect palms; upstairs dining room with brick walls is handsome and stylish; noisy but convivial.

SERVICE: Excellent but tends to slow a bit before main courses and when the check is requested.

DRESS CODE: None.

SMOKING REGULATIONS: No special policy.

FACILITIES FOR PRIVATE PARTIES: Upstairs dining room accommodates between twenty and thirty-five; also outside catering.

HOURS: Lunch, Sunday through Friday, noon to 3 P.M.; dinner, seven days, 5 P.M. to midnight. Closed most major holidays but open on Thanksgiving.

RESERVATIONS: Necessary.

PRICES: Moderate.

CREDIT CARDS: MC, V.

Few restaurants have become classics as soon after opening as did Carolina, the enchanting effort of Martin Yerdon and Eileen Weinberg, she one of the originators of the stylish and successful take-out food shop Word of Mouth. Since it opened in 1983, it has been among the rare restaurants in the Theater District worth a visit for its own sake, whether or not one is attending a performance. Basing their menu on the barbecues and seafood specialties of the South Carolina coast, and going along that coast as far as Boston, the owners blended influences and have evolved a style of cooking that is sui generis and, even more important, delicious.

There are three different atmospheres in which to have lunch or dinner, my favorite being the front room, where the handsome bar creates a club-like feeling. Although the back room is prettier, with its skylight, twinkling lights and a single palm that wall mirrors reflect as a veritable tropical forest, it is less comfortable for parties larger than four or even two. I prefer round or square tables for four or more and the added elbow room in the bar. The newer upstairs room is also a stylish and different setting, suggesting a Village brownstone floor-through, with natural brick walls, a mellow antique French screen and a certain air of privacy. It is also available for private parties and is one of the best-looking facilities for that purpose in the city.

And, of course, the food, much of which is based on the

no-nonsense smoker and mesquite-fired open hearth grill in the windowed kitchen that one passes going from entrance to back dining room. The most spectacular Carolina offerings are cooked in that smoker, most especially the huge, meaty and tender ribs and the meltingly fatty, succulent beef brisket (in the words of Leo Steiner of the Carnegie Deli, "If they want lean, they should eat turkey!"), the sweet sausage that with its mellowing roasted peppers is a delicious appetizer, and the breast of chicken that magically never dries out. With such dishes the barbecue sauce is the only mild disappointment, it being a bit sweet and tomatoey for my taste, but not too damagingly so. Barbecue in big nicely charred chunks nestles on lettuce for another lusty first course. Hot green chilies are the surprise ingredient in a somewhat solid, sustaining cheese soufflé, and the city's best crab cakes, made here with hints of mustard and mayonnaise, are as tantalizing a main course as they are when an order is shared as an appetizer. Corn chowder with flecks of smoky sweet pink ham and one of the town's best chili representations are also Carolina classics.

Broiling fish and seafood over the hot grill fires is a job not easily accomplished with success as those foods dry so quickly. But here the red pepper-zapped shrimp, the swordfish and salmon emerge juicy, their own natural flavors softly enhanced by smokiness. Cold grilled filet of beef with caper-dotted mayonnaise and red onion, and a delectably meaty pink ham baked with a bourbon basting and with cherry sauce, which I prefer on the side, are as dependable as the duck with green peppercorns and the barbecued lamb, when available.

There are also enticing side dishes, some to be ordered à la carte, others served as garnishes. One way or another, get the custardy corn pudding and the Carolina slaw and go easy on the marvelous butter and corn breads and biscuits in the basket, or you'll regret it when it is time for dessert. Imagine not being able to indulge in the earth-rich Carolina mudd cake, the crunchy pecan fingers dipped in bittersweet chocolate sauce or the ice cream with walnuts in maple syrup or with black currant sauce. For gentler palates there is fruit crisp in the best American tearoom tradition and, in the right season, old-fashioned biscuit strawberry shortcake, which is a meal in itself.

In fact, the single most consistent flaw at Carolina is that every dish is a meal in itself (the combined barbecue platter is an exception; it is three meals in itself). Even the light fish dishes seem heavy because of flavor more than substance. Somehow smoke and a similar spicing format makes for less contrast on the menu than is needed. Also, anyone not used to true barbecue should avoid having more than one dish cooked that way as it can be difficult for a novice stomach to digest, especially if much hard liquor has been consumed at the same time. Beer is a more judicious drink than wine with this food, not that wine is hard liquor, but it seems to have more acidic overtones than beer, and besides, its flavor is knocked out by the heftiness of the food.

The staff at Carolina could not be more sincere, polite or efficient. Slowdowns before main courses appear to be a kitchen problem, and at times there is also a slowness about bringing checks, which can be unsettling before theater. It is best to ask for those checks when desserts are served. Carolina serves lunch on Sundays, which is a fine option before matinees, and it is open late enough for post-theater eating, when great hamburgers are among other offerings.

THE COACH HOUSE

110 Waverly Place, between Washington Square Park and Sixth Avenue.
Telephone: 777-0303.

Favorite meals:
  Black bean soup with Madeira
  Roast duck with quince or other fruits on the side
  Grand Marnier bavarois
  OR
  Deviled crab cake
  Boneless black pepper steak
  American pecan pie
  OR
  Sausage with lentil salad
  Whole red snapper roasted with fresh dill sauce (FOR TWO)
  Apple tart Tatin

OTHER FAVORITE DISHES: Eggplant Provençale, mushrooms à la Grecque, poached striped bass in court bouillon, roast prime ribs of beef, rack of lamb, brochette of lamb, American chicken pie, chocolate cake, dacquoise, chef's custard.

SETTING: Handsome and much like an urbane club in an old coach house with English food and hunting paintings; Hayloft room is uncomfortable.

SERVICE: Impeccable but can be overbearing to unknowns.

DRESS CODE: Jacket and tie required for men.

SMOKING REGULATIONS: No cigars or pipes are permitted; no smoking in upstairs dining room.

48

FACILITIES FOR PRIVATE PARTIES: Small upstairs room accommodates up to thirty-two.
HOURS: Dinner, Tuesday through Sunday, 5:30 to 10:30 P.M. Closed Monday, major holidays and for the month of August.
RESERVATIONS: Necessary.
PRICES: Moderate to moderately expensive.
CREDIT CARDS: AE, CB, D, MC, V.

The Coach House is a restaurant that is part of my own private Greenwich Village history. When I began going to N.Y.U. in the mid-40s, the premises was known as Helen Lane's Tearoom and even then was a sort of homey, American tradition students saved for. Shortly after I moved to the Village, Helen Lane's became The Coach House, and for years I stayed away, hearing it was expensive. Going once, I knew immediately I would try to return often and did, though for the first ten years of my association I was just another customer and not even a food writer. Throughout I had nothing but wonderful food and impeccable service, albeit the tone and style of both changed through the years.

Starting with the history of the building itself—once the coach house of the Wanamaker estates—and the character it took on as Helen Lane's, the new owner, Leon Lianides, created an American menu with wonderful fried chicken and chicken pot pie, pecan pie, cornsticks and similar fare. An informal but professional staff served the food, and gradually the place developed a combination of urbanity and authenticity. Slowly the Greek-born Lianides introduced more Continental sophistications. Brick walls were trimmed in their present deep-but-subtly-bright Victorian red, and he began to collect 19th-century English paintings of food and horse scenes. Always impeccably maintained, with simple but graceful flowers and a buffet of desserts at the entrance, The Coach House soon took on the sophistication of the Guinea Grill in London. Steak au poivre as dark and enchanting as midnight, always perfect prime ribs of beef, rack of lamb done rose-red and crusted with parsley, garlic and breadcrumbs, and a fresh bright bouillabaisse took their places on the menu. Eggplant in a garlic and tomato sauce Provençale and plump white mushrooms à la grecque, simmered in oil with oregano joined appetizers such as crab cakes based on nuggets of the whitest Florida lump crabmeat and coarse, garlicky saucisson nestled alongside a cool lentil salad. Always there was the marvel of black bean soup, a velvety puree with overtones of smoked ham, best accented by a shot of lemon juice or a trickling of wine vinegar and olive oil.

Cornsticks are still passed and are as crunchy as ever, and

49

salads add refreshment by way of their tangy vinaigrette dressing.

Two exceptional fish dishes at The Coach House are the striped bass (which never tastes of petroleum) poached in a court bouillon with slivers of fresh vegetables and the whole red snapper roasted and then glossed with fresh dill butter. Duck is parchment crisp yet moistly flavorful, but I much prefer quince to cherries as its garnish. Chicken pie has remained a fixture on the menu, but fried chicken, alas, has disappeared. There used to be the best osso buco I have ever eaten served here and that too seems to be gone, but there are still occasional surprises in what was really one of the earlier outposts of the new American cuisine. (The other was The Four Seasons.) Dishes I have never liked at The Coach House include the fresh lump crabmeat that used to be sautéed with Virginia ham (the heating made the ham unbearably salty) and veal with chestnuts so sweet they wiped out the meat's delicate flavor. Now the crabmeat is sautéed with shrimp, but I have not yet tried it that way.

If the luster is slightly dulled and the format dated since The Coach House's heyday, those flaws do not extend to desserts. The velvety chocolate cake and the chewy hazelnut-flavored dacquoise, the country's best crunchy pecan pie and the airy Grand Marnier bavarois are always perfection, as is the chef's custard, really a bread pudding, which I prefer without its raspberry sauce. Apple tart Tatin, though delicious, does not always have the right glassy caramelization, but it is properly thick with tender, buttery apples.

Just as he respects America's ingredients and its culinary heritage, so Lianides was one of the first serious purveyors of American wines, and they are as well chosen as his French bottles. Italian wines are banally represented, but perhaps they are unnecessary in this context.

Failures at The Coach House are the service and treatment of certain unknown guests, whether because of their dress or whatever. I have had reports from people I trust on the cold indifference that can greet them and the short shrift they are given. Also, the balcony Hayloft room is claustrophobic and cramped, and service up there can be perfunctory and slow, all too bad in a New York landmark that still can set an exceptional table.

The Four Seasons, *see* The View, the Setting and the Scene

GROVE STREET CAFÉ

53 Grove Street, between Bleecker Street and Seventh Avenue
South.
Telephone: 924-9501.

Favorite meals:
Sweet red pepper stuffed with eggplant, capers, onions,
olives and croutons
Roast duck with red cabbage
Walnut ice cream with bittersweet chocolate sauce
OR
Seafood sausage
Grilled filet mignon in green peppercorn sauce
Chocolate almond torte with bitter chocolate icing

OTHER FAVORITE DISHES: Timbale of scallops and spinach in
chive cream sauce, sweet red bell pepper terrine, crab or
lobster salad (summer), pasta with tomato, cream and pancetta, gravlax, grilled Norwegian salmon, calves' liver Veneziana, Cornish hen with sausage and nut stuffing, grilled
loin veal chop with basil butter, apple-raisin tart, lime mousse
with brownie, flourless chocolate roll.

SETTING: Intimate boutique restaurant with candles, flowers
and provincial fabric on walls.

SERVICE: A bit precious but well meaning, friendly and efficient.

DRESS CODE: None.

SMOKING REGULATIONS: No cigars or pipes are permitted.

FACILITIES FOR PRIVATE PARTIES: Can accommodate fifteen to
twenty-six on Sundays and Mondays when restaurant is
closed.

HOURS: Dinner, Tuesday through Saturday, 6 to 10:30 P.M.
Closed Sunday and Monday and major holidays.

RESERVATIONS: Recommended.

PRICES: Moderate, especially since there is no liquor license
and you may bring your own wine.

CREDIT CARDS: None.

A small and intimate storefront restaurant with candlelight,
flowers and a sweet provincial print fabric on the walls makes
the Grove Street Café the sort of place every romantic wants
to find in Greenwich Village. Too often such places, when they
do exist, offer cutesy food or just plain bad cooking, and such
simplicity can come at punishing prices.

In that sense, Grove Street represents a dream come true. Not only does it have an intimate boutique feeling, but most of the food is delicious, and the moderate prices are even more so when you consider that diners may bring their own wine or whatever else alcoholic they care to drink. As a bonus, the restaurant is close to many off-Broadway theaters, and it is wise to reserve one of the dozen or so tables well in advance before such performances.

"New Continental" is far more accurate here than new American, but by any name most of the dishes are savory and nicely cooked, and always seem well chosen for the surroundings, a special harmony I prize. Most recently, I had a beautiful dinner that began with a sweet red pepper, lightly roasted with a caponata-like stuffing of eggplant, capers, onions, olives and crunchy little croutons. Roast thigh and breast of duck, trimmed with red cabbage as bright as a ruby and just as sparkling with its balsamic vinegar, onion and bacon overtones, was a superb main course, suitably finished off with the house classic dessert—a big scoop of walnut-studded ice cream bathed in a bittersweet chocolate sauce, and always sheer heaven.

Very good seafood sausage appears and reappears as an appetizer and is worth having as is the ethereally light sweet red pepper terrine. Crab and lobster salads tangy with a Louis dressing are favorite first courses in hot weather, and there is always a non-Italian-tasting but soothing pasta, which can be shared as an appetizer. My favorite in that department is the combination of corkscrew fusilli with cream, tomato and bacon. Good pâtés and gravlax are often on hand, and if the menu offers a timbale of scallops with spinach in a frothy chive cream sauce, don't miss it. After that, the grilled filet mignon with green peppercorn sauce is a fine counterpoint, to be followed perhaps by the delicately dry and airy chocolate almond torte with bitter chocolate icing.

Grilled Norwegian salmon with a variety of finishes and a winy, onion-rich calves' liver Veneziana have proved to be excellent choices. A dish I loved that seems no longer offered is the Cornish hen stuffed with sausage and nuts. In a telephone conversation, chef and partner Jim Reed said the kitchen was bored cooking that but may offer it again. They are entitled to that feeling, but it is a loss to guests.

Not all dishes work equally well at Grove Street, a certain creamy blandness and a few unfortunate combinations being the causes. Chicken stuffed with crayfish is an example of the bad-combination flaw primarily because of the fishiness of the crayfish, and veal with mustard sauce is much like hospital food. Overly sweet mint sauce can spoil an otherwise fine lamb chop, as it did here.

Desserts have not failed, and in addition to those already

described, good candidates are the apple-raisin tart, a light, flourless chocolate roll and lime mousse, although I am not quite sure I like this with a brownie.

HUBERTS

102 East 22nd Street, between Park Avenue South and Lexington Avenue.
Telephone: 673-3711.

Favorite meals:
Octopus and wakame seviche with avocado
Pan-fried Muscovy duck breast with spaetzle, salsify and pickled apricots
Espresso mousse with praline
OR
Shrimp and smashed cucumbers
Country captain chicken with basmati rice
Plum tart

OTHER FAVORITE DISHES: Gravlax, wild mushrooms in puff pastry or over grits, salad with duck confit, rabbit sausage, tuna sashimi, charred beef in plum sauce, wild mushroom soup, chicken and vegetable soup with dill, crab cakes with codfish, grilled tuna, rack of lamb, sirloin steak with wild mushroom sauce, mesquite-broiled squab, all sorbets and ice creams, lemon tart, chocolate fudge cake.

SETTING: Spare but atmospheric café-restaurant with felicitous, rose-glow lighting; chairs are handsome and comfortable, and noise level is fairly bearable; there is some discomfort from street lighting at certain window tables.

SERVICE: Friendly and efficient with a good-naturedly preppie tone.

DRESS CODE: None.

SMOKING REGULATIONS: Separate smoking and nonsmoking sections; no pipes or cigars anywhere.

FACILITIES FOR PRIVATE PARTIES: Small room accommodates between fifteen and twenty.

HOURS: Dinner, Monday through Saturday, 6 to 11 P.M.; Closed Sunday and major holidays.

RESERVATIONS: Recommended.

PRICES: Expensive.

CREDIT CARDS: AE, MC, V.

To be successful, eclecticism can be practiced only by those experienced in more traditional forms and disciplines, for though it may seem like the ultimate, anything-goes license, it fails if not done knowingly. In art, the wave of abstract expressionism was a signal to a lot of would-be painters that it was no longer necessary to know how to draw to succeed, when in fact, the best abstract expressionists are indeed good draftsmen. Similarly the new all-bets-are-off school of cooking has led to much bad food, based as it is on lack of experience (both in eating and cooking) and no foundation in technique. The wonder of Huberts is how magnificently culinary eclecticism can succeed when practiced by those who have a finely honed sense of aesthetics and craftsmanship.

This is by far the most intellectual representation of new American cooking, and both Karen Huberts, who runs the dining room, and her husband, Len Allison, who is the chef, have evolved from a rather sentimental Continental cuisine in a sentimental antique Brooklyn bar to their spare but atmospheric Gramercy Park restaurant, where they turn out subtle dishes that make one reevaluate former taste references and really think about the food. Usually what I think about the food is that it is wonderful, only occasionally feeling that the kitchen has gone too far, perhaps with the rareness of the mesquite-grilled lobster, or an overdose of saffron here and a bit of undersalting there. Considering the wide-ranging invention, those are minor protests. There is a strong and attractive Oriental bent to the cooking here, attributed not only to the owners' studies of Japanese and Chinese dishes and ingredients but to a Japanese chef and a Thai cook in the kitchen. But it is clearly Allison who choreographs the steps of combining influences.

An appetizer that typifies the best sort of inventiveness here is tender octopus, lightly cooked and served just a shade cooler than lip temperature and thinly sliced as for sashimi or sushi. Arranged over a glistening bed of translucent, seductively crisp and slippery wakame seaweed, the combination was further enhanced by soft avocado slices, which soothed the other textures, and all was brightened with a sunny dressing with a perfect orchestration of light oil, rice wine vinegar, mandarin and lime. Similarly, the aforementioned mesquite-grilled lobster, despite its rareness, was beautifully garnished with a ruffle of thinly sliced black radish that had its scrubbed skin left on for a fine etching of color, purely Oriental in inspiration. But the fine saffron sauce and noodles were more European in feeling. The entire combination, like the octopus, seemed wholly European despite the Japanese elements. Or perhaps more accurately, wholly Huberts. Windfall salad of seasonal greens with duck confit, which could have been just a little more plentiful and fatter, was nonetheless a delicious first course, as was the snowy rabbit sausage in a tomato mole that had a judicious hint of cumin. Cool, firm, shrimp with icy smashed cucumbers, tuna sashimi in a sherry and sesame oil dressing and, occasionally, gravlax have been other fine starters. Wild mushrooms may be sautéed and placed in puff pastry or strewn over grits, and plum sauce is the mellowing element for charred filet of Limousin beef.

Soups are lovely at Huberts, most especially one that harks back to the original Brooklyn restaurant, a blend of vegetables, chicken and dill. Karen Huberts sighs when anyone asks for it and intermittently puts it back on the menu, where it is as much a classic as the curried southern dish, country captain chicken with basmati rice. A puree of wild mushrooms in a soup resulted in a rich brown velvet-textured brew with earthy, almost smoky accents. Wild mushrooms also are the base of a rich sauce served with Black Angus sirloin steak.

Other favorites of mine from the past are fried cakes of crab mixed with codfish and mesquite-broiled squab, which profits from the non-drying heat of the Southwest wood. Grilled rack of lamb has the right light smokiness from the fire while remaining a perfect medium rare within. The new version is accompanied by goat cheese lasagna, which I have not tried, and it remains to be seen whether it will overcome my objection to hot strong cheeses.

Muscovy duck has always been beautifully handled, and a recent main course of that firm-textured, richly flavored bird indicated the kitchen's way with it is intact. Pan-fried and sliced rare, it was fleshed out with gritty but satisfying spaetzle, bands of salsify and pickled apricots.

Salads and vegetables are all as intricately planned as other elements of the meal, and desserts should be instant legends. Sorbets of jewel-like clarity include lovely rhubarb, strawberry, tangerine, and grapefruit cassis. Raspberry ice cream and an espresso mousse with crunches of praline were complex and soignée, while the plum tart with its top and bottom crusts of short cookie dough and its red plum filling was homey and nostalgic. Fudge cakes always turn out well here as do all ice creams, and the lemon soufflé tart revives the palate and the diner's spirits.

Karen Huberts sets a gentle and gracious tone in the dining room, and overall there is a peaceful air of restraint and careful aesthetic consideration. Pink walls, etched-glass lamp shades and handsome crafted chairs add to the atmosphere, only here and there perhaps too spare or marred by the glare of reflecting streetlamps coming through the uncurtained windows. Things can also get too noisy, but the preppily dressed waiters could hardly be improved upon. It would be nice to imagine this food served in the setting of a Japanese inn so the delicate play of flavors could be calmly appreciated. As an added civilized touch, there are a few decent half bottles of wine on the list.

Lola, *see* Cuban and Caribbean

Mary Elizabeth's, *see* Breakfast and Brunch

Maxwell's Plum, *see* The View, the Setting and the Scene

MEMPHIS

329 Columbus Avenue, between 75th and 76th Streets. Telephone: 496-1840.

Favorite meal:
  Barataria Bay crab cakes
  Marinated grilled duck with port-pepper sauce
  Black bottom pecan pie

OTHER FAVORITE DISHES: Barbecued ribs, spiced crawfish, Cajun popcorn, seafood gumbo, chicken and andouille gumbo, barbecued shrimp, southern fried chicken, apple molasses stuffed pork chop, banana sour cream pie, bread pudding with whiskey, New Orleans-style French toast and Louisiana crab cakes at Sunday brunch.

SETTING: Huge, noisy café with postmodern and Art Deco references.

SERVICE: Good natured and sincere but erratic and agonizingly slow in upstairs dining room.

DRESS CODE: None.

SMOKING REGULATIONS: No special policy.

FACILITIES FOR PRIVATE PARTIES: Will close part or all of restaurant to accommodate up to 140.

HOURS: Dinner, Monday through Saturday, 6 P.M. to midnight; Sunday, 6 to 10 P.M.; brunch, Sunday, noon to 3 P.M.

RESERVATIONS: Necessary.

PRICES: Moderate.

CREDIT CARDS: AE, CB, D, MC, V.

Memphis is a city in Tennessee. Memphis is an ancient site in Egypt. Memphis is a Milan avant-garde design group involved in furniture and interiors. Memphis is a huge, lively, head-splittingly noisy restaurant on Columbus Avenue serving, for the most part, Louisiana Creole-Cajun food, once or twice removed. Cajun bouillabaisse, Creole Caesar salad and pasta al pesto with Louisiana seafood are the most obvious examples of the culinary genealogy that typifies the menu.

Pay your money and take your choice. Is the slightly Egyptian arched doorway an indication of what Memphis means to the owners, or is the spare, vaguely Art Deco, postmodern interior an indication that Italian design was in mind? Surely the owners know that Memphis is not in Louisiana, but whatever the reason behind the name, some of the food is diverting and far better than much of what has passed for Cajun-Creole in these parts.

There is a typical packed Columbus Avenue singles scene at the long bar leading from door to dining room. (Incidentally, finding that door is no small task. Like so many other trendy restaurants, Memphis does not have a sign outside.) The main dining room downstairs, with its sleek silvery quality, is jammed and noisy but nevertheless pleasant, although why anyone needs thumping background music with the din of voices escapes me. Service is friendly but unprofessionally forgetful and lags at peak hours, most especially in the upstairs room, which is quieter but boring. Either you go to Memphis or you don't, but it's totally pointless to try to minimize the experience by sitting upstairs.

The kitchen's performance is uneven, but among appetizers that draw me back are the chunky, lean barbecued ribs with a spicy sauce and cool, creamy coleslaw and the crisp-fried Cajun popcorn, the peppery crawfish that here are nested on fried eggplant with a bright and brassy rémoulade sauce. Meaty lumps of crabmeat are mounded into the Barataria Bay crab cake, fleshed out with garlic crab fingers and a chive butter sauce. Crescent City pancakes with crabmeat and avocado were a sticky mess, oysters were served almost warm, and boiled crawfish lacked enough of the traditional crab-boil pickling spices. Two gumbos, one with seafood and the other combining chicken, andouille sausage and the cured-ham tasso, are peppery and delicious, but be sure to specify that you want them hot in temperature or they will surely arrive tepid and therefore dreary.

Barbecued shrimp in shells, adrift in a fiery sauce, are worth the peeling they require, and southern fried chicken has been nicely crisp yet moist on several tries. Cajun bouillabaisse, with its combination of shrimp, mussels, clams, crawfish and fish, is moistened by a light clear butter broth and is satisfying if short on shrimp and long on mollusks, so that the portion seems much larger than it is. Why restaurants here as well as in Louisiana have so much trouble with jambalaya is beyond

57

me; perhaps precooking and preheating requires more careful handling than they give it. Whatever the reason, the rule holds at Memphis; the jambalaya is a greasy, salty mass. Not so the fine marinated and grilled duck with a pepper-port sauce, roasted peppers and duck cracklings or the lusty apple molasses stuffed pork chop with cornbread dressing. Blackened redfish is fair, but its chive-lime sauce is a mistake. At brunch there are good crabcakes and New Orleans French toast with what are called Tennessee bacon slices (good, whatever that means) and honey-orange butter.

Desserts all have that Columbus Avenue overdone richness, but some of the better choices are the black bottom (chocolate) pecan pie, the banana sour cream pie, and bread pudding with whiskey.

ODEON

145 West Broadway, corner Thomas Street.
Telephone: 233-0507.

Favorite meals:
  Artichoke and leek soup
  Crisp roasted duckling with apples, white grapes and apple turnover
  Crème brûlée
  OR
  Goat cheese salad
  Cassoulet
  Lemon tart

OTHER FAVORITE DISHES: Vegetable ravioli in spicy broth, poached oysters in champagne sauce, Norwegian salmon with oysters, pan-sautéed filet mignon with three mustard sauce, paillard of beef, fettuccine with vegetables or pesto sauce or any cream sauce with ham or sausage but not with grilled shrimp, roast lamb, sautéed calves' liver with Madeira and currants or with shallots or with nuts, hamburger, thin apple tart, pecan tart, all egg dishes at brunch as well as buttermilk or potato pancakes.

SETTING: Art Deco cafeteria and bar turned café with a varied, handsome clientele; crowded and noisy.

SERVICE: Polite, informed, but painfully slow between appetizer and main course.

DRESS CODE: None.

Smoking regulations: No special policy.

Facilities for private parties: None.

Hours: Lunch, Monday through Friday, noon to 3 P.M.; dinner, seven days, 7 P.M. to 12:30 A.M.; supper, 1 to 3 or 4 A.M.; brunch, Saturday and Sunday, noon to 3:30 P.M.

Reservations: Recommended for lunch, necessary for dinner.

Prices: Moderate.

Credit cards: AE, V.

The reincarnated Art Deco cafeteria turned restaurant that is the Odeon is the only eating place that draws me to TriBeCa for its sake, and I include in that the new and much-touted Montrachet. The difference is that I know many places in the city where I can get the same sort of pleasant, nicely turned out quasi-French food that is served at Montrachet and there is no need to go way downtown for it, although I might go to that restaurant if I were in its neighborhood for other reasons. That detour from talking about the Odeon is not meant to be a gratuitous slap at Montrachet but rather an explanation of what I mean by loving Odeon for its own sake. The Odeon has a very special style, both in the room and the food. The handsome young crowd enlivens the atmospheric "moderne" dining room, which wears its casualness as well as its clientele wears the laid-back, enhancing costumes. I even prefer this ever so slightly to the same management's Café Luxembourg, but so slightly that I would have trouble giving them different ratings. Perhaps it's because the Odeon has mellowed more with time.

Odeon bristles with a stylishness that overcomes its noise and crammed-together tables, so that those apparent flaws become part of the spirit. Add to that a good-natured staff with a charm that helps, at least in part, to cancel out a lack of polished professionalism, and you have an engaging scene, one I especially enjoy at lunch, brunch and at a 7:30 to 8 o'clock dinner. Later hours are too hectic even for me. Reservations are honored promptly, a miracle of timing on the part of whoever coordinates them, given the large numbers of people.

Patrick Clark, who oversees the kitchen, has established an Odeon style in food, ranging from such simple bistro classics as steak frites to trendy new American presentations such as Norwegian salmon smoked over a wood fire and garnished with Wellfleet's briny oysters. There may be a sui generis artichoke and leek cream soup rich in overtones of both vegetables with a liaison of cream or vegetable ravioli in a lemony broth that suggests Southeast Asia more than it does Italy. Oysters lightly poached and glossed with champagne sauce have been house classics almost since the restaurant opened, and

59

though I have a slight preference for leeks as a garnish instead of the newer smoked duck breast, the meaty alternative does give one something to chew over, literally and figuratively. Pastas with creamy sauces flecked with solids such as ham, sausage or vegetables have been delicious non-Italian interpretations, but a recent version with grilled shrimp was a failure, the greasy charred shellfish being too overpowering for the delicate pasta. A salad with warm chèvre and toasted pine nuts is delicious primarily because the cheese is of the right medium ripeness and so is not stultifying when warm.

Duck, calves' liver and lamb have always been well handled here. The first, crisply roasted and adorned with apples, white grapes and an apple turnover, has roseate moist meat at the center and flavorful skin. Calves' liver with currants and Madeira sauce is done more successfully here than at Café Luxembourg for some reason, but in both places I prefer that fresh, pink-cooked meat with shallots or a light sprinkling of nuts. Paillard of beef is carefully grilled, and lamb, whether in the form of chops or a roast, is suitably garnished, most recently with braised endive and a zucchini flan. Paillard of chicken dries out because of its thin leanness.

Hamburgers are excellent, whether for lunch or late supper, and the Odeon has always done very good egg dishes, buttermilk or potato pancakes and corned beef hash for weekend brunches.

Lemon tart with a sting of fresh juice and a properly glazed crème brûlée custard are my favorite desserts, closely followed by a thin apple tart and a pecan tart rounded out with ice cream. (I've been a little rounded out by it myself.)

The one problem Patrick Clark has failed to solve in his years here is the slowness of the kitchen. There is still a long lapse between courses, but if the conversation is good, it might not matter. If you're in a hurry, you'll go mad. Also, a number of main courses are ungarnished, thereby making an à la carte side dish necessary, so prices are not always quite as low as they seem. That was true recently of both the liver and the Norwegian salmon.

The Pink Tea Cup, *see* Breakfast and Brunch

THE RITZ CAFÉ

2 Park Avenue, entrance on 32nd Street, between Madison and Park Avenues.
Telephone: 684-2122.

Favorite meals:
LUNCH
Oysters on the half shell
Creole eggplant stuffed with shrimp and crab
Lemon chess pie
OR
DINNER
Spring onion crab cake
Three smothered quail with dirty rice
Chocolate rum pecan pie

OTHER FAVORITE DISHES: Peppered scallops, cinnamon-jacketed rabbit, artichoke Rex, creole gumbo, roasted salmon with smoked shrimp, blackened swordfish, crawfish etouffee, drunken shrimp, Cajun meat loaf with tasso gravy (at lunch), Cajun cassoulet with duck, andouille and red beans, Jack Daniels chocolate ice cream with pecan diamonds, Creole cream cheese pecan pie.

SETTING: Formerly La Coupole, the dining room retains much of that Parisian café's decor and tone; large, spacious, lively and noisy, but quiet in private alcoves.

SERVICE: Occasionally inattentive but generally good and accommodating.

DRESS CODE: None.

SMOKING REGULATIONS: No special policy.

FACILITIES FOR PRIVATE PARTIES: None.

HOURS: Lunch, Monday through Friday, noon to 3 P.M.; dinner, Monday through Saturday, 5:30 to 11 P.M. Closed Sunday and major holidays.

RESERVATIONS: Necessary for lunch, recommended for dinner.

PRICES: Moderate.

CREDIT CARDS: AE, MC, V.

It has always seemed a pity to have a handsome restaurant close, then reopen with new decoration, as though it was the interior that failed rather than the food. Le Grand Café was one such loss, and for a while it looked as though the beautiful, doomed Art Deco re-creation of La Coupole was to meet the same fate. Fortunately when the premises were taken over by the operators of the Ritz Café, the original of which is in Los Angeles, they were shrewd enough to realize how easy it would be to adapt the high and wide Parisian café setting to the New Orleans big-restaurant look. A few partitions here and a change of mirrors there have accomplished the task, creating several different atmospheres in which to eat. There is a big oyster bar, where drinks, oysters and a few simple dishes are served. There are private alcove booths, very much in the New Orleans tradition, a sort of noisy, cramped inner "chic people" pen, and a more relaxed slightly quieter Outer Mongolia.

All of this lends itself to the very good versions of Louisiana-inspired food, much better in New York than in the Los Angeles original, if my one dinner at the West Coast outpost can serve as a fair experience.

If my favorite meal at the Ritz Café in New York is lunch, that is because one of the best dishes is available midday. The Creole eggplant stuffed with a near soufflé of shrimp and crab, liberally sprinkled with green onion (scallions, to most of the country), is a wondrous dish, and my only regret is that it is not also available for dinner. The Ritz Café is less crowded most nights, as lunch attracts a crowd from nearby publishing houses. That stuffed eggplant as well as the ruggedly down-home meat loaf with a salt-etched tasso ham gravy and sweet potatoes are two good reasons that the lunch crowd is so loyal.

There is still plenty of good eating at night, and in fact, with the exception of a few Cajun-Creole dishes prepared at Texarkana, this is the best Louisiana restaurant New York has had so far. Suitably enough, there are nice cold fresh oysters of various kinds, which are shucked to order, luscious crab cakes with green onions and a sprightly green tomato relish, and peppery but cool scallops such as Louisiana rarely sees. Artichoke Rex, named for the prestigious Mardi Gras crewe, I assume, has a more or less mustardy vinaigrette dressing that gets flavor and texture contrast from a generous heaping of minced sweet peppers and onion. Cinnamon-jacketed rabbit, a playful name for a nice creation of tender rabbit meat in crisp pastry turnovers, is diverting and satisfying.

Creole gumbo with chicken and seafood is unusually peppery and delicious if it has not cooked down too much and so become overly thick, much like a stew. It is a mystery why Northern cooks think that "thick" as applied to gumbo means that the liquid is dense. In my considerable experience with Louisiana food on its home ground, the thin soup is "thick" with solids such as vegetables, chicken, ham, seafood or sausage. It is also rarely hotly spiced, as the kitchen knows the Tabasco bottle is a rite Louisianians like to exercise for themselves. The other strange failure is the rémoulade sauce on the excellent but oversize shrimp. The authentic version relies on smaller shrimp, which can be tossed with the dressing, but even if one overlooks the shrimp size here, the sauce is a gross misrepresentation. It is closer to Russian dressing than to the brilliant coral, stingingly sharp Cajun original that depends on scallions, parsley, garlic, celery, oil, paprika, cayenne and plenty of Louisiana mustard for its character.

Blackened fish can be a travesty, the heavy spice coating and white hot pan often ruining the texture and the flavor of the fish. Done with restraint, it can be successful as it is at the Ritz with swordfish. Applied to steak, it can be excellent too, but the filet mignon used here does not stand up to the spices as well as the rib steak I have had at K-Paul's in New Orleans. Three tiny, moist quail, smothered (alas) with spices and nested on dirty rice (cooked with poultry giblets and livers, which do the dirtying), is one of the best main courses, closely followed by the roasted salmon with smoked shrimp and New York's best crawfish etouffee, that soup-stew with a heady rose-pink sauce. Drunken shrimp, inebriated in their beer broth for cooking, are accented with butter and crab-boil-type spicing. Cajun cassoulet, a hearty combination of red beans, duck and andouille sausage, is the right thing on a snowy midwinter evening. Disappointments came by way of red snapper with sautéed crabmeat, which had the unpleasant flavor of overheated grease, and also lamb chops with roasted garlic, mostly because the chops had the "black" flavor often imparted by a dirty grill.

Cheese-sharpened biscuits and cornsticks stung with pepper are dangerous diversions between courses; it is almost impossible not to fill up on them to the detriment of the large portions served here. Those large portions hold true for desserts too, and sharing them is a fine idea, whether you have the chocolate rum pecan pie, the Jack Daniels chocolate ice cream with crunchy pecan diamond confections, or Creole cream cheese pie crackling with pecans. There's a sort of crazy dessert about which I have not made up my mind. It is a compote of warm berries ladled over cognac ice cream, thereby melting it in its awkwardly tall wineglass. It's the sort of thing one polishes off while deploring it, a nursery dessert, which, like melted ice cream, is what kids always love.

Service is good at the Ritz Café except for the same old soft shoe about giving bad tables to unknown customers even if the place is almost empty. They are good, however, about honoring a request for a particular section when reservations are made, and I am much in favor of the alcoves.

Roxanne's, *see* The View, the Setting and the Scene.

TABLE D' HÔTE

44 East 92nd Street, between Madison and Park Avenues.
Telephone: 348-8125.

Favorite meal:
  Red pepper bisque
  Duckling with green peppercorn sauce
  Poached pear with caramel sauce
OTHER FAVORITE DISHES: Leeks in dill cream; salad with greens; fennel and chèvre; duck liver mousse; medallions of lamb with mustard, ginger and rosemary; tournedos with green peppercorn sauce; rabbit with Pommery mustard; chocolate pots de crème; lemon tarts; chestnut mousse.
SETTING: Tiny storefront café-restaurant with more or less American Colonial overtones; cramped and noisy but mildly so and with a certain charm.
SERVICE: Unprofessional but friendly and accommodating.
DRESS CODE: None.
SMOKING REGULATIONS: No special policy.
FACILITIES FOR PRIVATE PARTIES: Can close restaurant to accommodate up to twenty-four.
HOURS: Dinner, Tuesday through Saturday, 6 to 9:30 P.M., Closed Sunday, Monday, all major holidays and for the last two weeks in August.
RESERVATIONS: Necessary.
PRICES: Moderate.
CREDIT CARDS: None.

Although the name of this restaurant promises French food and the menu is for the most part reflective of that national cuisine, anyone expecting things to taste truly French will come away disappointed. The presentation and preparations are so essentially American and in the best sort of home-cooking tradition, it is safer to look for real French cooking elsewhere. What Table d'Hôte provides that I like is a unique experience in New York, a tiny storefront dining room that looks as though a good home cook put a few odds and ends of furniture together in her living room and hung a sign outside the house saying, "Dinner guests welcome." The mix-match of furniture, silver and dishes, more secondhand than antique, combines to create a sort of New England Colonial look, and the romantic lighting

64

and pretty sprays of flowers here and there add to the effect. Were I a young lover, this would be the restaurant I would like to call "Our place."

Nice and pleasant are the best adjectives for the fresh, cooked-to-order dishes, and given the moderate prices and very special setting, dining here makes for an unusual and uplifting New York experience. Not long ago I had a chiffon-textured, gently sweet red pepper bisque that was creamy and seductive, followed by moist, roseate duckling breast in a good, sharp green peppercorn sauce. Shoestring slim asparagus accompanied the duck but were unfortunately placed right in the sauce, so that everything tasted alike. That flaw marred other main courses here. Sliced poached pears, fired with ginger in a caramel sauce, added the right, refreshing contrast as dessert.

Other good appetizers at Table d'Hôte include the poached leeks in a bright dill sauce that needed just a dash of salt to have correct flavor, a subtle duck liver mousse with green peppercorns and a verdant salad combining watercress, radicchio, fennel and chèvre cheese, all with a tangy vinaigrette dressing. Creamed vegetable soups such as the leek and the spinach are much improved now that they are strained.

A thick loin veal chop that seemed to have been sautéed had an earthy, woodsy morel cream sauce to complement it. The sorts of main courses the kitchen has always done well are the rabbit with a brassy Pommery mustard sauce, medallions of lamb with mustard and ginger, and tournedos with a green peppercorn sauce, which I prefer to the mustard.

Certain flavor themes appear often in the menu as you can probably tell just from reading this. Green peppercorns, mustard and ginger appear just a little more often than they should on a small menu, as it makes planning a balanced meal a bit difficult. On the other hand, going to Table d'Hôte once in a while should not make that an overwhelming problem.

Desserts have the same gentle appeal, as though made by a talented amateur home cook, which is in no way meant as a put-down. It's the sort of flavor I prize in these days of over-professionalism and chefs who grind their axes on the customer's palate. Try the sweet little chocolate pot de crème, the pungent lemon tarts or the velvety chestnut mousse and find out. Vivek Bandhu and Lauri Gibson, who began this restaurant with a third partner no longer there, still express their love of cooking and serving in most convincing ways. Now if they could just find a way to ventilate the dining room... The house has a wine and beer license, but you can still bring your own bottle and pay a $5 corkage charge.

TEXARKANA

64 West 10th Street, between Fifth and Sixth Avenues.
Telephone: 254-5800.

Favorite meals:
  Southern-style pickled shrimp
  Barbecued tenderloin
  Fried okra (SHARED BY TWO TO FOUR)
  Rum pecan pie
  OR
  Seafood gumbo, if waiter brings it hot
  Roast suckling pig or breast of duck with jalapeño peppers
  Bread pudding with bourbon sauce

OTHER FAVORITE DISHES: Headcheese, charred raw beef, barbecued pork with lettuce leaves, venison sausage, jicama salad, kale soup, potato and green chili soup, orange and red onion salad, southern fried chicken, barbecued chicken, venison chop, calves' liver with bacon and scallions, barbecued lamb chops, barbecued veal chop, fried chicken salad, crab cakes, barbecued rib steak, stolen blackened fish, dirty rice, french fries, chocolate pecan tart, plum cake.

SETTING: Modern but with romantic French Quarter overtones and colors; crowded and noisy; bar is especially handsome as is the crowd frequenting it.

SERVICE: Staff is professional and accommodating, but the kitchen slows markedly at peak hours.

DRESS CODE: None.

SMOKING REGULATIONS: No special policy.

FACILITIES FOR PRIVATE PARTIES: Separate area can be set aside for parties of thirty-five to seventy-five.

HOURS: Dinner, seven days, 6 P.M. to midnight; late supper, Tuesday through Saturday, midnight to 3:45 A.M.

RESERVATIONS: Generally necessary.

PRICES: Moderate to moderately expensive.

CREDIT CARDS: AE, D.

Texarkana is the perfect name for the state of mind that holds sway in the kitchen of this stylishly handsome, convivial restaurant. With Abe De La Houssaye, a native Cajun who is the chef and a partner, that sensibility means combining such Louisiana traditions as gumbo and the suckling pig, cochon du lait, that he does each evening on a spit in the dining-room fireplace with Southwest overtones of green chilies, barbecued and southern fried chicken, then applying such ingredients and techniques to somewhat Continental dishes. He succeeds here far more than he ever did at his other restaurant, La Louisiana, even though the huge menu, crowds and difficult placement of the upstairs kitchen still make for an uneven performance.

The dishes I love at Texarkana have proved consistently excellent; those that fail also do so consistently. That suckling pig is one favorite, and portions must be ordered when reservations are made. There has been a sliding schedule of hours when that crunchy, mellow-meated piglet is served, so check when making reservations. Usually, the 8 to 8:30 time span is the safest. Before I get to that or other main courses, I nibble my way through the pickled okra and onions, the good, gritty cornbread, black-eyed peas and coleslaw. Then there are the fine appetizers, among the best being the charred raw beef in green chili sauce and the chunks of barbecued pork in a smoky sauce nested on lettuce leaves. Crawfish in a cocktail have never had flavor enough, but pickled shrimp in a vinegar, lemon and oil dressing almost make up for them. Cajun headcheese, much like the French pâté called rillettes, and a chewy, meaty venison sausage are other delectable starters.

More delicate appetites might prefer an icy jicama salad or the combination of oranges and red onions with vinegar, sesame oil and black pepper, a welcome palate freshener with the smoky meats. Goat cheese salad was disappointingly bland. Soups based on kale, or combining potatoes and green chilies, have a Tex-Mex lustiness, and seafood gumbo, better than other variations, can be fine if it is served hot. Remind the waiter that you want it that way because it can cool on the trip from kitchen to dining room.

Two moist, flavorful chicken dishes are the southern fried and the barbecued, pit grilled and glazed with pungent barbecue sauce. Catfish has lacked flavor, but the stolen blackened fish (stolen, one assumes, from Paul Prudhomme, who made the dish famous) is better, more delicately done than the so-called master's version. For the most part, though, I go to Texarkana for a meat fix, and there is that in spades in the thick, bloody barbecued beef tenderloin with green chili sauce and, even more, in the gargantuan, marvelous barbecued prime rib steak that two can easily share. (Or leftovers can be taken home to be enjoyed cold the next day.) Barbecuing is also well accomplished on veal or venison chops, neither drying out in the process.

In the mood for lighter fare, I might have the crab cakes or the fried chicken salad with nuggets of fried chicken tossed with greens and mushrooms and moistened with a honey-mustard dressing. Or for more stylish eating, there are the boned, crisp-skinned duck breast zapped with jalapeño peppers and the tender calves' liver with scallions and bacon.

Side dishes I tend to order include dirty rice (dirtied with giblets), or the slim, crisp french fries, the jalapeño and corn-meal dressing, or fried okra, depending on what is served with main courses ordered. All, however, are well worth trying.

Pacing myself to include dessert is a trick I have not yet quite mastered, given other enticements here, but we usually do some sharing on that last course. Rum pecan pie, bread pudding with bourbon sauce, chocolate pecan tart and a sur-prising (in this format) tart and juicy plum cake are among the temptations I have not always resisted.

Stunningly decorated with Southwest-sunset-pink walls and a balconied dining room that suggests a New Orleans court-yard, Texarkana is an attractive if jam-packed and noisy setting. The magnificent wooden bar was made by George Nakashima, the sculptor, who is the uncle of Mr. De La Houssaye's wife, Alene. It is a setting that draws a swinging uptown crowd late at night when limousines double-park outside. The balcony also has tables, but it is airless and out-of-it. Nice preppie waiters hold forth, often apologizing for the inevitable slowdowns.

The "21" Club, *see* The View, the Setting and the Scene

Windows on the World, *see* The View, the Setting and the Scene

YELLOW ROSE CAFÉ

450 Amsterdam Avenue, between 81st and 82nd Streets. Telephone: 595-8760.

Favorite meal:
  Texas ranch hot sauce with chips (SHARED BY TWO)
  Barbara Ann's southern fried chicken with fried okra and
    mashed potatoes
  Buttermilk biscuits
  Pecan pie
OTHER FAVORITE DISHES: Texas bowl of red chili, Cattle Annie's
  chicken-fried steak, smothered pork chops, chili and cheese
  burger, cornbread, french fries.

Setting: Simple, pleasant café with Lone Star flag as decorative focal point.

Service: Pleasant, accommodating and reasonably efficient except at peak hours when service slows.

Dress code: None.

Smoking regulations: No special policy.

Facilities for private parties: None.

Hours: Monday through Thursday, 11 A.M. to 11 P.M.; Friday, 11 A.M. to midnight; dinner, Saturday, 4 P.M. to midnight; Sunday, 4 to 11 P.M.; brunch, Saturday and Sunday, 10 A.M. to 3 P.M. Closed major holidays and last week in August.

Reservations: Not accepted, and the line forms by 6:45 P.M.

Prices: Inexpensive, with a $5 minimum after 6 P.M.

Credit cards: None.

The only thing that puts me off my feed at this engaging Texas outpost is the spelling of potato with an "e" at the end. That, and tomato with the same flaw, is becoming too standard on menus of restaurants run by young owners. My guess is that they arrive at that minor symptom of illiteracy by starting with the plural for both vegetables, and then simply dropping the "s," figuring they are home free. Not quite!

So much for the schoolmarm in me. From here on the eater takes over, and the meal I like to eat at the Yellow Rose Café is lunch, when this simple café-luncheonette, done in soft Southwest colors and adorned only by the Texas flag, is peaceful and felicitous. That, or early dinner, is best, because no reservations are accepted, and the dinner hour usually brings with it a waiting line. That good the Yellow Rose Café is not.

Good Texas-Southern home-style cooking is the mode, often with a disappointing blandness but always dependable with the dishes recommended here. Far and away the best is Barbara Ann's southern fried chicken, with a breading as crisp and greaseless as gold leaf and moist, flavorful meat within and only occasionally undercooked. It would be an improvement if the chicken were cut in smaller pieces before being breaded so there would be a better, crunchier proportion of bread to meat, but that is perhaps ungrateful carping about a dish so hard to find well prepared in this city. I always have it with some of the inspired, honest-to-God mashed potatoes and the vegetable I love, fried okra.

My main reason for ordering the Texas ranch hot sauce is the darling chips it comes with—tostadas stamped out in the shape of Texas. Guacamole also arrives with those chips and is fine if doctored with salt, pepper and hot sauce. Nachos are the sort I dislike, just a big mound of the chips with melted cheese all over them. I much prefer them individually topped and baked. Texas bowl of red chili, the meat properly cubed instead of ground, also could be spicier, but some Tabasco fixes things just fine. Chicken-fried steak (steak that is floured and pan-fried) is an idiosyncratic preference of mine; I know it's awful but I love it, but with cream gravy on the side. Barbecued ribs and chicken, as well as the messy and bland cheese enchiladas with green chili casserole, have been disappointing, but the tender, smothered pork chops with potato sauce are satisfying much the way the chicken-fried steak can be. Chili and cheese are enriching toppings on the house hamburger, and the coarse, mildly sweet cornbread and buttered hot biscuits are good enough to be destructive. I always opt for more biscuits and no dessert, taking my calorie credits where they produce the most mileage in taste.

Prices are so low that a $5 minimum is imposed after 6 P.M. In addition, there is so far no liquor license, so you can take your own beer or whatever. I kind of like having iced tea the year round, much in the spirit of Texas eating.

TIDBITS

Aurora, 60 East 49th Street, between Madison and Park Avenues, 692-9292, is the latest creation of master restaurateur Joseph Baum. Although it is too new to have wormed its way into my heart (comfortable but disjointed decor with very high prices), I have had a few memorable dishes prepared by Gerard Pangaud, late of a wonderful Parisian nouvelle bistro. Pheasant consommé, roasted pigeon with sweet garlic sauce and tournedos with red wine and marrow were the outstanding dishes, along with a sublime lemon hazelnut torte and a cinnamon apple tart with vanilla ice cream and wine granite.

Gotham Bar and Grill, 12 East 12th Street, between Fifth Avenue and University Place, 620-4020, is a high, wide and handsome pastel café-restaurant done to the nines in postmodernist symbols. Most food leaves me cold, but one luscious exception is the warm roasted quail salad, the boned, succulent quail bedded down on a round of pungent vegetables dressed with sherry vinegar and walnut oil.

Belgian

CAFÉ DE BRUXELLES

118 Greenwich Avenue, corner 13th Street.
Telephone: 206-1830.

Favorite meals:
Endive salad with ham
Waterzooi of chicken or shellfish
Belgian waffles with chocolate sauce (SHARED BY TWO)
OR
Mussels Marinières
White sausage with apples and onions (boudin blanc) or
Braised loin of pork with cabbage and apples
Poached pear in red wine

OTHER FAVORITE DISHES: Shrimp croquettes, chilled oysters, tomato stuffed with shrimp, fried Gruyère cheese with mustard (fondue Bruxelloise), mussel soup, cold poached salmon, hamburger, beef braised in beer (carbonnade flamande), fried sole in beer batter, Brussels fish stew, Belgian chocolate cake, ice cream with chocolate sauce.

SETTING: Handsome bistro-style café with starchy lace curtains and a bearable noise level; sophisticated and convivial small bar.

SERVICE: A bit precious but efficient and well meaning.

DRESS CODE: None.

SMOKING REGULATIONS: No cigars or pipes are permitted.

FACILITIES FOR PRIVATE PARTIES: None.

HOURS: Lunch, Monday through Friday, noon to 3:30 P.M.; dinner, Monday through Thursday, 6 to 11 P.M.; Friday and Saturday, 6 P.M. to midnight; Sunday, 6 to 10 P.M.; brunch, Saturday and Sunday, noon to 3:30 P.M.

RESERVATIONS: Always accepted; necessary on weekends.
PRICES: Moderately expensive.
CREDIT CARDS: AE, MC, V.

In just a few years, Café de Bruxelles has become one of the pleasantest restaurants in the city. It is a stylish bistro that invites conversation and conviviality in a handsome setting. Located on the triangle where Greenwich Avenue tapers into 13th Street, the restaurant follows that shape. The result is a tiny knifepoint of a bar, with a lively crowd. There is a long, narrow passageway dining room that some prefer because they can see who is entering and leaving. But because it is a passageway that includes a swinging kitchen door and a heavily trafficked stairway to check- and rest rooms, I find it unsettling. I much prefer the dining room with spacious tables and a view of the street through the windows hung with starchy white lace half curtains. Dark, bottle-green trim, glazed walls that have a peachy antique patina and bold, decorative modern art make for an urbane room that combines elements of the antique and the contemporary.

Add to that the very good, luxurious, hearty cooking of Belgium, with its French and Flemish overtones, and you have a thoroughly satisfying experience. Since Bruxelles was taken over by a new management, the kitchen performs with more consistency than it did originally.

Most of the great Belgian specialties are here. The braised beef stew, carbonnade Flamande, is seasoned with onions, nutmeg and the malty undercurrents of Belgian beer, and the big chunks of beef are lean and juicy. Waterzooi, the Flemish soup-stew of chicken or fish in an egg- and cream-thickened broth, is fragrant with leeks, white wine and lemon and gets a bit of crunch from julienne vegetables. The chicken waterzooi is delectable and the seafood version is sublime. (For those who wonder, sublime is better than delectable.) The Brussels version of bouillabaisse is nicely accomplished with lobster, mussels, scallops and shrimp in a saffron-gilded tomato broth, and sole Ostendaise is a thick, snowy fillet veneered by a greaseless, crackling beer-batter crust. Mussels are a Belgian obsession; at Bruxelles they are steamed in a white wine and garlic broth (marinières) or in a soup that has the absinthe accents of Pernod plus a brassy dash of saffron. Unfortunately, fried mussels, a great Belgian classic, have never been on the menu during any of my visits, and it is a sad omission. The mussels used here are farmed and so are never brackish and rarely sandy as they were in the early days of the restaurant.

Steak with pommes frites is a simple, sustaining main course, and in fact, the slim fries, so ubiquitous in Brussels, are served with all main courses, bunched in a paper cone and offered authentically with a mayonnaise dip. At times they are as golden and crisp as they should be; other times they are underfried and limp.

Boudin blanc, the delicate white sausage of finely ground veal and pork, is better in onion and applesauce than with prunes and apricots; it is available both at dinner and brunch. Loin of pork braised in vermouth and served with red cabbage and apples is miraculously nonsweet, the apples lending just the right foil to the richness of the meat. A velvety brown wild mushroom and cream sauce adds a satin touch to roasted quail garnished with wild rice; the quail, however, are sometimes overcooked.

Less interesting main courses include most other fish on the menu; both calves' liver and duck have been too sweet.

Before such heavy dishes, salad appetizers are best, and Bruxelles offers several that are intriguing—an endive and watercress salad with smoked ham; the salade Liègeoise of string beans, red onions, potatoes and bacon; and a goat cheese, walnut and greens combination. But all can be too heavily stung with vinegar; ask for such salads with very little vinegar. Heftier appetizers include a surprisingly good combination of snails with Roquefort butter (surprising to me because I usually dislike hot blue-veined cheeses with meat or fish). Fondue Bruxelloise arrives as crisp, small cheese croquettes with a mustard tang, and shrimp croquettes, though a bit bland, are gentle openers. Pâtés have been disappointing as has the innocuous tomato stuffed with shrimp.

My far-and-away favorite dessert is the thick, golden Belgian waffle with bitter chocolate sauce, but I have it only if I can share it with someone. Add to that a dollop of vanilla ice cream, and it is enough for three or four. Belgian chocolate cake and, for lighter going, pear poached in red wine are also good endings.

Lunch and brunch menus are beguiling, as Belgian dishes lend themselves well to those meals. Wine is available, of course, but I prefer the remarkable Belgian beer, my choice being the smoking, bracing Duvel.

Brazilian

BRAZILIAN PAVILION

316 East 53rd Street, between First and Second Avenues.
Telephone: 748-8129.

Favorite meal:
    Brazilian rum (cachaça) and lime juice cocktail (caipirinha)
    Codfish patties (bolinhos de bacalhau), when available
    OR
    Brazilian appetizer (sautéed shrimp with hearts of palm)
    Brazilian black bean and meat cassoulet (feijoada com-
        pleta), Wednesday and Saturday at lunch, daily for dinner
    Custard (flan)
OTHER FAVORITE DISHES: Soup of potatoes and kale or collard
    greens (caldo verde), broiled shrimp with garlic (camarao
    Paulista), shrimp Baiana in tomato sauce, hashlike fried
    chopped meat (picadinho), codfish with potatoes and eggs
    (bacalhau a gomes de sá), chicken fried with garlic (frango
    a bossa nova), roast leg of pork (pernil assado); fish stew
    (peixe a Brasileira).
SETTING: Trim, modern atmospheric dining room with bright
    colors, plants and green glass lamp shades; tables are close
    and both dining rooms are noisy when full.
SERVICE: Polite and helpful but very slow both at tables and
    at coat checkroom.
DRESS CODE: None.
SMOKING REGULATIONS: No special policy.
FACILITIES FOR PRIVATE PARTIES: Back dining room accom-
    modates up to fifty.
HOURS: Lunch, Monday through Friday, noon to 5 P.M.; dinner,

Monday through Thursday, 5 to 11 P.M.; Friday and Saturday, 5 P.M. to midnight. Closed Sunday and major holidays.
RESERVATIONS: Recommended.
PRICES: Moderate.
CREDIT CARDS: AE, CB, D, MC, V.

This is by far the prettiest and most stylish of the city's Brazilian restaurants, and though its food is not up to the level of Cabana Carioca's, many diners feel far more comfortable here and so are willing to forgo the more authentic fare. I go at times when I cannot get into the Cabana, or when I want to be on the East Side, or to introduce someone to Brazilian food in a slightly more familiar way. It is a large, bright and airy restaurant, with plaster white walls, lots of greenery in glass lamp shades, plants and waiters' jackets, and touches of royal blue-purple here and there. The front dining room, which includes the noisy, nonstop party bar, is the more spacious of the two; the back is more intimate if you define intimacy as being elbow-to-elbow with strangers. That crowding of tables makes it difficult for waiters to take orders and serve, something they do at a snail's pace anyway when the dinner hour is at its height. Just when you think they have forgotten your order entirely, it appears with apologies. But since that unfortunate drawback occurs only at peak hours, I try to go early or late.

I also try to get a reservation in the front room so I can sit comfortably as I sip a caipirinha, a refreshing, powerful cocktail based on cachaça (the Brazilian sugarcane rum) with lime juice and sugar, all shaken until frosty. A version prepared with lemon juice (batida de limon) is a little too sharp, but the batida de coco, made of cachaça and coconut milk, is rich and soothing, if slightly filling. With that drink I have some sliced, pan-sautéed Portuguese sausages if they are on hand or, on some days, the tiny fried codfish balls that Brazilians inherited from the Portuguese kitchens. More generally, I start with the aperitivos Brasileiros, a salad of shrimp sautéed in their shells with garlic, bedded down on hearts of palm with tomatoes, olives and crisp but tasteless iceberg lettuce; too bad romaine or escarole is not substituted. Other times I have the soup caldo verde, here somewhat thin, but nevertheless pleasant, with its collard greens, potatoes and nuggets of the Portuguese sausage linguiça.

Appetizers are not really essential because portions are huge as in all Brazilian restaurants and all main courses are fleshed out with rice and lovely stewed black beans. Shrimp are done in many intriguing ways in Brazil, and at this restaurant the best versions are the Baiana—simmered in palm oil and co-

75

conut milk with green peppers, garlic and tomatoes, a sauce similar to that used for moqueca de peixes, a soup-stew of fish and shellfish. Camarao Paulista, shrimp sautéed in garlic, is a fine choice if you have not had the similar appetizer. Plain broiled lobster is usually moist and fresh, and peixe a Brasileira—bass and shrimp in a peppery, garlicky tomato sauce— is a delicious stew.

Other fish dishes do not match these, nor does anything even vaguely Continental, such as veal cutlet Milanese or chicken "Francesa" with ham and cheese.

Picadinho, a comfortable sort of hash, is fine for tired stomachs. Chicken bossa nova—moist, tender chunks sautéed golden brown with a showering of garlic—is one of the better dishes as is the dried salt codfish, bacalhau gomes de sá, when it is offered as a Friday special. The well-soaked snowy codfish is cooked with potatoes and onions, then finished off with black olives and cut-up hard-boiled eggs.

And then, of course, there is feijoada, every Wednesday and Saturday for lunch and every night for dinner. This is Brazil's answer to cassoulet, based on the earthy, meaty black beans cooked with sausages and various cuts of fresh and smoked pork, all served with kale or collard greens, sliced oranges and the crackling manioc flour, farofa. The version here is tamer than that of Cabana Carioca and the cuts of meat a little less varied, but it is an easy way for a beginner to learn the ropes. Roast pork, a Wednesday and Saturday special, is generally moist and well flavored.

There are a lot of big fancy cakes on the dessert wagon, all of which are banal and seem impossible to negotiate after the hefty food. Fruit salad or flan is the most I can manage.

Portions are large and sharing is not discouraged; two people could share an appetizer and then a main course and eat inexpensively. There is sometimes terrible confusion at the coat checkroom when the restaurant is crowded, so be braced for it.

CABANA CARIOCA

123 West 45th Street, between Sixth and Seventh Avenues.
Telephone: 581-8088.

Favorite meals:
SHARED BY TWO
Brazilian rum and lime juice cocktail (caipirinha)

Clams in garlic broth
Brazilian black bean and meat cassoulet (feijoada),
   Wednesday and Saturday
OR
Chicken with okra, other days
Flan
OR
Soup of potatoes and kale or collard greens (caldo verde)
Grilled shrimp with garlic (camarao Paulista)
Fried potatoes and black beans
Flan

OTHER FAVORITE DISHES: Hearts of palm salad, shrimp in tomato sauce (camarão a Baiana), fish stew, oxtail stew with
   polenta, codfish with egg and potatoes (bacalhau a gomes
   de sá), roast chicken, codfish croquettes when available,
   chicken fried with garlic (bossa nova).
SETTING: Upstairs dining room is best and has a trim, clublike
   look; informal, with a convivial bar at which regulars also
   eat as they watch TV.
SERVICE: Seemingly brusque but really good natured and help-
   ful; nonregulars are discouraged from upstairs dining room.
DRESS CODE: None.
SMOKING REGULATIONS: No special policy.
FACILITIES FOR PRIVATE PARTIES: Private dining room accom-
   modates up to sixty.
HOURS: Lunch and dinner, seven days, noon to 11 P.M. Closed
   Monday and Christmas.
RESERVATIONS: Recommended, especially for upstairs.
PRICES: Moderate.
CREDIT CARDS: AE, CB, D, MC, V.

This favorite meeting place for New York's Brazilian community is jammed, lively and much like a private house party.
Because it specializes in lusty, delicious, moderately priced
food, and because the upstairs dining rooms are so small, in
recent years it has sprouted a neighboring annex, a few doors
east at number 133. I want to make it clear that the only Cabana
Carioca this review refers to, and the only one to which I go,
is the original upstairs dining room. The new outpost (Cabana
Carioca II) is run as a tourist trap, hustling diners in and out.
It presents the same menu as the original, but waiters announce
a forty-minute to one-hour wait for almost anything interesting.
Bum's rush, translated to Portuguese, would be a more suitable
name for this.

That over with, let's to the real Cabana Carioca, one of the
theater district's enduring delights. When making a reservation, always specify the upstairs dining room. Then walk the
narrow flight of stairs with its florid folk mural on the walls,

and you are in another world. Portuguese is the lingua franca; regulars eat, drink and watch color TV at a small active bar; and at the closely set tables in the dining room, friends and families share the enormous portions. Wood-paneled walls and spruce-green tablecloths give this an informal yet serious look, a promise the food fulfills.

A caipirinha, the Brazilian rum and lime juice cocktail, is a fine opener, especially if you nibble some chewy, fried garlic- and paprika-accented linguiça sausage. On days when fried codfish balls are available, they are even better appetizers. Hearts of palm salad with tomatoes and olives is enough for four even if you ignore the insipid iceberg lettuce upon which all of the goodies are bedded down. Soups are excellent whether you have the caldo verde, a kale, sausage and potato-thickened brew, the aromatic Alentejo garlic soup, or the near-soup that is clams steamed in a potful of verdant garlic and parsley broth. The last is best shared by two as the dozen or so huge clams in it constitute almost a meal in themselves.

Feijoada is the dish to shoot for, served Wednesdays and Saturdays. The black beans with tongue, smoked pork, sausages, oranges, kale and the nutlike farofa (toasted manioc flour) should satisfy a trencherman of any capacity. It is therefore not the best pre-theater choice for it will certainly cause drowsiness even as the curtain rises. If I have dinner at Cabana Carioca before theater, I prefer the shrimp Baiana (tomatoes, peppers, onions and garlic) or Paulista (sautéed in the shells with a haze of garlic). The dried salt codfish bacalhau is also a lighter choice, either braised with tomatoes or steamed with a sunny garlic egg sauce. Chicken is also light but rib-sticking when done bossa nova (fried with garlic), simply roasted, or in a tomato-based stew with fresh okra. Oxtail stew with polenta, available on some weekdays, is a dark, soul-warming and tender blend of onions, vegetables and meat in a sauce that gets body from the oxtail bones—a little greasy perhaps but wonderful on a cold wintry day.

Fish stew with a tomato and onion sauce is fine even if you do have to ignore the sometimes rubbery shrimp. Pot roast (carne assada) and roast suckling pig, when available, offer hearty options. Clams simmered with pork, Alentejo-style, a dish traditionally cooked in the hinged round casserole known as a *cataplana*, can be good if the clams do not toughen.

Steak and pork chops are too tough to be recommendable, and other dishes on the menu have proved to be lackluster.

As always with Brazilian food, main courses are accompanied by rice and black beans and round slices of fried potatoes, which add interest and heft.

Flan is the only dessert to consider, and Brazilian beer is the best accompaniment to the solidly flavored main courses.

Casual Eating—Cafés, Pattisseries and Luncheonettes

BREAKFAST AND BRUNCH

Café des Artistes, *see* The View, the Setting and the Scene
Elephant & Castle, *see* Cafés
Kiev, *see* Luncheonettes
Carnegie Delicatessen, *see* Jewish and Kosher
Patisserie Lanciani, *see* Patisseries
Sarabeth's Kitchen, *see* Cafés

Mary Elizabeth's, 6 East 37th Street, between Fifth and Madison Avenues (683-3018). The coffee shop attached to this classic, down-home tearoom operating since 1908, is among my favorite morning pit stops because of the crusty, yeasty crullers (doughnuts) and, when available, the "hearts" or centers stamped out of the crullers. Coated with cinnamon sugar and accompanied by the excellent coffee made here, the crullers and/or hearts (or for a change, one of the chewy honey buns) make any day look brighter. Breakfast is served Monday through Saturday, from 7 to 11 A.M. Closed Sunday and major holidays. This also operates as a take-out bakery.

Paris Commune, 411 Bleecker Street, between Bank and 11th Streets, 929-0509. Brick walls and Colonial blue wood trim create a pretty, vaguely French country setting. But there is nothing vague about the great breakfasts the kitchen creates seven days a week. Fresh juice, flaky croissants, batter-dipped French toast made of French bread, and substantial omelets

79

are there along with super portions of granola and oatmeal. I like this for business breakfasts on weekdays when the room is quiet and calm. Breakfast is served seven days from 10 A.M. to 4 P.M.

The Pink Tea Cup, 42 Grove Street, just west of Bleecker Street, 807-6755, is the sort of gentle café tearoom one hopes to find in the Deep South. Soul food is the feature as is the daylong special breakfast of eggs any style (I like mine fried) with grits, biscuits and spicy sausages or thick, half-chewy, half-crisp bacon. Breakfast is served from 8 A.M. to midnight, Sunday through Thursday and from 8 A.M. to 1 A.M. Friday and Saturday.

SoHo Charcuterie & Restaurant, 195 Spring Street, corner Sullivan Street, 226-3545. Rose-brick walls with white trim give this café a bright and airy look, especially inviting for Sunday brunch. There are fresh juices and very good egg dishes, my favorite being the scrambled eggs piperade with onions, peppers and sausages. French toast is gross and boring, but there are wonderful assorted platters of things such as herring, smoked fish and salads. Pâtés and other charcuterie leave much to be desired. Regulars here share orders and seem to have it down to a science. Breads are better than the overly rich cakes. Bloody Marys, virginal or otherwise, are spicy and well made. Prices are high but sharing is permitted, and there is an $8 minimum. Served from 10:30 A.M. to 4:30 P.M.

Also see Breakfast and Brunch listing in Restaurant Index.

CAFÉS

Elephant & Castle, 68 Greenwich Avenue, just east of Seventh Avenue, 243-1400, and 183 Prince Street, between Thompson and Sullivan Streets, 260-3600. At weekend brunches, as well as for lunch, dinner and late supper seven days a week, both of these pert and stylish café-luncheonettes turn out delicious omelets (I like the Mexican-inspired combination of Cheddar cheese, guacamole and tomato; the Provençale with zucchini, tomatoes and onions; and the bacon with scallions), beefy, juicy, nicely seared hamburgers (alas, no longer on kaiser rolls) and lusty chowders. Salads and sandwiches are always heftier than I expect (or want) them to be, and warm dishes tend to be overcontrived, but there are enticing appetizers that can be combined for a meal. Among them, the spicy chicken wings with blue cheese dip and the pasta with crushed olives and capers are my preferences. There are many teas to choose from, and in the larger, roomier and more inviting SoHo branch, there are wine, beer and full bar service. Speaking of service, it is friendlier and more efficient in the Greenwich Avenue original. Long lines form at both places as no reservations are accepted. Specific hours differ slightly, but both serve all meals described.

Il Nido Café, 875 Third Avenue, corner 53rd Street, 319-6122. An offspring of Il Nido, this shiny, very Milanese café, laid out in the polished lobby of a glassy new building, serves light lunches and early dinners, breakfast and all-day takeout. Cold food in the form of antipasto items is refreshing, light and decent, and there are a few hot dishes too, although I can't imagine eating any but the pasta in this setting. The real stars are the homemade Italian gelati, the creamy, custard-thick ice cream marvels of which the tantalizing bittersweet chocolate is the most seductive. Closed Sunday.

Sarabeth's Kitchen, 423 Amsterdam Avenue, between 80th and 81st Streets, 496-6280, and 1295 Madison Avenue, between 92nd and 93rd streets, in the New Wales Hotel, 410-7335. Sarabeth Levine, well known for her light, tearoom-style baking, now has two café-restaurants where brunches, lunches and dinners are served. I prefer them for weekday lunch or weekend brunch and am very partial to the newer, larger and bright pastel-painted Amsterdam Avenue location where sandwiches are better. Juices are fresh and egg dishes delicious, most especially the frittata with red peppers, scallions, Gruyère cheese, mushrooms and ham, served at Amsterdam Avenue, and the buttery cheese blintzes offered in both places. "Goldie Lox," scrambled eggs enfolding smoked salmon and cream cheese, is also diverting, and there is a spicy creamy tomato soup that makes the morning seem brighter. Pancakes, French toast and waffles are all fine, as is the juicy cider-soaked ham, which can be ordered on the side. Homemade peanut butter is a revelation, and salads (especially chicken) are fresh and substantial. Save room for some of the church-cake-sale muffins and desserts. Prune Danish, rugelach and poppy seed cake are my favorites. Napoleon pastry is too thick, and the marble and pound cakes are underbaked and undersalted for my taste. Honey and homemade jams are lovely touches with mild-flavored breads. There are full dinner menus with a variety of meat dishes, but neither of these places says "Dinner" to me. The Madison Avenue Sarabeth's is a little tacky and cramped, but I would go there if I was in that neighborhood and hungry.

It's the sort of home-style tearoom one would like to find in New England. Good luck!

Serendipity, 225 East 60th Street, between Second and Third Avenues, 838-3531. Except for the foot-long hot dog (see Hot Dogs), I go to this shop-cum-café for a rich dessert after seeing a movie in one of the nearby theaters. And each dessert is enough for two or three. Choices include drugstore sundaes, the monumental banana split and a variety of wonderful calorie-packed drinks, hot and cold. Cinnamon toast is soothing with afternoon tea. Monday through Thursday, 11:30 A.M. to 12:30 A.M.; Friday, 11:30 A.M. to 1 A.M.; Saturday, 11:30 A.M. to 2A.M.; Sunday, noon to midnight.

Terrace-five, fifth level of Trump Tower, 725 Fifth Avenue between 56th and 57th Streets, 371-5030. Though distinctly pricey, this tiny, tucked-away café has the charm of the undiscovered, never mind that reservations are necessary for peak lunch hours. Stylish and modern, with a small bar and two pocketsize outdoor terraces, where food is also served, its strengths are light salads and entertaining appetizers. Dinner is served as is hot food for lunch, but neither appeals to me in this setting. Tea does, however, and it is served Monday through Saturday. There is full bar service, and several good wines can be had by the glass. Closed Sunday.

PATISSERIES

Patisserie Lanciani, 271 West 4th Street, between 11th and Perry Streets, 929-0739, and 177 Prince Street, between Sullivan and Thompson streets, 477-2788. Although there are sometimes warm quiche with salad and croissant sandwiches at these places, I really go for coffee and cake—croissant, brioche or crumb buns with morning cappuccino or some of the richer pastries midday or late evening. Individual fruit or lemon tarts, the caramel and whipped cream extravagance known as the religieuse, and the chewy, soft-crisp French nut torte are my favorites. Eclairs are also good, and there are real old-fashioned charlotte russes—the little scalloped paper cups holding gen-oise cake and a swirl of whipped cream. Cookies are also but-tery and fragrant with spices. I generally go to the Greenwich Village branch on 4th Street, where the service is erratic. Ob-viously cakes can be taken out, but both cafés are pleasant.

Sant Ambroeus, 1000 Madison Avenue, between 77th and 78th Streets, 570-2211. This brass and mirrored local branch of the chic Milan pasticceria dispenses opulent and generally delectable cakes. Those made with chestnut purees and chocolate are especially good as are coffee and pound cakes and the eggy brioche loaves that approximate challah and so make good French toast. Other food tends to be tired and limp. The back café is swathed in puffy drapings, but the effect is bright and amusing, if a bit stifling. There is also a very Italian stand-up espresso bar that is popular and walk-away gelati of which I prefer the nougatine; most are improbably colored. Prices are high but that is to be expected midst the Madison Avenue art galleries and antique shops.

LUNCHEONETTES

A counter is essential to this format, as is takeout. There may also be tables and a menu that features what is most accurately billed as "hot eats," but with a difference.

Bleecker Luncheonette, also known locally as Italian Home Cooking, Bleecker Street, corner Carmine, with no apparent telephone number. From noon to 2 P.M. and from 5 to 7 P.M. on weekdays, this small luncheonette ladles out an extraordinary green minestrone full of vegetables such as potatoes, zucchini and string beans that seem to be bolstered with split peas. Pastas are overcooked but savory in an old-fashioned comforting way, and sausage with peppers is first-rate.

Chez Brigitte, 77 Greenwich Avenue, between Bank and 11th Streets, 929-6736, has only eleven seats at two counters and is uncomfortably elbow-to-elbow at the height of lunch and dinner. I go off-hours for light pea soup, juicy veal fricassee with paprika and softly overcooked vegetables, roast lamb or veal, veal cutlets or meatballs on plates or in sandwiches. Well-made omelets and scrambled eggs, the nice carrot and celery salad and silky crème caramel are other options. Monday through Saturday, 11 A.M. to 9 P.M. Closed Sunday, holidays and most of the summer.

Kiev Luncheonette, 117 Second Avenue, corner 7th Street, 674-4040. Open twenty-four hours a day, seven days a week, this Jewish-Eastern European-very New York eatery serves stupendous breakfast dishes around the clock. The best are the thick French toast made with egg challah and a pancake omelet with garlic- and pepper-sparked kielbasa sausage slices, which will see you through the day.

Viand Coffee Shop, 673 Madison Avenue, between 61st and 62nd streets, 751-6622. There are two lusty, delectable dishes here—the best turkey sandwich in town, freshly sliced from a whole bird roasted on the premises (I like mine without lettuce and with butter), and the best Greek coffee-shop rice pudding around. Served in a tulip glass with plump raisins and smoky dustings of cinnamon, it is enough for three people. I have either the sandwich or the rice pudding for lunch; both would be impossible. Monday through Saturday, 6 A.M. to 10 P.M. Closed Sunday.

Caviar

PETROSSIAN

182 West 58th Street, at Seventh Avenue.
Telephone: 245-2214.

Favorite meal:
  Années Folles (Crazy Years)
  Beluga, osetra and sevruga caviars
  Pressed caviar with blinis
  Smoked wild salmon
  Russian vodka
  Apple tart

OTHER FAVORITE DISHES: Salmon roe caviar; duck or goose foie gras.

SETTING: Think Belle Epoque opulence, and you'll be on the right track; marble, mink and mirrors set the stage in remarkably good if theatrical taste; inadequate lighting is the only drawback.

SERVICE: Professional, efficient and courteous.

DRESS CODE: Jacket and tie required for men.

SMOKING REGULATIONS: No special policy, and a pity with such delicate fare.

FACILITIES FOR PRIVATE PARTIES: It is possible to take over the entire restaurant or to have a small room that holds ten.

HOURS: Lunch, Monday through Saturday, 11:30 A.M. to 3:30 P.M.; cocktails, Monday thhrough Saturday, 3:30 to 6 P.M.; dinner, Monday through Saturday, 6 P.M. to 1 A.M.. Closed Sunday and major holidays.

RESERVATIONS: Recommended, especially for after theater.

PRICES: Expensive.

CREDIT CARDS: AE, CB, D, MC, V.

Yes, Petrossian does have real cooked food and it's French at that, but this luxurious haven's true reason for being is caviar, and I never get past it to try anything else. So to make things perfectly clear, I must say that this three-star rating applies only to the menu described. It would be hard to imagine any food bad enough to pull down the average, so sublime are the caviars and smoked salmon.

Petrossian in Paris is a stunning shop purveying the most impeccable caviar, smoked fish, foie gras and related king's ransom comestibles. That same tradition has crossed the ocean with one exquisite amplification: Now one can consume those solid-gold groceries on the premises. And what premises they are, all roseate marble with a mink-trimmed banquette here and there, sparkling mirrors and brass and an aura of irresistible decadence that suggests the Belle Epoque and the Roaring Twenties combined. Such special fare gets elaborate, intriguing equipment. There is a big ring on a stand to hold three small glass dishes for the caviar sampling, and a silver and vermeil paddle spoon, much like an Egyptian palm, to spoon caviar into one's mouth or to spread it on toast. (That toast, by the way, is the reason Petrossian gets three stars instead of four. At these prices we deserve more than limp, bodiless American white bread toast even if the bread baking has to be done in the restaurant kitchen.) My favorite meal here has a name— Années Folles ("Crazy Years")—and at this writing it goes for $98 a throw. It is worth every cent. First comes the big three-ring circus of caviars: thirty grams each of the best silken, diamond gray beluga, which is the largest of the eggs, the slightly smaller, topaz-colored osetra and the tiny beads of charcoal gray sevruga. With these there are episodes of toast, the cold being replaced by the warm. Butter is also served, but I find it masks the flavor of the caviar, and I allow only an occasional droplet of lemon juice for variety. I also like to eat the caviar straight, nibbling on toast now and then to renew my palate. Alas, the dim lighting here. With eye appeal so much a part of caviar connoisseurship, Petrossian is too dark for the diner to appreciate the color variations.

The next remove, as they used to say, is my personal favorite, fresh pressed caviar or pajasnaya, a thick, licoricelike spread with the most intense, quintessential caviar flavor. Accompanying it are puffy, light yeast blinis, correctly made with wheat instead of buckwheat flour, and a few cloudlets of crème fraîche. If I am with someone else, one of us orders the pajasnaya and the other has the red salmon roe caviar so we can have even more variety.

Smoked wild salmon so thinly sliced that it seems more like the glaze on the plate itself is the final offering, also with toast. Only Danish smoked salmon at its best competes with this rosy, sweet and gently woodsy fish. Apple tart is all I can contemplate following this elegance, but I would prefer home-made Italian lemon granita, the water ice that would truly clean and cool.

There is a variety of champagnes, offered mostly by the bottle but also by the glass. My preference is iced Russian vodka, the best caviar enhancer.

There are other lovely smoked fish here—trout, sturgeon and so on, as well as duck or goose foie gras, whole and un-pâtéd, which is the way to eat either. As for cooked dishes, perhaps I'll live long enough to try them, when I have had enough caviar.

There are less extravagant caviar portions that range in price from $19 to $53. Années Folles is a wonderful after-theater or opera supper, and Petrossian stays open late enough for that indulgence. The best time to stop by, as far as I am concerned, is whenever I decide I can afford the splurge. This is a retail shop too, so all of the goodies, paddle spoon included, can be had at home, a nice touch in this age of carry-out prepared foods.

Chili, Ribs and Barbecue, Hamburgers and Hot Dogs

CHILI

Carolina, *see* American

Corner Bistro, 331 West 4th Street, corner Jane Street, 242-9502. This neighborhood bar, with tables in back, cooks up an above-average, mild beef chile with red beans. Open seven days from noon to 4 A.M. Closed Thanksgiving Day.

Lone Star Café, 61 Fifth Avenue, corner 13th Street, 242-1664. Although there is a music charge in the evening, at lunch and early dinner anyone can walk in and try the fiery "bowl of red," diced beef chili that can be ordered in first-, second- and third-degree hotness, that last being my favorite. But I do ask them to hold the cheese, a topping I dislike with chili. Lunch is served Monday through Friday, 11:30 A.M. to 4 P.M., and dinner from 5:30 P.M. every night, with a music charge, starting about 7:30 or 8:00.

Manhattan Chili Co., 302 Bleecker Street, near Seventh Avenue, 206-7163. One of the better things to happen to the Village in a long while, this casual café in Southwest pastels offers a variety of satisfying chili variations to be eaten on premises or as takeout. My preferences are the Texas Chain Gang version, which is the hottest, with diced beef, jalapēnos, tomatoes and beans, and the Real McCoy, diced chunks of beef zapped with two types of chili powder (hot and hotter) and, as the menu says, no beans, no tomatoes, no bull. Salsa fresca and Calico corn muffins are good go-withs, but the coleslaw and guacamole are innocuous. Brunch is served on weekends, lunch and dinner seven days. Open late. There is a pretty trellised garden where food is served in warm weather.

88

Smokey's, 230 Ninth Avenue and 24th Street, 924-8181, 685 Amsterdam Avenue, at 93rd Street, 865-2900. Chili has a chewy, torn texture that is lusty; spicing is mildly hot, but stir in some of the house hot sauce to fire it up. Noon to 10 P.M., seven days.

Yellow Rose Café, *see* American

RIBS AND BARBECUE

Carolina, *see* American

Lone Star Café, *see* Chili for address and hours. Hickory smoked ribs are fresher, hotter and better at night than during day, but sauce is sweet and commercial.

Memphis, *see* American

Smokey's, *see* Chili for address and hours. Ribs are the thing here, with the regular big lean meaty and tender specimens generally better than the baby back ribs because the smaller size dries out. Sauce is inspired and available mild, medium and hot. Try the hot cautiously if you are a newcomer to it as it is incendiary—and my favorite. Two can also be blended, and all are available takeout so you can baste your homemade barbecue with it.

HAMBURGERS

Café de Bruxelles, *see* Belgian

Carolina, *see* American

Corner Bistro, *see* Chili for address and hours. Freshly ground beef in a huge burger is one of the very best, and still only $3.50 plain. Combined with chili, it's a gourmet meal if the gourmet is starving. Lunch, dinner, supper, seven days.

Diane's, 249 Columbus Avenue, near 72nd Street, 799-6750. Delicious fresh burgers properly cooked weigh seven ounces and are bargains ($2.95) in this casual luncheonette-café. Seven days, 11 A.M. to 2 A.M..

Elephant and Castle, *see* Cafés

Hamburger Harry's, 157 Chambers Street, between West Broadway and Greenwich Street, 267-4446. Mesquite-broiled

89

burgers of moderate size ($3.25) are delicious here but disappointing at the 45th Street Theater District outpost. The only added topping I like is the combination of guacamole with spicy pico de gallo sauce, and it's worth the extra 50 cents to get the burger on a toasted English muffin. Sunday through Thursday, 11:30 A.M. to 11:30 P.M.; Friday and Saturday, noon to midnight.

Taste of the Apple, 1000 Second Avenue, between 52nd and 53rd Streets, 751-1445. Huge seven- to eight-ounce burger, well cooked, juicy and fresh, is $2.70 at this writing and may be the most economical protein fix in town. Monday through Thursday, 11 A.M. to midnight; Friday, 11 A.M. to 1 A.M.; Saturday, noon to 1 A.M.; Sunday, noon to midnight. Closed major holidays.

HOT DOGS

Gray's Papaya, 2090 Broadway, corner 72nd Street, 799-0243. This old-style open luncheonette grills a meaty beef hot dog that is a steal at 50 cents. There's papaya juice if you can stand it, but I prefer the frothy piña colada for old time's sake.

Katz's Delicatessen, 205 East Houston Street, at Ludlow Street, 254-2246. Huge sandwiches are cheap and famous, but the quality of meat is disappointing. Not so the crisp grilled beef hot dogs (not skinless these, but crackling in natural casings), on rolls with hot sauerkraut and lots of yellow deli mustard. The scene late night is strictly New York, though hours are shorter than they used to be. Sunday through Thursday, 8 A.M. to 11:30 P.M.; Friday and Saturday, 8 A.M. to 1:00 A.M.

Paley Park, 53rd Street between Fifth and Madison Avenues. A wall-wide waterfall, ivy and chairs and tables make William Paley's gift to the city a treasure. The hot dogs are said to be Sabrett made to Paley's taste. What's most special about them is their freshness, the sizzling grilling they get and the toasted rolls. Then too there's iced tea, coffee or soft drinks and a sylvan oasis. Closed in January and part of February.

Serendipity, see Cafés for address and hours. Skip hamburgers and go for the slender foot-long hot dog, which I like plain with mustard, but you can have yours also with chili and chopped onions.

Chinese

Chinese food is so much better, more varied and less expensive in Chinatown than elsewhere that I rarely venture north of Canal Street to eat it. Uptown Chinese restaurants tend to be overpriced and banal, a condition not mitigated by the recent appearances of highly touted, lackluster, Americanized additions such as Pig Heaven, Fu's and Auntie Yuan. The last does have a few good appetizers, but that is hardly enough to draw me to those costly environs.

Four exceptions to the rule appear below, and I go to them when I want to eat in their neighborhoods—the midtown East Side and, most of all, Lincoln Center.

One of the most frustrating things about eating Chinese food is having all the dishes ordered arrive at the same time. Not only is the table overcrowded, but some dishes get cold and unpleasant. This almost always happens in Chinatown, no matter how one pleads for a few dishes at a time, and it often occurs uptown as well. The reasons for this are custom and the Chinese method of kitchen organization. It is easier for cooks to prepare the complete order for each table than it is to keep track of which table is ready for what. It helps a bit to order only a few dishes at a time, but at the busiest times, Chinatown restaurants prohibit that. If it makes you feel any better, this is not discrimination against occidentals; Chinese families get the same treatment and seem undisturbed.

As much as I love the food in Chinatown, I detest the dirtiness of the area and wonder why ours cannot be as clean as San Francisco's. I rarely go to Chinatown on Friday or Saturday nights, and if I do go on Sunday, I do so at about seven. Weeknights and Saturday lunches are my favorite times, as restaurants are less hectic and messy. Weekday lunches are wonderful, but I never get down there at that time unless I am on jury duty.

Most Chinatown restaurants now sell domestic and Chinese beer, and all have soft drinks. A few have full bars (as do all uptown Chinese restaurants), so it is a good idea to ask what is available when you call. It is also a good idea to check on credit cards. The policy in Chinatown changes rapidly and is always somewhat nebulous (a few restaurants restrict the use of cards to a minimum bill, and so on). English is clearly understood and spoken in all of the restaurants mentioned here, but it is also conveniently forgotten when the staff wishes to rush customers.

As a fairly dependable general rule, I find that it is best to skip dishes listed as chef's specials or suggestions on Chinese menus. They usually turn out to be gussied-up tourist creations, rarely as good as standards on other parts of the menu. Clues lie in ingredients; beware of an abundance of red and green peppers and carrots, American broccoli and dishes that are sweet and sour or made with ketchup. Also any that have "everything" in them, an obvious attempt to appeal to touristic palates.

BEIJING DUCK HOUSE RESTAURANT

144 East 52nd Street, between Lexington and Third Avenues. Telephone: 759-8260.

Favorite meals:
>SHARED BY TWO
>Tientsin bok choy with special hot sauce
>Peking duck
>Fresh fruit
>OR
>SHARED BY FOUR TO SIX
>All of the above plus
>Smoked fish
>Fried dried scallops with seaweed
>Shrimp in hot and spicy sauce
>Eggplant with garlic sauce and pork

OTHER FAVORITE DISHES: Spiced cold beef, duck song, hot and sour soup, meat and vegetables with Tientsin mung bean sheets, diced chicken in hot sauce with peanuts, sliced beef with watercress, pork with garlic sauce, string beans with minced pork, hot bean curd with minced beef, hot fish with crispy skin.

SETTING: Informal, disorderly dining room a notch or two above a Chinatown luncheonette setting; housekeeping needs improving.

SERVICE: Adequate, if impersonal; can be impatient when rushed or near closing time.

DRESS CODE: None.

SMOKING REGULATIONS: No special policy.

FACILITIES FOR PRIVATE PARTIES: One room that accommodates between twenty and twenty-six.

HOURS: Lunch and dinner, Sunday through Thursday, 11:30 A.M. to 10:30 P.M.; Friday and Saturday, 11:30 A.M. to 11:30 P.M.

RESERVATIONS: Necessary.

PRICES: Moderate.

CREDIT CARDS: AE, D, MC, V.

Beijing, the new way to say and spell Peking, is one of the offsprings of the Chinatown Peking Duck House that specializes in carved-at-the-table Peking duck that need not be ordered in advance. Unfortunately, the Chinatown original has become unrecommendable and is no longer a favorite of mine. Crepes for the Peking duck are dry and leathery, the dining room is a mess and the help rude. This East Side branch, as well as Peking Duck West, has maintained much higher standards.

The setting is only slightly more put together than Chinatown restaurants. There is carpeting (often soiled) and some attempts at decor, but in general an informal café atmosphere prevails. The staff is adequate and becomes pushy only at peak hours. The star on the menu is the Peking duck. A whole one must be ordered, and it appears, crisp, golden and greaseless, to be carved by a chef who wields a cleaver as deftly as a surgeon should. Skin and meat are carved together, making this an unauthentic version of Peking duck, for which skin and meat should be separated. But rolled into a rice-flour pancake with hoisin sauce and a spray of scallion and cucumber, the flavor is so sensational I have never regretted the lack of authenticity. The carcass, still with lots of meat, is carried away unless it is requested by diners, and when I am a diner, it always is. Or, again on request, it can be cooked with cabbage into a mild, soothing soup served as a last course. If only two people are eating, the duck is about all they will be able to manage, and it is a satisfying meal at that. But there are other good dishes here to be shared before and after the duck.

Tientsin hot and salty pickled Chinese cabbage is a bolting palate awakener, and spiced cold beef, much like corned beef, is another piquant first course. A cool-and-warm tossing of meat and vegetables with gossamer mung bean noodles glossed with a chili soy sauce is delicious, as is the deep-fried seaweed with crackling, fried, dried scallops. Chewy, caramelized

93

smoked fish and the hot and sour soup are other first courses I choose here. An improvement at the Beijing Duck House is the new willingness to spice food really hot when requested. Previously the kitchen staff had a timid hand, but recent insistence proved more rewarding, even though I was not recognized. What does persist is a tendency toward greasiness.

Spareribs and spring rolls are lackluster, as are soups other than the hot and sour and the duck and cabbage.

If for any reason I do not want Peking duck, or if we are six or eight, other dishes I order include the duck song, lettuce leaves wrapped around moist, meaty strips of duckling moistened by a light sauce; the diced chicken with crunchy peanuts in hot chili sauce; sliced beef pepped up with sautéed watercress; nuggets of tender pork in a light brown garlic sauce; or cushions of bean curd stir-fried with crumbles of beef in hot sauce, which really should be fiery to work. Hot fish with crispy skin, in a meaty garlic, ginger and chili oil sauce, is also good, as are the eggplant with garlic and the hot and spicy shrimp. Fruit is about all I can manage after the complex aromatic fare.

HWA YUAN SZECHUAN INN

40 East Broadway, between Catharine and Market Streets.
Telephone: 966-5534.

Favorite meals:
SHARED BY TWO
Hot spicy Chinese cabbage
Wined chicken
Pork meatball casserole
Oranges
OR
SHARED BY SIX
All of the above plus
Aromatic spiced beef
Stuffed eggplant
Carp with hot sauce
Noodles with hot brown meat sauce
Dried sautéed string beans with ground pork
OTHER FAVORITE DISHES: Shredded chicken with pepper sauce; sliced kidney with chili and ginger sauce; smoked fish; preserved duck; hot and sour soup; braised fish head casserole; shredded beef or pork with hot green pepper; chunked

chicken either with ginger sauce or hot sauce; sautéed kidneys, bean curd, chicken or pork home-style; eggplant with bean sauce; cold noodles with sesame sauce.

SETTING: Postmodern Chinese with dark wood and brick; has more style than the usual Chinatown setting.

SERVICE: Efficient, patient and helpful.

DRESS CODE: None.

SMOKING REGULATIONS: No special policy.

FACILITIES FOR PRIVATE PARTIES: Downstairs dining room accommodates up to eighty.

HOURS: Lunch and dinner, Sunday through Thursday, noon to 10 P.M.; Friday and Saturday, noon to 11 P.M.

RESERVATIONS: Necessary for six or more.

PRICES: Inexpensive.

CREDIT CARDS: AE, CB, D, MC, V.

The menu at this lively Chinatown outpost is really two menus intertwined—one offering the food Chinese customers eat, the other aimed at tourists. This was not always so and would be a pity except that the kitchen turns out the more authentic dishes with results so enticing, they cannot be matched at many places in town.

What I always avoid are the dishes listed as the "chef's new specialties." Recently deviating from that resolve, I ordered lobster with spicy ginger wine sauce, not suspecting it would have the cloying red sweet and sour sauce. The lobster was fresh and tender, but the sauce overpowered it completely. So back to the nonspecials, avoiding almost all that are Cantonese, definitely not the kitchen's strong point.

What that leaves is a dazzling array of delicious cold appetizers, an assortment of which would make a wonderful meal. Freshly cooked shredded chicken napped with a tingling sesame and chili oil sauce or the cool wine-marinated breast of chicken are full of flavor and would be perfect for a summer cold buffet. (All of this is sold takeout.) Thinly sliced preserved duck looks as though it were cured with Mercurochrome, but the thinly sliced meat, edged with fat and skin, is succulent and teasingly salty. So is the pickled aromatic spiced beef and the crisp, hot spicy cabbage. Sliced kidney seasoned with ginger and chili and the chewy, slightly sweet smoked fish are also worth trying. Hot and sour soup is consistently rich and properly fiery, especially if you ask to have it that way, but I usually forgo it in favor of one of the bubbling casserole soup-stews served here. Wire-bound stoneware casseroles arrive seething with boiling broth enriched by silken hanks of bean thread noodles, all sorts of vegetables and mushrooms, and five big, puffy pork meatballs. Fish head casserole with similar trimmings is a second choice, and others are based on bean curd or assorted meats and vegetables. Not long ago, my husband and I began with the wined chicken, the cabbage and then had this casserole. That copious meal cost exactly $20.50 for two, and we could easily have done without the chicken and spent $6.25 less.

Because they are so substantial, these casseroles must be considered a main course for two, or a soup course for four to six. Ordered that way, they can be preceded by a few of the enticing appetizers.

Among main courses, home-style, meaning a savory brown sauce, is the preparation that produces delectable results with kidneys, bean curd, chicken or pork. Hot, meaty sauces on fish, like the incomparable, fiery carp cooked here, is almost always at Chinese tables, and it is an extraordinary dish. Shredded beef or pork with hot green peppers, and crisply roasted chicken cut into chunks and bathed with ginger or hot sauce are among the house's best efforts. Good accompaniments include the string beans sautéed with pork and, when available, balls of fried, pork-stuffed eggplant. Scallion pancakes, also an occasional daily special, are thick, crisp and satisfying. Noodles are specialties here, cold with sesame oil as a refreshing appetizer or hot with brown meat sauce that can be mild or peppery.

I avoid anything with baby shrimp; they are frozen, translucent and tasteless. Also skip the greasy moo shu pork. But flaws like these leave more than enough pleasurable eating.

Remodeled after a fire, Hwa Yuan is now attractive, with brick walls and a sort of postmodern motif, Chinese-style, on one end wall. There are white tablecloths and a slightly more put-together look than one expects in this location and at these prices. There is a big downstairs dining room, but I do not like it because it seems musty. I therefore wait for a table in the street level dining room and make reservations there when there are six or more people in our party. Such reservations are honored and even held for a while after the appointed hour, as we found out recently when stuck in a traffic jam.

PEKING DUCK WEST

199 Amsterdam Avenue, at 69th Street.
Telephone: 874-9810 or 799-5457.

Favorite meals:
SHARED BY TWO
Tientsin bok choy (Chinese cabbage) with special hot sauce

Sugar-coated walnuts
Peking duck
Pineapple
OR
SHARED BY FOUR TO SIX
All of the above plus
Barbecued beef
Dried scallops with seaweed
Lobster in hot and spicy sauce
Crispy string beans with pork

OTHER FAVORITE DISHES: Smoked fish, meat and vegetables with Tientsin mung bean sheets, cold noodles with sesame sauce, lobster in hot and spicy sauce, steamed sea bass, dried sliced beef with orange flavor, sliced beef with watercress in hot sauce, homemade noodles with bean sauce, hot bean curd with minced beef.

SETTING: Once attractive, modern dining room has grown dull and is in need of sprucing up; tables are large and well spaced; noise level is comfortable but lighting is too dim.

SERVICE: Usually polite and helpful but can become perfunctory at busy times.

DRESS CODE: None.

SMOKING REGULATIONS: No special policy.

FACILITIES FOR PRIVATE PARTIES: None.

HOURS: Lunch and dinner, Sunday through Thursday, 11:30 A.M. to 10:30 P.M.; Friday and Saturday, 11:30 A.M. to 11:30 P.M.

RESERVATIONS: Recommended before Lincoln Center performances.

PRICES: Inexpensive to moderate.

CREDIT CARDS: AE, D, MC, V.

Just about the same flaws and advantages described for the Beijing Duck House apply to this branch, close to Lincoln Center. It is, in fact, one of my choices for dinner when I am going to a performance, and the Peking duck shared by two makes a wonderful pretheater dinner. It would also be fine as a late supper, but the restaurant is open late enough for that only on Friday and Saturday.

When the Peking Duck West opened, it had a handsome, upholstered modern dining room, but since that time the setting has become dull and shabby. It wouldn't take much to restore it to sprightliness. Also, the private rooms unfortunately no longer function as such, and so the restaurant has a depressing half-closed feeling.

Even so, that hot golden duck, carved at the table by a deft, cleaver-wielding chef, is inspired. The crisp skin and moist meat rolled into big, hot rice-flour crepes that have been slathered with hoisin sauce and garnished with slivers of scallions and cucumber makes for sublime eating. Ask to have the chopped carcass to nibble on, or order it cooked with cabbage into a last-course soup. Or take it home and have it cold for breakfast and forget what you read in *Fit for Life*.

As at the Beijing Duck House, there is some greasiness in stir-fried dishes, and here, too, there are some sweet and sour dishes to avoid. That said, I can in good conscience recommend a number of other delectable dishes, all moderately priced. Nice, fresh, big walnut meats caramelized with sugar to crackling succulence have an engaging bite and flavor and are lovely with drinks. Bok choy, the gentle, flavorful Chinese cabbage, gets fiery pickling with chili oil and salt, and among other fine appetizers are the cold noodles with sesame-chili sauce and the slivered meats and vegetables tossed with slippery Tientsin mung bean noodles. Beef that is marinated and barbecued on a stick is delicious, as are the nutlike fried, dried scallops mingled with crisp-fried seaweed. Fish smoked in a sugar glaze is edible, skin, bones and all.

Skip rather disappointing soups and save room instead for the tender, fresh lobster developed carefully in the pork and chili sauce that has an astringent belt of ginger, the chewy dried beef with a bitter orange glaze, and the easygoing sliced beef sautéed with wilted watercress, then zapped with a hot garlic sauce. When dieting, I have the delicate steamed sea bass that gets a touch of ginger and scallion. Noodles with crisp bits of cucumber in bean sauce and the bean curd with minced beef are inexpensive, satisfying dishes, as is the crisp string beans tossed with crumbles of lean pork. Forget fried bananas, which almost always taste of overheated oil, and choose instead the fresh pineapple.

SAY ENG LOOK

5 East Broadway, between Oliver and Catharine Streets. Telephone: 732-0796.

Favorite meals:
SHARED BY TWO
Fried fish roll in bean curd sheet
Eggplant with meat in spiced sauce
Lion head pork ball
OR

SHARED BY FOUR TO SIX
All of the above plus
Beef with scallops
Shanghai spareribs
Broccoli with oyster sauce

OTHER FAVORITE DISHES: Fried whole fish with seaweed, prawns in hot spiced sauce, Tai chi chicken in spiced sauce, chicken in brown sauce, dried beef sautéed, shrimp with kidney, hot and spicy carp, dry sautéed string beans, bean curd in spicy meat sauce, ho sai sea or fish head casserole, casserole of chicken and cellophane noodles, pan-fried noodles with mixed topping. Beer and wine are available. Bring your own hard liquor.

SETTING: Garish but substantial red lacquer decor; downstairs dining room is more comfortable and in all ways preferable to upstairs.

SERVICE: Generally good, if rushed when busy; impatient upstairs, where food is apt to be cold.

DRESS CODE: None.

SMOKING REGULATIONS: No special policy.

FACILITIES FOR PRIVATE PARTIES: Upstairs dining room can be reserved for between seventy and one hundred.

HOURS: Lunch and dinner, Sunday through Thursday, 11 A.M. to 10 P.M.; Friday and Saturday, 11 A.M. to 11 P.M.

RESERVATIONS: Necessary for more than six; rarely honored for less than four.

PRICES: Inexpensive to moderate.

CREDIT CARDS: AE, MC, V.

Shanghai food is the specialty at this very good, very moderately priced Chinatown Mecca. If it is not quite as wonderful as it used to be (most especially on busy weekend nights when the crush is on), it is still a fine option for some unusual food. The main dining room on the street level is done up to a fare-thee-well in old-style Chinese red lacquer. Though gaudy, it is at least "decorated," which in Chinatown has to be considered a plus. Although the upstairs dining room has been given brief decorative consideration, it is uncomfortable. The service up there ranges from indifferent to rude, and the food is rarely hot. My rule for Say Eng Look, then, is to go Monday through Thursday for dinner, or for an early lunch on other days, and always to sit downstairs.

One of the best dishes in the city, regardless of price, cuisine or location, is the fried fish fillet rolled in a sheet of bean curd and fried to tissue-crispness. Crunchy and peppery, it is a lusty appetizer, but for anyone eating alone it would make a main course, along with one of the fine vegetable dishes such as the eggplant in a spicy meat sauce or the broccoli with brown, pungent oyster sauce. Another amazing seafood creation is the fried whole sea bass, scored for crispness and moistness, and topped with cellophanelike flakes of fried seaweed. Shanghai spareribs, really lean and meaty marinated pork chops, are beautifully cooked. Lion head, huge but airy ground pork meatballs braised with green vegetables in a gingery brown sauce, is a soothing, subtly satisfying main course, and for contrast, when the group is large enough, I like the hot spicy carp, its sauce fleshed out with ground pork and its chili-based sauce accented by ginger.

Two very good chicken dishes are Tai chi chicken in spiced sauce stir-fried with black mushrooms and the chicken in a gentle, meaty brown sauce. Dried beef, chewy and mellow in a light sauce, is enlivened by scallions, ginger and garlic. If you like spicy sauces really spicy, ask for them that way. The kitchen will comply, thereby doing justice to dishes such as the prawns or shrimp in hot sauce and the bean curd in meat sauce. For palates of milder inclinations, there is a stir-fry of beef with scallops and the improbable but intriguingly textured combination of shrimp and thinly sliced pork kidney.

Unfortunately, two dishes that used to be excellent have become disappointing—the crisp aromatic duck, somewhat like Peking duck but served with steamed buns, and the Peking duck itself. A recent order did not seem freshly roasted, and the crepes were stiff and crumbly. If available, the sweet glazed and braised pork loin with watercress suggests a hint of star anise and is delicious, but you will have to ask for it as it has never appeared on the menu. Pan-fried noodles tossed with a mix of shrimp, pork and vegetables are better than fried rice.

Wire-bound stoneware casseroles hold a variety of one dish soup-stews of amazing heartiness and richness. Try the fish head version, with bean thread noodles and Chinese cabbage, or the ho sai sea, a broth plumped up with balls of pork and fish, noodles, vegetables, shrimp and julienne strips of omelet. Guests may bring their own wine even though there is a limited list offered, along with beer; many carry in hard liquor. Oranges become dessert in the standard Chinatown fashion.

SHUN LEE PALACE

155 East 55th Street, between Third and Lexington Avenues.
Telephone: 371-8844.

Favorite meals:
SHARED BY TWO
Tangy spicy shrimp
Fried dumplings
Lobster Szechuan, out of the shell
Dry sautéed shredded crispy beef
Fruit
OR
SHARED BY FOUR TO SIX
All of the above plus
Hot and sour cabbage
Broccoli with garlic sauce
Smoked duckling with scallion pancake

OTHER FAVORITE DISHES: Hot and sour soup, cold duck with spicy Hunan sauce, crispy stuffed prawns, spicy crispy sea bass, shrimp or lobster with black bean sauce, Peking duck, velvety shrimp puffs.

SETTING: Neon gives an Art Deco touch to corny, traditional Chinese-screen-type decor for a mismatched blend; most-comfortable seating is in back dining room.

SERVICE: Professional and prompt but pushy toward unknown guests.

DRESS CODE: None.

SMOKING REGULATIONS: No special policy.

FACILITIES FOR PRIVATE PARTIES: One private room holds between twenty and thirty.

HOURS: Lunch and dinner, seven days, noon to 11:30 P.M.

RESERVATIONS: Necessary.

PRICES: Moderately expensive.

CREDIT CARDS: AE, CB, D.

Shun Lee Palace, along with Shun Lee West, Shun Lee Dynasty and Hunam on Second Avenue and 46th Street, were all creations of T.T. Wang, perhaps the most talented and innovative Chinese chef New York has known so far. Abetted by Michael Tong, who ran all his dining rooms, this wizard of a chef-owner introduced us to a new era in Chinese cooking, one that went well beyond the egg roll, egg drop, wonton, subgum, one-choice-from-A cuisine we were used to. He also introduced staggering prices for Chinese food, all of which we got used to because of the excellence of his cuisine. Since Wang's death, Shun Lee Dynasty has closed, and Michael Tong is occupied only with the two remaining Shun Lees. Both have remained among my favorites. This one, the Palace, was the most opulent until recently (see Shun Lee West), and it is still among the more luxurious Chinese restaurants. Never mind that the mix-match of Art Deco neon and modern ceilings clashes with the old-time flashy opulence of gold and Chinese-screen motifs. The effect is pleasant enough even if the details bring a shudder to anyone with a finely honed sense of design.

This is one restaurant where I am sometimes recognized, sometimes not, and there is a difference, less in food than in service. For reasons that still remain a mystery, unknown guests are offered the least desirable tables even when the place is empty. Only when they ask for a better table do they get one, and even then it can take several requests to get into the quieter, more orderly back dining room. One night we were first seated in the raised alcove smack up against a noisy party of ten. We asked to be moved and were offered a mingy table at the entrance to the dining room right in the busy path to the kitchen. Again we asked for a larger table in the almost empty dining room and got it. "Of course," said the host. But if "of course," then why not in the first place? We had a similar experience on our last visit.

The other difference is in the pushiness of captains. To unknown guests they quickly suggest assorted appetizers with drinks. That is a quick way of taking care of the first course. What guests then miss is some of the best choices and the fun of putting the hors d'oeuvre assortment together themselves. Similarly, family service is discouraged, with captains dishing out food and so heaping dishes of varied foods and flavors all over one another. Ask for family service, and the meal will be more enjoyable.

With so many cavils, it might seem surprising that this is a favorite. What makes it so is the very good food and the fact that the staff can be brought to heel in short order. The rewards of the effort are many, beginning with the remarkably bright and cool hot and sour cabbage, which can awaken even the tiredest palate; the cold hacked chicken nestled in a sesame and chili sauce; and the tangy, spiced shrimp, topped with an almost Mexican-type sauce of coriander, scallions and chili peppers. Crescent dumplings filled with meat are delicious fried (really both steamed and fried) and surpass any dim sum in Chinatown for freshness and hotness. So do the stuffed fried prawns. Velvety shrimp puffs, crunchy with bamboo shoots and water chestnuts, are fine as main course or appetizer. Hot and sour soup is full of delicate goodies—slivers of meat and bean curd, black mushrooms and peas—but make it clear that you want it very spicy, assuming, of course, that you do. Otherwise it will be thick and rich but bland. That insistence on hotness is essential to be taken at your word here.

Peking duck is absolutely authentic and masterly done— the glassy veneer of skin as crackling as it should be, the meat moist and rich, the scallions and hoisin sauce adding just the right flavor contrasts to the packet rolled in fresh hot rice-flour

102

crepes. Another marvel of a duck dish is the sweetly woodsy smoked duck, served at room temperature and complemented with a crisp-fried scallion pancake—a really intriguing combination. And as an appetizer, there is yet another cold duck with a spicy Hunan sauce, well worth trying.

Lobster prepared in a spicy Szechuan sauce or in a more mellow fermented black bean puree can be had in or out of the shell; that last, with an extra charge, is a blessing even for the most serious lobster buffs, who have to admit that with such sauces, extricating meat from shell is not fun.

Dry sautéed shredded beef is something like pajasnaya, the fresh pressed caviar connoisseurs love. The dryness lends a concentration of flavor that emerges in the chewing. Vegetables are nicely done, most especially the broccoli with garlic sauce and the dry sautéed string beans.

Considering how many excellent dishes this kitchen turns out, it is hard to understand why so many others—especially the stir-fried meats—are so greasy and tasteless. Hunan lamb, Wang's amazing chicken and Lake Tung-Ting shrimp are enduring examples.

Allow me to wind up on a positive note, much as my usual meals there usually do. Crispy whole sea bass could not be improved upon. The fresh, plump fish is crisply deep-fried, then blanketed with a gingery, hot Hunan meat sauce. This is, by the way, an excellent restaurant at which to have a banquet, especially if Michael Tong does the planning—excellent *and* expensive.

SHUN LEE (WEST)

43 West 65th Street, between Columbus Avenue and Central Park West.
Telephone: 595-8895.

Favorite meals:
SHARED BY TWO
Tangy spicy shrimp
Mongolian oxtail soup with vegetables
Smoked duckling with scallion pancake
Szechuan broccoli
Sesame snow ball
OR
SHARED BY FOUR TO SIX
Szechuan wonton

Hacked chicken
Hot and sour cabbage
Smoked duckling with scallion pancake
Crispy sea bass Hunan-style
Dry sautéed beef
Frogs' legs with scallions and hot pepper
Fresh fruit

OTHER FAVORITE DISHES: All dumplings, spicy chicken soong, honey baby ribs, crispy shrimp balls, Szechuan sesame noodles, Peking hot and sour soup, prawns with garlic and scallions, Szechuan lobster, Peking duck, steamed salmon with ginger and scallions, stuffed bean curd in hot Szechuan or mild oyster sauce, eggplant Szechuan.

SETTING: Stunning and dramatic new interior done in black with stylish touches; long, attractive bar.

SERVICE: Excellent when guests are known; can be perfunctory to unknowns, especially late in the evening.

DRESS CODE: None.

SMOKING REGULATIONS: No special policy.

FACILITIES FOR PRIVATE PARTIES: None really, but a few exceptions are made for the side room at off hours; it is a good idea to ask.

HOURS: Lunch and dinner, seven days, noon to 12:30 A.M.; Sunday brunch is being planned for the new café.

RESERVATIONS: Recommended for lunch; necessary for dinner, especially before and after Lincoln Center performances.

PRICES: Moderately expensive.

CREDIT CARDS: AE, CB, D, MC, V.

For a bit of history and background on this Lincoln Center restaurant (formerly called Shun Lee West), see the introduction to the previous review of Shun Lee Palace. This too is a T.T. Wang-Michael Tong production, and right now it is far and away the most spectacular-looking Chinese restaurant in the city. Redecorated in 1985, it first seemed to me to look like a gaudy New Jersey nightclub. The main dining room is all tiers of black velour, and around the ceiling cornice winds an almost endless, stiffened-fabric white dragon glowing from within. But by my third visit, I became enchanted. The black shell, with its white accents of tablecloths, is a dramatic backdrop against which women dressed in black, white or bright red become a wonderful design. Even hands tipped with red lacquer nail polish look deliberately planned. Men look fine, if less dramatic, unless they are in black tie.

Because of this stunning decor, this is one uptown Chinese restaurant I would visit for its own sake, especially if I were with anyone who is design conscious. Actually, I feel the food is a shade better and more consistent at Shun Lee Palace, but the setting here makes up the difference, so both get the same rating.

Service is excellent, but I have always been known. That means no one pushes assorted appetizers or automatically messes up the food by dishing it out on plates. There are wonderful dumplings, including all of the steamed, fried, mild and spicy variations. All are better, fresher and hotter than even the best found in Chinatown. This is also true of crispy, fried shrimp balls, curry turnovers, the spicy stir-fried chicken soong and honey baby spareribs. Try the cool, pungent hot and sour cabbage, Szechuan noodles glossed with sesame oil, or remarkably tangy spicy shrimp (better than those at Shun Lee Palace), with a verdant sprinkling of coriander, parsley and garlic for an almost Mexican-style green salsa. Hacked chicken is freshly cooked and moist, and the combination of sesame and chili oils blends into an enticing sweet-hot sauce. Both hot and sour soup, thick with meat, bean curd and mushrooms, and the very original crocks of Mongolian oxtail and vegetable soup, much like heartening stew, are delicious.

Unfortunately, a number of old favorites have disappeared from this menu; but luckily the lean, cool woodsy smoked duck with warm scallion pancakes has survived. So has the crispy sea bass, greaselessly deep-fried and burnished with Hunan hot sauce. (Ask to have food really spicy here and you'll get it; otherwise it will be relatively mild.) Salmon is unusual on Chinese menus in New York; here it is lovely steamed with ginger and scallions, emerging moist and distinguished by its own flavor. I prefer chewy, dry shredded crispy beef with its pungent sauce to the candy-sweet orange-flavor variation.

Frogs' legs with scallions and hot pepper are tantalizing when available. Peking duck is utter perfection, the crepes always freshly made and soft, the duck skin glassy and crackling, the meat moist and flavorful. Rolled with hoisin sauce and slivered scallion, it is the city's best and, as lagniappe, does not have to be ordered in advance. There is also fine lobster, either in ginger-scallion sauce or with black beans, and both versions can be ordered out of the shell, a blessing for anyone all dressed up to go to Lincoln Center.

Inexplicably, I find that most stir-fried meat dishes (Hunan lamb or veal, for example) are soaked with grease and totally characterless. The same is true of the overly large sizzling scallops that are fried and served with vegetables. Singapore curried rice noodles are also below par, but young chow pan-fried noodles with pork and shrimp are all they should be.

Sesame snow ball is a strange warm dessert that looks startlingly like eyeballs—a sort of white puff with a sweet dark filling in a thin syrup. One bite goes a long way. Honey apple fritters invariably taste of overheated oil. Fresh fruit or ice cream is preferable.

Siu Lam Kung

18 Elizabeth Street, between Canal and Bayard Streets. Telephone: 732-0974.

Favorite meal:
SHARED BY FOUR TO SIX
Fried bean curd stuffed with shrimp
Pork chops with chili pepper and salt
Bird's nest and crabmeat soup
Roasted chicken
Lobster with ginger and scallions
Braised duck with Chinese mushrooms
Oranges

OTHER FAVORITE DISHES: Sliced pork and vegetable soup, sliced abalone with vegetables, braised abalone with oyster sauce, roasted squab special-style, baked chicken with salt, steamed chicken with ham and Chinese broccoli, pork chops Peking-style or with pepper and black bean sauce, baked salted shrimp, boiled shrimp, shrimp with scrambled eggs, conch with scallops and vegetables, squid with chilies and salt, mixed seafood in bird's nest, crabs with ginger and scallions, steamed or fried flounder, braised bean curd with black mushrooms and vegetables, broccoli with oyster sauce, fried rice, pan-fried noodles with pork or shrimp, braised turtle and eel in black bean sauce (ordered twenty-four hours in advance), steak with broccoli.

SETTING: Recently redone, pleasantly modern dining room, with usual noisy, disorderly jam-packed scene.

SERVICE: Perfunctory at busiest times but generally good natured, helpful and fast.

DRESS CODE: None.

SMOKING REGULATIONS: No special policy.

FACILITIES FOR PRIVATE PARTIES: None.

HOURS: Lunch and dinner, seven days, 11:30 A.M. to 11:30 P.M.

RESERVATIONS: Necessary and honored with reasonable promptness.

PRICES: Inexpensive to moderate.

CREDIT CARDS: None.

Few restaurants in Chinatown have attracted such a steady line of eager eaters as this one. Even when reservations are made, there is usually at least a short wait, and parties of two to four often have to share larger tables. Since it first earned three stars, much has happened to this large, bustling Cantonese restaurant. There have been changes in partner-owners, and clones opened across the street and on Mott Street. Now there seems to be just this one, across the street from the police station and next to the Chinatown arcade. The others were never as good as this, and it is the only location I go to. Whether because of the changes or overexpansion, there was a lapse in quality for a while. But on recent visits, during which I had no clue that I was recognized, I found the food spectacularly good, with only a few exceptions: Black bean sauce on all seafood was too thickly cornstarched, and beef tended to be sinewy and tough.

Turtles and eels swim in a window tank here, and they are not mere decoration. All can be served if ordered twenty-four hours ahead. The turtle meat is tender, slippery and briny, braised in a light brown sauce, and the meaty, clean-tasting eel is equally good fried, braised with vegetables or cooked with black beans. (In this case, the sauce is just fine.) Both specialties are favored by the many Chinese who hold family banquets here. At those banquets it is possible to see many dishes; then you can order them by pointing. Sharing tables affords another opportunity to learn of other new choices.

Despite the Cantonese kitchen, the menu does not offer the usual wonton-spare rib-egg roll trinity or other similar clichés. Instead you can start with puffy, creamy square pillows of bean curd, stuffed with shrimp and lightly, crisply fried, or the pork chops, pounded thin and simmered with pepper and black beans or stir-fried with chilies and salt. Ordered Peking style, they arrive crisply fried, with only a spiced salt dip for seasoning. Shrimp either plain boiled in shells or baked with salt are also good to begin with (not that you can be sure they will arrive before main courses), and there are a couple of delicious soups—one with sliced pork and vegetables, the other a luxurious richness of bird's nest flecked with crabmeat. Soup orders are huge and rarely a good idea for two, as much will be wasted. Abalone, which can be as tough as rubber washers, here is pounded and simmered to tenderness and is fine with vegetables or braised with oyster sauce.

Conch, the shellfish the Italians call scungilli, can also be tough but not here, especially as served with scallops and vegetables. Stir-fried seafood of all sorts nests in a crisp fried basket of grated taro root, another understandable favorite at Chinese tables. For an original and altogether pleasing lunch main course, there is sweet pink shrimp folded into softly

107

scrambled eggs, to which I like to add minced scallions.

Other good seafood dishes include the pearly, fresh steamed flounder brightened with ginger and the fried version, so crisply done it can be eaten small bones and all. Scallions added to the clear broth around the fish lend sprightly flavor contrast. Lobster is sea fresh and full of flavor, and the ginger-scallion sauce over it provides the right complement.

Chicken is wonderful in several forms, my favorites being the crisp-skinned, golden, roasted version and the gentler, sunny, salt-baked variation. Delicate too is the chicken steamed with shavings of salty Virginia ham and firm, slightly bitter Chinese broccoli. Crunchy but moist roast squab is excellent but be ready to have it head and all. There is a sensational duck dish that defies the American passion for crispness in that bird. It is braised slowly, tenderly, with spices that include star anise and black Chinese mushrooms to lend an earthy, almost smoky accent. Steak with broccoli is about the only beef dish I order here, and it has never been disappointing.

Very good vegetable combinations round out this menu. Among favorites are the snowy bean curd tossed with black mushrooms and Chinese vegetables, the broccoli with oyster sauce and, when in season, something called yocca cooked with fermented bean curd. Some waiters know this when asked, others claim never to have heard of it. I always try and hope for the best. It is much like dandelion greens and profits from a dose of garlic. Shrimp or pork fried rice and pan-fried noodles with the same toppings are comforting fillers worth saving room for. Consider them dessert, as oranges are the only alternative.

Y.S. (Hop Woo) Restaurant

17 Elizabeth Street, between Canal and Bayard Streets.
Telephone: 966-5838.

Favorite meal:
Shared by four
Spicy pork chops with chili and salt
Lobster with ginger and scallions
Roasted chicken (half)
Fried flounder
Sautéed Chinese broccoli with oyster sauce
Oranges

OTHER FAVORITE DISHES: Special West Lake with beef soup; lobster, clams, shrimp or crabs with black bean sauce; shrimp or baked crabs with ginger and scallions; baked prawns with chili and spicy sauce; baked chicken with salt; fried quail with honey sauce; roasted squab; steak with Chinese broccoli and special sauce. Chinese beer is available; take your own wine or hard liquor.

SETTING: Bright, pleasant, bustling room; tables near door and kitchen are uncomfortable.

SERVICE: Prompt, helpful and efficient.

DRESS CODE: None.

SMOKING REGULATIONS: No special policy.

FACILITIES FOR PRIVATE PARTIES: None.

HOURS: Lunch and dinner, seven days, 11 A.M. to midnight.

RESERVATIONS: Accepted for parties of eight or more if they are carefully made in person well in advance.

PRICES: Inexpensive to moderate.

CREDIT CARDS: None.

Directly across the street from Siu Lam Kung, Y.S. is said to have a chef who worked at that exceptional place and left at the peak of its popularity. Both restaurants are Cantonese and so have many similar menu items; therefore, before long, a line was also gathering here. But though this simple, crowded and fairly pleasant place has about ten or twelve first-class dishes, the rest of the food is innocuous. My husband and I were in the habit of eating the same dishes all the time and so one day decided to make different choices, with totally disappointing results.

But what it does well, it does very, very well, and because it is easier to get into than Siu Lam Kung and has such low prices and friendly service, I go often and am happy to stick to the proven favorites. Among soups, that means a gentle, soothing version of the good old egg drop standard, here called special West Lake with beef soup. The West Lake region of Suzhou is known for its light and frothy egg concoctions, and the flakes of egg in this beef broth wrap around crumbles of beef and shreds of coriander. It has a mild flavor that restores frayed nerves and settles one's palate for the more complex flavors and textures to come. Appetizers as such (the usual barbecues, egg rolls and fried wonton) are eminently skippable. Instead, create your own first course with the spicy pork chops, a variation on spareribs, that are dry-fried to lean meatiness, then showered with green chili peppers and salt. You might be able to get those chops before the soup, so you can nibble on them with beer or any hard liquor or wine you may take along. Lobster is always fresh and tender at Y.S. and best with a thin, heady sauce that combines fresh ginger and slivered scallions, the same combination that works so well on shrimp and the crunchy, fatty baked crabs.

Fermented black beans, one of the world's best-tasting ingredients, create the sauce for another fine lobster dish, as well as for clams, shrimp or crabs. At times that sauce can be a bit overly slick with cornstarch, so ask for very little of that binder when ordering. (Some is needed to make the sauce stick to shellfish, but a little goes a long way.)

Slivers of green chili peppers and salt complement many simple, savory and sauceless foods, such as the pork chops already mentioned. That combination also sparks baked prawns, sautéed squid and sautéed scallops with equally intriguing results. The fried flounder is a miracle of greaseless, crackling crunchiness. The flesh of fish stays moist, while skin and even bones are so crisp they flake. The fine bones along the fins are as irresistible as salted peanuts.

Oddly enough, the three or four duck dishes I have tried here have all tasted stale and greasy, yet other poultry has been excellent. Perhaps more chicken is sold and so is more freshly cooked. Whatever the reason, it would be hard to beat the golden roasted chicken, with its crisp skin and moist meat, or the softer, succulent sunny yellow chicken baked in salt; both are served with a spicy seasoned salt dip. It's a tossup between these two, and I alternate, ordering a half of either. Another surprise dish, beautifully done, is fried quail in honey sauce. One quail per person ($2.75) is another good appetizer choice. The meat is tender, and the honey glaze adds a nice caramelized zest. Similarly, roasted squab ($7.95 each) is an adventure into crunchiness and juiciness. It arrives with head intact, so if you are squeamish in the American manner, be forewarned.

Hearty appetites that are unsatisfied without beef should be happy with the steak topped with sizzling Chinese broccoli in a rich brown sauce. The same firm, slightly bitter Chinese broccoli in oyster sauce is one of my favorite vegetables. Another that appears here seasonally, and which is not on the menu, is called hong choy, related to the Chinese cabbage bok choy but closer in appearance and taste to watercress. It is usually available in late spring to early summer and is served stir-fried with a bit of garlic, much like Italian escarole. Cut-up oranges are again the only dessert and always seem right.

Yun Luck Rice Shoppe

17 Doyers Street, between Mott Street and the Bowery.
Telephone: 571-1375.

Favorite meal:
>SHARED BY FOUR TO SIX
>Periwinkles or spareribs in black bean sauce
>Pink pepper shrimp
>Steamed flounder
>Golden Peking roast chicken
>Buddhist delight mixed vegetables
>Beef with broccoli
>Pan-fried noodles

OTHER FAVORITE DISHES: Steamed chicken, salt-baked chicken, fried flounder, lobster or crabs Cantonese, heart of broccoli with oyster sauce, squid with sautéed vegetables, mixed seafood in bird's nest, fried sea bass with vegetables (hong shu yu).

SETTING: As plain pipe racks as they come, complete with oilcloth on tables; busy and lively.

SERVICE: Good natured and helpful; some waiters need help with English.

DRESS CODE: None.

SMOKING REGULATIONS: No special policy.

FACILITIES FOR PRIVATE PARTIES: None.

HOURS: Lunch and dinner, Sunday through Friday, 11:30 A.M. to midnight; Saturday, 11:30 A.M. to 1 A.M.

RESERVATIONS: Necessary for five or more.

PRICES: Inexpensive.

CREDIT CARDS: None.

Chinese outnumber non-Chinese by at least 15-to-1 here, and the English menu is far more limited than the Chinese. Many of my favorite dishes do not even appear in English but are always forthcoming when ordered. For that reason, I rate this one star only; it is just not fair to limit the menu in that way. Whenever I go, I spot new dishes at Chinese tables. Then I ask waiters what they are, make notes and order them next time. That way I have built up a dependable repertory of delicious dishes so inexpensive it is often cheaper to eat here than to cook at home.

Yun Luck used to be excellent. The best dishes were offered to all, and they were prepared with dazzling consistency. But success takes a toll, and so there were good days and bad days (probably because of the switching of good chefs to bad), and I reduced the rating to two stars. Now it rates only one, but as with Y.S., that still means quite a bit of very good eating.

Considering how pro-Chinese the management is, the staff is amazingly patient and helpful with others. They suggest and explain dishes, always bring something else if it is requested after the main order, and good-naturedly take back anything not properly prepared, as they did when I sent back some clams in a black bean sauce too gluey with cornstarch.

You will not find golden Peking roast chicken on the menu, but it is always available and always impeccable. I ask to have it cooked as it is for Chinese, meaning that the skin is not so crisp that the meat dries out. A showering of those crazy, pastel-colored shrimp wafers always accompanies this chicken (as in all Chinatown restaurants) for reasons that remain inscrutably Oriental. Never mind, though, the anise- and pepper-scented salt dip lends this delectable chicken a tingling lift, as it does to the other whole or half chickens, steamed or salt baked. All of those chickens are so good, I have ordered them whole, taking uneaten halves home for the next day.

Plump fresh sea bass (hong shu yu), crisply batter fried and decked out with shreds of pork, black mushrooms, vegetables, and icy water chestnuts in a light brown oyster sauce, is dependably good.

Whole flounder, dewily fresh and greaselessly fried to parchment crispness, is a delight as is the steamed version, a delicate silken masterpiece with flesh cooked to the consistency of a just-set custard and accented by ginger and scallion. Pink pepper shrimp, sautéed with salt, is a traditional favorite here as are the tiny sea snails, periwinkles, in a black bean sauce. The meaty little bodies must be extricated from shells with toothpicks or long satay skewers, but diligence is well rewarded. Crabs or lobster in a Cantonese egg, pork and garlic sauce is delicious as are the tender, scored curls of squid stir-fried with vegetables and the mixed seafoods (shrimp, crabmeat, squid and fish dumplings) with vegetables in a deep-fried nest of grated taro root. Buddhist mixed vegetables with ginkgo nuts, lotus root, lily buds and so on is a silky, soothing specialty.

Avoid all clichéd Cantonese soups and appetizers here and dishes listed as "chef's suggestions," excepting only seafood in bird's nest and the sea bass.

DIM SUM AND OTHER CHINESE TIDBITS

A specialty of Southern China and Hong Kong, dim sum are the "heart's delights" that you eat while you *yum cha*—

112

drink tea. The array of steamed and fried dumplings made with various types of rice- and wheat-flour doughs, and the small dishes such as stewed spareribs with garlic, peppers stuffed with shrimp, taro pancakes, various innards and chicken or duck feet, along with big puffy filled steamed yeast buns, make up the repertory.

Traditionally these delicacies are served in huge cafeteria-like dining rooms, but instead of customers going to the food, it comes to them on little carts rolled by waitresses. You point to what you want, and at the end the empty dishes and steamers are tallied to arrive at the bill.

As this custom has become more popular in Chinatown, the dim sum have become less good, an unfortunate development. Flushed with the easy success of satisfying parvenu dim sum eaters, more and more Chinese cooks turn out carelessly made versions. The best of this sort of thing are at the two Shun Lees, but they are not served in the traditional manner, merely as appetizers ordered from the kitchen.

The most authentic and best dim summery in Chinatown is the *Lan Hong Kok Seafood House*, 31 Division Street (226-9674). It is small and decorless, in fact downright raunchy, but it is a great favorite with Chinese for dim sum from 7:30 A.M. to 4 P.M. every day. Because the room is small, waitresses carry trays, and not too many dishes are on each. That assures hotness and freshness. In addition, the dim sum are very well flavored. Meat fillings are copious and coarsely chopped for good texture, the lion head pork balls with ginger are garnished with wilted watercress (or what looks and tastes like that green), and the pinwheels of crisp, shredded taro root packed around flat minced pork are masterpieces. Stuffed crab claw (the stuffing around instead of in the shell) and slivers of roast pork or duck folded into yeast buns are equally good.

There is a full Cantonese menu with a number of inexpensive, sustaining noodle, meat and vegetable soups.

H.S.F., standing for Hee Sung Feung, at 46 Bowery, just south of Canal Street (374-1319), is my second choice even though it is not as impeccable as formerly. Sometimes overcooked, the dumplings do, however, have more flavor than most others in Chinatown, and they arrive at tables steaming hot, a necessary requirement for most of the offerings. It is also a bit easier for novices to negotiate than Lan Hong Kok.

The only category to avoid at H.S.F. is the crisp-fried specialties such as shrimp toast, fried pork dumplings, sesame chicken, etc. Those always are tepid and ooze grease. Steamed shrimp dumplings either in transparent rice- or opaque wheat-flour dough, shu mai, which are tulip-shaped pork dumplings, and slippery crepes filled with chicken, beef or shrimp are all delicious. So are fried crab claws, fried bean curd sheets filled with vegetables, shrimp stuffed green pepper sautéed at the table on a grill cart and the half-steamed, half-fried dumplings finished in the same way. Bowls of hot and sticky fried rice with pork; nuggets of spareribs in garlic and black bean sauce; roast pork, chicken and duck; and spicy squid are also good.

One of my special favorites is paper shrimp, big butterfly wings of starchy rice paper holding a shrimp filling at the base. It does not come out of the kitchen too often, but ask as soon as you sit down and some will be forthcoming. H.S.F. has a neat and enticingly illustrated leaflet of dim sum at each table, and you can point to what you want and the waiters will generally get it. Sweet pork or red bean paste in steamed buns and a variety of soups are also satisfying. If you are in a large group, finish up as Chinese do, with an order of pan-fried noodles with seafood. That and beer or tea should hold you for the day.

Dim sum are served seven days a week at all of the places mentioned, starting at 7:30 or 8 A.M. and going through the afternoon until 4 or 5 P.M.

There are also good selections at the *Nice Restaurant*, 35 East Broadway between Market and Catharine Streets, 406-9510, and at *Sun Tong Gung*, 28-30 Pell Street between Mott and Elizabeth Streets, 513-0622, but by the time waitresses work their way around to all of the tables, the food is cold and, therefore, unpleasant.

Another emergency stop I rely on is at *Hsin Yu*, 862 Second Avenue, at the corner of 46th Street (752-8943). Primarily a neighborhood takeout place, there is also a small, attractive café-dining room with big windows overlooking the street. There are delicious fried, pork-filled dumplings here and wonderfully pungent hot and sour soup. Diced chicken with peanuts in hot pepper sauce is another soul-stimulating choice, but the dumplings and soup are usually enough. It is best if two share the eight big dumplings, then each have a bowl of soup. When I am alone, I just leave half of the dumplings as they do not travel well.

Cuban and Caribbean

SABOR

20 Cornelia Street, between West 4th and Bleecker Streets.
Telephone:243-9579.

Favorite meals:
Escabeche of fish with vegetables
Pot roast stuffed with chorizo sausage (carne estofada)
Key lime pie
OR
Empanadas filled with chorizo sausages
Shrimp in green sauce (camarones en salsa verde)
Baked coconut bread pudding with sherry and cinnamon
(coco quemado)

OTHER FAVORITE DISHES: Zarzuela of mussels in tomato sauce;
marinated squid (calamares picantes); salt codfish with potatoes and vegetables in tomato sauce (bacalao à la Vizcaina); zarzuela of shellfish; ground sirloin with olives, capers
and raisins (picadillo); chicken in prune sauce (curri de pollo
con ciruelas pasas); flan; fresh sliced pineapple; cappuccino
ice cream.

SETTING: Small, closely packed bohemian bistro that is attractive, if noisy.

SERVICE: Slow and inexplicably tight lipped but not rude unless
a complaint is made.

DRESS CODE: None.

SMOKING REGULATIONS: No special policy.

FACILITIES FOR PRIVATE PARTIES: Can close restaurant for groups
of about thirty.

HOURS: Dinner, Sunday through Thursday, 6 to 10:30 P.M.; Friday and Saturday, 6 to 11:30 P.M. Closed only on Christmas
Eve and Day.

115

RESERVATIONS: Recommended.
PRICES: Moderate.
CREDIT CARDS: AE, MC, V.

No one who ate a lot of wonderful Cuban food in pre-Castro Havana will for a moment consider the offerings at Sabor truly Cuban. Rather they are done with a sort of learned restraint, much as though they were based on good recipes in a progressive womens' magazine. Yet this small, pretty Village bistro, with its cream-colored brick walls and plum wine trim, does serve up the only really decent representation of this cuisine that I have found in New York. Tables are very closely set and are cramped, and the room is noisy, especially when music is played full blast, but it is that sort of place, and one should go, as I do, not trying to have a long, serious heart-to-heart with dinner companions.

Even with the strangely tight-lipped waitresses, who without being rude impart a sense of near hostility, the food is worth the gaff. They are never really argumentative unless something such as a badly made drink is sent back, in which case they may tell you why you are wrong. Drinks here are all badly made, by the way, including both daiquiris and margaritas, so a bottle of Dos Equis beer is a wiser choice, and it stands up well to the richly seasoned food, at prices so moderate the house imposes a $9 minimum.

To light eaters, that could mean two of the very good appetizers, perhaps the crisp empañada turnovers filled with spicy chorizo sausage and the escabeche, a nice chunk of firm fish pickled with olives and vegetables and served overflowingly on a small lettuce-lined plate. A larger plate would make eating more comfortable. Or the starter might be mussels in a saffron-piqued tomato sauce or the cool, marinated squid, just chewy enough in its pungent peppery dressing. One night special fritters were offered, either of shrimp and crabmeat or chicken with ham. I asked if I could have a combination and the waitress gave me a cold "No." I thought perhaps each order was one large fritter, but when six or seven small puffs arrived, I could not understand why the combination had not been possible. As it was, the chicken and ham I chose (because I was having shrimp for a main course) were pleasant, if too soft inside. I have a feeling the shellfish would have been better.

Cream soups tend to have the flavors of eggnog, what with seasonings of sherry and nutmeg, so I skip them. The well-soaked salt codfish bacalao is served here à la Vizcaina, a lovely stew of potatoes, vegetables, capers and olives in tomato sauce, and there is the equally good shellfish stew zarzuela, combining clams, mussels, shrimp, scallops and squid in a spicy tomato broth. Firm, snowy shrimp in a fluffy parsley and garlic

116

green sauce is one of the better dishes. It is very good with the steamed white rice and stewed black beans that accompany all the main courses. Red snapper, however, in a sourish lime juice and garlic sauce is far less pleasant, especially when the fish is small and little more than skin and bones.

The same escabeche that is offered as an appetizer can be had in a larger main course portion and is a welcome option on a hot night.

Picadillo is a sort of Spanish hash, ground sirloin tossed with olives, capers and raisins and wholly satisfying here. The best meat dish is the carne estofada, a pot-roasted beef stuffed with chopped chorizo sausage, olives, capers, raisins and prunes. Its sauce is bolstered with pureed vegetables and lightened with dashes of sherry and fresh orange. Lŏmo de puerco, a pork roast, has the impossibly sweet overtones of hot pineapple and sherry in its sauce, so I avoid it.

Prunes also are in the curry sauce on chicken, a surprise and a delight, although mushrooms midst all of this seem strangely out of place. An order of fried plantains was limp and grease soaked and a far cry from the crisp wonders that used to be served at bars in Havana and Veradero Beach.

Individual tarts of Key lime pie and light flan, the custard burnished with caramelized sugar, are easygoing desserts. Lustier and yet soothing is the coco quemado, a sort of coconut bread pudding with sherry and cinnamon, served hot with a soft whipped cream topping. Brazo gitano, an insipid, soft cake roll drenched with custard, Grand Marnier, sherry and orange sauce, is close to a mini-trifle and cloying.

It is hard to understand why the two young women who own this place, Gail Lewis and Ronnie Ginnever, do not make a greater effort to get real Cuban bread and serve stain-the-cup Cuban coffee. Both are available in New York, most especially the coffee, and Puerto Rican or even a good, dry and light Sicilian bread would be closer to the mark than the characterless Italian loaves they offer.

TIDBITS

Caribbean food is said to be a new rage in New York, meaning there are about three restaurants serving it. Although I have not been to any of the places avowedly offering the food of that area, I did have a very good meal at the new *Lola*, where Jamaican and Caribbean influences are exercised on what is known as new American cooking. Owned by a former partner of Pesca, Lola too has theatrical peach-glow walls washed by colored filters of stage lighting and a romantic little fake garden showing through the windows. Yvonne "Lola" Bell, the partner who is said to have created the recipes, has adapted her Jamaican parents' dishes to this format. The cooking, however, is done by Chef Jeffrey Loshinsky, formerly of Pesca. Among very good dishes I had were little giveaway piquant Cheddar cheese crackers, supposedly after a recipe from Lady Bird Johnson, the wonderfully greaseless, flavorful fritters of shrimp and potatoes dipped into a fiery creole mayonnaise, and tissue-thin onion rings. Bermuda chowder would have been better with a fish other than the oily tuna, a touch I do not remember at Pesca, but there was no fault to be found with a seafood stew that combined scallops, clams, lobster and shrimp in a clear saffron, wine and tomato bouillon or with a delicate curry of chicken and shrimp garnished with crisp waffles to soak up the sauce, which, like that of many dishes here, has a nice needly sting. A good spicy sting ruined by oversalting was a flaw in the one-hundred-spice Caribbean fried chicken, alas, for it was otherwise well cooked. Pumpkin mousse served in a big tuile cookie cup was a more interesting dessert than the fresh fruit plate or the bland ricotta gelato.

Lola, 30 West 22nd Street, between Fifth and Sixth Avenues (675-6700), is open for lunch and dinner Monday through Saturday and also serves late supper. Sunday hours vary, so call ahead.

Ethiopian

THE BLUE NILE

103 West 77th Street, just west of Columbus Avenue.
Telephone: 580-3232.

Favorite meal:
SHARED BY TWO TO FOUR
Red lentil salad (azefa)
Kale and potatoes with spices (yegomen wot)
Chicken in hot sauce (doro wot)
Spicy beef tartare (kitfo)
Lamb in curry-style sauce (yebeg alitcha)

OTHER FAVORITE DISHES: Peas in hot sauce (yekik wot), chick-pea puree (shuro wot), stewed red lentils (yemesir), beef stewed in hot sauce (tibs wot).

SETTING: Spacious, attractive downstairs dining room with a pretty bar, colorful Ethiopian artifacts, and exquisite basket tables and carved three-legged stools at which food is served native-style.

SERVICE: Gracious, helpful and efficient.

DRESS CODE: None.

SMOKING REGULATIONS: No special policy.

FACILITIES FOR PRIVATE PARTIES: Four rooms that can accommodate between fifteen and eighty-five.

HOURS: Dinner, Saturday through Thursday, 5 to 11 P.M.; dinner, Friday and Saturday, noon to midnight. Closed major holidays.

RESERVATIONS: Not accepted.

PRICES: Inexpensive to moderate.

CREDIT CARDS: AE.

Although as represented in New York no one would rank the Ethiopian kitchen as being among the world's finest, it does at least offer a number of delicious and diverting dishes, all truly exotic, in the strictest sense of that word. Borrowing from Indian and Arabic cooking, and adding a number of their own creations, the Ethiopians offer a menu that will appeal to anyone who likes subtle spicing and soothing textures. Sheba was the first such restaurant in New York, and there on Hudson Street, close to the Holland Tunnel, food was served at tables and chairs. The same management then branched into Abyssinia, a tiny place still operating in SoHo, where food is served as in Ethiopia, at colorful basket pedestal tables as guests sit on carved wood stools with three splayed legs. Now Sheba has closed, and again the same owners opened another restaurant, The Blue Nile, also serving native-style. The food is as good as it was at Sheba (Abyssinia, for some reason, never quite measured up), and this new setting is far more comfortable and handsome. There is a trim bar, beautiful Ethiopian artifacts and Coptic-style religious hangings and decorations, and the service is graceful and helpful. True, the squat stools are not recommended for knees over forty, but negotiating them will result in an interesting dinner. It is a good idea to wear pants rather than skirts for this culinary adventure.

No utensils are used. Instead, food is picked up with pieces of a spongy, crepelike bread called injera. The first time I saw it laid out in a wide flat basket, I assumed it was our napkins. Most of the food is stewed or in a currylike sauce, so that the small pieces and their sauces are easily picked with torn-off sections of the injera. As in India and other countries where eating is out of hand, it is considered correct to use only the right hand. Among dishes designated as appetizers, my preference is for the azefa, a lentil salad spiked with onions, bitter mustard seeds, green chili peppers and lemon juice. Kidneys marinated in red wine were overly strong, and a house salad seemed to have been invented to pacify the American passion for such greenery.

If in a party of six or more, start also with the kitfo, beef tartare that profits from a mixing with spiced butter and chili powder and is best when ordered hotly seasoned. For a smaller group, this can be included among main courses.

Kale simmered with potatoes and green peppers and aromatically spiced is a good foil for dishes such as doro wot, stewed chicken and hard-boiled egg in a fiery berberé sauce, the only problem with that dish being the large pieces of chicken with bones that are hard to handle with the bread. Yebeg alitcha—chunks of tender lamb mellowed in an exotically spiced sauce of turmeric, ginger, onions, garlic and white pepper—and the tibs wot—beef cubes tenderized in a hot sauce that

120

includes fenugreek, garlic, onions and spices—are easier to handle, as is, of course, the kitfo. Chick-pea puree (shuro wot) with overtones of basil and ginger and the yekik wot (peas in hot sauce) are good company to meat dishes for parties of four or more. Portions are not large, and sharing is convivial since all eat from the same injera-lined tray. Other dishes on the menu are dull by comparison, and occasionally even the best creations seem to have been made too long before they were served. On one occasion, the doro wot had obviously been scorched.

Desserts are the Columbus Avenue repertory of heavy, overly rich pies and cakes. Too bad no fresh fruit or sherbet is on hand.

Beer provides a refreshing contrast to this food, and as a less caloric alternative, have a Scotch and soda, as I do.

French–With an Explanation

Once asked what his religion was, Woody Allen answered, "Jewish, with an explanation." It is a remark that came to mind as I tried to categorize restaurants by the type of food they serve, most especially where nouvelle French and new American come together. Is a French restaurant one in which the kitchen staff is French? If that were true, La Tulipe and Chanterelle would not be in this category. Or does it matter if choices are described on the menu in English, French or Franglaise, or that a certain percentage of dishes are French inspired? In that case, Odeon and Café Luxembourg would qualify.

The only solution, when in doubt, was to follow my own perception of a restaurant and let the chips fall where they may. Odeon and Café Luxembourg appeal to me as new American, and so that is where I have put them. In an attempt to make sense out of this stew of confusion, I have indicated the categories of those restaurants that might be looked for under a French heading. That, and the detailed index, should solve the problem.

It is, of course, more important to know if the food is good than to know which category it fits into, but expectations are very much a part of my evaluations. If something is billed as French, I expect something different from food that is called Continental, new American or abstract expressionist, which is what much of it has become. None of this adds up to the most burning issue of our times, but it is a question raised by the current wave of culinary eclecticism that tends to make all food alike, at least in the "hottest" restaurants. Anyone going only to such places will have a hard time knowing whether the city is Munich, Paris, London, New York, Chicago, San Francisco or Los Angeles. It's fillet-of-sole-bonne-femme time, all over again.

One sad omission from this chapter is Le Cherche-Midi, Sally Scoville's delicious little bistro, which closed just as this book was going to press. Her fragrant Provençale dishes and most especially the wonderful walnut-honey tart will be missed.

122

The restaurant had improved so much since its opening that I looked forward to giving it three stars, and it is a loss.

Le Bernardin, *see* Seafood

LE BIARRITZ

325 West 57th Street, between Eighth and Ninth Avenues. Telephone: 757-2390.

Favorite meal:
   LUNCH ONLY
   Salade Niçoise
   Gigot of lamb with beans (flageolets)
   Rice pudding

OTHER FAVORITE DISHES: Assorted hors d'oeuvres; artichoke vinaigrette if it is a fresh, bright green; quiche; roast chicken with cèpes or chanterelles; calves' liver à l'anglaise; brains with black butter (cervelles au beurre noir); braised shank of veal (jarret de veau); crème caramel; chocolate mousse; salad of fresh fruits in red wine.

SETTING: Beautifully kept, charming red dining room hung with gleaming copper pots; noisy at crowded lunches but comfortable.

SERVICE: Well meaning but generally absentminded or distracted.

DRESS CODE: None.

SMOKING REGULATIONS: No special policy.

FACILITIES FOR PRIVATE PARTIES: None.

HOURS: Lunch, Monday through Friday, noon to 3 P.M.; dinner, Monday through Saturday, 5 to 10:30 P.M. Closed Sunday and major holidays.

RESERVATIONS: Recommended, especially for lunch.

PRICES: Moderate.

CREDIT CARDS: AE, CB, D, MC, V.

This is a restaurant I am wary about recommending lest the reader hit it on one of its more pixilated days and decide that I, too, must be crazy. It is a maverick of a bistro, beautifully kept and inviting, with warm red walls and rows of brightly polished copper pots, and it is one of the last places left at which to find those old bistro flavors. But there are bad days when the service slows to an absentminded smile and when the kitchen has a heavy hand with the Grand Marnier that is poured into the otherwise magnificent rice pudding.

But I risk such hazards to sample what the place does best, and that means *lunch only*. Le Biarritz gets a big midday crowd, largely from publishing and broadcasting offices in the vicinity, and the food at that time of day is fresh and sprightly. At night it can be as woebegone as the staff. Walking in, I always glance at the assorted hors d'oeuvres laid out on a buffet near the entrance. If all looks bright, colorful and not sodden, I know things will go well. Not many places in town offer this classic array—a substantial salade Niçoise, with the right little Mediterranean black olives and pink tuna, or the céleri rémoulade, with the good firm bite and mustardy mayonnaise dressing. Even the sardines are moist and plump, and the slices of French garlic salami are always paper thin and pungent. If the artichokes are nice and green, rather than limp and bronzed, I start with one, valuing the leaves as vehicles for a creamy, mustard vinaigrette dressing.

Quiche at lunch has a puffy soufflélike filling, and after that I might have roast chicken with tarragon or cèpes or chanterelles, the wild mushrooms that lend their own earthy color and flavor to the cream sauce. Gigot, that marvelous French roast leg of lamb, is always rose pink, and its juices flavor the jade green beans, flageolets, just firm and garlicky enough. Even more classic bistro dishes are the simple fresh calves' liver anglaise sautéed in butter in a light, golden breadcrumb dusting, the calves' brains in butter called black but really a deep-nut brown, and braised shank of veal with herbs, so tender it melts from the bone. Even broiled lamb chops with watercress and butter are done right here as are traditional desserts such as crème caramel and chocolate mousse. There can be a good apple tart, and there is always cut fresh fruit macerated in red wine. But by far the best dessert is the thick, creamy rice pudding that gets a bittersweet accent from a strip of orange rind and a droplet of Grand Marnier. But on days when the hand that pours slips, that liqueur can ruin the dessert.

LE BISTRO

827 Third Avenue, between 50th and 51st Streets.
Telephone: 759-5933.

Favorite meals:
Leeks, artichoke or asparagus vinaigrette

Saddle of venison with chestnut puree (selle de venaison) in season, or rack of lamb (carré d'agneau)

Rice cake with vanilla-rum sauce (gâteau de riz)

OR

Hot sausage with potato salad (Saucission chaud, pommes persillées)

Roast squab chicken with tarragon (poussin de grain rôti à l'estragon)

Apple tart Tatin

OTHER FAVORITE DISHES: Pâté; cold mussels in mustard sauce (moules à la sauce moutarde); snails (escargots de Bourgogne); cream of lentil soup; onion soup; cream of pea soup (potage Saint-Germain); sautéed fillet of sole (sole meunière); frogs' legs with garlic (cuisses de grenouilles Provençales); beans with duck, lamb and sausage (cassoulet); veal chop with apple and Calvados (côte de veau à la Normande); poached salmon; calves' liver Bercy; steak au poivre; veal stew Marengo; grilled lamb chops; pear in red wine; chestnuts with ice cream (coup aux marrons glacé), crème caramel, fruit sherbets.

SETTING: Faux Art Nouveau that is mellowing with age; packed and noisy at lunch but pleasantly easygoing for dinner.

SERVICE: Excellent.

DRESS CODE: Jacket required for men.

SMOKING REGULATIONS: No special policy.

FACILITIES FOR PRIVATE PARTIES: None.

HOURS: Lunch, Monday through Friday, noon to 3 P.M.; dinner, Monday through Saturday, 6 to 9:45 P.M. Closed Sunday and major holidays.

RESERVATIONS: Necessary for lunch, suggested for dinner.

PRICES: Moderate.

CREDIT CARDS: AE, CB, D, MC, V.

Le Bistro that I like is a dinner restaurant when the pseudo-Art Nouveau near-Gigi setting is relatively relaxed and the noise level is bearable. Even better is Le Bistro on Friday and Saturday nights because its traffic pattern goes against that of most fashionable restaurants. Weekday lunches fill this place to wall-creaking capacity, and it is difficult to make oneself heard, even to a waiter. But the night crowd seems to come from the neighborhood and also must stay home or go out of the city on weekends. Hence this is a find.

It is a find for more than mere peace and availability of seating space, although given the crush in so many places these days, those considerations might almost earn it a high rating. Add to that very good, solid bistro cooking with just enough stylish touches at moderate prices, and you understand why it is a night-off favorite for many French chefs, including the city's leading pâtissier, Maurice Bonté, who is a regular. Le Bistro is, in fact, a landmark, having been at its present address more than twenty-five years, following twenty years across from its present site. Since buying the place almost ten years ago, George Hayon has kept its traditions and developed his own loyal following. The young American-born, French-Italian chef, Bill Santini, also accounts for that following, as he cooks rings around many wet-behind-the-ears superstars.

What I am loyal to is dishes like the cold leeks, artichokes or asparagus sharpened with a mustard-vinaigrette dressing, the coarse hot garlic sausage sliced alongside parsley-sprinkled French potato salad, the pâtes that recall the little charcuteries one used to be able to take for granted in France, and always fresh, bright mussels in mustard sauce. Unfortunately, at a recent dinner mussels marinière were so sandy they were inedible, a pity because their garlic-white wine broth had all the right overtones. At times the céleri rémoulade can be too strongly touched with mustard, but generally it is a nice companion to thin slices of dry, hard salami. Being a soup freak, I rely on several here, including the cream of lentil, lobster bisque, onion soup and the cream of pea that is Saint-Germain.

Simple fish dishes such as the fillet of sole sautéed meunière and the poached salmon, which is moist and flavorful, are preferable to more complex daily specials. Bouillabaisse appears on Friday with, one suspects, leftovers on Saturday. Choosing it one Saturday night, I was disappointed to find it fleshed out with sole, a disastrous touch if ever there was one. It also included some striped bass that tasted of kerosene, as that fish tends to do when it swims in polluted waters.

There has been little fault to find, however, with frogs' legs in the traditional Provençale glossing of garlic butter and a touch of tomato or with the gently soft white beans baked with lamb, sausages and confit of duck and goose. It is, in fact, one of the best cassoulets in town and far richer than those that are undercooked, leaving the beans a little stony and unable to absorb the flavors of garlic and thyme. With that dish, a little too mushy is better than a little too firm. Apples and Calvados mellow a tender pink veal chop prepared à la Normande, and the shallot-butter sauce Bercy lifts fresh, pink calves' liver to simple perfection.

Other classics here, done as one expects to have them, are steak au poivre in a good, dark fiery sauce gritty with crushed peppercorns, the aromatic stew that is veal Marengo, and such nearly disappeared choices as civet of rabbit, nut-brown roast chicken with tarragon, and saddle of fresh venison, rose at the center and garnished with a velvety, smoky sweet chestnut puree. At times the kitchen has a heavy hand with salt, most especially with a wild duck dish I had there recently; the duck was also wildly overcooked. Watch out for escalopes of veal with lime (do I detect a nouvelle urge rearing its limey head?) and lotte with coriander. That last could be fine, depending on how judiciously the coriander is dispensed.

Glassily caramelized apple tart Tatin and a nice soft pear developed in red wine are fine desserts, but I have a hard time getting past the gâteau de riz au rhum vanillé, translated on the menu as "rice cake." That flat-footed phrase does not begin to do justice to this golden brown, subtly creamy cross between rice pudding and cake, with its heady rum-vanilla crème anglaise sauce. It reminds me of a childhood I wish I had had. Properly silken crème caramel, and that Frenchiest of sundaes, coupe aux marrons, offer further evidence that the old-time culinary religion still has its worshipers.

Café des Artistes, *see* The View, the Setting and the Scene

CAFÉ 58

232 East 58th Street, between Second and Third Avenues.
Telephone: 758-5665.

Favorite meal:
Mussels marinière
Grilled pig's foot (pied de porc grillé)
Green salad
Baked apple

OTHER FAVORITE DISHES: Asparagus vinaigrette, snails, céleri rémoulade, pork pâté (rillettes), poached egg in aspic (oeuf en gelée), sautéed sweetbreads, rack of lamb, frogs' legs, steak au poivre, rabbit with mustard sauce (lapin à la moutarde), calf's head vinaigrette (tête de veau), brains in black butter (cervelle au beurre noir), grilled blood sausage (boudin grillé), skatefish with brown butter and capers (raie au beurre noir), cold poached bass or salmon, apple tart, ice cream bombe (bombe glacée pralinée), pear in red wine, crème caramel.

SETTING: Though convivial the dining room is depressing, with murky acoustical ceiling, plaid fabric that needs changing on walls and inadequate ventilation.

SERVICE: Fleetingly attentive; generally distracted and at times forgetful.

DRESS CODE: None.

SMOKING REGULATIONS: No special policy.

FACILITIES FOR PRIVATE PARTIES: None.

HOURS: Lunch, Monday through Saturday, noon to 4 P.M.; dinner, Monday through Saturday, 4 P.M. to midnight; Sunday, 5 to 11 P.M.

RESERVATIONS: Necessary for lunch and for dinner on weekends.

PRICES: Inexpensive to moderate.

CREDIT CARDS: AE, CB, D, MC, V.

I wonder if any nouvelle cuisine dishes invented since that trend began about thirty years ago will ever stir the same nostalgic longings as do the traditional French bistro dishes. Can the little roundels of rare meat fanned with undercooked snow peas, carrots and turnips really inspire the same sort of taste memory as smooth, fat mellowed rillettes of pork, or a lusty coarse pâté, or snails sizzling in a shallot-and-parsley-butter bath? Herb-scented pink gigot of lamb with flageolets, garlicky frogs' legs, pig's foot grilled beneath a crackling breadcrumb and mustard crust that keeps the meat slippery, moist and tender, and the snappy casing on the subtly puddinglike grilled blood sausage boudin, give one more flavor complexities to remember than all but two or three nouvelle inventions.

That is why I regularly go in search of that good old bistro flavor in New York. (In fact, it is now almost as hard to find in Paris.) Several friends, foremost among them Geoffrey Beene, share this predilection, and so we keep one another informed of finds and go together to see how close we can come to finding the beloved flavors of the past. Café 58, subtitled Bistrot Français, is one of the more satisfying sources. What would make it even more satisfying, and well worth two stars, is better bread, more consistency in the kitchen and a redoing of its dreary interior. Despite the warm glow and hum of activity, the room is depressing, primarily because of a fluffy-looking red acoustical ceiling and some fading tartan fabric on the wall, which suggests a phony men's bar in a chain hotel. Even at these low prices, the management could afford a refurbishing, no matter how simple.

Seating, however, is comfortable in the typical crowded bistro fashion. Typical too is the offhand, sometimes distracted service, with staff members occasionally forgetting something, such as the rouille sauce for a bouillabaisse. It doesn't take much to turn them around, however, and the effort is worth it.

There are not many places where one can have a three-course lunch of solid bourgeois fare for between $11.50 and $16.50, or dinner from $14.25 to $18.50. Many appetizers and

128

desserts carry supplemental charges, but even without making those choices it is possible to have a fine meal. Example: Begin with oeuf en gelée, a softly poached egg, its yolk still runny, caught in an amber aspic, or the rillettes of pork. For a main course, it might be sweetbreads sautéed with a crisp veneer of flour, calf's brains fragrant with nut-brown butter or a little red casserole of tender rabbit sparked by a mustard cream sauce. The delicious warm baked apple and a pear simmered in red wine (perhaps a bit firmer than it should be) are fine possibilities for dessert.

Among classic bistro appetizers that carry extra charges are the snails heady in their aromatic butter, asparagus glossed with a nice tart vinaigrette sauce, cleanly plump mussels good in the garlic and white wine broth that is marinière-style, or cold with a spicy sauce ravigotte. Leeks and artichokes tend to be overcooked, and the pâté maison is too bland as are the few soups I have tried, but that still leaves more than enough dependable choices.

A daily special I always hope to find at lunch is raie au beurre noir—skatefish gleaming under a burnished butter sauce sharpened with capers. But even if it is not available, there is much to choose from in addition to main courses already mentioned. My far-and-away favorite is the pig's foot, an endlessly delectable crunch of crisp fat, succulent gristle, flavorful meat. Tête de veau, the cooked calf's head, again with the seductive textural contrast of meat, fat and chewy cartilage in a vinaigrette sauce, is also a personal preference. Not everything has equal appeal here. I have always found the choucroute garni—that Alsatian mix of sauerkraut, pork and sausages—to be overcooked and stale tasting, and the condition of bouillabaisse on weekends is a sometimes thing. Ditto any fish other than the skate and the cold poached bass or salmon. Calves' liver could be fresher at times, and late in the evening cold hors d'oeuvre on the buffet become limp and greasy.

Beef for the steak au poivre is not the tenderest but has a good meaty edge to it, and the sting of the black peppercorn makes up for a lot. Even Kleenex would be delicious that way.

Experience has taught me to stick to the desserts recommended above. Others on the menu are lackluster.

There is a fairly good choice of moderately priced wines, but in the bistro spirit the house should have better choices en carafe. There should also be better pickings on the cheese "plateau."

The same management plans to open a clone, Café 79, on 79th Street, between Amsterdam Avenue and Broadway. Perhaps it will be functioning by the time this book is published.

Café Luxembourg, *see* American

CHANTERELLE

89 Grand Street, corner Greene Street.
Telephone: 966-6960.

Favorite meal:
   Grilled seafood sausage
   Rack of lamb with cloves of garlic
   Assorted cheeses
   Orange-flavored chocolate torte (reine de saba)
   OR
   Ravioli filled with crabmeat or wild mushrooms and truffles
   Roast squab
   Assorted cheeses
   Apple tart

OTHER FAVORITE DISHES: Crab or crayfish bisque, sorrel soup,
   seafood terrines, asparagus in puff pastry, white beans with
   sausage and meats (cassoulet), red snapper in lime butter,
   bass in mustard dill sauce, shad roe with rhubarb and leeks,
   beef with marrow and red wine, coffee ice cream, fruit tarts,
   chocolat pavé, poached pears in Sauternes sabayon.

SETTING: Spacious, romantic dining room with theatrical lighting; there is adequate space between tables and a benign
   noise level.

SERVICE: Prompt and efficient although pretentious in tone.

DRESS CODE: Jacket and tie required for men.

SMOKING REGULATIONS: No special policy.

FACILITIES FOR PRIVATE PARTIES: None.

HOURS: Dinner, Tuesday through Saturday, 6 to 10:30 P.M.
   Closed Sunday, Monday, major holidays, for the first week
   in January and all of July.

RESERVATIONS: Necessary well in advance.

PRICES: Expensive.

CREDIT CARDS: AE, MC, V.

Young American wonder chefs who are today's premature
superstars have generally been disappointing, reveling as they
do in their own bizarre creations and considering any detractor
a Philistine. Midst such disarray of standards, it is reassuring
to have David Waltuck, a graduate of the Culinary Institute of
America, who opened this handsome SoHo restaurant in 1981.
During that time he has carefully invented dishes and honed
them to near perfection. His wife, Karen, who runs the dining
room, seems to have gotten rid of an early insecurity that led

to an embarrassing pretentiousness. The result is a delight both for those who love good food and beautiful surroundings.

Halfway between new American and French nouvelle, the food here is delicate and pretty in presentation and in flavor. The dining room itself, set in a former lingerie shop, has a magnificent sugar-white pressed-tin ceiling as pretty as a valentine, and the peach-pink walls are dramatically shadowed by streetlamps shining through the windows, which creates a theatrical backdrop. And, wonder of wonders in New York today—the tables are large and set comfortably apart from one another, making for elbow room and a low noise level, which makes conversation comfortable.

The menu changes often, so recommendations made here must be taken as indications of what the kitchen does well. A few dishes are almost always available, among the best being the grilled seafood sausage in a pale pink cream sauce, lightly blushed with tomato. A while back this specialty emerged from the broiler toughened; more recently it was delicate and gentle. All seafood terrines are delights, whether of fresh or smoked salmon with pike or marblings of caviar, and so are ravioli with a variety of fillings, my favorite being the crabmeat version. I have not had the mushroom and truffle variation but hope it is as as good as its $10 surcharge on a $55 dinner promises it to be.

Seafood bisques and vegetable cream combinations have the sheer but substantial texture they should have, but I usually bypass them for one of the more intriguing openers.

Nut-brown cloves of garlic cooked to the gentleness of butter flavor the rare-roasted rack of lamb for one of Chanterelle's more enduring favorites. Beef with cèpes and venison in a classic, peppery sauce poivrade offer confirmed meat eaters the satisfaction they require. Duck and squab are two birds beautifully prepared. I still remember a crisp-skinned, pink meat squab in a subtle red wine sauce, hoping it will reappear on the menu when I go back. Scallops with roe and shad roe with rhubarb are forerunners of a later poached salmon, its richness polished with the tartness of cranberries. Lime and ginger can appear too frequently here and are used too strongly. A refreshing green salad is a liaison between the main course and one of the very best cheese assortments around, served with wonderfully crusty sourdough rolls. Each, however, carries an excessive surcharge on the $55 dinner—$5 for the salad, $10 (!) for the cheese.

There are usually three desserts, which always include a lovely, satiny homemade ice cream (watch out for the overly strong ginger) and the orange chocolate torte, reine de saba. Poached pear in Sauternes-brightened sabayon, a buttery apple tart or an astringent lemon tart may be others.

All sorts of sign-off goodies arrive, compliments of the house, and there are silken dark chocolate truffles, crackling tuiles and mosaics of petits fours.

LE CIRQUE

58 East 65th Street, between Madison and Park Avenues, in the Mayfair-Regent Hotel.
Telephone: 794-9292.

Favorite meals:
LUNCH
Spaghetti primavera
Grilled chicken with mustard (poulet grillé aux graines de moutarde)
Crème brûlée
OR
Assorted pâtés and terrines (except vegetable terrine)
Lobster salad
Bread pudding with vanilla sauce
OR
DINNER
Any salad with sautéed sweetbreads or salmon or scallops
Langoustine or other shellfish and ravioli in court bouillon, shared by two
Pheasant Souvaroff with foie gras and truffles (special order in advance)
Coconut soufflé with bitter chocolate and Armagnac sauce
OR
LUNCH OR DINNER
Salad of radicchio, oak leaf lettuce, mâche, etc., in season
Bouillabaisse (on Friday)
Lemon tart
OTHER FAVORITE DISHES: Fettuccine with white truffles, aspic of calf's feet and head (tête et pieds de veau en gelée), duck liver sautéed with sherry vinegar, sautéed wild mushrooms, all smoked fish, carpaccio of raw beef, red snapper seviche, grilled langoustine, snails in casserole, all soups except hot or cold carrot, quenelles of pike, fried goujonettes of sole, grilled flounder with mustard sauce, salt codfish au gratin (brandade de morue), grilled red snapper with dill, sweetbreads sautéed with capers but without pink peppercorns, quail with foie gras on field salad, roast squab in casserole, veal kidneys grilled with herbs, grilled paillard of

beef, entrecôte with marrow and red wine, calves' liver with shallots, roast rack of lamb, roast chicken, assorted boiled meats and vegetables (bollito misto, usually on Thursday), calf's head with ravigote sauce, noisettes of venison with mustard and morels, roast saddle of veal, fruit tarts, petits fours.

SETTING: Dated and corny perception of elegance suggests "dining salon" in a Continental hotel; tables are packed together and noise level is high; all tables are uncomfortable.

SERVICE: Generally excellent but can be perfunctory toward unknowns; impossible to be elegant in these cramped quarters.

DRESS CODE: Jacket and tie required for men.

SMOKING REGULATIONS: No special policy.

FACILITIES FOR PRIVATE PARTIES: Separate attractive room, L'Orangerie, accommodates between twenty and seventy.

HOURS: Lunch, Monday through Saturday, noon to 2:45 P.M.; dinner, Monday through Saturday, 6 to 10:30 P.M.. Closed Sunday, major holidays and for the month of July.

RESERVATIONS: Necessary well in advance.

PRICES: Expensive.

CREDIT CARDS: AE, CB, D.

Apparently any restaurant at which Alain Sailhac is the chef is bound to become one of my favorites. Long before his name was known, when he was the chef at Le Cygne, I rated that restaurant four stars in *The New York Times*. Then he went to Le Cirque, and a kitchen that had been lackluster, stodgy and wildly overrated under a previous chef rose to Sailhac's extraordinary heights. His talents are able to shine to the fullest, in large part, because of Le Cirque's owner and guiding genius, Sirio Maccioni, probably the single shrewdest restaurateur in New York today. Because of his pride in showing what his restaurant can offer, and Sailhac's wide range of culinary abilities, Le Cirque right now has the best menu in New York, and I say that even though I rate the overall dining experience at Lutèce one star more.

What compromises the experience at Le Cirque is the madhouse celebrity zoo of a dining room, and nothing short of Sailhac's talent and the house menu could induce me to go there. The setting in the Mayfair-Regent Hotel is corny and dated, but that is a minor detail as decor has always mattered less than food to me. Its effect is pleasant enough even if the anthropomorphic monkey murals and garish lighting fixtures suggest the Continental dining-salon of a fallen grandeur hotel. The nightmare element at Le Cirque is the jammed-in crowd, the dizzying noise and the action in the aisles, with trays sailing overhead 'midst the waving, nodding and kissing of its devotees, most of whom are dressed as flashily as the room itself. Sit on a banquette and you are tightly wedged as in a stock, and if you have an aisle chair, know that it will be kicked all night long, eight to the bar. Sirio Maccioni acknowledges this crush and always says he will remove some tables, but the only furniture moving I ever see is more chairs being added, to cram yet another guest or two around an already tight table arrangement. There is also the nagging knowledge that I would like Le Cirque less if I were not known there. Reliable reports on indifference on the telephone when reservations are called for, and of the dullness of seating in outer Siberia, persist, although they are much less marked than they were eight or nine years ago. That Siberia is inevitable with so many high-rolling movers and shakers among regulars. If you owned a restaurant and took in something like $500 a week from a customer, would he or she be the one to get the table near the kitchen? In truth, there should be no bad tables in expensive restaurants, and a little more space between them would help a lot here. If I have taken off at length about this, it is because I feel Maccioni is selling his kitchen short, a hard point to make with him since he plays to a packed house almost every noon and night.

And so I go, getting one of the so-called better tables, ignoring the teased and sprayed bouffant blond hairdos once dubbed "Le Cirque," and try to escape fumes of perfume and cigars. A glance at that menu and I am a goner anyway, for it combines deftly composed new creations in the light nouvelle vein (langoustine with ravioli in a diamond-clear court bouillon and a deceptively simple, simply perfect salad of lobster nested on the salty, verdant French seaweed pied-pousse are two cases in point) with solid bourgeois classics (entrecôte with marrow and red wine in the true Bordeaux tradition and the Saturday lunch special, brandade de morue au gratin, are only two examples, but among the best). Not only does Le Cirque offer this wide-ranging French menu, but it is adorned with some exquisite Italian specialties as well, dishes Maccioni is especially proud of as he is of his upper class Italian wines, not a surprise for this native of Montecatini. Now if only there were English translations...

There was a time when all great restaurants had large menus. That became a foolish pursuit as the costs of operation soared and some dishes invariably got short shrift. Enter the boutique menu that often leaves the diner too few options at the price. For in an expensive restaurant, one pays for possibilities, and in that respect few places can rival Le Cirque.

Seasonal products such as various wild mushrooms, the white truffles that are the earthy glory of Alba, langoustine or true scampi, a bright-eyed branzino flown in from Italy, and

134

the first fraises des bois from France are among the provender exhibited to clientele to be prepared in a variety of ways. Here not all get a fair shake as there is much less bearing of nature's gift toward the back of the house, for which note five demerits. But ask and you shall be shown, and to be sure, note what is on the large hors d'oeuvre buffet when you enter and stop at the checkroom. That is where the lovely terrines and pâtés, the cold mussels in their red onion dressing, the impeccable cured fish and meats, and the red snapper seviche rest until ordered. Glistening meat and chewy cartilage of calf's head polished in flavor and texture by a properly sharp vinaigrette dressing is another bistro delight. Among warm appetizers, few can vie with the combination of wild mushrooms with shallots sautéed in butter or New York State foie gras glossed with sherry vinegar.

Pasta never appears on the menu because, Maccioni says, his French chefs do not want to be connected with a spaghetti house. It's their mistake, for few pasta creations in town match the spaghetti primavera (flowerets of broccoli, bits of zucchini, mushrooms and tomato, and toasted pine nuts in a light froth of cream and chicken stock) or the fettuccine with wild porcini mushrooms or with a generous grating of the ripe-scented white truffles. I hardly ever make it to soup at Le Cirque, which is my loss, because all are excellent excepting only the carrot because I just do not like carrot soup.

I cannot remember having a fish dish much less than perfect here, whether as simple as grilled sole or flounder with mustard sauce or as complex as quenelles with a touch of salmon caviar in their sauce. Goujonettes of sole may be a shade less crisp and flavorful than those at Le Cygne, but that still places them far above average. Poached scallops or lobster in a leek-and white-wine-graced court bouillon broth, grilled red snapper with an airy flourish of dill, and various versions of poached and grilled salmon are always delicate and rich, although I prefer the grilling done sans skin.

I especially like daily specials, not only the inspired Friday bouillabaisse, with its lobster, clams, mussels and snowy firm-fleshed fish enlivened by a garlic- and cayenne-laced rouille sauce but the brilliant, succulent mixed boil (bollito misto) of beef, veal, tongue, chicken and brains along with vegetables and a vivid, oily green sauce sprightly with parsley and capers. Other times it may be osso buco or navarin of lamb or seasonal offerings such as roast partridge with juniper or venison with wild mushrooms. Poultry is my most frequent main course at dinner, in one form or another: quail in confit with foie gras, crunchy squab roasted with garlic cloves as golden as butternuts, grilled chicken crackling under a mustard glaze and gloriously simple roast chicken in casserole. One of my beloved old-time haute classics, pheasant Souvaroff, can be ordered for two a few days in advance. The plump bird is braised with foie gras and great knobs of whole black truffles, touched with Madeira and sealed under a bread crust so all aromas are sealed in. Opened in the dining room, the crust issues forth a great cloud of truffles- and foie-gras-scented steam, sustaining in itself. This dish used to be magnificent at the long-gone Café Chauveron, but even that masterpiece is superseded by Sailhac's. Duck at Le Cirque is better with peppercorns or with apples and Calvados than with newer combinations of cassis and ginger, and roast veal is better than veal chop overly complicated with wild mushrooms or the escalope mired in sweet red pepper sauce. But that still leaves more delights: sweetbreads with capers, calves' liver with shallots, and grilled kidney, a nicer cooking method for those succulent organs than sautéeing because the charred skin stands in good contrast to the roseate interior.

Baked desserts hardly seem in order after the very rich food that goes before, but the lemon tart is light and sunny. Soufflés are sometimes undercooked, but a recent one, flavored with coconut and sauced with bitter chocolate and Armagnac, will do until perfection comes along. Bright sherbets and a fine crème brûlée are always good choices, and at lunch there is often a real down-home (down-home in France, that is) bread pudding with the satiny vanilla sauce crème anglaise. There are enticing little petits fours and bonbons, but a distracting habit of giving all diners an assorted dessert platter with so many cakes and creams wipes out taste memories of the main meal and is overkill in a final form.

Even with the big French wines the house stocks, I tend to prefer Italian offerings except with the most formal of French dishes, such as the pheasant Souvaroff. There are also some good buys captains will point out if they are pressed. At lunch, and occasionally at dinner, there is a dangerously delicious Parmesan toast passed round more than once. Try to resist seconds or you will regret it midmeal.

LE CYGNE

★★★

55 East 54th Street, between Madison and Park Avenues.
Telephone: 759-5941.

Favorite meals:
LUNCH
Country-style pâté

Fried slivers of sole with mustard sauce (goujonettes de sole Dijonnaise)
Fruit salad with liqueurs
OR
DINNER
Hot cream of mussel soup (billi-bi)
Braised sweetbreads with chanterelles
Raspberry soufflé
OR
Cold seafood terrine
Chicken in champagne sauce with morels
Apple tart

OTHER FAVORITE DISHES: Assorted hors d'oeuvres; smoked salmon; duck terrine; oysters or clams, cold or baked with white wine and mushrooms (des gourmets); seafood in puff pastry; snails with wild mushrooms; potato and sorrel soup (crème Maximoise); frogs' legs with garlic; soft shell crabs Provençale; red snapper with basil; squab with artichokes and cèpes; roast duck Smitane; loin of lamb with rosemary; loin of veal with wild mushrooms; steak au poivre; rack of lamb with sage; veal or beef roast from the wagon; chocolate, coffee or Grand Marnier soufflés; fruit sherbets; raspberry tart.

SETTING: Beautiful postmodern impressionistic dining room with flower murals that create a graceful backdrop; noise level is bearable though some seating is cramped; upstairs dining room is more spacious and best for parties larger than four.

SERVICE: Excellent.

DRESS CODE: Jacket and tie required for men.

SMOKING REGULATIONS: No special policy.

FACILITIES FOR PRIVATE PARTIES: Three rooms including a wine cellar that holds between twelve and twenty-two and the upstairs dining room, which can accommodate from fifty-five to sixty-five or be divided for twenty-five to thirty-five.

HOURS: Lunch, Monday through Friday, noon to 2:30 P.M.; dinner, Monday through Thursday, 6 to 10 P.M.; Friday and Saturday, 6 to 11 P.M. Closed Sunday and major holidays and for the month of August.

RESERVATIONS: Necessary, especially for Friday and Saturday nights.

PRICES: Expensive.

CREDIT CARDS: AE, CB, D, MC, V.

The attractions of Le Cygne include the bearable noise level, the comfortable seating and the graceful new dining room with its impressionistic floral murals and a luminous postmodern decor that strangely enough suggests a dining room aboard a luxury yacht. In addition, there is an even more spacious dining room on the second floor, which is comfortable for parties larger than four, as tables are more spacious and more widely spaced. Service is gracious, correct and genuinely concerned and the food prepared by the new chef is lovely. Lovely, but not breathtakingly exciting, which is why I would give this three stars, not four.

Even so, that means a lot of excellent food, including the city's crispest, most succulent goujonettes (thin slivers) of fried sole and the snowiest, tenderest leg and stuffed breast of veal, sliced from the wagon in the dining room. Other Le Cygne masterpieces include, in season, soft-shell crabs sautéed in Provençale herbs with an authoritative belt of garlic and altogether delicious soups, among them a tangy billi-bi in which the saltiness of mussels is gentled by heavy cream (I prefer the hot to the cold). When crème Maximoise is available, I have a hard time choosing, loving that mix of cream, potato, sorrel and leeks.

It is, in fact, a hard choice between appetizers and soups here, what with an hors d'oeuvres wagon bearing delectable pâtés, mussels in a mustard-gilded mayonnaise, truffled seafood pâté and various vegetable salads. Enticements not on the wagon include chilled clams and oysters with a shallot-sparked mignonette dressing, snails in the authentic Burgundian blend of shallots and parsley, sweetbreads braised in mild vinegar, and puff pastry filled with lobster or other shellfish. There is often some sort of fish or fish mousse en croûte, either as first or second course. Grilling is artfully accomplished here, whether on sole that is served with mustard sauce or on the paillard of beef, both luncheon favorites.

Frogs' legs with garlic butter and red snapper with basil are far better than the more complex fish cookery here. Sautéed sweetbreads have always been good, and now chanterelles add a lovely textural contrast. Neither the braised chicken in champagne cream sauce with morels or the caneton Smitane (duck in a white wine and sour cream) are surpassed in the city. Similarly, veal with wild mushrooms and braised squab with artichokes are the sort of dishes the kitchen has always done well. But here too honey vinegar has crept into a duck on which I must reserve judgment. Sautéed kidneys, calves' liver with shallots and rack of lamb with sage are far more blessedly predictable and the kind of dishes I choose at Le Cygne.

Soufflés are lofty and full of flavor, and this is one place that does a great job on hot raspberry soufflés. The fruit retains its flavor through the baking, and is finished with a splash of framboise and fresh whole berries. Mocha is the other standout among soufflés.

Baking has never been a strong point here, but there are more than enough fruit salads, crème brûlées, sherbets and

138

mousses to do a diet in, and the raspberry tart is above average.

Le Cygne is a place I would choose for business lunches or a dinner with a long lost friend—an occasion on which quiet, peaceful surroundings allow for a comfortable conversation.

La Gauloise

502 Sixth Avenue, between 12th and 13th Streets.
Telephone: 691-1363.

Favorite meals:

Mousse of shrimp with Nantua sauce (flan des crevettes Nantua)

Roast rabbit with tarragon mustard (lapin rôti à la moutarde d'estragon)

Custard and cherry tart (clafouti aux grillottes)

OR

Hot pâté in crust (tourte du vieux Bugey)

Grilled chicken with herbs

Chocolate marquise

OR

Artichoke vinaigrette or string bean salad

Alsatian sauerkraut with pork and sausages (choucroute garni)

OR

White beans baked with duck, lamb and sausages (cassoulet)

Crème brûlée

OTHER FAVORITE DISHES: Terrine of chicken livers, oysters on the half shell, galantine of pheasant with green peppercorns, tabbouleh with scallops, mussels with coriander and saffron or ravigote, fricassee of snails, vegetable soup, sweetbreads with julienne of orange and green peppercorn sauce, duck breast with green peppercorn sauce, roast confit of duck with roasted potato cake, steak with béarnaise sauce, salmon in pastry crust, loin of lamb with shallots, calves' liver with shallots, venison, veal kidneys with mustard sauce, all egg dishes, profiterolles with vanilla ice cream and chocolate, chestnut parfait.

SETTING: Handsome, faux-antique bistro with dark wood, mirrors and Art Deco lighting fixtures; cramped and noisy in certain areas when full.

SERVICE: Friendly, polite and efficient.

DRESS CODE: None.

SMOKING REGULATIONS: No special policy.

FACILITIES FOR PRIVATE PARTIES: Will accommodate thirty to sixty-five on Mondays when restaurant is closed.

HOURS: Lunch, Tuesday through Friday, noon to 3 P.M.; dinner, Tuesday through Sunday, 5:30 to 11:15 P.M.; brunch, Saturday and Sunday, noon to 3 P.M. Open Thanksgiving Day, but closed other major holidays and Monday.

RESERVATIONS: Recommended.

PRICES: Moderate. The pretheater dinner served from 5:30 to 6:45 P.M., Tuesday through Friday, is $16.50 for three courses.

CREDIT CARDS: AE, MC, V.

In an age of superstar chefs, imagine one of consummate skill both with classics and innovations who is said to be shy and retiring, and must be, for how many dedicated eaters have ever heard of Thierry Moity? A native of Nantua, he holds forth in the kitchen of La Gauloise, a handsome mirror-and-wood paneled bistro that has, in the six or so years since it has opened, become a landmark for solid bourgeois cooking modified by stylish innovations. Originally owned by Jacques Alliman and Camille Dulac, it is now the sole property of Mr. Alliman, as Mr. Dulac left to become a partner in Le Chantilly. Because Alliman is Alsatian, many specialties of the region appear on the menu, making this a brasserie and bistro combined.

I have a certain preference for this place at lunch as it is less crowded and quieter than at dinner and invites lingering. But many of the best specialties are on the night menu, and so I brave the noise and try to sit where it is the least intrusive. That can mean the bar if not too many people are waiting, the two tables at the front window or the deeper recesses of the dining room. The midpoint, being perceived as the chicquest, is the least comfortable.

The menu is a delicate interweaving of traditional and nouvelle-inspired fare. Among appetizers, for example, are such delectable standbys as artichokes or asparagus in a sunny vinaigrette dressing; a variety of pâtés that change frequently but whether of game, duck, chicken livers or pork have the authentic charcuterie bite and savor; ice-cold and clear oysters; and snails that are best in a fricassee that is redolent of garlic and has a nutlike crackle. Soupe du pêcheur may be a rose-pink lobster bisque thick with cream and bristling with the overtones of coral and lobster butter, or a rosy fish soup, lighter than lobster but delicately subtle and sustaining. Vegetable soup also appears as a pink puree, thickened with the vegetables themselves and glossed with cream.

Add to these some recent additions, such as taboulé de St.

140

Jacques, a salad of bulgur, parsley and mint adapted from the Lebanese tabbouleh and here topped with lightly poached scallops, then ringed with paper-thin slices of cucumber for a brightly counterpointed combination. Mussels with coriander and saffron are more sophisticated than the usual ravigote, also done well here, and the flan des crevettes, a hot shrimp mousse, swims in sauce Nantua with just the right shellfish accents. Tourte de vieux Bugey is a house classic, and my only caveat concerning it is its heaviness. A lusty tourte of game or poultry in a crust, finished with a red wine sauce, it is better suited to a main course. However, if it is to be followed by the fine grilled sole or the grilled chicken with herbs, it should not be too overpowering.

If winter is my favorite season for La Gauloise it has to do with two of the best specialties—the juniper-brightened sauerkraut, pork and sausage dish that is Alsace's choucroute garni and the mellow, garlicky baked white beans with duck confit, lamb and sausages that is cassoulet. Both are beautifully accomplished here. Grilling is always done properly, whether for the chicken or the entrecôte in a pungent tarragon béarnaise. The kitchen has a way with rabbit too, rendering it most succulent when the fillet is wrapped around a parsley and spinach filling, then given a brassy finish of tarragon mustard. It is equally good as a more classic roasting with mustard sauce. Magret de canard, the rare roasted duck breast, is lovely with green peppercorns, a sauce I prefer to the honeyed innovation, and the preserved duck confit, crisped in its own flavorful fat and bedded down on a golden pancake of potatoes, is perhaps the best house duck of all.

Sweetbreads, plump and fresh, are sautéed to an almost crisp glaze, then sharpened with green peppercorn sauce and gilded with julienne strips of orange peel. The only flaw with the combination is its intensity, making it very rich going for a full main course. That intensity flaws several dark, demi-glace-based sauces and is something the kitchen should guard against. Thick cuts of salmon baked, but not overcooked, in flaky pastry is preferable to the paillard of salmon, which invariably dries out. Shallots add a satiny flavor to both loin of lamb and pink sautéed calves' liver, and veal kidneys in a traditional mustard-red wine sauce have always been fresh, crunchy and roseate at the center.

The only desserts I tend to dislike at La Gauloise are the fruit tarts, because they are too thickly glazed with gelatinlike coverings, and a pear charlotte in which the flavor of fruit and custard lie heavy on the tongue. But the soft rich chocolate marquise and the puffy profiterolles with vanilla ice cream and bitter chocolate sauce are superb options, as is the crème brûlée, with its burned sugar topping, and the lovely clafouti, that halfway cake-custard that is wonderful with cherries, plums or peaches.

Brunch includes a number of the house appetizers and grilled dishes plus good versions of the expected egg specialties.

La Grenouille

3 East 52nd Street, between Fifth and Madison Avenues. Telephone: 752-1495.

Favorite meals:
LUNCH
Assorted hors d'oeuvres
Quenelles of pike in champagne or fennel cream sauce
Raspberries with Grand Marnier sauce or fruit sherbet
OR
DINNER
Cream of pea soup Saint-Germain
Roast chicken in champagne sauce or with morels
Soufflé harlequin, half coconut, half chocolate
OR
Roast lobster with beurre blanc Nantais, shared by two
Fillet of lamb with vegetable tian
Pudding Canadien (maple syrup pudding), in winter

OTHER FAVORITE DISHES: Littleneck clams Corsini, cassolette of clams with thyme, all pâtés and terrines, hot sausage with potato salad, egg in aspic, lobster bisque, fish soup, lobster or scallops à la nage, grilled sole with mustard sauce, poached chicken with horseradish and coarse salt, roast chicken with tarragon, frogs' legs with garlic and tomato, calves' liver Bercy or anglaise, steak with marrow and red wine sauce, duck Rouennaise, veal chop Grand-mère or variation, pheasant and venison in season, oeufs à la neige, gratin of fruits, apple tart Tatin, orange chocolate cake.

SETTING: Elegantly posh, high-style setting with flattering lighting and flower arrangements out of Flemish still lifes; tables are cramped and too close together; noisy.

SERVICE: Professional and polite, if at times perfunctory toward unknowns.

DRESS CODE: Jacket and tie required for men.

SMOKING REGULATIONS: No special policy.

FACILITIES FOR PRIVATE PARTIES: None.

HOURS: Lunch, Tuesday through Saturday, noon to 2:15 P.M.; dinner, Tuesday through Saturday, 6 to 11:30 P.M.. Closed

Sunday and Monday, all major holidays, and for the month of August through Labor Day weekend.

RESERVATIONS: Necessary, generally well in advance.
PRICES: Expensive.
CREDIT CARDS: AE, CB, D, MC, V.

I have often wondered if the fashionable regulars who frequent La Grenouille really know how good the food is. Certainly they go for love of the setting, with its flattering lighting, the sparkle of mirrors that reflect pale green walls and bouquets so exquisitely lavish they cost the management some $90,000 a year, at last report. But much the same crowd alternates between La Grenouille and a few other restaurants so poor it's hard to believe they could eat food so good, then accept anything so bad. I felt that especially when the Grenouille crowd went to Orsini, now closed, or in the evening to Mortimer's, a monument to the preppie WASP palate if ever there was one.

Do they know, for example, that these quenelles of pike are, day in day out, the best the city has ever known? That is true whoever the chef may be and whether those sublime pike dumplings are in a cream sauce enhanced with champagne, vermouth or fennel. Do the slim denizens of the haute couture world spring for the calories in the potage Saint-Germain, the bright green cream of pea soup La Grenouille raised to new heights, or in the oeufs à la neige, the opulent cloudlets of poached egg whites adrift in a vanilla sea of crème anglaise and topped with a golden lacing of spun sugar?

And are they willing to risk the hazards of garlic on the breath so they can nibble on the tiniest, sweetest frogs' legs, sautéed with tomato and garlic? Do they shy away from the cholesterol in the gentle scallops à la nage, shimmering under a mantle of heavy cream and brightened with slivers of celery and carrots?

Lunch is the scene here, even though many famous diners are on hand at dinner. Somehow the tension and competition shine through midday and the pace is quicker. Then too, there are more delicate dishes for lunch, with the lustier specialties offered at night. Lunch, by the way, means 1 o'clock, and the posh dinner hour begins at 8:30. Go earlier either time and you'll miss most of the show, although you'll probably get better service.

In truth, I must admit that La Grenouille, like Le Cirque, is a place I enjoy much more since I have become known there. Before recognition at La Grenouille, I always had excellent food, but the service varied from excellent to overbearing. I will never forget one meal when a party of eight was placed around a table just comfortable for five. This is by way of a caveat, especially if you are in a party larger than four; it is difficult for more than that number to be comfortable within these premises.

After some twenty years La Grenouille had a change of chefs, but Gisèle Masson, widow of the restaurant's founder, and their son, Charles, have managed to make the change almost invisible. Sampling the elegant mixed hors d'oeuvre, I would not have detected a change in the kitchen. The cool cucumber salad gentled with cream, the firm shrimp in pink creamy dressing, the snowy bass that never tastes of kerosene, and thinly sliced sausage and celerí rémoulade are as perfect as always. Terrines and pâtés have the right hints of pepper and garlic, and in season tiny haricots verts are barely cooked and marinated in oil and vinegar. Poached eggs in aspic, their yolks runny in the herb-glossed gelée, are other lunchtime favorites.

Hot saucisson with warm French potato salad is a lusty appetizer at lunch, and for dinner I like the littleneck clams Corsini, with their parsley, garlic butter and white wine.

In addition to the famed house potage Saint-Germain, there is a fine lobster bisque, which at times has a hint of tarragon and cognac and a rich, coral Brittany fish soup with vermicelli and subtle garlic overtones. The lovely billi-bi has been replaced by a soup of frogs' legs, an innovation I have not sampled but which could be delicious, as it is at Lutèce. Grilled fish with mustard sauce is a dependable classic as are all lobster dishes, most especially the whole roast lobster with a froth of white butter sauce. Sautéed fish has been overcooked frequently here so I avoid it.

A veal chop is difficult to cook well as the meat tends to dry as it is being sautéed. Part of the trick is the right thickness (about one and a half inches), and the other is the right heat in the skillet and the right hand at the helm. With new chef or old, that combination is in order here, and whether garnished with vegetables, tomatoes and tarragon for the printanier version, or with rounds of potatoes, shallots and onion (Grand-mère), the côte de veau is one of the best main courses. So is duck, whether done in the traditional red wine sauce Rouennaise or with cassis so well handled it is not overly sweet.

Braised venison and steak au poivre have the juicy, meaty overtones that satisfy real meat lovers, and roast chicken in champagne cream is one of those simple, immaculate dishes that no inventiveness can improve. A new chicken on the menu that I have not tried gives me pause as it includes grapes in a sweet and sour sauce, just as the new duck combines lemon and kumquat. Eating will be believing, but I hope neither innovation denotes a turn toward sweetness. That is not a danger with the herbaceous fillet of lamb accompanied by a Provençale tian or flan of baked eggplant, zucchini and tomato, nor

144

with the lunchtime masterpiece of poached chicken with coarse salt and horseradish sauce, a dish I am addicted to.

Harlequin soufflés, half one flavor, half another, have always been house specialties, and none is better than the coconut-chocolate combination. As alternates there are coffee, vanilla, lemon and Grand Marnier, all of which I prefer to raspberry. A fluffy Grand Marnier sauce is wonderful on fresh raspberries, and from time to time there is a velvety orange chocolate cake. In winter pouding Canadien is offered—a sort of soufflé flavored with brown sugar, cinnamon and maple syrup, out of character for La Grenouille, perhaps, but delectable nonetheless.

Given my enthusiasm for this lovely restaurant, it might be in order to explain why it gets three stars instead of four. One reason is the newness of the chef and the menu changes that are in the air. (Could one be a tendency to oversalt?) Second, though I love what La Grenouille does, I feel the menu has a certain pat quality about it. This is not an eater's restaurant in the sense that Lutèce and Le Cirque are, meaning that no one ever comes over to say, "I have a lovely something or other I would like you to try," or, "Is there anything special I can make for you?" Nor does the chef ever send out a small pride-and-joy that he has invented and wants to delight a customer with. So while this is the restaurant I would go to if I wanted to wear my prettiest dress, or if I wanted to show someone the chicquest of the chic and still eat wonderfully well, usually I choose to spend my money at either of the two other places. Wines, by the way, are exorbitant, with few good, moderately priced choices.

LUTÈCE

249 East 50th Street, between Second and Third Avenues.
Telephone: 752-2225.

Favorite meals:
 LUNCH
 Alsatian onion tart
 Alsatian sauerkraut with pork and sausages (choucroute garni), when available
 Apple charlotte
 OR
 DINNER
 Sautéed foie gras with apples

145

Fish soup with crabmeat
Roast chicken with herbs
Rhubarb tart when available, or lemon bavaroise
OR
Snails baked in brioche
Cream of frogs' legs soup
Roast pheasant or venison, in season
Lemon succès maison

OTHER FAVORITE DISHES: Foie gras in brioche, home-marinated salmon, mousse of duck with juniper, three fish in brioche, all pâtés and terrines, artichoke stuffed with mushrooms, snails Alsatian-style, bay scallops méridionale, salmon or bass in puff pastry, truffles with foie gras in croissant, pumpkin soup, cream of pea soup, roast lobster, casserole of crabmeat, scallops Provençale, turbot with lemon butter, chicken or veal with morels in cream, veal kidneys in red wine sauce, fillet of lamb with peppercorns, filet mignon or noisettes of veal in puff pastry, all game dishes, chicken sauté au Riesling, sweetbreads with capers, chartreuse of cabbage with duck or pheasant, roast duck with peppercorns (not fruit), sirloin steak in red wine sauce, cold raspberry soufflé, praline ice cream bombe, orange chocolate cake, cassis sherbet, all other desserts except gratinée fruit if on the menu.

SETTING: Four rooms in town house duplex; simple, charming country bistro with generally good space between tables and bearable noise level in most rooms.

SERVICE: Generally excellent, but there are intermittent reports of rudeness or indifference from guests the staff considers unimportant.

DRESS CODE: Jacket and tie required for men.

SMOKING REGULATIONS: No special policy.

FACILITIES FOR PRIVATE PARTIES: Limited but possible if planned well in advance.

HOURS: Lunch, Tuesday through Friday, noon to 2 P.M.; dinner, Monday through Saturday, 6 to 10 P.M. Closed Sunday and for lunch on Monday; in June and July also closed on Saturday. Closed all major holidays and for the month of August through Labor Day weekend.

RESERVATIONS: Necessary three to four weeks in advance, depending on day and time.

PRICES: Expensive.

CREDIT CARDS: AE, CB, D.

Restaurant-conscious New Yorkers of a certain age may find it hard to believe that twenty-five years have passed since the opening of Lutèce, the grand bistro on two floors of an East Side townhouse. The invention of the pompous and conten-

146

tious but brilliantly theatrical and nervy André Surmain (now the owner of Le Relais de Mougins in France and a branch in Palm Beach), it did not reach culinary glory until the original chef and early partner, André Soltner, took over completely. To give credit where it is due, Soltner profited by the stage Surmain set for him, but without the master chef's consistently impeccable performance, Lutèce would probably have disappeared long ago. First known as the most lavish and expensive French restaurant in New York, it is now acknowledged by virtually all critics as the country's best, and by fans as one of the least pretentious. Expensive though it may be, Lutèce offers greater value than other dining places in its price category, and it is easy to spend more money unsuspectingly at a few other improbable spots such as "21," and The Four Seasons to name only two. That is especially true at lunch, when Lutèce has a $29 prix fixe that is, by comparison, plainly and simply a steal.

Were I forced to choose a single New York restaurant to dine in, this would have to be it for reasons I shall try to explain with two stories. The first has to do with an interview I had many years ago with Jean Didier, then the editor of a now extinct French restaurant guide, the *Guide Kleber*. That rating system included a black caldron topped with a crown, just a step below its top rooster symbol. When traveling through France, I consistently found satisfaction in restaurants bearing that mark and I told that to Didier. "That means you like to have all of your superb right on the plate," he said. In truth, he had my number.

Years later I had a conversation with fashion designer Mollie Parnis, who asked me to name my favorite French restaurant. When I answered Lutèce, she said, "Well, now let me tell you something. I went there a few weeks ago with a very important man who owns a large newspaper chain. I had never been before, and I don't care if I never go again. I didn't know anyone there, no one was beautifully dressed, the room was not glamorous, and the only thing anyone talked about was food." And there in a nutshell is why I love Lutèce. Not that I do not like the beauty of La Grenouille or its equally beautiful crowd, but food is what Lutèce is all about, and that's what I care about when I eat.

Certainly the dining rooms are attractive enough, my favorite being the small first room downstairs or either of the two upstairs dining rooms and my least favorite being the enclosed garden. There is nothing seriously wrong with that trellised pink room with its Paris café chairs; it's just that I prefer the intimacy of the other settings. Right from the entrance, with its charming bar, which has tiny café tables, green checked curtains and a festive Jean Paget mural of Paris, Lutèce suggests a country restaurant with an easygoing charm. Pass the open

147

window of the kitchen, where Soltner and his chef de cuisine, Christian Bertrand, nod starchy white toques blanches as they finish dishes and greet customers, you instantly feel relaxed and in good hands.

Soltner himself comes out of the kitchen frequently to tour the dining rooms, make suggestions, take orders and then to check on the meal's progress. He is as likely to do this with newcomers as with regulars, and his wife, Simone, who oversees the dining room, among other things, tries to seat first-timers near celebrities. Among such, Lutèce can count Woody Allen, Jack Lemmon, William Paley, Henry Kissinger and more. The regular clientele ranges from out-of-towners in near frumpy clothes to last-of-the-big-spender Seventh Avenue types and on to the fashionable wearers of the St. Laurents, Armanis and Beenes. Here, as in all truly great restaurants, what customers have in common is not social standing or profession but their love of food, and that is what they (and I) come to have and talk about. Sorry, Mollie.

Proud of his Alsatian culinary heritage, Soltner often features dishes of that region, lightening them and garnishing them with unexpected flourishes. Classic French dishes of other regions as well as almost daily revisions of more or less nouvelle-style presentations add up to an irresistible and varied repertory. My own dilemma when I plan a meal at Lutèce is whether to opt for the old tastes that I adore or chance a new one. If left to my own whim, it would be the former, but Soltner always seems hurt if I do not try a new dish or two. Rarely am I sorry.

If left absolutely to my own choice, a perfect lunch would be the Alsatian onion tart always among midday appetizers, followed by his choucroute garni were it a special. Nowhere else is the blond sauerkraut more subtly scented with juniper and Riesling nor the kraut itself cooked just tender but juicy. Three or four kinds of white and red wursts accompany this as does the most stunning array of pork cuts, including smoked and fresh meat from body and foot to provide the right contrast of soft and firm textures with just enough fat to give it all a luxurious gleam. The star of the assortment for me is the sautéed quenelles of liver Soltner adds along with tiny, perfectly boiled potatoes. A variation on that dish includes roast pheasant when in season, and the bird is so golden and moist, I can forgo some of the other meats to make room for it.

Another wonderful Alsatian specialty sometimes featured for lunch is chicken sauté au Riesling, laced with cream and adorned with tiny dumplings of marrow and semolina.

No one has a better hand with foie gras, and the lush New York State product is here sautéed with sliced apples; at times that combination is scooped into small hollowed brioches. The

148

same eggy, crusty yeast roll is the new vehicle for snails, baked right in the brioche complete with parsley and shallot butter.

Pâtés and terrines of pigeon mousse, foie gras, pork and veal or game, or a combination of fish and shellfish, are equally extraordinary as is the almost daily special of salmon or bass, perhaps with a mousse, baked en croûte. Crusts are much favored in Alsace, and Soltner is as fine a baker as he is a chef.

Cool salmon marinated at Lutèce and polished with a few drops of oil, bay scallops méridionale sautéed with Provençale herbs, truffles and foie gras rolled into a flaky croissant, and simple classics such as asparagus vinaigrette and artichokes stuffed with mushrooms make the first-course choice a wonderful puzzlement.

And that's without even considering soups, a course I rarely miss here. (Soltner gladly divides a series of his appetizers into tiny portions so a small bowl of soup becomes possible.) Some days it is the cream of frogs' legs with tiny puffs of fish dumplings, and another it may be the incredible soupe de poisson au crabe, a more or less Provençale fish soup given zest with nuggets of sea-fresh crabmeat. Pumpkin soup gets just enough cream to give it a peachy glow, and the cream of pea soup Saint-Germain suggests liquid jade.

If not soup, I might have the pungent crabmeat in a tiny cassolette or share some sautéed scallops with the Provençal trademarks of garlic and herbs. From the simplest Dover sole meunière through the light mousseline of fish with a Nantua sauce coral pink from its shellfish to the roast lobster with its beurre blanc sauce, most fish dishes are sublime. The few that disappoint are those based on what are called around town escalopes or paillards of fish—paper-thin slices that invariably stick to the plate and do not have enough texture to hold their flavor.

Much to Soltner's consternation, I often automatically order my preferred main course at dinner—the roasted baby chicken with herbs. It is immaculately rendered, with the meat juicy and just falling from the bone (there's no nonsense about bloody-at-the-joint fish or chicken here, thank God), and with its skin greaseless and faintly crisp but slightly silken. Or if I am feeling traditional, it might be the filet mignon in puff pastry, which has been on the menu almost since the day Lutèce opened, or sweetbreads in hot brown butter sparked with capers. Roast duck is lovely here too, but I prefer it with peppercorns rather than with fruit or fruity vinegar. Morels give a smoky patina to cream sauce that mellows noisettes of veal, and a classic red wine sauce adds an astringency to sliced, sautéed veal kidneys.

There might be a surprise such as a miniature chartreuse with duck or pheasant, the tender bird meltingly delicious in

149

its leafy covering. I wish I could still get rack of lamb persillé at Lutèce as I favor that parsley-garlic-breadcrumb crust to the caramelized honey glaze, although it adds minimal sweetness and is pleasant.

Nowhere in the city can I find more subtly handled game or rabbit, whether in light mustard sauces, the dark-as-midnight stews that are civets, or roasted and garnished with wild mushrooms.

It can probably go without saying that André Soltner also provides the loveliest vegetable and potato creations to round out main courses, and all of the noodle-spaetzle variations are heaven. One touch I love is the topping of cooked fresh noodles with a few golden crisp strands that have been browned in butter, a custom Soltner learned in his mother kitchen in Alsace. The crisp noodles add intriguing textural contrast by way of a nutlike crunch.

All that and dessert too, and a glance at the array in the garden dining room should hint at the divine perplexity of choosing. One day it may be the apple tart Tatin, perfect if humidity has not melted the caramelized glaze or, even better, an apple charlotte, the barely firm fruit centered in a crisp, toasted bread housing and swathed with vanilla-perfumed crème anglaise. Other fruit tarts, especially those based on Alsatian originals, are wonderful, and I always hope for one with blue plums or rhubarb. Puff pastry layered with berries and cream and the light, lemony succès maison are usually on hand.

Chocolate mousse is dark, bittersweet and frothy, and the praline ice cream cake, with its crackling bits of sugared filberts, is cooling and rewarding. So is the frozen raspberry soufflé and the thin, moist chocolate cake brightened by orange. I avoid gratinée fruits if they are on the menu as warm fruits thinly sliced do not appeal to me, but I have no trouble with a hot soufflé, of which the chocolate is an enduring first choice.

What makes eating at Lutèce entertaining is the little extras Soltner sends over—a bit of sautéed foie gras or langoustine when you have ordered none, an extra dessert or a half cup of soup, just to try. He is inclined to do this more with customers whose tastes he knows, but he usually makes some effort along those lines even with newcomers. After dessert that means buttery crisp cookies and bonbons, the best of which are the glazed orange sections that inform the palate in the most benign of ways that a wondrous meal has come to an end.

Soltner has a stupendous wine cellar, with some 40,000 bottles stored in a nearby building, and they reach into the thousands in price with many in the mid-hundreds. He prefers customers to drink more modest bottles to their heart's content and has a suitable list of such choices. His pride is the Alsatian

150

Rieslings and tokays. He also stocks a fire-and-ice framboise that should, I suppose, be considered the trou Alsacien, the drink that, like Normandy's Calvados, burns a hole to make more room for food.

And as a bonus midst all that French splendor, Soltner has the good taste to include English translations on his menus. Le Cirque, take note! The time is now!

La Metairie, *see* Middle Eastern, North African and Armenian

Odeon, *see* American

QUATORZE

240 West 14th Street, between Seventh and Eighth Avenues. Telephone: 206-7006.

Favorite meal:
Salad of chicory with bacon and hot vinaigrette
Sautéed calves' liver with shallot sauce
Crème caramel

OTHER FAVORITE DISHES: Alsatian onion tart; jambon persillé; smoked chicken breast with horseradish cream; Alsatian sauerkraut with pork and sausages (choucroute garni); grilled herbed chicken; grilled salmon with sauce Choron; beans with duck, lamb and sausage (cassoulet); apple tart.

SETTING: Handsome Parisian brasserie-bistro decor with Art Deco touches; very noisy and crowded, with an active bar.

SERVICE: Professional and efficient, if sometimes perfunctory.

DRESS CODE: None.

SMOKING REGULATIONS: No cigars or pipes are permitted.

FACILITIES FOR PRIVATE PARTIES: None.

HOURS: Lunch, Monday through Friday, noon to 2:30 P.M.; dinner, seven days, 6 P.M. to midnight. Closed Christmas Day.

RESERVATIONS: Necessary.

PRICES: Moderate.

CREDIT CARDS: AE.

If ever a restaurant exceeded my expectations, it is this one. Trying to create a new dining room that looks mellow and old and as though it had always been in place without becoming corny or overly theatrical was the first unlikely effort. Yet the dark maroon wood trim, creamy walls, mirrors, French posters and Art Deco wall sconces establish a brasserie-bistro setting, somewhere between the Parisian classic Lipp and La Goulue on the Upper East Side. The noise and Brasserie-packed tables, and the hectic scene at the bar, are all drawbacks but are certainly typical of similar spots in Paris. Then take an owner named Peter Meltzer, formerly a food photographer, and an Italian-American chef, Mark Di Giulio, founder of the Bridge Café, and again low expectations are in order on an almost totally French menu.

Yet because the chef is capable and understands the simple, bistro-brasserie classics, it works very well, for the most part. Now if only I could have a table whenever I wanted one, how lovely life would be. But with the stretch limousine crowd hot on the trail (it shows what can happen when 14th Street becomes Quatorze), reservations are needed anywhere from a few hours to a week in advance, varying with the day and the hour. A few times when I have wanted to eat early, say before the theater, I have walked in at 6 or 6:30 and was told I could have a table if I left by 8—a fair bargain under the circumstances. It is an easy trip up Eighth Avenue to the theater district from this location and so it usually works well. Service is generally crisp and efficient but can be distracted, with waiters looking off in the distance as they take orders. There is also the annoying attempt to give away poor tables first even if the room is empty, something that happened on a few occasions when I was not recognized.

But the food has been consistently good whether I was known or not. The appetizer salad of ice-crisp chicory, its bitter bite gentled by nuggets of meaty bacon and a hot, sharp vinaigrette dressing, is a refreshing starter, and large enough to be shared by two. Jambon persillé, the chunks of ham set in a garlic and parsley aspic, is sliced instead of being properly scooped from a bowl. Nevertheless, the flavor combines delicacy and substance. Though not particularly French, the smoked chicken breast with horseradish cream is delicious, and the Alsatian onion tart is soft, fragrant and satisfying. Unfortunately, the house terrine had the wet softness of pet food, and oysters were warm.

Thin slices of calves' liver, sautéed to rosy perfection and glossed with a bittersweet mantle of shallots, is a main course I find hard to resist. But other temptations do win out, from time to time, among them the nicely done choucroute garni, the Alsatian classic of juniper-scented sauerkraut piled with various cuts of pork, sausages and boiled potato. As presented at Quatorze, the dish is a little heavy on sausage and short on meat, but all is fine otherwise. The better-than-average cassoulet has plenty of pork, duck confit and coarse cotechino sausage midst the white beans that need just a little more garlic to achieve perfection. Fettuccine with artichokes and fennel or with tomato and basil has been too oily and salty with too much sauce in proportion to pasta.

Grilled chicken, which is properly moist within and herbed outside, is a menu regular. Duck, unfortunately, has tasted either reheated or overcooked, and all fish except the grilled salmon with sauce Choron has been disappointing. As simple as crème caramel is, it is not easy to find an excellent interpretation—properly set yet soft and slightly floppy, its essential egginess modified by vanilla and caramelized sugar sauce. That is how it appears here, and it rivals the wafer-thin baked-to-order apple tart as the best dessert. Chocolate regal, declared a specialty on the menu, is a dark wet cake of the sort I detest. The gooey texture suggests it was not baked at all but is rather like raw dough, a state immature palates favor.

There is a modest wine list befitting the cuisine, but there should be more choices by the glass, carafe and half bottle.

La Ripaille

605 Hudson Street, between West 12th and Bethune Streets. Telephone: 255-4406.

Favorite meal:
> Mousse of broccoli with lemon butter
> Sautéed veal kidneys in mustard sauce (Emincé de rognons de veau sautés à la Dijonnaise)
> Crème Caramel

OTHER FAVORITE DISHES: Chicory salad with garlic croutons and bacon (petite frisée aux croutons à l'ail et bacon), seafood sausage in sweet pepper sauce (boudin des fruits de mer), fettuccine with smoked salmon (fettuccine à la crème de saumon fumé d'Ecosse), paupiettes of salmon with basil (paupiettes de saumon poché, sauce au basilic frais), leg of lamb with white beans (gigot aux flageolets), grilled rack of lamb with herbs (le carré d'agneau grillé aux fines herbes), mignonettes of beef or steak au poivre, fresh fruit desserts, dark chocolate mousse (mousse au chocolate noir), frozen raspberry souffle and profiterolles.

SETTING: Rustic French bistro, relaxed and charming; noise level is high and small tables are uncomfortable.

SERVICE: Good, if occasionally pretentious.

DRESS CODE: None.

SMOKING REGULATIONS: No special policy.

FACILITIES FOR PRIVATE PARTIES: Will open on Sundays or close other days to accommodate private parties of between thirty and fifty.

HOURS: Dinner, Monday through Saturday, 5:30 to 11:00 P.M. Closed Sunday, Christmas Eve and Day, and Labor Day weekend.

RESERVATIONS: Recommended.

PRICES: Moderately high.

CREDIT CARDS: AE, MC, V.

This is an endearing bistro that I am happy to have near my home. It is small, intimate and atmospheric and follows the decor established by Charles Chevillot in his original Village version of La Petite Ferme. That means rough white plaster walls, farm tools, a pseudo-hayloft and an imposing old grandfather clock that has never tolled for me, hélas. La Ripaille is a medieval French word meaning a feast and revelry, and judging by the loyal clientele and the air of conviviality, Patrick and Alain Laurent, the brothers who own this restaurant, have succeeded in making the promise of the name come true.

There is a nice sense of proportion between menu and surroundings, a harmony not always found these days. Every dish seems just right for the place, from the delicate broccoli mousse with a lemon-sharpened butter sauce that has become a house classic to the dark chocolate mousse served with crunchy homemade biscuits. Although the original sublime fruit tarts have long since disappeared and a sweetness via that accursed ingredient, raspberry vinegar, has crept in here and there, for the most part there is nothing but improvement since La Ripaille opened.

First courses may include such traditional offerings as a smoky lentil soup with meaty slivers of bacon and a salad of spiky chicory with garlic croutons and warm bacon. Tomato and fresh basil give stylish lift to the flavors of plump snails, and fettuccine with smoked salmon, dill and cream is as enticing a starter as the seafood sausage nestling in a rose pink sweet pepper sauce. There are, from time to time, lovely cold vegetable cream soups, vegetables vinaigrette and wild mushrooms, all to be watched for as they appear in season on this oft-changing menu.

Among lusty main course classics, I love the kidneys in mustard sauce, which are always fresh and cooked to the right ruby redness at the center, the mignonettes of beef, preferably au poivre, and grilled rack of lamb with thyme and rosemary. Frogs' legs are nothing short of wonderful in their garlic, parsley and tomato sauce, but the bones tend to loosen and work their way into rice that is beneath them. This makes for difficult but worthwhile eating. Magret de canard, the thick, meaty duck

154

breast in a sauce of port and figs, is miraculously nonsweet, and that combination should work almost as well with kiwi when that version is on the menu. (Since kiwi has virtually no taste, how can it hurt?) Veal sautéed with morels, shrimp braised with leeks, and sole wrapped around a mushroom duxelles provide other delectable options. Rolls of salmon poached and brightened with basil, and roast leg of lamb, its juices mingling with white beans, are other favorites. There is a tendency to overload main course plates here, making meat hard to cut.

Orange adds a sunny touch to the classic crème caramel, and the lemon tart finishes a meal with the right palate-restoring bite. White chocolate mousse is as awful here as anywhere else, and floating island, last time I had it, was too soft and its vanilla-egg sauce anglaise too watery. Better choices are the bitter chocolate mousse, strawberries with crème fraîche frozen raspberry souffle or the profiteroles.

Roxanne's, *see* The View, the Setting and the Scene

Table d'Hôte, *see* American

TERRACE

400 West 119th Street, at Morningside Drive, in Butler Hall. Telephone: 666-9490.

Favorite meals:
Asparagus vinaigrette
Steamed and baked lobster, Georges Garin
Crème brûlée
OR
Mousse of smoked fish
Rack of lamb
Grand Marnier soufflé

OTHER FAVORITE DISHES: Oysters in champagne, seafood in puff pastry, lobster bisque, onion soup, veal chop with morels, quail or partridge with red cabbage, poached salmon, endive and arugula salad, chocolate mousse, chocolate cream torte, lemon meringue tart.

SETTING: Elegant and romantic candlelit dining room with beautiful view over the city; tables for two are less comfortable than those for four; noise level is bearable even with harp or piano music at dinner.

155

SERVICE: Attractive, polite, helpful and efficient.
DRESS CODE: Prefers jackets on men, but rule is not enforced.
SMOKING REGULATIONS: No special policy.
FACILITIES FOR PRIVATE PARTIES: Separate room accommodates between twenty and sixty; for larger parties it is possible to reserve the entire restaurant on Sunday and Monday.
HOURS: Lunch, Tuesday through Friday, noon to 2:30 P.M.; dinner, Tuesday through Thursday, 6 to 10 P.M., Friday and Saturday, 6 to 10:30 P.M. Closed Sunday and Monday but open most major holidays.
RESERVATIONS: Suggested for lunch, necessary for dinner.
PRICES: Moderately high to expensive.
CREDIT CARDS: AE, CB, D, MC, V.

The Terrace is a restaurant I love to take first-timers to for a surprise. Most people cannot believe it even when they are in the midst of it. Located atop the Columbia University residence Butler Hall, it has a sparkling, three-sided view that takes in Upper Manhattan, the Hudson River and the George Washington Bridge. The large, beautiful dining room shimmers with candlelight, mirrors and glass, and this is one place where background music (classical harp or piano) is more welcome than intrusive. Also open for lunch, it offers a different but no less felicitous view by day. Elaborate floral bouquets and comfortable seating (except for parties of two, who get short shrift) add to the inviting effect. Belying the too-oft-proven adage that rooms with a view have poor food, this one has many excellent dishes produced by a kitchen that seems to have settled in solidly since the death of its founder and chef, Dusan Berniç. Now operated by his widow, Nada, with the kitchen in charge of Dominique Payradeau, the former sous-chef under Berniç, the restaurant is on an even keel with food much in the style of its originator.

The only problem with the menu is reading it in the too dim candlelight; a second or larger candle at each table would enable one to more easily find the way to the lovely appetizers of smoked fish mousse (originally haddock but more recently smoked trout) or the baked oysters lightly puffed under a mantle of champagne sauce. Shellfish in puff pastry with a wine-accented cream sauce and brightly firm asparagus are other fine first-course options. Those asparagus are better in a vinaigrette dressing than with hollandaise, primarily because the hollandaise is so meagerly applied. Lobster salad is worth the thirty-minute wait required for it if you are not too hungry and want to relax with a drink anyway. Appetizer pasta with vegetables sampled awhile back was milky and bland, and the sauce for snails with walnuts were oversalted.

Lobster bisque, though slightly overthickened, had exactly

156

the right crackling shellfish flavor and was served blessedly hot; too often that soup arrives tepid in most restaurants. Onion soup is another steamy winner and almost a meal in itself.

Apparently Berniç had a way with lobster that he imparted to his assistant, for another first-class experience is lobster Georges Garin. This steamed and baked combination, glossed with Pernod butter, is named for the owner of the erstwhile, extraordinary Parisian restaurant Chez Garin. Equally dependable is the rack of lamb lightly touched with garlic and always roasted medium rare as ordered. Fortunately, the luscious meat is saved from the candying effects of mint sauce, neatly contained in a mushroom cap and thereby rendering that cap inedible as far as I am concerned. Game birds are deliciously moist, and both the boned morsels of quail and the roast partridge are served with wonderful red cabbage—at once winy, sweet and sour and just firm enough. Little flans and timbales of vegetables garnish some dishes. Noisettes of veal, once dry, now emerge from the sauté pan petal pink inside under a beige cream sauce of morels, but wild rice still presents a problem; as usual, it is woody and cold.

Duck is not quite up to other dishes, and a couple of my favorite desserts seem to have disappeared, most sadly the ethereal banana mousse cake and the nut-crunched Linzer torte. But that still leaves lofty, aromatic soufflés, a perfect crème brûlée, its custard like satin under a glassy burnt-sugar veneer, and the bittersweet chocolate mousse, which I much prefer to the albinoid interloper. There is also a thin-layered chocolate torte with a light cream filling that might make me forget the much missed banana masterpiece, but not quite.

The wine list has very good choices at a wide price range. There is valet parking, and the valet will also call a cab.

La Tulipe

★★★

104 West 13th Street, between Sixth and Seventh Avenues.
Telephone: 691-8860.

Favorite meals:
    Mussel soup with tomatoes and cream
    Squab with couscous
    Cheese
    Warm apple tart
    OR
    Zucchini fritters

157

Red snapper steamed with vegetables en papillote or soft-shell crabs meunière, when in season

Vanilla ice cream with hot chocolate and toasted almonds in a pastry shell (La Tulipe Marie-Louise)

OTHER FAVORITE DISHES: Smoked trout or fish mousse, sorrel soup, wild mushrooms on toast, game terrines, eggplant Provençale, sautéed sweetbreads, lamb chops or noisettes with herb or mustard butter, roast chicken with garlic, breast of chicken with morels, navarin of lobster, venison medallions, confit of duck with lentils, peach Melba, chocolate cake with crème anglaise.

SETTING: Urbane and stunning brownstone dining room with plum-colored walls and chic bar; extremely noisy; tables are much too closely set.

SERVICE: Generally efficient and helpful but still too pretentious; can be very slow between appetizer and main course.

DRESS CODE: Jacket and tie preferred for men but not required.

SMOKING REULATIONS: No cigars or pipes are permitted in the dining room.

FACILITIES FOR PRIVATE PARTIES: None.

HOURS: Dinner, Tuesday through Sunday, 6:30 to 10 P.M. Closed Monday, major holidays and for the last three weeks in August and the first week of September.

RESERVATIONS: Necessary well in advance.

PRICES: Expensive.

CREDIT CARDS: AE, CB, D, MC, V.

Charm is the word that comes instantly to mind when I think of La Tulipe, the small, sophisticated French restaurant on a tree-lined street in Greenwich Village where the Darrs—Sally (in the kitchen) and John (in the dining room)—have nurtured this establishment into being one of the city's best. The only detractors from that charm are a pretentiousness that seems to pervade the staff, head-splitting noise and, generally, slow service.

But the food is so good, and the town house dining room so attractive, I am willing to forgo some comfort to enjoy what is best. And that is a lot in this cuisine that combines nouvelle presentation with classic flavors. Plum-colored walls enlivened by mirrors, soft yet adequate lighting and beautiful flowers make this a flattering and urbane setting. The small front café, with its zinc-topped bar, is a felicitous, very Parisian spot in which to have an aperitif and wait for friends. A small banquette has been added to that room for those who like to eat in the bar.

The menu is not large, and though it changes often, it always includes a few house specialties served almost since the place opened in 1979. That is a good idea, because frequent guests require new choices while those coming back only occasionally usually do so for remembered tastes.

Among my favorite remembered tastes are appetizers of zucchini fritters, long slender fingers of that vegetable fried in a crisp veneer of breading and grouped perhaps a bit too cutely in a basket, a picturesque holdover, no doubt, from Mrs. Darr's stint in the test kitchen of *Gourmet* magazine. But the bright green flavor and delicacy of that appetizer cannot be faulted. There is usually a fish mousse among first courses, and it has always been first-rate, whether of smoked trout, scallops or a roll of smoked eel. Terrines of game, such as venison, or of pork and tongue, have the right al dente bite and the aromatic herbal overtones. Eggplant Provençale, baked with tomato, cheese, oregano and thyme, blends the enticing combination of Italianate-Provençale seasonings. A salad of shrimp sparked with ginger and scallions, though pungent and fresh, seems out of harmony with the rest of the food here and also numbs the palate for the wine—a bit too Southeast Asian to be offered here.

Variations on sautéed sweetbreads and foie gras appetizers are well handled, and cream of mussel soup, blushed with a bit of tomato and tinged with saffron, has the right counterpoints of saline pungency and the gentling of cream. Only once was it too watery, a flaw now obviously corrected.

My single favorite dish at La Tulipe, season permitting, is the soft-shell crabs meunière, which may just be the world's best. Tiny crabs, each about the size of an infant's hand, are lightly floured and gilded in hot butter. But the real miracle of timing is the nut-brown butter poured over them. Mrs. Darr begins by placing butter in a small copper saucepan and melting it to a halfway point in the kitchen. The crabs are brought to the table along with the saucepan, its buttery contents still cooking, to be poured over the crabs in a haze of nut-sweet perfume. Never once has the butter been less than perfect, and because heavy copper retains heat, it could easily burn were the timing even two seconds off. There is a short season for the kind of crabs Mrs. Darr insists on—usually from April to mid-July, at the latest.

Less of a high-wire act and more frequently on the menu are tender, succulent morsels of roast squab ringing steamed couscous with raisins and pine nuts. A variation is grilled squab nested in braised cabbage and "batons" (sticklike slices) of vegetables. Another house classic is red snapper decorated with slivers of carrot, leeks and zucchini, all emerging buttery and tender after steaming in a big paper papillote.

Grilled rack of lamb with mustard butter, accompanied by butter-gilded slices of potatoes, is as solidly satisfying. So is any dish made with the rich preserved duck confit Mrs. Darr prepares, smoky lentils being the best accompaniment.

Breast of chicken stuffed with morels, navarin of lobster with tomato and tarragon, and puffy pink venison medallions nicely bittersweet with orange rind and gentled with celery root puree are among other personal favorites.

A salad of lacy mixed greens gets just the right sort of winy vinaigrette dressing, and there is always an earthy, ripe goat cheese to go with it, an un-French combination of courses perhaps but a delicious one nonetheless.

Desserts are irresistible, excepting only the apricot soufflé, which has a choking sweetness. I skip that in favor of the hot, baked-to-order wafer of an apple tart, the true floating island (a huge fez of meringue adrift in a crème anglaise sea), and La Tulipe Marie-Louise, a "tulipe" of a thin, butter-crisp cookie filled with homemade vanilla ice cream, hot bitter chocolate sauce and toasted almonds. There is also a velvety dark chocolate mousse with contrasting overtones of Grand Marnier, to which a textural counterpoint is added by way of whipped cream and shaved chocolate.

When La Tulipe opened, the prices seemed outrageous, but as they have not increased in proportion to the rest of the New York scene, they now are merely high. Considering the consistent high quality of the food, a $57 prix fixe that includes appetizer or soup, main course, salad, cheese, dessert and coffee can no longer be declared exorbitant by players in the New York restaurant game. In addition to everything else, the Darrs have now added a giveaway appetizer (amuse-gueule sounds fancier), a croustade topped with brandade de morue, Provence's seductive, creamy whip of salt codfish with garlic. And with coffee they serve the fragile, butter-thin curved cookies known as tuiles. Also, no choice on the menu carries a supplemental charge. The only problem will be for those who do not want a full meal. Exceptions are made for someone who might want one or two courses, but only if he or she is with others who have the full table d'hôte.

Wines are still expensive here, but there are a few more moderately priced choices than formerly. It was a struggle to decide between three and four stars for La Tulipe. I decided on the former because of the noise, the pride that translates as pompousness and the slow service. It's too bad the Darrs do not maintain a dress code. The room is so smartly handsome and most of the guests dress to it, only to feel foolish seated next to someone in shirt sleeves.

Greek

XENIA

871 First Avenue, between 48th and 49th Streets.
Telephone: 838-1191.

Favorite meal:
Ouzo
Greek antipasto (cold salads)
Baby lamb Yuvetsi (baked with orzo and tomato sauce)
Retsina wine
Floghera (warm phyllo dough and custard pastry)

OTHER FAVORITE DISHES: All cold appetizers that include the pungent fish roe (taramosalata), the sauce of sour cream with cucumber (tzatziki), stuffed grape leaves (dolmadakia), eggplant puree (melitzanosalata), marinated baby octopus (octapodaki); all hot appetizers (mezedakia) that include grilled liver, sweetbreads and meatballs; spinach pie (spanakopita); fillet of striped bass in tomato sauce (spetsiota); fried squid (kalamarakia); broiled scampi; eggplant baked with ground lamb (moussaka); potted baby lamb (kapama); shish-kebob of lamb; baby lamb chops; mixed grill of sweetbreads, liver and lamb chops; halvah. The melted cheese appetizer, saganaki, is worth trying as a curiosity.

SETTING: Cheerful modern dining room with atmospheric folkloric touches provided by Greek handicrafts; outdoor terrace for lunch and dinner, May through September.

SERVICE: Friendly and helpful but sometimes slow between appetizers and main courses.

DRESS CODE: None.

SMOKING REGULATIONS: No special policy.

161

Facilities for private parties: Can accommodate up to one hundred.

Hours: Lunch, Monday through Friday, 11:30 A.M. to 3 P.M.; dinner, Monday through Friday, 5 to 11 P.M.; Saturday and Sunday, noon to 11 P.M.. Closed Thanksgiving and Christmas Day.

Reservations: Recommended.

Prices: Moderate.

Credit cards: AE, D.

Considering how dim, undecorated and murky most Greek restaurants in New York are, Xenia is a surprise and a joy. Greek Island white plaster walls trimmed with what look like terra-cotta pink bricks, brightly colored rugs and fabrics, and rustic furniture give this an inviting country air. The big bar and the small backyard terrace that is a sort of valley midst the peaks of surrounding buildings lend urbanity. Add to that a friendly and helpful staff, and you might not even notice that service can slow down markedly at the busiest hours.

The slowness bodes well for the food, for most of it is broiled, and the delay indicates it is broiled from scratch when ordered. That freshness is typical of all the food here and again sets this apart from most Greek restaurants in the city. Having gained the reputation of being cheap, Greek food is usually turned out cheaply—cooked far in advance and so overcooked in the re-heating. But not at Xenia, in my experience.

To get into the full mood, and to be able to stand the bouzouki music sometimes piped into the room, I like to start with an ouzo, the milky-white, licorice-flavored aperitif Greeks drink with water and a little ice. There will be some nice briny olives coming along with that and very good appetizers. If two or more are dining, it is a good idea to have one order of assorted cold appetizers and another of the assorted hot mezedakia and share. The first combines all the lovely dips and salads the Greeks specialize in. Among those is the creamy whip of red fish roe lightly glossed in oil (taramosalata) and an equally seductive puree of eggplant (melitzanosalata). Sour cream flecked with cool, chopped cucumber and fragrant with dill and garlic (tzatziki) is a lovely dip for the Greek pita bread. (It is also wonderful with the grilled baby lamb chops or the lamb shish kebob. That is not a traditional combination in Greece although it is in Turkey, an association probably best not mentioned on these premises. Just order tzatziki on the side when you have those grilled meats.) Neatly rolled grape leaves with a lemony, oily rice-and-herb filling and tender marinated slices of baby octopus round out the cold appetizers.

For hot appetizers, Greeks like to grill lamb innards on skewers just as they do the meat itself, and a version of that makes

162

up the mezedakia—sweetbreads, liver and pungent little meat-balls, which at Xenia are sautéed. The sweetbreads can be a bit dry, but they have a nice, nutty flavor.

Saganaki sounds more interesting than it tastes, but it is amusing. Earthy sharp cheese is melted in a small gratin dish and arrives at the table all buttery and bubbling hot. A little lemon juice is added, and the soft cheese is scooped up with pita, a pleasant diversion with drinks. Spinach pie layered with flaky phyllo dough makes a delicious dinner appetizer or a lunch main course.

Egg lemon soup with rice is one of my favorite dishes, but ordering it at Xenia has proved chancy. The key seems to be the time of day. It is light, clear and heady at lunch, but by night apparently cooks into a starchy mass. As I usually go to Xenia for dinner, I skip it.

Among main courses, I especially like the fillet of striped bass baked with a thick sauce of tomatoes, chunks of onions and olive oil, which is served with rice. Like all main courses, it is also served with vegetables and a salad. But since the vegetables are almost always overcooked and the salad is based on iceberg lettuce, I leave those foods untouched, still content with the value received. Broiled striped bass is overcooked, but scampi (really shrimp done scampi-style) emerge from the broiler firm and redolent of oil and lemon. Concoctions such as shrimp Santorini baked with feta cheese are exaggerated here, but the simple, crisp and tender fried squid is perfect and, by the way, another possibility as an appetizer.

Moussaka, the Greek national dish based on eggplant baked with a filling of ground beef mixed with tomato and topped with a soufflélike blend of eggs and cheese, is always done to order at Xenia and is excellent. So is the baby lamb Yuvetsi, a huge braised knuckle of meat that is falling-apart tender. It is nestled on the rice-shaped pasta, orzo, that absorbs the to-mato sauce and meat juices. Kapama, potted lamb with a red wine, tomato and meat sauce, is only slightly less exceptional, but I prefer orzo to the rice usually served, and so order it that way.

Marinated lamb shish-kebob and a mixed grill of sweet-breads, liver and lamb chops are just fine and the broiled baby lamb chops brushed with herb-scented olive oil is equally good, but it is not always possible to get them medium rare. Insist-ence in that direction pays off. Pastitsio, a baked macaroni and meat combination, is something I love, but not the heavy ver-sion here.

Fancy dishes are the kitchen's weak points, but the simple food is rarely disappointing. Fresh halvah and, even better, the sensuous, warm floghera—flaky phyllo filled with warm cus-tard—are by far the best desserts.

White wine seems better than red with Greek food, and at Xenia I like the resin-flavored retsina, which provides an astringent touch to the oily food. If you dislike the piney overtones of retsina, try white Hymettus.

TIDBITS

Good Greek food is hard to come by in New York. A limited option now in the Theater District is *Pantheon*, 689 Eighth Avenue between 43rd and 44th Streets, (664-8294). Most of the food there is overcooked and tired, especially at dinner, but the cold appetizer assortment, supplemented with a sublime stewed artichoke with oil and lemon, makes a fine pre-theater meal. (Closed Sunday)

Hungarian

CSÁRDA

1477 Second Avenue, corner 77th Street.
Telephone: 472-2892.

Favorite meal:
  Brains and eggs or giblet soup
  Stuffed roast chicken
  Apricot palacsinta (crepes)
OTHER FAVORITE DISHES: Marinated herring, sausage with green peppers and onions (lecsós kolbász), stuffed cabbage, stuffed pepper, noodle soup, beef or veal goulash with nockerl, chicken paprikash, lecsós roast pork, calves' liver paprikash, chicken in the pot, cheese or apple strudel.
SETTING: Rustic Hungarian inn that is comfortable and atmospheric.
SERVICE: Concerned, efficient and sincere.
DRESS CODE: None.
SMOKING REGULATIONS: No special policy.
FACILITIES FOR PRIVATE PARTIES: None.
HOURS: Dinner, Monday through Friday, 5 to 11 P.M.; Saturday, lunch and dinner noon to 11 P.M.; Sunday, noon to 10 P.M. Open all major holidays.
RESERVATIONS: Accepted for more than three.
PRICES: Inexpensive to moderate.
CREDIT CARDS: AE.

For many years one of the city's best values, Csárda remains a delight. It is a solid, full-fledged restaurant, with immaculate red-and-white tablecloths and an efficient and cheerful staff, and it offers a great deal of very good food at amazingly low prices. One samples the various rugged, Hungarian home-style dishes feeling satisfied and with no sense of deprivation at having eaten on the cheap. The small dining room, with its plaster white walls, peasant pottery, rugs, plants, and the polished little service bar and comfortable rustic wood chairs create a romantic Balkan tavern setting. Midst that, there are the motherly but professional waitresses dispensing cheer both by way of their personalities and the rich hot food they serve up in copious portions. So copious, in fact, that the sharing of main courses is allowed for an extra $4 service charge.

Not everything is wonderful here all the time, but because I like this place enough to have mastered the ropes, I can find my way to a three-star meal. That, averaged out with the occasional good or fair meal, accounts for a two-star rating. I try to go to Csárda on the busiest days—Thursday through Sunday—for though there may be a short wait for a table and slightly slow service at peak hours, the food is always at its best at such times. Off nights in the dining room seem to mean off nights in the kitchen, when the roast duck and the roasted veal shank will not be their freshest, juiciest and most sprightly. If I do go on a slow night, I stick to the meats that are simmered in sauce—one of the goulashes (beef or veal) or such paprikash specialties as veal, chicken, the sublime calves' liver or the schnitzel. Anything paprikash comes with the tiny dough dumplings known as nockerl that soak up the lusciously rich paprika and sour cream sauces.

Usually I begin with a hearty appetizer and either of two good Hungarian red wines—the deep ruby Egri Bikavér (Bull's Blood) or the Hajósi cabernet. Both put California red wines at the same price level to shame. Among my favorite starters are the firm, sharply saline marinated herring mantled with sour cream that gets an icy crunch from slivers of onions, or the combination of garlic sausage sautéed with green peppers, onions and paprika (lecsós kolbász). There are also the great fist of stuffed cabbage with a tender meat filling on a nest of paprika-zapped sauerkraut and the delectable scrambled eggs with snowy nuggets of calf's brains mellowed with sautéed onions. Both the stuffed cabbage and the brains may also be had as main courses. Chopped liver tends to be bitter, but the stuffed pepper is a close rival to the cabbage.

Or soup. Especially if there is giblet soup with vegetables and mushrooms in a paprika-brightened broth. But even the chicken noodle standard is a warming opener. Warming, by the way, is what all this food is, and Csárda is a place I prefer in fall and winter.

With all this goes a basket of breads that look better than

166

they taste and a nice fresh cucumber salad that would be even more welcome if it were less sweet.

The one dish that never fails me is the superb half of roast chicken that is stuffed in a particularly flavorful way. Thyme-scented bread with flecks of liver is placed between skin and breast meat, there to remain moist as it flavors the meat and helps the skin to turn thin and crisp. All of the goulashes and papri-kash dishes already mentioned are choices I depend on, and with which I am rarely disappointed. Similarly, the lecsós roast pork with paprika sauce is generally moist and flavorful, and the chicken in the pot with noodles never has the overboiled, stale-grease accent it gets in less careful kitchens.

Two of my favorite dishes are the roast duck and the enor-mous roast veal shank, but again only when the action is heavy and the cooking fresh. I have learned that no time is right for most of the breaded or broiled meats as they tend to be dry, tasteless and tough.

Warm cheese or apple strudel or the thin crepes known as palacsinta filled with apricot jam and sprinkled with chopped walnuts are lovely. Not so the chocolate-covered palacsinta or the cherry strudel.

GREEN TREE HUNGARIAN RESTAURANT

1034 Amsterdam Avenue, corner 111th Street.
Telephone: 864-9106.

Favorite meal:
    Chicken matzo ball soup
    Chicken paprikash
    Napoleon

OTHER FAVORITE DISHES: Borscht, fried potato pirogen, Hun-garian and szeged goulash, stuffed cabbage, stuffed pep-pers, chicken fricassee, stuffed roast chicken, apple strudel, cream puff. Wine and beer only.

SETTING: Bohemian atmosphere in what is a cross between a luncheonette and a café, with a convivial young crowd.

SERVICE: Good natured and concerned but sometimes slow when most crowded.

DRESS CODE: None.

SMOKING REGULATIONS: No special policy.

167

FACILITIES FOR PRIVATE PARTIES: None.
HOURS: Lunch, Monday through Saturday, noon to 3 P.M.; dinner, Monday through Saturday, 3 to 9 P.M.. Closed Sunday and major holidays.
RESERVATIONS: Not accepted.
PRICES: Inexpensive.
CREDIT CARDS: None.

Despite a $7 or $8 cab ride there and back, I find the Green Tree an exceptional buy, and it is a restaurant I like to go to once in a while just to enjoy the bohemian student café atmosphere, the bright and cheerful room and the nurturing staff. Of course there is some good food too, and at the prices charged, it is a near miracle. Because the place caters to students of nearby Columbia and Barnard, as well as to the staffs of St. Luke's Hospital and the Church of St. John the Divine, there are all sorts of specials available at very low prices. The management even gives a free bottle of beer to students who dine before 7:30. Cagily enough, the management also refrains from bringing out the two or three super homemade desserts until after that time, saving the wonderful cream-filled napoleon and cream puffs and the warm, flaky apple strudel for the more profitable guests. Or so it has seemed. But the young people and the relaxed neighborhood regulars create an amiable café de quartier that makes me wish I lived in the quartier.

My toughest choice is whether to begin by sharing some of the chewy, mellow potato pirogen, available boiled or, as I prefer, fried, capped with sour cream or to have what is unquestionably the city's best chicken soup with matzo ball. The soup tastes of root vegetables, and the matzo ball is light but yet has enough substance so one feels it against the edge of the spoon—perhaps the Jewish counterpart to the Italian al dente state for pasta. If I am with three or four people, we might share some pirogen and have soup anyway, but that blissful state does not often occur as my husband and I tend to go up to the Green Tree for Saturday lunch or a weekday dinner on impulse. Cold beet borscht is also good; it's even better if you ask for a wedge of lemon and squeeze some of its juice into the winy soup, then add a cloudlet of sour cream. Cherry soup, unfortunately, is sweeter than it used to be and has less character.

A good general rule in a restaurant as inexpensive as this one is to steer clear of meat cuts that are unlikely to be both good and cheap. That means no steak or roasts, but rather poultry, stews and braised dishes—preparations that were, in a sense, created to accommodate toughness with long simmering. Among such at the Green Tree are the chicken paprikash, with its fluffy sour cream and paprika sauce and a version

168

known in kosher homes as chicken fricassee—the same preparation essentially, minus sour cream. But that makes a big difference in creating a thinner, more peppery sauce. That, as well as the fine, juicy beef goulash, comes with light little nockerl dumplings. Spicier szeged goulash is nestled against sauerkraut. Roast chicken with a fragrant herb bread stuffing is delicious as are the seductive combination of scrambled eggs with brains and onions, and stuffed cabbage or peppers. Breaded veal cutlet is one exception to the no-costly-meat rule. It is crisp, lusty and full of meaty flavor. Dishes that seem to be at equal risk in all Hungarian restaurants in town are the roast duck, pork and veal shank. All can be excellent when freshly cooked and moist, but they tend to be held over from one day to another if they are not sold, with unappetizing results. Usually, a waiter will tell you if they are freshly cooked, so it's worth asking.

Vegetables, salads and breads are eminently skippable as are heavy potato pancakes. But with sauerkraut, nockerl and mashed potatoes, as well as with the other good food at low prices, Green Tree remains a fine value. How many places offer so much satisfaction at $7.50 to about $12 for a three-course meal and coffee? Save room for one of the desserts mentioned above, and to be sure they are not sold out, reserve what you want when you order the meal. Beer is favored by many regulars, but the Hungarian red wine Egri Bikavér, (Bull's Blood) is less filling and a better complement to the food.

MOCCA HUNGARIAN RESTAURANT

1588 Second Avenue, between 82nd and 83rd Streets.
Telephone: 734-6470.

Favorite meal:
  Breaded mushrooms with tartar sauce
  Stuffed cabbage
  Rum cake with chocolate sauce and nuts (somloi galuska),
  SHARED BY TWO OR EVEN FOUR
OTHER FAVORITE DISHES: Sausage with green peppers and onions (lecsós kolbász), fried cauliflower à la Mocca, chopped liver, marinated herring, chicken noodle soup, stuffed roast chicken, beef or veal goulash, stuffed pepper, Wiener schnitzel, warm cheese or apple strudel.
SETTING: Simple, crowded informal dining room, one step above a luncheonette, with glass tops over tablecloths.

169

SERVICE: Good natured if sometimes distracted and slow.

DRESS CODE: None.

SMOKING REGULATIONS: No special policy.

FACILITIES FOR PRIVATE PARTIES: None.

HOURS: Lunch, seven days, 11:30 A.M. to 4 P.M.; dinner, seven days, 4 to 11 P.M. Open all major holidays.

RESERVATIONS: Recommended, especially for dinner on weekends.

PRICES: Inexpensive, especially at lunch when a three-course special is $4.95.

CREDIT CARDS: None.

What I enjoy at Mocca, in addition to the soul-warming food at almost impossibly low prices, is the relaxed conviviality of the clientele and the simple approach of the management. This is really a cross between a luncheonette and a café, with glass tops covering tablecloths, paper napkins and a seating arrangement that is elbow-to-elbow. But with candlelight on tables at night, a shot of slivovitz or a bottle of Egri Bikavér, the Hungarian red wine, the atmosphere is that of a big friendly family gathering. In contrast is the new Mocca Royale the same management opened next door as an attempt to become fine and fancy—and thereby a near disaster. The Royale has a corny but not amusing come-on complete with awful Gypsy music and a poor ventilating system and food is twice the price.

Never mind though, because the real action is at the inexpensive original, where it is still possible to have a relaxed friendly lunch for $4.95. It may begin with golden, fragrant chicken noodle soup, then go on to a mellow, meat-stuffed green pepper or stuffed cabbage on paprika-spiced sauerkraut or the juicy, spicy goulash with flecks of nockerl dumplings. Even at that price, the dessert is palacsinta, the crepes filled with apricot preserves and topped with ground walnuts. Not a lunch for every day, perhaps, but something I like to do once in a while if I am going to theater or a concert in the evening and do not want to eat beforehand. That lunch is enough to carry anyone through to a post-theater hamburger or pizza. The scene is friendly at noon too, with neighborhood people dropping in, and service is even warmer and friendlier than at peak dinner hours.

But even in the evening Mocca is a wonderful buy, especially since all portions are generous enough to be shared, something my husband and I do with appetizers and desserts. Fried, breaded foods are much better as appetizers here than as main courses, for reasons I cannot fathom. The breaded mushrooms or flowerets of cauliflower, both with tartar sauce, are never greasy or too dark, failings that often spoil main courses such as liver or breaded veal knuckle. Lecsós kolbász, the rich sauté of garlic sausage, green peppers and onions with paprika, is a delicious starter as is the marinated herring and the stuffed cabbage. In addition to the noodle soup, there may be a heady brew of giblets, vegetables and paprika, or a lusty goulash soup that is almost a meal in itself. There is always a nice, cool cucumber and onion salad giveaway, and unlike many others in town, it is not too sweet.

As in other inexpensive Hungarian restaurants, the braised dishes are the most dependable, which here mean veal or beef goulash, my preference being the former, the stuffed cabbage or pepper, and the roast chicken with a peppery, herb-scented stuffing layered between skin and breast meat. Lecsós roast pork with a paprika sauce and, when available, smoked pork tenderloin with beans have also been satisfying as has the Wiener schnitzel, an exception to the no-fried-main-course rule. I avoid anything that has a cream-style sauce here, finding the results too starchy. That includes all paprikash preparations, unfortunately, and the veal medallion with garlic. On busy days—Saturday and Sunday—roast duck or veal shank can be delicious—huge, moist, tender and flavorful. But on off days both carry the discouraging overtones of reheating.

Hot cheese or apple strudel, both exuding the enticing scent of vanilla, are fine desserts as is the somloi galuska, an almost insanely irresistible indulgence of sponge cake oozing rum, chopped walnuts, a dark chocolate sauce and whipped cream. *That* can be shared by four.

It's a good idea to check on accompaniments to food, or you can wind up with quite a lot of cabbage in one form or another. One night my husband began with an appetizer of stuffed cabbage after which he had duck. How could he have known that sauerkraut accompanied the duck and the vegetable served on the side was, you guessed it, cabbage? On the other hand, cabbage is really the only vegetable the kitchen does well, so perhaps this is a good place to fill up on it. Still, turning out a very good three-course meal for as little as $12 is no small accomplishment, and so Mocca can be forgiven stylistic lapses.

Indian

BOMBAY PALACE

30 West 52nd Street, between Fifth and Sixth Avenues.
Telephone: 541-7777.

Favorite meal:
SHARED BY TWO
Flour crisps with potatoes in yogurt (alu papri)
Seekh kebob
Butter chicken
Vegetable and rice biryani
Leavened wheat-flour bread (nan)
Yogurt and cucumber sauce (raita)
Mango ice cream

OTHER FAVORITE DISHES: Spicy chicken soup (murgh shorba);
mulligatawny soup; chicken tandoori; lamb with spinach
sauce (saag gosht); lamb pieces in piquant sauce (boti kebob masala); beef, lamb or chicken vindaloo; tandoori chicken
in spicy sauce (chicken tikka masala); chicken in mild spiced
cream sauce (chicken shahi korma); roasted, seasoned
eggplant bharta; lentil sauce (dhal); cauliflower and potatoes
in spices (aloo gobi masala); pistachio ice cream (kulfi).

SETTING: Large, dark and once handsome decor now in need
of sprucing up; booths afford privacy; large, lively cocktail
area.

SERVICE: Efficient, polite and helpful.

DRESS CODE: None.

SMOKING REGULATIONS: No special policy.

FACILITIES FOR PRIVATE PARTIES: Upstairs dining room seats
up to 125.

Hours: Lunch, seven days, noon to 3 P.M.; dinner, seven days, 5:30 to 11:30 P.M.

Reservations: Recommended, especially for lunch and before theater.

Prices: Moderate to moderately expensive. Weekday buffet lunch upstairs is $9.95 without dessert.

Credit cards: AE, CB, D, MC, V.

The kitchen of this spacious, quiet and restful restaurant has had its ups and downs. Several years ago, it was bristling with spirited cooking, sharply distinguished flavors and an overall verve. Though still among my favorite Indian eating places, that glow seems slightly diminished. Even the decor needs a going-over.

Nevertheless, there is more than enough deliciously prepared food and enough roomy, widely spaced tables to draw me, especially before or after theater and for business lunches. At lunch the buffet meal served upstairs is a good buy—$9.95 for all anyone wants of very decent choices.

I have found it unwise to order anything assorted here, such as the appetizers of vegetable fritters and turnovers, and the mixed tandoori grill of chicken, prawns and the ground lamb sausages, seekh kebobs. Each of the grilled meats is fine if ordered individually, but less attention is paid to the assortment. Among appetizers I still enjoy while sipping a Scotch and soda or a beer is the alu papri, the crunchy flour fritters tossed with potatoes in spiced, pungent yogurt sauce. Soups are as good as ever—the "pepper water" mulligatawny with its light lentil puree and the murgh shorba, a garlic-, ginger- and cardamom-accented chicken soup.

Many of the breads ooze oil here, and so I rely on two that are as crisp and greaseless as they should be—the nan, which is much like a pizza dough baked on the stone walls of the tandoori oven, and the roti, a yeast bread made of whole-wheat dough.

The spiced marinated tandoori-broiled foods are well-turned-out, with their typical improbable red coloring and their nicely moist insides. The seekh kebob, livened with raw onion slivers, is delicious as is the quartered tandoori chicken. Among the dishes Westerners would broadly call curries are several that are lush and flavorful. Softly cooked spinach blankets tender lamb (saag gosht), and a more piquant sauce of tomatoes and onions mellows chunks of tandoori lamb (boti kebob masala). Vindaloo, the fieriest curry of all, can be had hotly seasoned if you ask for it, and it is lovely on chicken, lamb or beef. A drier curry, korma, is based on a mildly seasoned cream sauce and is just right for the chunks of boneless chicken simmered in it. Tandoori chicken, cut in bits and simmered in a sweetly

173

spiced tomato-cream sauce (chicken tikka masala), is soothing.

Vegetable curries are so rich they almost seem to include meat. One I like at Bombay Palace is the aloo gobi masala, a combination of cauliflower and potatoes gilded with turmeric. Flecks of vegetables brighten the rice biryani, and tandoori-roasted eggplant (bharta) is mashed with browned onions and fragrant herbs. To cool the palate while sampling these heavy spicings, there is the yogurt, cucumber and mint sauce, raita; stewed lentils (dhal) mellow the rice. As in all Indian restaurants, there are intriguing chutneys and relishes, my own preference being for the lethally hot onion chutney and the extinguishing minted green yogurt.

Syrupy Indian desserts leave me cold. But there are a few refreshing creamy alternatives, among them the pistachio ice cream, kulfi, the peach-colored mango ice cream and a soft, pureed rice pudding, kheer.

DARBAR

44 West 56th Street, between Fifth and Sixth Avenues.
Telephone: 432-7227.

Favorite meal:
SHARED BY FOUR
Chick-pea, potato and onion salad (channe ki chaat)
Onion fritters (onion bhajia)
Chicken in a coconut curry sauce (mughlai korma)
Lamb with spinach and coriander (saag gosht)
Crab malabar
Rice with vegetables, saffron, raisins and nuts (shahi sabz biryani)
Yogurt and cucumber sauce (raita)
Deep-fried bread puffs (poori)
Pistachio and rosewater ice cream (kulfi)
OTHER FAVORITE DISHES: All appetizers; Hyderbad chicken and potato soup; tandoori lamb (boti kebob); boneless tandoori-grilled chicken in tomato, onion and butter sauce (murgh tikka masala); chicken with lemon and cinnamon (murgh Madras); chicken with green peppers, tomatoes and onions (murgh Jalfrazie); sliced lamb in yogurt, onion and tomato sauce (khara pasanda); lamb with yogurt, cream and almonds (rogan josh); cheese cooked with spices (paneer Jalfrazie); cauliflower and potatoes in curry spices (aloo gobi masala); grilled eggplant in sauce (bayngan bhurta); rice

with lamb, raisins and nuts (Shahjehani biryani); vegetable bread (vegetarian paratha); onion-stuffed bread (onion kulcha); cardamom-flavored rice; creamy rice pudding (kheer).

SETTING: Downstairs is romantic, pukka-sahib Indian with beautiful fabrics, pierced wood screens, gleaming brass and copper; noisy and stuffy but alcoves are comfortable; upstairs dining room is attractive but uncomfortable.

SERVICE: Excellent downstairs; slow and indifferent for dinner upstairs.

DRESS CODE: None.

SMOKING REGULATIONS: No special policy.

FACILITIES FOR PRIVATE PARTIES: Upstairs room seats up to forty. Will close entire restaurant for parties up to two hundred.

HOURS: Lunch, seven days, noon to 3 P.M.; dinner, Sunday through Thursday, 5:30 to 11 P.M.; Friday and Saturday, 5:30 to 11:30 P.M. Saturday and Sunday lunch is served buffet only.

RESERVATIONS: Recommended, especially for lunch, before and after theater.

PRICES: Moderately expensive for dinner; moderate for lunch; upstairs buffet at lunch is $9.95.

CREDIT CARDS: AE, CB, DC, MC, V.

Darbar, a relatively recent addition to the New York scene, is also one of the more welcome. It is a stylish little supper club of a restaurant with romantic decorative accessories, seductive if eventually wearing background music and a gracious staff—downstairs. At two dinners upstairs I felt quite differently and so sit there only for buffet lunch. Because it is on a sort of landing, the upstairs makes one feel left out, and at night waiters do nothing to alleviate that feeling, bringing food slowly and usually cold.

But back downstairs all is luxury and charm. True, there could be better ventilation in some corners, and the best tables are for four or more, in private alcoves, but the colorful, rich and fresh food dispels minor discomfort.

Unlike those in many Indian restaurants, the fried vegetable fritters (pakoras) and turnovers (samosas) are clear and distinguishable here, as are the chicken pakoras, marinated in yogurt, then fried in batter. Onion bhajia is a masterpiece, a forerunner, perhaps, of Tony Roma's onion loaf but an ethereal version, lightly floured and as crackling as gold leaf. Puckery tamarind sauce sharpens yogurt that is folded into chick-peas, potatoes and onions for the appetizer salad (channe ki chaat), and crab Bombay is a cool, curried salad, lightly spiced. With the exception of the zesty chicken and potato soup, creamy with coconut and piquant with lemon (hyderbad murgh shorba), soups are not quite worth the better food they displace. I prefer to save room for the nuggets of tandoori grilled lamb (boti kebob), which is the moistest and most flavorful of the grilled specialties, and for the murgh tikka masala, tandoori chicken pieces in a pink and spicy tomato and onion sauce.

Lemon and cinnamon are the complementary seasonings for chicken in the South Indian murgh Madras, and a light green pepper, tomato and onion saucing enriches the chicken in murgh Jalfrazie. Yogurt tenderizes lamb in two fine dishes—the khara pasanda, which also contains onions and tomatoes, and the rogan josh, sweetly accented with almonds. Most unusual and intriguing is crab Malabar, perfumed with fennel and green coriander, mixed with tomato.

Indian vegetarian dishes are so satisfying one has no sense of deprivation when eating them, the spices filling the mouth to lend a sense of completeness. The best examples here are the cheese cooked with spices (paneer Jalfrazie), the curried cauliflower and potatoes (aloo gobi masala) and the grilled eggplant (bayngan bhurta). Rice biryanis are rich as Croesus whether you choose the simple vegetable version, the lamb with raisins and nuts or the herbed Punjabi special. All are made with basmati rice, which adds its characteristic sweet-nut flavor. Not all breads are equally good. I concentrate on the vegetarian paratha and the onion-filled kulcha. Cucumber, mint and yogurt are combined in the cooling raita sauce, and there are lively chutneys, my favorite being the onion and the mint.

As always, I steer away from sugary Indian desserts and opt for the rice pudding, kheer, and the rosewater and pistachio sherbet-ice cream, kulfi.

If Darbar rates two stars instead of three, it is because of the difference between food and service upstairs and down, the stuffiness of the downstairs dining room and an occasional lapse in the kitchen that renders all sauces virtually identical. Then too, they fail to make food truly spicy when requested, even for the vindaloo curries.

MOGUL 57

327 West 57th Street, between Eighth and Ninth Avenues.
Telephone: 581-1774 or 581-1032.

Favorite meal:
SHARED BY TWO
Assorted vegetable appetizers

Nargis kofta
Tandoori-grilled chicken
Lamb with spinach (lamb shag)
Tandoori chapati flatbread
Raita
Rosewater and pistachio ice cream (kulfi)

OTHER FAVORITE DISHES: Tandoori ground lamb kebobs (sheekh kebob); cauliflower and potato curry (alu gobhi); grilled and mashed eggplant (bharta); mild chicken curry (chicken moghlai masala); lamb with medium spicy gravy and onions and tomatoes (lamb do piaz); vegetable and rice biryani; fancy pilaf (Shah Jahani pilaf); breads such as nan, onion kulcha, paratha tandoori; chutneys; rosewater custard (firni).

SETTING: Artful, atmospheric Indian decor with brass, pierced wood screens and a beautiful stained glass window in the long bar area; comfortable at most tables.

SERVICE: Good.

DRESS CODE: None.

SMOKING REGULATIONS: No special policy.

FACILITIES FOR PRIVATE PARTIES: There is a covered garden that can be reserved in summer; half of the dining room can be screened off to seat up to eighty.

HOURS: Lunch, seven days, noon to 3 P.M.; dinner, Monday through Saturday, 5 P.M. to midnight; Sunday, 5 to 11 P.M.

RESERVATIONS: Recommended.

PRICES: Moderate.

CREDIT CARDS: AE, D, MC, V.

Because it was so difficult to find a place for a good, pleasant and reasonable dinner in the area of the Coliseum, I was disappointed when Shah Jahan closed a few years ago. It offered nicely prepared Indian food and was one of the better options in this neighborhood. Only recently did I discover that it had, in fact, moved and changed its name, thereby escaping me. Now called Mogul 57, and under the same management, it is on 57th Street between Eighth and Ninth avenues in the location old New York hands may remember as Mont St. Michel. There is a nice little covered garden for summer dining, an atmospheric dining room with all of the de rigueur Indian trappings such as pierced screens, gleaming brass and wall hangings. There is also a huge bar and across from it a gorgeous stained glass window installed by this management for the sparkle it gives to the otherwise gloomy area. All in all, it is a delightful hideaway, not yet discovered by the hungry hordes.

The kitchen is completely competent and has unusually good assorted appetizers. The items themselves are the standard Indian vegetable fritters (pakoras) and turnovers (samosas), but they have more flavor than most. Assorted meat appetizers of tandoori-grilled chicken pieces (tikka) and the ground lamb sausages (sheekh kebob) are also well seasoned and moist, and if two dine together, it is a good idea to share both assortments. Onion bhaji, Indian fried onion rings, need a more sprightly seasoning and more careful frying.

Nargis kofta is basically a main course, but I like to share it as an appetizer. It is a personal favorite and does not often appear on Indian menus around town. It is somewhat like Scotch eggs—hard-boiled eggs, covered with a packing of ground lamb and then sautéed in Indian curry spices. On the Mogul 57 menu it is described as meatballs stuffed with hard-boiled eggs, but to me it is hard-boiled eggs encrusted with meat, an example of culinary epistemological dualism.

Tandoori broiling is generally good here, excepting only the assortment. Better to order the half chicken or the sheekh kebob individually as they get more careful attention. Standard curries are pleasantly if not quite brilliantly executed. Vindaloo, the hottest of all, here is too mild even if a request for true hotness is made, but those prepared Jalfrezi, with tomatoes, onions and green peppers, work perfectly with chicken or beef. A gentle chicken curry, moghlai masala, is a lovely blend of tomato, cream and sweet spices. Spinach and herbs are blended into a mellow sauce for lamb or shrimp shag, and do piaz, a spicy sauce with onions and tomatoes, is fine with lamb or shrimp.

With these curries come the lusty pilaf and rice biryanis, the most elaborate being the Shah Jahani pilaf with chicken, saffron, eggs, and almonds. Simpler, and my preference with a complex meal, is the vegetable biryani. Vegetables such as the spiced cauliflower and potatoes (aloo gobi masala) and the roasted eggplant puree (bharta) are just two of the delicious concoctions that can be ordered as side dishes, or as part of a vegetarian platter or thali.

All of the fancy Indian breads are good, and whether to have the plain nan or the most elaborate kheema nan stuffed with lamb depends on what other dishes are ordered. The cucumber-yogurt sauce, raita, the soothing lentil puree, dal, and a jewellike range of chutneys add the intriguing flavor counterpoints that distinguish Indian food. One problem persists from the Shah Jahan days: The food is served tepid instead of hot, and the spicing should also be hotter. The rosewater custard, firni, and the almond and pistachio ice cream, kulfi, are the best desserts.

Raga

57 West 48th Street, between Fifth and Sixth Avenues.
Telephone: 757-3450.

Favorite meal:
SHARED BY FOUR
Lentil crisps with potatoes in pungent yogurt sauce (dhal papri)
Assorted hot appetizers
Lobster malabar
Tandoori-grillled chicken
Lamb vindaloo
Roasted and mashed spiced eggplant (baingan bhurta)
Rice with fruits and nuts (Kashmiri pullao)
Puffed whole-wheat bread (puri)
Flat bread stuffed with onions (onion kulcha)
Assorted chutneys
Yogurt and cucumber sauce (raita)
Mango ice cream

OTHER FAVORITE DISHES: Shrimp in a spicy creole-type sauce (shrimp Goa); salmon steak in ginger- and garlic-flavored tomato sauce (machali masala); tandoori chicken pieces in tomato-butter sauce (murg tikke makhani); chicken with green peppers, onions and tomatoes (murg Jalfrazie); tandoori-grilled minced lamb (reshmi kebob); all lamb dishes; all rice specialties; all vegetarian specialties; flatbread baked in tandoor (nan); cardamom and saffron ice cream (kulfi); rice pudding (kheer); chocolate-cinnamon ice cream.

SETTING: Handsomest Indian restaurant in the city; formal, elegant, spacious; dramatically decorated with carvings, musical instruments, colorful fabrics; alcoves are good for private conversations but are usually reserved for parties of five or more; try to avoid smaller tables for four in back of dining room; bar area is especially comfortable.

SERVICE: Poor at lunch; at dinner it ranges from decent to indifferent.

DRESS CODE: None.

SMOKING REGULATIONS: No special policy.

FACILITIES FOR PRIVATE PARTIES: Downstairs room accommodates from twenty to fifty.

HOURS: Lunch, Monday through Friday, noon to 2:45 P.M.; dinner, Monday through Friday, 5:30 to 11 P.M.; Saturday, 5 to 11 P.M.; Sunday, 5 to 9:45 P.M.

RESERVATIONS: Recommended, especially for lunch.

PRICES: Moderate to moderately expensive. Executive lunch is $15 and pretheater dinner, served from 5:30 to 7:30 P.M., is $19.75.

CREDIT CARDS: AE, CB, D, MC, V.

When Raga is good, it is very, very good and when it is bad, it is probably lunchtime. This is a restaurant I love for dinner but dislike for lunch. It is hard to understand why this is so, considering the solid citizens it attracts midday. Perhaps regulars get preferential treatment. But back to that later.

Dinner at Raga is a thorough joy. The palatial dining room, with its carved wood doorways, columns and partitions, its beautifully striped silks, and the array of lavishly crafted and painted Indian musical instruments such as sitars, flutes, veenas and rubabs. The name Raga denotes a particular style of Indian music, and the musical theme is reiterated on most evenings, when live musicians play traditional pieces on these instruments.

The best tables set in romantic alcoves are for five or more, five being the most comfortable number. Otherwise there are cushiony banquettes. Only a few square tables in the back are too small for four, primarily because of all the breads, relishes and rice dishes set down to make Indian food the delight it is.

Few cuisines light up the palate the way this one does. Spices such as chile, cardamom, turmeric, black and brown mustard seeds, various peppers, cinnamon, cloves and ginger are contrasted with onions, garlic, mint and tart tamarind. Soothing notes are to come by way of cool yogurt and the lentil sauce dhal to be spooned over the rich rice pullaos and biryanis. Basmati rice, with its sweet-nut flavor, is the basis for these dishes, and bits of lamb, vegetables, peas or dried fruits and nuts add crunch and substance.

Most of this is handled expertly at Raga, with only the few lapses noted below. It is one place that does a fine job on assorted appetizers, the fritters known as pakoras and the vegetable turnovers that are samosas. Pieces of chicken marinated in yogurt and fried in batter are delicious (murg ke pakore), and the best of all is dhal papri, nutlike crunches of lentil-flour crisps tossed with potatoes and a tamarind-zapped yogurt sauce. Only two appetizers are disappointing—crab Goa, which is well spiced but based on fishy threads of crabmeat, and the hideous oysters Bombay. It is hard to believe the kitchen starts with freshly shucked oysters, so curled, gray and metallic-tasting are these specimens; at a recent lunch the oil in their sauce was rancid.

On to more pleasant thoughts. Tandoori chicken, with its red coloring and brassy spicing, and the tandoori-broiled ground

180

lamb kebobs (reshmi kebob) arrive moist and succulent. An unusual and delectable dish is the machali masala, two thick, very fresh salmon steaks gentled in a golden sauce of ginger, garlic, tomato and onion, all applied with enough finesse to allow the salmon's own richness to come through. Another fine seafood choice is lobster Malabar, with a sauce much like that of the salmon but a bit creamier. One daily special, shrimp Goa, in a sort of creole sauce, was good too, flawed only by a slight oversalting. But the shrimp were firm and fresh.

Vindaloo, the hottest of all curries, can be truly blistering if you insist on it that way when ordering, but be sure you mean it. I prefer that sauce on lamb, a version nicely executed here.

There are several good chicken dishes, among them the tandoori-broiled pieces that are simmered in a creamy, spiced tomato sauce (murg tikke makhani) and another with green peppers, tomatoes and onions (murg Jalfrazie). Lean and fresh chunks of lamb in a verdant spinach sauce (gosht palak) or in herbed yogurt (gosht dahiwalla) combine heft with subtlety and are especially good with the rice dishes and the plain, pizzalike tandoori bread, nan, or the balloon puffs, puris. Other breads tend to be greasy.

Vegetarian specialties are excellent here, my favorites being the roasted eggplant (baingan bhurta), the cauliflower with potatoes (aloo bhaji) and the mixed vegetables with herbs and spices (subzi Jalfrazie). Add to all of this a red-hot onion chutney, the sharp mango chutney and the comforting cucumber and yogurt sauce, raita, and you have makings of a sublime meal. Even desserts are fine—"even" because they are usually cloying in Indian restaurants. But the almond and saffron ice cream, kulfi, the creamy rice pudding, kheer, and both the mango and chocolate-cinnamon ice creams are coolly refreshing. Indian beer is best with this food, and spiced tea is the right finish.

Given the general excellence of Raga in so many directions, it could well deserve three stars. What intervenes, however, is the service, which at best is adequate. At night there can be a certain impatience on the part of the staff, especially if they are in a hurry to wrap things up and go home. At my lunch experiences, service has bordered on the horrendous. Guests (especially women sans men) are directed to poor tables even when the better ones are empty. Orders are confused or forgotten, main courses may be brought before appetizers, and there is a long lapse between first and second courses. The food is less good midday and hints at too much precooking.

Having been in business since 1977, the management should have had time to straighten this out so that the beautiful food in the beautiful room will be just as beautifully served.

TANJORE

1229 First Avenue, between 66th and 67th Streets.
Telephone: 535-8718.

Favorite meals:
SHARED BY TWO
Lentil-flour crisps, potatoes and sweet chutney in yogurt
(Tanjore chat)
Tandoori-grilled chicken
Spicy lamb curry (lamb vindaloo)
Vegetable and rice biryani
Cucumber and yogurt sauce (raita)
Pistachio ice cream (kulfi)
OR
SHARED BY FOUR TO SIX
Assorted appetizers
Spiced cold chicken (chicken chat)
Tandoori-grilled cubes of lamb (boti kebob)
Tandoori chicken pieces simmered in butter-tomato sauce
(chicken tikka masala)
Lamb with spinach sauce (lamb sagwala)
Shrimp in gingered creole-type sauce (shrimp Jalfrezi)
Rice and vegetable biryani
Mango ice cream

OTHER FAVORITE DISHES: Fried chicken wings (pakora); grilled
pieces of lamb with onion on thin bread (kati kebob); spiced
vegetable soup (shorba); all breads; all rice dishes; all vegetable dishes; tandoori-grilled ground lamb (seekh kebob);
chicken with spinach, garlic and ginger (tikka sagwala); hot
curried chicken (chicken vindaloo); chicken in butter-tomato
sauce (makhni chicken); cubes of lamb in spiced onion and
tomato sauce (Tanjore rogan josh); onion chutney; mango
chutney; creamy rice pudding with nuts and raisins (kheer);
spiced yogurt drink (salted lassi).

SETTING: Simple, attractive storefront café-restaurant with
greenery and mirrors; ventilation could be improved.

SERVICE: Polite, helpful, prompt and concerned.

DRESS CODE: None.

SMOKING REGULATIONS: No special policy but tries to put non-
smokers together.

FACILITIES FOR PRIVATE PARTIES: Can accommodate up to thirty.

HOURS: Lunch, Monday through Saturday, noon to 3 P.M.; din-

182

ner, Monday through Saturday, 5:30 to 11 P.M.; Sunday, 1 to 11 P.M.

RESERVATIONS: Necessary for dinner on Fridays and Saturdays and for more than four any night.

PRICES: Inexpensive to moderate.

CREDIT CARDS: AE, MC, V.

Right from the first nibble of the spicy, crisp lentil-flour wafers, papadum, you know something marvelous is about to happen. Nothing is ordinary at this delightful restaurant, and if the menu is somewhat more limited than those of other Indian restaurants, and the decor less elaborate, the food is by far the best—each dish carefully crafted and sparkling with character.

Ever since the dashingly handsome Ashok Seth opened this cheerful little storefront café-restaurant, it has turned out fresh, tantalizing food. And when the request for "double dynamite" is made, the curries can blister your gullet. Anyone less insistent than double dynamite will get those sauces mildly needling but not really hot; the kitchen applies a cautious hand because so often Americans ask for really hot spicing and then cannot eat it. "Dynamite" or "double dynamite" indicates that you're not just whistlin' Dixie.

A really dazzling appetizer is the Tanjore chat, round, crisp puffs of lentil flour, tossed with diced potatoes, onion, sweet chutney, herbs and a sourish tamarind sauce that contrasts with the yogurt. Chicken chat, marinated breast meat sunny with lemon and coriander, is a close second. All the fried vegetable pakoras and pastry turnovers (samosas) are impeccably done, and chicken wings pakora, marinated, battered and fried, put their Buffalo cousins to shame. Tender nuggets of tandoori-grilled lamb and onions served in thin bread (boti kebob) is another substantial and tantalizing first course.

I remember the spiced, slightly tart vegetable soup, shorba, as being one of the best versions in the city. Incredible Indian breads—the pizzalike nan that bakes crusty in the tandoor oven, the version filled with lamb (keema nan) or an even heftier specialty fleshed out with chicken—are among the winners. Puffed-up puris, cheese-flavored batura and aloo paratha layered with potatoes are just a few personal favorites. All rice biryanis and the peas pullao are moist, aromatic and tantamount to main courses, especially the Shajahani biryani, with tandoori-grilled chicken fillets, nuts, herbs and bits of scrambled eggs. Basmati rice is used throughout, imparting its unique sweet-spice overtones to any combination.

Vegetarians should have a field day here, for their favorite foods get varied and flavorful attention. Mixed vegetable curry, cheese in a spiced spinach sauce (saag paneer), curried cauliflower and potatoes (aloo gobi masala) and stewed black lentils in light cream (kali dhal) all can be had singly or on the combined tray or thali.

Large quarters of marinated, spiced chicken grilled in the tandoor are moister and have more flavor than the boneless bits (tikka). Cubes of lamb (boti kebob) and ground lamb (seekh kebob) are other good tandoori grills. I prefer them to shrimp, which dry out, or to the assorted mixed grill.

Bits of tandoori-grilled chicken mellow in tomato-cream sauce (chicken tikka masala) or a gingery spinach cream sauce (tikka sagwala) are sprightly, as is the buttery chicken labeled makhni.

Double dynamite is the correct way to order vindaloo, and it's a curry equally enticing with chicken and lamb. Milder palates will appreciate fragrantly spiced lamb rogan josh or the lamb sagwala, in a froth of spinach. Korma is the mildest, creamiest of curries, and though the sauce is nicely turned out at the Tanjore, on one occasion the lamb itself seemed to have been cooked too long in advance. But large, firm and snowy shrimp were perfection, accented by the Jalfrezi blend of green pepper, onion and tomato in a gingery sauce.

Lively dips and chutneys are house triumphs. There is a green blend served with the giveaway pappadums that is much like Mexican tomatillo sauce, another that has a brassy tamarind belt and a bright-red onion chutney that looks like chopped rubies and tastes like flame itself. After that the freshest, richest kulfi, the ice cream flavored with pistachio and rosewater, and the even creamier rice pudding, kheer, studded with nuts and raisins, are welcome, as is the peach-colored mango ice cream.

Lassi, a thin yogurt drink, is lovely with this food. I favor the spiced or plain variations to the sweet. Otherwise, I like Indian beer.

Mirrors and greenery add style to this café-restaurant. I just wish it would move to my neighborhood so I could dine there once a week.

Indonesian

Tamu

340 West Broadway, corner Grand Street.
Telephone: 925-2751.

Favorite meal and favorite dishes:
Rijsttafel, SHARED BY TWO, as follows:
Beef and chicken satays
Gado-gado vegetable salad
Madura chicken soup (soto ayam)
Chicken in spicy coconut cream sauce (opor ayam)
Beef stew with coconut cream (rendang)
Codfish in a turmeric sauce with garlic and ginger (ikan bumbu Bali)
Shrimp braised with mushrooms and coriander (udang tumis)
Shrimp in coconut curry (sambal goreng udang)
Bean curd and bean sprout salad (asinan)

SETTING: Think of *Rain* and Sadie Thompson, and you'll be right on target; very "tropical islands," with batiks and basket lamp shades.

SERVICE: Well-meaning and courteous but generally slow.

DRESS CODE: None.

SMOKING REGULATIONS: No special policy.

FACILITIES FOR PRIVATE PARTIES: None.

HOURS: Dinner, seven days, 6 P.M. to midnight; brunch, Saturday and Sunday, 1 to 4 P.M.

RESERVATIONS: Necessary on weekends; recommended every day for parties of four or more.

PRICES: Moderate.

CREDIT CARDS: AE, CB, D, MC, V.

185

Whether the Dutch invented the rijstafel concept when they ruled over what was then known as the Spice Islands or whether they simply named it "rice table," this Indonesian meal is one of the more exciting gastronomic experiences. Or can be, when it is freshly, carefully prepared, as it generally is not. Tamu in SoHo does a nice job on this meal, although a dinner at the newer branch on 14th Street near Eighth Avenue was a disaster of stale, bland food. Anything written here refers to the downtown original only.

It is a pretty, soaring two-tiered restaurant swathed in inky, waxy batiks and hung with basketry lamp shades. Bamboo chairs, brick walls hung with watery Balinesian-style nature paintings and pierced leather shadow puppets bring to mind a stage set for Somerset Maugham's classic *Rain*, although I can't remember if that is where the story was set. This is the sort of place I like to take young people who are interested in all sorts of exotic food customs. It is just right for a large group who can sit around and share a progression of the hot and cold, fiery and mild salads, curries and grills that are paraded out in the name of rijstafel. That meal costs about $40 or $42 for two, but food for two is enough for three; it follows that four orders suffice for six and to that can be added a few nonrijstafel items, such as the spicy broiled chicken (ayam panggung) fragrant with bay leaf, caraway and coriander and the curried fillet of sole (ikan kuning). Or order extra soups along with a few of the chicken or beef satays.

Once you order rijstafel, you just sit back and let it happen. The meal begins with cool salads of mixed vegetables with peanut sauce (gado-gado) and an equally titillating mix of sharply pickled vegetables (acar). Madura chicken soup (soto ayam), lightly aromatic with lemon grass and adrift with noodles, chicken and vegetables, is mild and pleasing. Then comes a grill-type warmer on which a dozen or so tiny oval dishes are set; they drip sauce on the grill and get so hot you will find it hard to serve yourself. Never mind. Just grasp the dishes with a napkin and keep spoons off the warmer, and you can manage. The dishes described above under "Favorite meal" are the ones you get. Pork satays are usually too dry and never seem fresh, and lamb dishes are greasy and too strong. But beef and chicken are moister and have better flavors. Anything with green chilies will be as fiery as you might expect, but other dishes tend toward blandness. Ask for them spicy if you want them that way; it is also possible to get a red chili relish sparked with garlic and lemon that adds interest.

The best time to go to Tamu for rijstafel is on the most crowded nights—Fridays, Saturdays and Sundays—because the food is more likely to be fresh. On off nights, the obviously reheated and reheated stews leave much to be desired. So do

186

all desserts, including grease-soaked fried bananas. Fresh fruit would be preferable. I wish the xylophone-like gamelan music, with its liquid plink-plunk, would supplant the mix-match recordings generally played. (At 14th Street, there is a cocktail lounge white lacquer piano with a vocalist singing '30s and '40s American hits.)

Beer is the best drink with this food. With Indonesia being the home of Java and Sumatra coffees, it's a pity the management doesn't make more of those beans. The brew served is weak, watery coffee-shop standard.

Italian

New York has come a long way since veal parmigiana and ravioli with meat sauce, witness the range of dishes in the restaurants that follow. Italian food has, in fact, replaced French as our number-one source of fashionable culinary excitement, primarily because it is more in keeping with the easy-going, less exacting life-style practiced these days. What New York still needs is some of the simple, savory dishes of Umbria and a reawakening of the Neapolitan favorites, this time rendered fresher, lighter and just once more with feeling.

CENT' ANNI

★★★

50 Carmine Street, between Bleecker and Bedford Streets, just west of Sixth Avenue.
Telephone: 989-9494.

Favorite meals:
  Baked soup of beans, cabbage, leek, toast and cheese (zuppa ortolana)
  Broiled squab diavolo
  Salad Cent' Anni, SHARED BY TWO
  Chocolate cake with chocolate curls, SHARED BY TWO
  OR
  Seafood salad (insalata di pesce), SHARED BY TWO
  Wide pasta with rabbit, onions and tomatoes (pappardelle al coniglio), SHARED BY TWO
  Veal chop with sage
  Tirami sù
  OTHER FAVORITE DISHES: Sautéed wild mushrooms; beans stewed with tomatoes and garlic; buffalo mozzarella with herbs; roast pepper with anchovies (peperoni arrostiti); raw

188

beef carpaccio; fettuccine with smoked salmon in cream; capellini with lobster and clams; wide pasta with porcini mushrooms; pasta shells with bacon, tomato and onion (amatriciana); red snapper Livornese with clams and mussels; grilled marinated pheasant or chicken; grilled rack of lamb (costolette di agnello); mixed grill with rabbit, lamb, quail and sausage (grigliata mista); cold zabaglione.

SETTING: Simple, pleasant, modern storefront diningroom with closely set tables; moderately noisy.

SERVICE: Friendly, polite and helpful.

DRESS CODE: None.

SMOKING REGULATIONS: No special policy.

FACILITIES FOR PRIVATE PARTIES: None.

HOURS: Lunch, Monday through Friday, noon to 2:45 P.M.; dinner, Monday through Saturday, 5:30 to 11:30 P.M.; Sunday, 5 to 11 P.M. Closed Christmas, New Year's and Thanksgiving Days and for two weeks toward the end of July when there is a street festa in the area.

RESERVATIONS: Necessary.

PRICES: Moderate to moderately expensive.

CREDIT CARDS: AE.

Raffish food, Tuscan and otherwise, in a relaxed storefront café setting is the combination that draws me time and again to Cent' Anni. This simple, bright modern trattoria, with its close-set tables, generally reasonable noise level and stylish casualness, is the setting for new culinary wonders both lean and lavish.

From the small stand at the doorway, where desserts and seasonal provender are displayed, a waiter will bring the latest porcini or oyster mushrooms to tempt a diner, and either is earthy and succulent, sautéed alone or wound into some buttery pasta. Bay scallops, lobster, shrimp and squid get an efficacious bathing of olive oil, lemon, parsley and crunches of celery for the seafood salad, and carpaccio here has a verdant, pungent green parsley-basil sauce rather than the bland, creamy topping of the Harry's Bar original. An assorted cold antipasto can include chewy, peppery prosciutto that exudes the ripeness of age and tiny rounds of buffalo mozzarella, as good with roasted peppers as they are with fresh or sun-dried tomatoes. Beans are among the glories of the Tuscan kitchen, and two preparations at Cent' Anni show them off at their best. Simmered all'uccelletto with tomato and garlic, they are served ever-so-slightly warm as an appetizer. Or they can be baked into the meal-in-itself soup zuppa ortolana, along with cabbage, leeks, toast and a dusting of grated Parmesan.

Not usually a fan of fettuccine with salmon, I find that dish exquisite as prepared in this kitchen. Thick chunks of the

189

smoked salmon, mildly woodsy and moist, are tossed with the green and white pasta along with a sheer cream and butter sauce. Big, chewy rigatoni or hollow shells can be had at times all'Amatriciana with prosciutto, tomatoes and onions or with a simpler filetto di pomodoro sauce or earthy porcini. Forced to pick my favorite pasta at Cent' Anni, I would deliberate between the wide, flat noodles called pappardelle with a rich topping of rabbit, onions, carrots and tomatoes or the fine capellini with tomato, lobster and clams, hoping only that this will be the most difficult choice I ever have to make in my life.

Rabbit alla Fiorentina is again simmered with onions, carrots and tomatoes enlivened by white wine for a main course, and there are particularly good grilled birds—all butterflied, marinated and charred so that the skin takes on a herbaceous burnishing while the meat remains elegantly dewy. Pheasant, Cornish hen and, best of all, squab are prepared this way and served with sautéed potatoes, heady with rosemary, and a simple vegetable such as string beans, spinach or escarole—the sort of accompaniment that goes to virtually every table. The lustiest appetites will be not only satisfied but enchanted, as I have been with the mixed grill—rabbit, lamb, sausage and quail—for a meaty binge that might thrombose Jane Brody but never fails to delight me.

A thick, near animal that is the gigantic veal chop is sautéed and sauced with fresh sage and white wine for a main course of stunning proportions, both in size and flavor. For lighter eaters there is red snapper, either grilled and brushed with oil and lemon or simmered with clams, mussels and a touch of tomato and capers, Livornese-style.

Less beguiling are such complications as veal with oil, mushrooms, artichokes and tomatoes, a case of overkill, and a highly touted osso buco, which though acceptable was cooked short of the fall-off-the-bone tenderness that makes the dish the dream it is. Its sauce, however, was velvety and balanced, but I have a hard time contemplating that dish without a slab of grilled polenta or some risotto to absorb the meat juices and gravy. Fruit tarts have been dull, but tirami sù, the layering of soft sponge cake, custard and coffee cream dusted with cocoa, is cool and gentle. There is a lovely chocolate layer cake topped with thick curls of milk chocolate that I believe to be Hershey's. If not, it's a dead ringer and as utilized here raises usually insipid milk chocolate to new heights.

DA SILVANO

260 Sixth Avenue, between Houston and Bleecker Streets.
Telephone: 982-2343 and 982-0090.

Favorite meals:
LUNCH
Sautéed artichokes with buffalo mozzarella
Quill-shaped pasta with bolognese or tomato sauce (penne
strascicate or marinara)
Crème caramel
OR
DINNER
Bread salad (panzanella)
Tortellini in cream, SHARED BY TWO
Florentine pot roast in wine (stracotto)
Cold zabaglione

OTHER FAVORITE DISHES: Chicken livers with capers and anchovies on toast (crostini); seafood salad (insalata di mare);
spaghettini with capers and anchovies (puttanesca); cannelloni with ricotta and spinach; linguine with white clam
sauce; pasta with porcini; osso buco; Cornish hen marinated
in oil and grilled (pollastrello alla diavolo); steak pizzaiola;
veal chop with chicken livers, wine, tomatoes and peas (lom-
batina San Frediano); roast quail; calves' liver with sage;
berries.

SETTING: Informal, attractive café with brick walls, plants and
natural wood; meals can also be had in the sidewalk café,
weather permitting. Noisy.

SERVICE: Usually excellent but can be indifferent and brusque
to unknowns.

DRESS CODE: None.

SMOKING REGULATIONS: No special policy.

FACILITIES FOR PRIVATE PARTIES: Generally none, but occasionally closes for a private party.

HOURS: Lunch, Monday through Friday, noon to 3 P.M.; dinner,
Monday through Thursday, 6 to 11:30 P.M.; Friday and Saturday, 6 P.M. to midnight; Sunday, 5 to 11 P.M. Closed Thanksgiving and Christmas Days.

RESERVATIONS: Recommended generally and necessary on
weekends.

PRICES: Moderate to moderately expensive.

CREDIT CARDS: AE.

The day I finish this book and hand the last chapter to my patient publisher, I am going to go to Da Silvano for lunch. This rustic but stylish trattoria, with its plants, brick walls and comfortable sidewalk café is just right for a long, laid-back celebratory lunch to mark release from bondage. At that time of day it is just crowded enough, usually with an attractive art and design crowd, and the sunlight reflected on the walls and the gentle pace, along with flavorful, enticing food, should relieve some of the tension deadlines create.

Not that I don't like this outpost of Tuscan cooking by night, of course. In fact, the only hours I avoid are the early ones, when there can be a crush of off-Broadway theatergoers. Eight is about right, as that means I will be out before the late, swinging and noisiest contingent walks in. The dishes I like best at Da Silvano are the Tuscan standards, almost always better than the innovative daily specials that tend to be too gussied-up. At lunch there is usually a house giveaway of pungent, peppery salumeria—ham and sausages of various sorts, including a fine mortadella, the original bologna. After that there might be sautéed artichokes with garlic and oil, which the house garnishes with a small puff of buffalo mozzarella, or some firm asparagus vinaigrette. Panzanella, a Florentine bread, oil and tomato salad, is a cooling, soul-soothing first course, and the salad of calamari and mussels with black olives, capers and anchovies could be a dinner appetizer or an enticing main course for summer lunch. At my hungriest I have the crostini—thick, toasted bread with a velvety topping of mashed chicken livers, capers, anchovies and onions, a dish that always reminds of a favorite Florence restaurant, Sostanza.

Meaty bolognese sauce enriched with cheese is delicious on the short penne, while tomatoes, garlic, olives and capers enliven the nice oily spaghettini puttanesca. Lighter tomato sauces on rigatoni, and tender tortellini satiny with cream and cheese are also done well here as is the cannelloni, with its ricotta and spinach filling, topped with cream sauce and gratinated until a bubbling golden brown. Although not exactly Tuscan, linguine with white clam sauce is properly accomplished.

Stracotto, that long-simmered north Italian pot roast of beef, here is as fork tender as it's supposed to be, and the winy tomato sauce is the real reward for that patient simmering. Cornish hen or squab, butterflied and marinated in oil and cayenne pepper, is grilled to moist succulence, and in only one of about six tries was the squab dry. Chicken livers, white wine, peas and tomatoes blanket a thick veal chop sautéed San Frediano-style, and anytime osso buco is on this menu, it is worth ordering.

A grilled paillard of chicken is always dry, that cut being totally inappropriate for that cooking technique anyway. Probably it is a house concession to dieters, who should perhaps reorder their priorities.

Seafood has never been the kitchen's strong point, and that includes an order of soggy soft-shell crabs and tough grilled shrimp. Better the lavishness of veal scallopine with shavings of white truffles, roast pork with rosemary or calves' liver, any style.

Nice bright salads and vegetables are always on display and well prepared, but other than a light, custardy crème caramel and a cool whip of eggy, Marsala-spiked zabaglione, desserts disappoint.

ENNIO & MICHAEL

504 LaGuardia Place, between Bleecker and Houston Streets. Telephone: 677-8577.

Favorite meal:
Seafood salad (insalata di mare), SHARED BY TWO
Gnocchi marinara, SHARED BY TWO
Sautéed chicken with garlic and vinegar (pollo all'arrabbiata)
Homemade cheesecake

OTHER FAVORITE DISHES: Fried zucchini (zucchini fritti), clams casino or oreganata, roast peppers, stuffed mushrooms, mozzarella and toast with anchovy sauce (spiedini alla Romana), all pastas, filet mignon with eggplant and mozzarella (medaglioni di manzo), broiled veal chop, shrimp fra diavolo, arugula salad, homemade cannoli.

SETTING: Trim, tailored and attractive diningroom with well-spaced tables and fairly moderate noise level.

SERVICE: Excellent.

DRESS CODE: None.

SMOKING REGULATIONS: No special policy.

FACILITIES FOR PRIVATE PARTIES: None.

HOURS: Dinner, Tuesday through Saturday, 5:30 to 11:30 P.M.; Sunday, 3 to 10 P.M. Closed Monday and major holidays.

RESERVATIONS: Necessary on weekends for four or more; recommmended at other times, especially before off-Broadway theater.

PRICES: Moderate.

CREDIT CARDS: AE.

Seldom does one find a restaurant that manages to combine some of the favored old Southern Italian flavors with a certain nuova stylishness in a trim, tailored modern setting. Combining those elements is what has made Ennio & Michael popular ever since it opened in its original Bleecker Street home.

Not only is it a popular dining place for those going to one of several off-Broadway theaters in its neighborhood, but it has a loyal following among knowing Villagers, a loyalty that testifies not only to the very good food but to the service that matches it.

As a general rule, I stick to Neapolitan-style dishes here, knowing they will have none of the oily, cooked-down thickness that put that regional cuisine in bad repute. What I have learned to avoid is complicated creations that combine too many elements into a sort of Chinese stir-fry kind of dish, about which more later.

Black olives, parsley, lemon and light olive oil moisten and spark the mixed seafood salad that includes snowy squid, octopus and shrimp, an opener that my husband and I like to share and that, on a hot night, makes a fine main course. Slivers of fried zucchini gilded with a light flour coating never taste of grease and are always hot. Standard appetizers in above-average preparations include home-roasted peppers, herb-stuffed mushrooms, and clams baked with striplets of bacon (casino) or with a toasty topping of garlicked breadcrumbs (oreganata). There is also one of the town's better interpretations of spiedini alla Romana, the skewered bread and mozzarella temptation that is fried and swathed with a lemon anchovy sauce. That, with a salad, is another fine light main course and just right before theater.

Not long ago, we had some of the lightest puffiest potato gnocchi here, the airy dumplings mantled in a froth of a marinara sauce. The short wide tubes of rigatoni alla matriciana—a sauce of tomato, prosciutto and onions—was a close second. Spaghetti puttanesca (whore's spaghetti because the simple sauce is said to be easy for a busy working girl to prepare) has the right needling of salty ripe Gaeta olives, basil, oil and garlic, and the large green dumplings tortelloni get a more refined treatment via a cream-lightened tomato topping. Vegetables for the pasta primavera are somewhat overcooked, but they result in a different sort of dish—soft, gentle and with a seductive meld of flavors. The short slim penne are tossed with a spicy tomato sauce heightened with a shot of hot vodka. An appetizer and pasta would make a fine meal, but for anyone who wants to go on there are some good choices. But for this course one has to tread more carefully because it is where Ennio & Michael can go astray.

After rich openers it is probably just as well that the house's

194

best efforts are its simplest—the superb, thick and lean but tender grilled veal chop, the sautéed chicken with garlic and a dash of vinegar to cut the oil, and properly fiery fra diavolo tomato sauce on firm, fresh shrimp—a bit greasy sometimes, but always delicious.

Two more lavish dishes turn out well and are fine if one has eaten sparingly of earlier courses; the veal parmigiana proves that dish can be an occasional diversion (and one kids are mad about), and similarly, there are medallions of beef sandwiching mozzarella and sautéed eggplant between them. Other scaloppine have been disappointing here, and a recent dish of chicken, sausage, onion, mushroom, peppers and potatoes inspired the Chinese comparison. It was far too wet, the pieces of everything were too small, and it was heaped on a small plate in a discouraging overkill.

A light yet substantial Italian ricotta cheesecake and homemade cannoli have been wonderful since the restaurant began and still are. Prices are most moderate, and to make it even better, there is only a 50 cent surcharge for half orders of pasta.

FELIDIA

243 East 58th Street, between Second and Third Avenues.
Telephone: 758-1479.

Favorite Meals:
LUNCH
Pasta with game sauce (fuzi all fortuna del cacciatore), half portion
Grilled Italian striped bass with garlic, parsley and olive oil (branzino)
Mixed green salad
Fresh fruit or berries
OR
DINNER
Assorted cold fish appetizers
Pasta with wild mushrooms (pappardelle with porcini), in season and SHARED BY TWO
OR
Risotto with white truffles or squid ink, SHARED BY TWO
Roast pheasant or roast veal
Fresh fruit
OTHER FAVORITE DISHES: Crostini of polenta with porcini mush-

rooms in season; sautéed wild mushrooms (porcini saltati); green and white pasta with mushrooms (paglia e fieno al funghi); cornmeal polenta with game; pasta with mushrooms, sausage, tomato and ricotta (occhio di lupo alla boscaiola); seafood risotto; pasta al pesto; fried calamari; red snapper with polento; calves' liver Veneziana; sweetbreads with lemon sauce (animelle di vitello); veal cutlet Milanese, Valdostana or pizzaiola; chicken with peppery wine sauce (arrabbiato).

SETTING: Tiles and natural wood create a stylish, casual modern dining room with urbane overtones; tables are uncomfortably cramped, noise is deafening, and lighting is inadequate in some areas.

SERVICE: Good but awkward because of tight space, so that there is much reaching across diners; sometimes slow before main course.

DRESS CODE: Jacket required for men.

SMOKING REGULATIONS: No cigars or pipes are permitted.

FACILITIES FOR PRIVATE PARTIES: One private room seats up to fifty.

HOURS: Lunch, Monday through Friday, noon to 3 P.M.; dinner, Monday through Saturday, 5 P.M. to midnight. Closed Sunday and all major holidays.

RESERVATIONS: Necessary.

PRICES: Expensive.

CREDIT CARDS: AE, CB, D, MC, V.

Felidia is a restaurant I enjoy going to now and then despite itself, because its kitchen, overseen by Lidia Bastianich, does some unusual dishes of her native Friuli that are delicious and not available in abundance elsewhere. Versions of the cornmeal porridge polenta served with truffles, wild mushrooms, game or red snapper, as well as various risotto dishes, are the attractions here as are a variety of game dishes and innards.

For such dishes that are best eaten in fall and winter, I will withstand considerable discomfort from the jam-packed dining room, with its deafening din and generally inadequate lighting. When my husband could not read the wine list at one dinner, Mrs. Bastianich produced a flashlight she had at the ready, a necessity that should have told her brighter lighting is in order. (You also need a flashlight to read the check, perhaps even more to the point.) The setting, with pink terra-cotta tiles, white walls and polished natural wood, is pretty enough, suggesting a Mexican Greek island with Italian provincial overtones, but pretty is as pretty does, and this does not quite work.

A purer strain of inspiration is reflected in the menu, and a fine starting point for a meal is the focaccia, a chewy, yeasty pizzalike flat bread, fine with aperitifs. Bruschetta, toasted bread brushed with oil, is offered most times and is a good foil for the best appetizer, an assortment of beautifully fresh and sparkling seafood salads that unexpectedly includes tripe vinaigrette; it is one of the few interpretations of the spongy innard that I can get down. (Even then, I put a piece in my mouth and wash it down with wine, as though I were taking an aspirin.) That, of coure, is a personal dislike, but even I know this tripe is very well prepared. Good prosciutto is sometimes made of boar, and wild mushrooms in season are sautéed in oil and butter with a touch of lemon. They are even better topping a toasted slice of polenta. Wild mushrooms gentled with cream also have a nice bite with the green-and-white noodle combination paglia e fieno (straw and hay), and again, polenta appears as a stick-to-the ribs course with game such as venison, pheasant, quail or a mix of several.

The big round pasta known as wolf's eyes—occhio di lupo—holds a rich sauce of ricotta and sausage within the tubes to release a marvelous mouthful when chewed, and fuzi, a homemade, short bow-tie-pasta twist, also gets a smoky, earthy elegance from game sauce. Homemade pasta with a toothsome bite is wonderfully complemented by a pesto blend. When white truffles or porcini are in season, I like them here in risotto.

There is a thickly cut, beautifully roasted veal rustico at Felidia that is much in the Abruzzese style of roasting and cutting, and that same meat is dependable in breaded cutlets fried Milanese-style or sandwiched with prosciutto and Fontina cheese, then fried Valdostana-style. Pizzaiola, the pizzaman's blend of tomato, garlic and oregano, is a surprise in this context and is lightly, delicately accomplished as a sauce for veal. Greaselessness and freshness distinguish the fried calamari rings and tentacles, and a peppery wine sauce is what angry chicken—pollo arrabbiato—is fired up about. On a more delicate note, there are white, moistly sautéed sweetbreads bright with a lemony dressing and grilled branzino—Italian striped bass—dressed with fresh lemon and oil. Calves' liver Veneziana and osso buco are far above average.

As good as the dishes mentioned are, other common preparations are blandly executed, tasting of overheated grease or lacking salt.

Baked desserts have seemed overly rich after previous courses, so fresh fruit is a more appropriate choice.

Late lunch—say about 1:45—is the optimum time at Felidia, when it is bright enough so one can see, only half-crowded so one can move and hear.

The upstairs balcony dining room, is still a kind of Upper Siberia, but there is a stunning new room for private parties.

GEORGINE CARMELLA

165 Mulberry Street, between Grand and Broome Streets.
Telephone: 226-3999.

Favorite meals:
  Fried red peppers with anchovies (peperoni con alici),
    SHARED BY TWO
  Spinach risotto, SHARED BY TWO
  Roast quail with garlic, bacon and rosemary (quaglie allo
    spiedo)
  Cheesecake (pizza di ricotta)
  OR
  Raw beef (carpaccio), SHARED BY TWO
  Spaghettini alla carbonara, SHARED BY TWO
  Seafood in wine with basil and tomato (zuppa di pesce)
  Tirami sù

OTHER FAVORITE DISHES: Mozzarella with fresh or sun-dried
  tomatoes, grilled eggplant with ricotta (melanzane alla griglia), clams baked with garlic (vongole gratinate), spinach and
  egg drop soup (stracciatella Romana), ravioli with sage butter (ravioli al burro fuso e salvia), chicken roasted with garlic
  and vinegar, veal chop Milanese with fried capers, veal sautéed with wild mushrooms and cream (scaloppine bos-
  caiola), all salads, raspberry tart, chocolate hazlenut torte.
SETTING: Casual but stylish and romantic storefront café with
  comfortable seating despite a high noise level when full.
SERVICE: Excellent if occasionally a bit precious.
DRESS CODE: Jacket required for men.
SMOKING REGULATIONS: No cigars or pipes are permitted.
FACILITIES FOR PRIVATE PARTIES: None.
HOURS: Dinner, Tuesday through Sunday, 6 to 11 P.M. Closed
  Monday and Christmas Eve and Day.
RESERVATIONS: Recommended.
PRICES: Moderate to moderately expensive.
CREDIT CARDS: AE.

If this rosy pink storefront restaurant were in Greenwich
Village or on the Upper East Side, no one would be able to get
near it without a two-week-in-advance reservation. So while
its many fans may be pleased to have it hidden away in Little
Italy, I suspect that the owner and guiding light in the kitchen,
Georgine Cavaiola, would be pleased to have it otherwise. The

198

notion that Little Italy is the wrong place for a great Italian restaurant may seem odd, but the trouble with Georgine Carmella in its present location is its stylish, exquisite food. Tourists going to Little Italy (and believe me, only tourists go these days) expect larger-than-life Italian eating places serving larger-than-life food. Or they go to one of the old-time famous places, which are no longer what they once were.

The sort of nuova cucina presentations based on traditional preparations and flavors is too sophisticated for the standard clientele in these parts and has been since it was opened in 1983 by Ms. Cavaiola and her associate, Carmella Seijas, who, unfortunately, died several years ago. It is not often one finds Italian food so prettily and delicately arranged, yet tasting exactly as remembered from traditional regional kitchens. Even an appetizer as simple as fried sweet red peppers, silky with oil and garnished with anchovies and Ligurian olives, arrives looking as though it might have been arranged by a Japanese chef. Toasted slices of eggplant glossed with oil and mellowed with ricotta, baked or steamed clams with the right heady proportion of minced garlic, and the raw beef carpaccio frilled with arugula reflect classic dishes, newly styled. Juicy mozzarella may be had at times with sun-dried tomatoes or, in season, with fresh, and it is also delicious alongside the fried peppers, anchovies and all. At times the menu offers perfect clams Posillipo in a sheer tomato broth, while at other seasons it may be grilled porcini or a fluffy spinach and egg drop soup, stracciatella Romana, showered with grated cheese.

By far my favorite pasta here are the delicate, round ravioli filled with ricotta and spinach and sauced with sage-flavored butter and cream. Filaments of angel's hair pasta have the correct fine texture for such light sauces as the primavera or fresh tomato, while the short quill pasta penne are just right arrabiata-style, with a spicy tomato sauce. The pasta menu varies from day to day, but if I'm lucky, I get there when the risotto is made either with spinach, asparagus or champagne, and I always hope that a once-tried dish of shell-shaped cavatelli with oil-and-garlic-sauced broccoli will make a reappearance. Midst all of this lavishness, the humble spaghettini alle vongole—with white clam sauce—is as good as any you'll find in town. The spaghettini alla carbonara with its thin polishing of egg, cheese and bacon is the best I know this side of Rome.

Because she is creative, Georgine Cavaiola changes dishes frequently on the menu, so not all of these favorites are always available. But if quail are to be had, have them. Nowhere are they more succulently roasted and veneered with rosemary, bacon and garlic. Roast baby chicken is similarly seasoned, and that same bird with garlic and vinegar takes on lusty overtones. Wild mushrooms, prosciutto and cream combine for the boscaiola sauce that moistens sautéed veal scaloppine, and for the simpler side of things, there is a crisp veal cutlet Milanese served with a plum tomato salad sprigged with basil.

Grilled scampi, scallops in cream and white wine and an inspired zuppa di pesce, that mixed soup-stew of shellfish, tomato and basil, are brightly fresh and aromatic. Sweetbreads with lemon and capers and calves' liver Veneziana have also been well turned out.

Refreshingly crisp, clear green salads, braised or grilled radicchio and sautéed spinach are some of the better side dishes.

There are not many desserts, but if one is the raspberry tart, don't miss it. Failing that, have the dark moist chocolate hazelnut torte, the feathery Italian cheesecake or the tirami sù, that currently popular layering of cake with coffee-flavored cream and chocolate.

The wine is very well chosen both for variety and price.

LATTANZI

361 West 46th Street, between Eighth and Ninth Avenues. Telephone: 315-0980.

Favorite meals:
 LUNCH
 Mixed antipasto
 Grilled scampi
 Fresh fruit
 OR
 DINNER
 Artichokes cooked in olive oil with garlic (carciofi alla Giudea)
 Homemade wide noodles with fresh tomato sauce (tortelloni al pomodoro), SHARED BY TWO
 Broiled chicken with rosemary
 Cold zabaglione
 OR
 DINNER
 Fine pasta with shellfish (cappelletti con frutti de mare), SHARED BY TWO
 Grilled veal chop
 Napoleon, SHARED BY TWO
 OTHER FAVORITE DISHES: Mixed green salad (insalata mista), smoked thin beef with arugula and Parmesan cheese (carpaccio affumicato), homemade mozzarella with tomatoes

200

and basil, mussels in tomato broth (muscoli in brodetto), all pastas, chicken with peppers and onions in tomato sauce (pollo capriccioso), squid with tomato and peas (calamari Lattanzi), veal parmigiana, all desserts. From Roman Jewish menu served after 8 P.M.: Dried beef with marinated zucchini (carne secca), combination appetizer, fettuccine with braised beef (stracotto), green lasagne, red snapper with raisins and vinegar (orata con uvetta), grilled lamb chops with rosemary and garlic (agnello al rosmarino), ricotta cheesecake (cassola).

SETTING: Bright, attractive, brick-walled dining room with brassy, bright accessories and a big open grill.

SERVICE: Polite, professional and helpful.

DRESS CODE: Owner describes as "proper attire" without being specific as to restrictions.

SMOKING REGULATIONS: No pipes or cigars are permitted.

FACILITIES FOR PRIVATE PARTIES: None.

HOURS: Lunch, Monday through Friday, noon to 2:30 P.M.; dinner, Monday through Thursday, 5 to 11 P.M.; Friday and Saturday, 5 P.M. to midnight. Closed Sunday and all major holidays.

RESERVATIONS: Recommended, especially for lunch and before theater.

PRICES: Moderate to moderately expensive.

CREDIT CARDS: AE.

The second-best thing gastronomically to happen in the Theater District in years (the first is Carolina just next door), Lattanzi is a bright, stylishly rustic, brick-walled restaurant that puts on one of the most entertaining shows in town, local playwrights, actors and directors notwithstanding. The kitchen is good enough to attract an audience for its own sake, although its major appeal is to the lunch and pretheater crowd who want to be in the area. But from 8 o'clock on, it becomes a peaceful yet lively option for some delicious and innovative food, of the manner this same family has created in its other restaurants. (For the genealogy of Lattanzi, see Trastevere.) After 8 is also the time for the special menu of Roman-Jewish classics, an intriguing cuisine from what is said to be history's oldest continuous Jewish community.

But even without those esoteric specials, the menu is full of enticements, only a bit less opulent and a bit less magical than those at the original Trastevere. Many of the same pastas appear here, just as succulently executed, but main courses are lighter and are generally grilled, a good idea considering the work or pretheater schedules of most of the clientele.

One Roman Jewish special that is on all menus is carciofi ala Giudea, artichokes here sautéed in olive oil with garlic.

Although delicious, this preparation is not authentic, the real version being whole artichokes pressed open and deep-fried to golden crispness while the hearts remain soft and rich. (I have only once seen that dish properly done in New York and that was at Sandro's, 420 East 59th Street, 355-5150, a relatively new restaurant at which only this dish proved exceptional.) Nevertheless, the good oil and fresh artichoke hearts make for an enticing first course. Carpaccio of smoked beef that is still rare is a nice change from the standard raw meat and has arugula and Parmesan accompaniments. Homemade mozzarella with tomatoes is as tempting as the shiny mussels in a heady tomato broth. Sautéed porcini mushrooms have had the unpleasant aftertaste of overheated oil, and the assorted antipasto is heavy going before most other courses.

It would be sad to miss one of the pastas, and orders can be split for a $1 charge. Here, as at Trastevere, half orders before main courses should be possible even without sharing. Cavil aside, we can go on to the fresh fettuccine Lattanzi tossed with peas, mushrooms and cream; the thick strands of bucatini Amatriciana, meaning there is a satisfying sauce of tomato, onion and Italian bacon; and my beloved linguine with white clam sauce, steamy hot, aromatic with garlic and full of the seaside freshness only clams can impart. Fine spaghettini is easily twirled around flecks of vegetables bound by a gossamer cream sauce (capellini primavera), and the floppy tortelloni are simple, classic and lovely in a marinara sauce. Porcini served with fettuccine is worth having in season.

The same sublime fish soup-stew, zuppa di pesce, with its mussels, clams, fish and squid, is made here as at Trastevere, and squid alone gets a slightly different treatment, being more lightly presented with tomato, garlic, peas and basil. Grilled herbed chicken and chops are particular specials, always moist within and gently charred without. Scampi-style shrimp, whether grilled or sautéed with oil and garlic, are among the lightest of main courses. The menu, by the way, offers to prepare dietetic or vegetarian dishes on request, but don't let that worry you. The chef's heart and soul are firmly committed to lusty dishes.

The Roman Jewish menu has its own diverting repertory, including a crostini of chicken livers on toast with artichokes and a combination appetizer that includes marinated eggplant, fresh mozzarella and the fried rice balls, suppli al telefono. Literally, that means telephone wires, referring to the stringiness of the melted cheese in the rice croquettes.

Zucchini wilted in olive oil is tossed with the short quill-shaped penne, and little ears, orecchiette, is the pasta best suited to the topping of tuna fish, tomato, olive oil and garlic on the same menu. Pasta keeps me away from the soups on this menu—but maybe one day I'll be strong and deviate. Stracotto is a gentle, crumbling, long-cooked pot roast, and it is an enrichment on fettuccine, while green lasagne layers with artichokes, onions and tomatoes is a Roman-Jewish-vegetarian delectable that grinds about as many axes as one dish can be expected to.

As improbable as red snapper with raisins and vinegar may sound, the result is surprisingly good, with a delicate sweet-sour balance well-known in all Jewish cooking. Veal scaloppine with artichokes, roast chicken and lamb with rosemary and garlic are other temptations on this special menu.

The regular Lattanzi menu includes the same napoleon and cream puff miracles as at Trastevere, and the Jewish menu adds yet another—cassola, a sort of ricotta cheese and egg combination, between a cake and thin soufflé. Incidentally, Jewish does not mean kosher here, as anyone familiar with that dietary requirement can tell by the presence of cheese and meat on the same menu.

The help at Lattanzi tend to be better to unknowns than at Trastevere, and prices are slightly lower. Both pluses.

LUSARDI'S

1494 Second Avenue, between 77th and 78th Streets. Telephone: 249-2020.

Favorite meals:
Fried zucchini or squid, SHARED BY TWO
Penne with pressed tuna roe (alla bottarga), half portion
Veal chop with sage (salvia)
Berries with cold zabaglione
OR
Ravioli with walnut sauce, half portion
Chicken with tomatoes and mushrooms (chicken Abruzzese)
Berries with balsamic vinegar
OTHER FAVORITE DISHES: Buffalo mozzarella and ricotta with artichokes or roasted peppers; crostini of polenta with beans and porcini; carpaccio with green sauce (salsa verde); mushroom salad; fish croquettes; veal with tuna sauce (vitello tonnato); corkscrew pasta with basil, tomato and cream (fusilli ai tre sapori); bucatini with tomato, onions and prosciutto (bucatini Amatriciana); linguine with white clam sauce; penne with basil, tomato and mozzarella (penne tricolori); risotto

with walnuts or porcini; tagliatelle with porcini; rigatoni with sausages; tortellini alla panna; tortelloni with spinach and four cheeses (tortelloni de spinacci ai quattro formaggi); tortelloni with pumpkin and sage (tortelloni de zucca alla salvia); mixed seafood fry (fritto misto di mare); chicken sautéed with garlic (scarpariello); veal piccatina; veal paillard alla Dino; veal chop Valdostana or Milanese; all vegetables and salads; crème brûlée; caramel custard.

Setting: Handsome, tailored and urbane dining room that suggests a stylish Florentine osteria; tables are not too cramped and noise level is moderate; lighting is exceptionally pleasant, but chairs can be uncomfortable if you stay through four courses.

Service: Professional without being pretentious and with an attractive, casual but efficient tone.

Dress code: Men are preferred in jackets, but no code is enforced.

Smoking regulations: No special policy.

Facilities for private parties: Lunchtime only when entire restaurant can be closed to accommodate between twenty-five and seventy.

Hours: Lunch, Monday through Friday, noon to 3 P.M.; dinner, Monday through Saturday, 5 P.M. to midnight; Sunday, 4 P.M. to 11 P.M.

Reservations: Recommended for lunch, necessary for dinner.

Prices: Moderate to moderately expensive.

Credit cards: AE, CB, D, MC, V.

When it comes to style, no Italian restaurant in New York, as of this writing, can match Lusardi's. It is perfect for its time and place, with a casual but handsome dining room and bar that suggest an upscale wine tavern-trattoria as it might be in Rome, Florence, Milan or, of course, New York. Cream-colored walls with dark, stained wood trim, the racks of wine, and waiters wearing ties, shirts and aprons make for a modern, practical but businesslike tone, much in the tradition of the Italian steak house.

The food matches the spirit of the room, an elusive subtlety that I prize, with choices that range from the most traditional dishes, such as linguine with white clam sauce, through Tuscan-style dishes of the moment (tortelloni with pumpkin and sage) and all sorts of nut and porcini risottos and pastas, to house inventions such as the grilled veal paillard alla "Dino," which gets an anointing of balsamic vinegar a second or two before it is taken from the fire, thus taking on a mild sweet-sharp patina.

There are no regional culinary snobbisms reflected in this menu, as the food of all Italy appears at some time or another on the menu, with the kitchens of Naples, the Abruzzi, Rome, Tuscany, Emilia and Liguria as the standards. However, all are styled and presented in a manner essentially Lusardian, which is perhaps the most a restaurateur can wish for. This has been true since the restaurant opened in March 1982 and continues even though the original chef is now at Sistina. Since his successor, Lamberto Terrosi of Pisa, has his sea legs, the food is better than ever. Only one dish that was a personal favorite is not quite up to its former savory self, and that is the flattened, fried small chicken that is cooked under a brick weight (mattone) and is called, therefore, chicken mattone. More salt and black pepper and a touch of olive oil to forestall dryness would do the trick. That is a small cavil midst so many other fine choices.

There are a few seasonal appetizer specials not listed on the menu, a selection that would be even more enticing if waiters quoted prices. One night it might be sautéed porcini or grilled radicchio alongside tiny, fresh buffalo mozzarella and a cloudlet of tangy ricotta, or in winter it could be a toasted crostini of polenta topped with braised white beans and mushrooms. Carpaccio appears in two variations, one with paper-thin slices of raw beef dressed only with oil and vinegar and arranged on arugula salad, while the other, which I prefer, has a grass-green oil-based sauce sprightly with capers, parsley, basil and garlic.

Mussels steamed in white wine, clams raw or baked oreganata, and high-quality prosciutto and the air-cured beef bresaola can be had singly or in combination. Seafood salad has not always been fresh, so I now avoid it. But I have never been disappointed by the vitello tonnato with thin slices of pale veal mounded on arugula in an enticing pyramid, napped with a sheer tuna sauce. That and some pasta would make a fine meal, and the veal alone is a lovely summer lunch dish.

That veal is too rich a forerunner to pasta, so it is a good idea to refrain when you want to try some of the gorgeous possibilities. Among the best are the short-pasta penne mixed with an oil and butter sauce that includes mashed bottarga, the pressed, air-cured tuna roe that imparts a caviarlike flavor. Say no to cheese if it is offered as it will ruin the flavor of the roe. The three colors in the tricolori sauce on penne are the red of tomatoes, the green of basil and the white dicings of buffalo mozzarella, and the three flavors—tre sapori—folded into the corkscrew pasta fusilli are basil, tomatoes and a binding of sweet cream. The large, chewy bucatini have the proper heft to carry the amatriciana sauce of tomato, prosciutto and onion, while tagliatelle, fresh and medium in width are the more delicate accompaniment to porcini. Tortellini in cream and linguine with white clam sauce are nonetheless enticing for being omnipresent around town, and the more unusual large tortelloni are as good with spinach and four cheeses as with pumpkin in a creamy and sage dressing. Walnuts are pounded into the cream sauce for ravioli, somewhat in the manner of Ligurian pansotti, and walnuts too add a meaty fresh-air flavor to risotto. Only occasionally are pasta dishes lacking in salt, and since all are cooked to order, it's wise to state whether you want yours with or without that salting. Without is unthinkable as far as I am concerned, but those whose doctors have warned them off can have it their way.

Frying is immaculate here—light, golden, greaseless—as is true for the slivered zucchini, the rings and tentacles of squid and the mixed seafood fry, which did indeed need a sprinkling of salt when last tried.

Oddly enough, the meat main courses include two or three clichés, the dated chicken Castelli Romani (breast of chicken with artichokes, mushrooms, cream and white wine, and a hodgepodge) and veal sette colli (the same as Castelli Romani minus cream). I prefer dishes with fewer complexities and more character than what might well be dubbed "rich American eaters' preferences." Take, for example, the nuggets of chicken, bone and all, as sautéed in oil with garlic to make the scarpariello specialty or the same chunks browned in olive oil and finished with tomato and mushrooms in the manner of the Abruzzi. Veal scaloppine appears in an Emiliana portfolio, stuffed with prosciutto and cheese and then fried, for a dish timid palates will probably enjoy, as do I when tired and in need of something gentle. That mood might also suggest the perfectly executed veal piccatina, and if you think it's easy to get the scaloppine golden brown at the edges while remaining moist within, try to find it that way in this city. Lemon and capers sharpen the butter-and-oil glossing. A thick veal chop with a pocket holding ham and Fontina cheese, topped with a light brown sauce, is the lusty and delicious veal chop Valdostana, and the crisp-crusted veal Milanese is as simple but as remarkable a triumph here as the piccatina. Sage lends a dry, herbaceous flavor to the well-trimmed, succulently moist sautéed veal chop.

Simple well-cooked vegetables such as whole string beans or sautéed escarole are served family-style with all main courses.

Considering how far the kitchen goes to be sure everything is just right, it's a pity it doesn't go a step further and make all of the desserts in-house. As decent as the store-bought cakes may be, they are now tired and overpowering finishes, and the homemade tirami sù here is an overly soft and creamy mush, pleasant though its flavor is. Cold zabaglione with or without berries is a better choice as are crème brûlée, crème caramel, or berries doused lightly with sugar and either lemon juice or balsamic vinegar. As for that commercial ice cream tartufo, it sells the rest of the menu short.

There is an usually careful wine list at Lusardi's, and one gets the feeling that the owners worked hard to get the best possible representations in all price categories, from $15 to $88. Only a few more half bottles would be welcome, but with so many good choices at $20 or less, it is not a serious omission. But the absence of vintage years on the less expensive choices is.

NANNI

146 East 46th Street, between Lexington and Third Avenues. Telephone: 697-4161.

Favorite meals:
LUNCH
Seafood salad
Baked ziti with eggplant (ziti al forno alla Siciliana)
Fresh fruit
OR
DINNER
Fettuccine with prosciutto, peas, tomato and cream (alla Nanni), half portion
Chicken sautéed with garlic and white wine (pollo scarpariello)
Zabaglione
OTHER FAVORITE DISHES: Baked clams areganata; linguine with white clam sauce (linguine alle vongole); fusilli or spaghetti with tomato, onion and prosciutto (all'amatriciana); ravioli malfatti; manicotti with cheese; clams or mussels in tomato broth; veal cutlet Milanese; broiled veal chop; sautéed escarole.
SETTING: Intimate, trattoria-tavern feeling that is casual but urbane. Tables are closely set, but noise level remains magically moderate except at peak lunch hours.
SERVICE: Friendly, accommodating, professional and civilized.
DRESS CODE: None.
SMOKING REGULATIONS: No special policy.
FACILITIES FOR PRIVATE PARTIES: None.
HOURS: Lunch, Monday through Friday, noon to 3 P.M.; dinner, Monday through Saturday, 5:30 to 11 P.M. Closed Sunday and major holidays.

207

RESERVATIONS: Necessary.
PRICES: Moderate to moderately high.
CREDIT CARDS: AE, CB, D, MC, V.

We may not be able to go home again, but we certainly can go back to Nanni, one of New York's homiest yet urbane and professional, old-timey Italian restaurants. With its white walls, dark wood trim, travel posters, red and white tablecloths and shelves of wine bottles around the room, this low-ceilinged, masculine eating place suggests a small osteria or wine tavern. There is a clublike feeling to the intimate surroundings enhanced by the crowd of obvious regulars who gather at lunch and dinner, and if the tone is essentially masculine, it is for that reason appealing to women—or at least to this woman.

Owned by the renowned Abruzzese chef Luigi Nanni, who also has the more pretentious and pricey Al Valletto, this restaurant offers all the dishes that were standards about twenty years ago when it opened. In an interview for *Vanity Fair*, Federico Fellini told me that he misses "the soft and gentle flavors of the past." In a sense, that is what Nanni dishes up, with pastas and soups overcooked by today's standards, yet mellow with the soft blending of flavors. His food reminds me of Louisiana cooking—most especially gumbo—which nouvelle-minded critics seem to prefer full of firm ingredients. Yet a truly soul-satisfying gumbo is one that has been reheated, softness being the soothing touch. And so here, with the thick, restorative minestrone and all the pastas that are a shade more mellow than al dente and so wrap themselves around their satiny sauces with ease. Among those pastas, my favorite for lunch is the baked ziti with eggplant, Sicilian-style—a main course that is just right after the house seafood salad, never on the menu but always on hand. That too is a little soupier than would be considered stylish today, but it is also so damned good I never let a drop of its oil and lemon dressing go back un-sopped by the chewy Italian bread.

Perfect linguine with white clam sauce, a dish on which I qualify as the world's leading expert, is dished up with well-salted pasta (oh, happy day), plenty of chopped clams and golden garlic and, for garnish, two clams in their shells. Just a dash of hot red pepper flakes is needed to attain gastronomic Nirvana, as far as I am concerned. Various pastas, such as the filled rings cappelletti, fettuccine or the fine capellini, may be had alla Nanni, with a nicely sticky cream-tomato sauce flecked with peas and prosciutto. The cappelletti version with a green salad, makes a satisfying main course. The others are better as first courses, being lighter since they are not filled with meat. Ravioli malfatti are really dubbed "badly made" because they have no pasta covering but are, instead, dumplings of the spin-

208

ach, egg and cheese that usually fill ravioli. Here the name is applied to ravioli that are conventional except in a few respects—they are larger, floppier and more irregularly cut. I suspect matagliati—badly cut—would be more to the point. Still more to the point is their deliciousness, nestled as they are under a creamy pink tomato sauce that perks up with a sprinkling of cheese. Even those clichéd manicotti, filled with ricotta and topped with a smooth tomato sauce, can be soul-warming when the world has been cruel.

Clams and mussels as fresh as sea breezes are heaped in bowls and are wonderful dipped into their garlicky tomato broth for another house triumph.

Meats can be disappointing, generally because they are tough. That was true recently of very dry pork chops that were not helped by their spicy pizzaiola sauce and of osso buco that needed a sharp knife for cutting, an unthinkable requirement with meat that should almost fall from the bone. In the past, grilled chops have been far better choices as has been the veal cutlet Milanese with its golden breading. Nuggets of chicken sautéed with garlic and white wine (scarpariello) are better with bone-in pieces, and it is offered both ways. Sautéed escarole with garlic is a bright contrast with meat dishes.

Cheesecake here is awful—gummy and insipid. Better to have fresh berries, with or without the winy warm egg froth that is zabaglione.

Nanni is the kind of raffishly serviceable trattoria every neighborhood needs, but satisfaction will depend on the amount you spend. Order a lavish meal with an expensive wine, and you'll suddenly feel as though you should have gone someplace else. Order modestly, and you'll feel you had a bargain. It's that kind of place.

IL NIDO

251 East 53rd Street, between Second and Third Avenues.
Telephone: 753–8450.

Favorite meals:
LUNCH
Green tortellini in cream, half portion
Red snapper with clams
Pears and Parmesan cheese in season, or homemade
chocolate ice cream
OR

DINNER

Assorted cold antipasto

Spinach and cheese dumplings with tomato sauce (ravioli malfatti), half portion

Mixed fry of sweetbreads, brains, veal, calves' liver and lamb or goat chop (fritto misto all' italiana), SHARED BY TWO

Mocha meringue cake

OTHER FAVORITE DISHES: Prosciutto, the cured beef bresaola, mushroom salad (insalata di funghi freschi), baked clams (vongole oreganate), broiled scampi, mussels marinara, clams in tomato broth (vongole alla Capri), carpaccio, crostini of polenta with mushrooms, all soups, all pastas except spaghetti carbonara, fried squid (calamaretti fritti), shellfish marinara, mixed seafood in broth (zuppa di pesce), chicken scarpariello, brains (cervella) or sweetbreads (animella), veal kidneys (rognone trifolato), grilled veal chop, veal cutlet Milanese, paillard of beef, all vegetables, arugula and endive salad, homemade ice creams, zabaglione, cheesecake (torta di formaggio), tirami sù.

SETTING: Beautifully elegant country restaurant with mirrors and etched-glass panels; most tables are comfortably spaced, but noise level is high and there is an occasional ventilation problem.

SERVICE: Always wonderful for well-known customers, but there are some reports of rudeness to unknowns.

DRESS CODE: Jacket and tie required for men.

SMOKING REGULATIONS: No special policy.

FACILITIES FOR PRIVATE PARTIES: None.

HOURS: Lunch, Monday through Saturday, noon to 2:15 P.M.; dinner, Monday through Saturday, 5:30 to 10:15 P.M. Closed Sunday and major holidays.

RESERVATIONS: Necessary.

PRICES: Expensive.

CREDIT CARDS: AE, CB, D, MC, V.

Il Nido is as close as New York gets to having a four-star Italian restaurant. All it would take is the replacing of a dozen or so overly complicated, dated chicken and veal main courses with lighter, cleaner and more subtly herbed specialties that might be Tuscan, Venetian, Ligurian or Abruzzese in style. This beautiful, polished little restaurant, with its paneled mirrors, etched glass and the generally professional and accommodating staff, raises an aesthetic question I have long pondered: the difference between the classic and the dated where food is concerned. The best comparison can be made with clothing fashions, in which, for example, an A-line dress is considered dated but a silk shirt and a turtleneck cashmere sweater are classics.

On the Il Nido menu the classics are all of the appetizers, fish and pasta offerings and the meats such as golden fried veal cutlet Milanese, the chicken scarpariello or the sautéed sweetbreads and brains. But things such as chicken or veal "sette colli," wet sautés of meat with artichokes, mushrooms and white wines, are the culinary A-lines. The difference, I suppose, is that the dated dishes are those once considered at the cutting edge of a trend. In the case of Italian food in the United States, the sette collis represent a special era that peaked about five years ago. In the beginning we had only what has come to be called "red" Italian cooking, based on the tomato-sauced dishes of Naples. Then about thirty-five years ago, Northern Italian food was introduced, and the color was white and creamy. Examples of such are fettuccine Alfredo, risotto Piemontese and meats such as vitello tonnato and calves' liver Veneziana.

Then came the Il Nido era and the masses of mushrooms and white wine and, for good measure, some even glued together with melted mozzarella. Given the current rage of nuova cucina, the clichés-to-be are the fruited risottos, the nearly raw grilled birds, the overabundance of sage and rosemary, and pasta or rice only half-cooked and therefore unpleasant and flavorless. Fortunately, Giovannetti stands fast against such travesties, but I suspect he has painted himself into a corner with his longtime menu specialties. They probably have strong appeal to the backbone of his clientele—conservative eaters who are upper-middle-class in age and income. By taking their favorite dishes off the menu to make way for others, he risks losing the audience most able to pay his sky-high prices.

But because the menu is so large, it is full of wonderful choices, despite its shortcomings. Appetizers I especially like include the grilled crostini of cornmeal polenta that is topped with sautéed wild mushrooms, the carpaccio with a green sauce far more suitable to it than the creamy bland mayonnaise-type dressing of the original dish, and all sorts of sprightly hot shellfish appetizers such as baked clams, mussels and clams in tomato broth and the impeccable prosciutto and the air-cured beef bresaola, sautéed wild mushrooms or raw mushrooms in a lemony olive oil dressing. In season the fragrant white truffles of Alba are as heavenly in a raw salad as they are shaved over fettuccine or risotto, although they carry outrageous prices compared with those at several other places in town. There is only one appetizer I dislike at Il Nido and that is the house version of spiedino alla Romana because the bread is always wet at the center and the anchovy sauce is so heavy it wipes out the flavors of toasted bread and melting mozzarella.

Pasta e fagioli, that lusty soup of short ditali and beans in a tomato-pink herbed base, here takes on elegance without losing character. Clear, heady broths are the vehicles for spinach and egg or the meat-filled cappelletti, and minestrone is so full of vegetables and flavor one might almost be tempted to have it instead of pasta.

Almost, but not quite. How to resist the airy dumplings of spinach, egg and cheese that are ravioli malfatti—"badly made" because they have no pasta covering—trimmed with a light sauce of fresh, barely cooked tomatoes, or the good, chewy tortellini in a glossing of cream or the lacy capelli d'angelo— angel's hair—that is easily twirled around bits of shellfish or vegetables and cream? Lasagne with green pasta and a bolognese filling, linguine tossed with the matriciana sauce of tomato, prosciutto and onions, and the white and green straw and hay that is paglia e fieno with cream and ham provide further embarrassments of choice. Gently soft polenta can be had bolognese-style, and risotto here has always been perfectly cooked, firm but never with a crackle at the center of the rice kernels, meaning that each grain has been fully developed in broth, wine and whatever flavors it should absorb. "Whatever flavors" could be seafood, tomato, asparagus, saffron or wild mushrooms, the determining factor usually being the season. Again there is only one dish I rule out among pastas and that is the carbonara. Here, as usual in this country, that dish is a far cry from the Roman original. There, it is a spare, almost greasy-with-butter tossing of pasta in which egg clings to the strands of spaghetti, coating them with a rough finish and holding bits of bacon and heavy showerings of coarse black pepper. Americans apparently regard this as a creamy dish and, in the bargain, like onions with it. For the superb originals, I recommend the restaurants Al Moro and La Carbonara in Rome.

Anyone who feels it is necessary to go to a fish restaurant to get great seafood should know about Il Nido. The assortment and freshness are incomparable and so is the preparation, whether as simple as fried squid or as subtle as the imported Italian striped bass, branzino, that may be roasted and dressed with lemon and oil, or simmered in a translucent tomato brodetto. Red snapper in brodetto with clams is a lunchtime favorite of mine, and once when I was there with a dieting friend, the kitchen produced a sublime, oil-free variation, relying on tomato and a dash of white wine to keep fish and mollusks succulent as they bake in cartoccio—a big envelope of foil. When the little pink Mediterranean triglie are available, they are worth trying grilled, and the house also does a properly hefty fra diavolo sauce for lobster or shrimp.

Most Americans who go to Italy come back disappointed with meat dishes, finding them lacking in interest. But most Italian meat is simply cooked—grilled, fried or roasted and not too often sauced because it follows rich antipasti and pastas. That is why at Il Nido I generally have some of the sautéed innards or, if my husband is in the mood to share it with me, the mixed fry of sweetbreads, brains, liver, veal and a lamb or goat chop, with which we usually have some fried zucchini. That or grilled veal chop or a paillard of beef (veal being too dry for this sort of cooking) are my choices.

I have never tried a game or rabbit dish at Il Nido, probably because I don't go often enough, but more should be in evidence.

Desserts have improved markedly in recent years, but in fall, when pears are ripe and juicy, none surpasses that fruit peeled and sliced and arranged with chips of aged Parmesan cheese and shelled walnut meats. It is really my idea of an elegant finish, especially when followed by a glass of Giovannetti's pride, the golden dessert wine Vin Santo, served with crunchy almond biscotti.

Those with sweeter longings will be happy with the warm, airy whipped egg and Marsala zabaglione, the ice cream homemade around the corner at Il Nido's new café (see Cafés), of which the vanilla, nougat and dark chocolate are destructively alluring. There is also a marvelous, nearly indescribable dream of a mocha, almond and crushed meringue cake that must be eaten to be believed.

Prices are supremely high here, and that includes the array of excellent wines.

I much prefer the front dining room at Il Nido to the even more crowded, even noisier back area, and at certain tables in need of ventilation, there can be eye-stinging fumes from the source of heat on the tableside cooker. That does not happen often, which is lucky, because it would ruin what is perhaps the single most felicitous Italian dining experience in New York.

POSITANO

250 Park Avenue South, corner 20th Street.
Telephone: 777–6211.

Favorite meals:
   Mussels sautéed with garlic, oil and parsley (cozze alla Praianese)
   Quail with fennel and cognac with polenta (quaglie alla Iride)
   Berries with cold zabaglione
   OR
   Pasta with sausage, mushrooms and tomato (marille Positanese), SHARED BY TWO
   Braised rabbit with celery and onions in white wine (coniglio alla Saracena)
   Chocolate almond torte (torta di mandorle)

OTHER FAVORITE DISHES: Sliced mozzarella with tomato (nuova Caprese); arugula and mushroom salad (prataioli); pasta with chicken, herbs and tomato (canneroncini); rigatoni with tomato cream sauce and pimiento (rigatoni ambrosiana); penne with bacon, escarole, olives and capers (penne alla giudea); risotto with porcini; lobster with tomato, celery and potatoes (aragosta Pachialone); swordfish with vinegar, herbs and olive oil (pesce spada alla griglia); shrimp sauteed in shells with garlic, olive oil, tomato and hot peppers (gamberoni haum! haum!); alla Vichinga; fish soup (zuppa de pesce); squid sautéed with olive oil, garlic and red wine (calamari alla Cicciluzzo); cold poached salmon with diced vegetables (salmone multicolore); veal chop with cherry tomatoes, leeks and ginger (costoletta bizzantina); New Zealand mussels with tomato and cream; chicken livers grilled with garlic, parsley and lemon (fegatini di pollo alla patriota); sautéed escarole; string beans; tirami sù.

SETTING: Airy modern café in limpid pastels with tiered seating; noisy and hectic especially around and overlooking bar; quieter and more relaxed in side booths.

SERVICE: Friendly and good natured but often very slow.

DRESS CODE: None.

SMOKING REGULATIONS: No special policy.

FACILITIES FOR PRIVATE PARTIES: None.

HOURS: Lunch, Monday through Friday, noon to 3 P.M.; dinner, Monday through Thursday, 5:30 to 11:30 P.M.; Friday and Saturday, 5:30 P.M. to 12:30 A.M. Closed Sunday and major holidays.

RESERVATIONS: Necessary.
PRICES: Moderately expensive.
CREDIT CARDS: AE, CB, D, MC, V.

Just as the town of Positano on Italy's Amalfi coast is built
up on a mountainside in ledges, so this namesake restaurant
was designed with tiered seating. Even the butter emphasizes
that point, stamped out as it is in a mini-three-stepped design.
Limpid Mediterranean pastels and clear, comfortable lighting
add to the graceful effect but are not quite enough to dispel
the hectic and noisy activity that prevails every night. Owned
by TV commercial director Bob Giraldi and his production
partner, Phil Suarez, this café-restaurant has become a hangout
for denizens of the advertising world, most of whom are cas-
ually and attractively gotten up to stand four deep at the bar.
The only oasis of quiet is a downstairs row of booths, which
is where I like to sit unless I am with someone who wants to
catch the scene. In that case, the upstairs balcony tables are
the ones to reserve.

Usually the kitchen of a restaurant as "in" as this one doesn't
exert itself unduly, but at Positano the chef, said to be from
that Campagna town, offers unusual and enticing dishes, many
of which are beautifully prepared. Weaknesses are appetizers
and desserts, but there is a lot of very good and savory eating
in between, most notably among pastas. Half orders are not
permitted, but sharing a full order is, and so that is how we
usually begin. Some of the more delectable choices have included the risotto smoky with a resounding belt of porcini
mushrooms adding heft to the juicy, just barely tender rice,
and the marille (sort of a double penne with an extra flap)
tossed with sausage, mushrooms and tomato. A tomato cream
sauce with pimiento and celery gentle big, chewy rigatoni, and
canneroncini, a short-cut macaroni that is sauced with chicken,
hot peppers and tomato, is a sustaining main course. Penne
alla giudea—Jewish-style—seems perversely named considering that its sauce includes bacon, but there is nothing per-
verse about the complex, intriguing combination of ingredients,
among them escarole, black olives and capers. Less successful
are greasy farfalle (bow-tie pasta) with overcooked, bitter zucchini.

Those who prefer a lighter first course, or who want pasta
as a main course to be preceded by something, have slim pickings. The only good options are the mussels sautéed with garlic,
parsley and hot peppers; the larger, milder New Zealand mussels in tomato cream sauce; the mozzarella with tomato and
grilled mushrooms (nuova Caprese); and a salad of mushrooms
and arugula. The toasted bread bruschetta here is drowned
with a heavy tomato sauce that makes it simply wet bread, and

215

a salad of artichoke leaves and shrimp arrives watery and bland. Other green salads need more careful drying so the wet leaves do not shed their dressing, and better draining would also improve the main course of bitter broccoli di rabe served with sausages. Better sausages would help too; those said to be homemade have little flavor other than salt, and their meat was too finely ground, for a most un-Italian result.

Two main courses that have been extraordinary at Positano are the quail with fennel and cognac garnished with slices of cornmeal polenta and the lean, succulent rabbit braised with celery, onions, white wine and woodsy herbs. Almost as good is the butterflied veal chop sautéed and topped with cherry tomatoes and slivers of leeks, all profiting from a delicate hint of ginger. Grilled chicken livers with garlic, lemon and parsley are crunchy and delicious, if at times overcooked and therefore dry; ask for them pink and return them if they are overdone. Those livers, by the way, would be even better in smaller appetizer portions. Even now it's a fine idea for four people to share an order as a starter.

Fish lovers have much to choose from here, with the tender, fresh lobster out of its shell and sauced with tomato, celery and hot peppers, all bedded down on sliced potatoes (aragosta Pachialone) or the grilled shrimp in their shells that are sparked with hot peppers and glossed with olive oil, parsley and tomato. Whole baby squid sautéed in oil and red wine (calamari alla Cicciluzzo) are tender and spicy, and there is often a fine Friday fish soup, zuppa de pesce, in a garlic- and basil-heightened tomato broth. A little more shellfish would add brinier overtones. Swordfish remains moist and glistening when broiled with a basting of olive oil and vinegar (pesce spada alla griglia), and cold salmon with a diced vegetable salad is a refreshing choice for lunch or summer dinner. Red snapper has been less successful, what with its overcooking and overpowering splashes of vinegar.

With most dishes, vegetables must be ordered à la carte; two very good choices are the firm, just tender string beans and the brightly sautéed escarole smothered with garlic in oil.

Ice creams are ordinary as is much of the baking. The only sweet finishes worth their calories are the chocolate almond torte that is a Capri specialty (torta di mandorle) and the tirami sù—layered sponge cake with mascarpone cheese, zabaglione sauce and powdered chocolate. Berries plain or with a froth of cold zabaglione are perhaps the safest alternative.

The wine list is well chosen, if slightly overpriced; a particular favorite is the Umbrian red wine Rubesco di Torgiano Lungarotti "Riserva" 1975 at $22. There is also a decent variety of whites and reds by the glass.

216

The young staff is friendly and helpful, but the kitchen seems to be the reason for the often painful slowdowns at peak hours.

RAO'S

455 East 114th Street, corner Pleasant Avenue.
Telephone: 534–9625.

Favorite meals:
 Seafood salad, SHARED BY TWO
 Pasta with marinara sauce and ricotta, SHARED BY TWO
 Chicken with lemon sauce
 Fresh fruit
 OR
 Fresh broccoli salad
 Linguine with white clam sauce, SHARED BY TWO
 Pork chops with vinegar peppers
 Fresh fruit

OTHER FAVORITE DISHES: Baked clams; roast pepper salad; clams in tomato broth; all soups combining pasta with various beans; all pasta; escarole or broccoli with garlic and oil (aglio olio); chicken fried with garlic, onions and vinegar peppers; veal, beef or pork chop pizzaiola; broiled veal chop; sausages broiled or with peppers and onions; shrimp fra diavolo or arreganate; squid (calamari) in red or white sauce.

SETTING: Small, bohemian bar and grill with only eight tables and year-round Christmas decorations adding a festive touch.

SERVICE: Highly personal and superb, once they let you in.

DRESS CODE: None really, but most regulars wear jackets.

SMOKING REGULATIONS: No special policy.

FACILITIES FOR PRIVATE PARTIES: None.

HOURS: Dinner, Monday through Friday, 6 to 10 P.M. Closed Saturday, Sunday and major holidays.

RESERVATIONS: Necessary for first-timers about three months in advance.

PRICES: Inexpensive to moderate.

CREDIT CARDS: None.

Rao's is undoubtedly the most special Italian restaurant in New York. It's virtually a private club because of its large, loyal following, its limited capacity of eight tables and its short workweek. Determined always to reserve a few tables that can be booked on short notice by regulars, the management doles out reservations to newcomers so stringently that a call two to four months in advance is not excessive. Whether you think it is worth all that depends upon how you feel about finding a unique classic, totally without pretense or obeisance to fashion, and how much you like no-frills Southern Italian food, fresh and lustily prepared.

In a way, Rao's is much like another of my favorites, Chez L'Ami Louis in Paris, because I feel that when cook-owner Vincent Rao (now in his 80s) and his wife, Anna, retire, there will be nothing to replace this, just as Antoine Magnin at L'Ami Louis is the last of a breed. The Rao's nephew, Frank Pellegrino, who has become a skillful restaurateur and host, will undoubtedly have another successful restaurant, but trying to copy this without the originators could be a drastic mistake, inviting only invidious comparison.

Rao's is much favored by Woody Allen, among other serious eaters, and he cast Frank Pellegrino in a role in his delicious film *Broadway Danny Rose*. Still, Frank remains levelheaded enough to run the dining room single-handed, sitting at each table to write the order, making suggestions and warning against over-ordering, taking reservations and generally being a sort of one-man-band restaurateur, all with charm and aplomb.

In the kitchen, tall, ramrod-straight Vincent Rao, cowboy hat in place, grills his incomparable chicken to charred perfection, then sauces it with lemon. He sautés the veal chop and fires up sausages with pungent vinegar cherry peppers while the equally imperturbable Anna, never a pale blond hair out of place, pitches in with pastas, salads and desserts. Anyone who thinks fast, good cooking can be done only in a shower of confusion should glance in here. I have a feeling that Mr. and Mrs. Rao are the only people who indeed can make omelets without breaking eggs.

That is not all that is unusual about this New York landmark. Its location gives lie to the oft-heard excuse of failed restaurant owners, namely that they were ruined by being in a bad neighborhood. Looking at Rao's, as well as at Sammy's and Peter Luger's, one has to believe that going to improbably disastrous sections is in itself a kind of reverse chic, witness the big fancy cars parked out in front of each. At Rao's you will want a car of some sort, for this deserted slum neighborhood, formerly a thriving Italian community, is hardly the place to take a stroll looking for a taxi. But any car you bring will be safe, as Rao's seems to have reached a detente with local troublemakers. A glance at the outside of this tiny corner bar and grill, which usually has letters missing from its shabby sign, and the sheets of metal covering windows in the rest of the building, and it would not be hard to feel that you have come to the wrong address and that the street name, Pleasant Avenue, is someone's grim idea of a joke.

But that sort of setting intrigues me, not only at Rao's but also at the other two places mentioned. Standing outside in these dismal neighborhoods, one has to think they have been abandoned by all inhabitants. But step inside the doors, and you find a bright, warm, convivial interior, humming with activity and fragrant with reassuring aromas of hot food. At Rao's it is always Christmas, thanks to the colored lights and tinsel the management keeps the year round. There is a long bar, where customers wait for tables or friends of the management drop by for drinks, and then the eight small, immaculately set tables stand against the dark walls that suggest years of varnishing and revarnishing.

The menu has much the same sure, simple and satisfying quality as the room, and it is the sort that is a forerunner of such great Italian steak houses as the Palm. It is essentially a grill and hot-stove kitchen, where everything is cooked to order and nothing prepared in advance. That means no lasagne or ravioli or tortellini, no stews or roasts. Vincent Rao is basically, in effect, a master short-order cook, and anyone wanting to know how to rustle up a magnificent meal in thirty minutes could learn a lot from him. The "60-Minute Gourmet" would not indicate impressive speed to him. What he needs is the right, thin strong pans and enough heat; his eye and hand take care of the rest.

The rich and soul-nourishing results are appetizers such as the satiny, sweet and pungent salad of slivered roast peppers just oily enough to smooth the bite of the anchovies that accompany them, clams baked in their shell with a garlicky breadcrumb topping or simmered in a light tomato "zuppa." By far the most brilliant first course is what is here called fish salad, a tossing of sea-fresh lobster and crabmeat with tender rings of squid and magenta-tinged octopus bits, and the chewy, smooth conch meat, scungilli. Celery, lemon juice, mild olive oil and parsley do the rest, which is plenty. I can never let a drop of that dressing go back to the kitchen, sopping it up with the good crusty Italian bread provided.

Which leaves me already half-sated by the time I choose soup or pasta. But I manage, as the house is good about half portions, sharing and other civilized practices. Clear, fragrant broths may be adrift with escarole and white beans, and the thicker soup-stews combine short tubular pastas (I prefer ditali) with peas (piselli), or white beans (fagioli), smoking brown lentils or chick-peas (ceci). A light glossing of tomatoes, garlic and mellow onions flavors these restorative soups, best eaten in fall and winter.

But it's a tough choice between those and the pastas when

219

I consider the perfection of the linguine with white clam sauce which always has the right amount of nut-brown chips of garlic and plenty of salt, or the similar sauce minus clams and known as aglio olio—garlic and oil—a favorite of mine when it is sprinkled with hot red pepper flakes. Or short pasta tossed with broccoli, oil and garlic or spaghetti or linguine marinara, which I like very much with a little ricotta stirred in for a creamy thickening touch. Filetto di pomodoro is a simple, quick-cooked tomato and onion sauce very good on spaghetti, any twisted pasta, the short, wide rigatoni, or slimmer, quill-shaped penne.

Aglio olio also works magic on firmly cooked broccoli or blanched and sautéed escarole, vegetables that take on new meaning with that dressing. There are five ways to have chicken at Rao's, but the two I always choose are the grilled with the sunny, sharp lemon sauce and the fried that is zapped with garlic, onions and hot and pungent vinegar cherry peppers. Those same peppers lend their fresh sting to pork chops and to sausages that can be had alone, or with, the chicken.

The more delicate veal scaloppine dishes are disappointing here, the Marsala, piccata and Francese versions among them. That sort of delicacy is just not what the kitchen does best, and so that same pink and tender meat is better ordered with pizzaiola sauce (tomatoes, garlic, oregano), or breaded and fried Milanese-style, or as our old friend veal parmigiana, a comforting, nostalgic choice when done as well as it is here.

There is good, beefy steak and again the pizzaiola sauce can be had as an enhancement. Grilled veal and pork chops are flavorful and rarely dry out, and fried sweet peppers and onions give lean, plump, fennel-seasoned sausages the classic treatment. Again, lighter shrimp dishes impress me less than those baked with garlic, breadcrumbs and oregano (arreganate) or in a hot and spicy fra tomato sauce. Fresh tender rings of squid in white (garlic and oil) or red (tomato—did you think it would be beets?) sauce are delicious plain or sheer heaven atop some steaming al dente linguine.

Frank wisely suggests a fresh fruit platter after such filling fare, and with a commercial tartufo as the only alternative, who could argue? Modest Italian wines are all the house offers, with a Chianti Riserva being as classy as it gets. But those strong, fresh wines go well with this food, despite Woody Allen's predilection for the Lafite-Rothschild he always carries with him. Prices are so low you'll hardly believe it, but everything is à la carte, so it can add up faster than you might suspect.

SISTINA

1555 Second Avenue, between 80th and 81st Streets.
Telephone: 861–7660.

Favorite meals:
Fried zucchini (zucchine fritte), SHARED BY TWO OR MORE
Tortellini in cream, half portion
Italian striped bass with clams, mussels and tomato (branzino del capo cuoco)
Tirami sù
OR
Risotto with four cheeses (ai quattro formaggi), SHARED BY TWO
Grilled, herbed chicken (Sisto IV)
Sautéed spinach (spinaci saltati)
Pear in red wine

OTHER FAVORITE DISHES: Sautéed scampi when available; sautéed porcini or other wild mushrooms when available; veal with tuna sauce (vitello tonnato); crostini with mozzarella, tomato and anchovy; crostini of cornmeal polenta with porcini; vegetable soup (zuppa di verdure); rigatoni with vegetables; linguine with shellfish; Mediterranean fish soup (caciucco); fried calamari; veal cutlet Val d'Aosta; veal cutlet Milanese; veal nodini with herbs.

SETTING: Small, posh supper-club look; just a little cramped and at times noisy; lighting is flattering and felicitous.
SERVICE: Polite, informed and professional.
DRESS CODE: Jacket required for men.
SMOKING REGULATIONS: No cigars or pipes are permitted.
FACILITIES FOR PRIVATE PARTIES: None.
HOURS: Lunch, Monday through Friday, noon to 2:30 P.M.; dinner, Monday through Saturday, 5 P.M. to midnight; Sunday, 5 to 11 P.M.
RESERVATIONS: Necessary, especially for dinner.
PRICES: Moderately expensive.
CREDIT CARDS: AE.

In keeping with the current vogue to make new "in" restaurants hard to find, Sistina's sign is practically invisible, being only a tiny engraved brass plaque unlighted on the front of the building. But that sign is worth seeking out more than most, for unlike so many of the new and the in, Sistina also has delicious, rich, North Italian food and a lively, friendly dining room. The setting suggests a small, posh, private supper club, with a pleasant roseate glow and a convivial tone that manages to dispel the drawbacks of a slightly cramped and noisy room. The only pretentious touch is what looks like a Xerox copy of Michelangelo's "hand of God" detail from the famed fresco on the ceiling of the Sistine Chapel. It is an obvious reference to the origin of the restaurant's name, but a reproduction so tacky that were Buonarroti to see it, he might well regret all those years on the scaffolding.

However art critics feel about this, there should be little to displease food buffs, for the food prepared by chef-partner Antonio Bruno (formerly of Lusardi's) is by and large delicious and diverting. His brother Giuseppe, also a Lusardi graduate, oversees the dining room, and two other brothers trained in top New York restaurants, divide assorted chores. The result of all this experience is a consummate professionalism that keeps things running smoothly, if with a certain absence of the urbane style that distinguishes Lusardi's. (It is difficult not to compare these two restaurants, given the background of Sistina's owners and the following they attract because of their former association.)

One of the most appealing sights in the room is the display of glistening seafood, often flown in from Italy and available in a number of simple-to-complex preparations, and seasonal enticements such as wild mushrooms and white truffles, fresh asparagus and fruit. I like to munch on some gilded slivers of fried zucchini or rings of squid that need only a dash of lemon and salt while waiting for the pastas to be cooked up and sauced. Or, if I am not going to have pasta, I might begin with a richer appetizer—say the pink and tender vitello tonnato, the cool meat mantled with a creamy tuna sauce—or one of the intriguing crostini—either of polenta topped with sautéed porcini or the baked combination of fresh tomato with a cushion of mozzarella. So far I have made only one disappointing pasta choice, that being a very salty, overly creamy spaghetti alla carbonara. Otherwise, solid satisfaction has been the result of trying the meat-filled circlets tortellini in cream, the large rigatoni with vegetables, or linguine in a light, saline tomato-seafood sauce. Risotto is beautiful whether made with asparagus or four cheeses. The grains of rice are firm and juicy, but not crackling at the center as when underdone. Spinach-filled ravioli, also with four cheeses, is another fine alternative, as is the light vegetable soup that gets added zest from grated cheese.

Fish is especially well handled, none more so than the imported Italian striped bass branzino baked in cartoccio—a parchment packet—with clams, mussels, tomatoes and herbs.

The Mediterranean fish soup caciucco is rich with shellfish, snowy fish and a fragrant tomato broth.

Simple and superb are the flattened, pepper-grilled chicken Sisto IV, piney with rosemary, and the lemon-glossed shrimp, grilled scampi-style. On a more lavish scale there is the veal cutlet Val d'Aosta, the veal sandwiching Fontina cheese and prosciutto before being lightly fried with what seemed like a hint of shallots. Veal pounded to tenderness for the cutlet Milanese has a greaseless veneer of breading, while woodsy herbs spark sautéed nodini (thick slices from the fillet) of veal.

Lightly wilted spinach, grilled radicchio and refreshing salads are restoratives. Unfortunately, too many dishes are garnished with tomato and lettuce, giving them the look of drugstore plates (is there anyone else around who remembers when drugstores served food at counters?) That touch typifies the stylistic lapses that differentiate this from Lusardi's, but I am willing to live with that for this level of culinary prowess.

There is a light, creamy tirami sù (I feel as though I have written that dessert name for every Italian restaurant in this chapter, so it will probably soon disappear from menus, having achieved cliché status) with nice counterpoints of coffee and chocolate, cream and cake, and a refreshing pear poached in wine. The chocolate cake is good but nothing more, and the crème brûlée has been too liquid.

The menu suggests, "Please ask the prices of daily specials." Why not just tell them or, better yet, write them out on a menu clip-on?

TRASTEVERE RISTORANTE

309 East 83rd Street, between First and Second Avenues.
Telephone: 734–6343.

Favorite meals:
   Antipasto of vegetables (antipasti di vegetali), SHARED BY
     TWO
   Linguine with white clam sauce (linguine con vongole),
     SHARED BY TWO
   Chicken with peppers, onion and rosemary (pollo alla Ro-
     mana)
   Napoleon, SHARED BY TWO
   OR

Brochette of mozzarella and prosciutto with anchovy sauce (spiedino alla Romana), SHARED BY TWO
Combination fish and seafood stew (zuppa di pesce)
Cream puff

OTHER FAVORITE DISHES: Mussels in tomato and garlic broth (cozze in brodetto); vegetable soup (especially broccoli with tomato); all pastas; chicken with garlic, white wine and mushrooms (pollo alla Gaetano); veal cutlet with tomato salad (vitello Trastevere); squid in spicy tomato broth (calamari Trastevere); tartufo.

SETTING: Tiny, cramped but romantically atmospheric trattoria with bohemian overtones.

SERVICE: Generally excellent but can be brusque toward those wanting half orders of pasta; at times check is presented before it is requested.

DRESS CODE: Jacket and tie required for men.

SMOKING REGULATIONS: No cigars or pipes are permitted.

FACILITIES FOR PRIVATE PARTIES: Can close for parties of up to thirty-two.

HOURS: Dinner, seven days, 5 to 11 P.M. Closed major holidays.

RESERVATIONS: Necessary.

PRICES: Moderate to moderately expensive.

CREDIT CARDS: AE.

Of the four restaurants now owned by the Lattanzi family, this is the first, the best and in every way my favorite. Small, bohemian and with a particularly Roman charm, this dark, slim pocket of a brick-walled, candlelit trattoria, with prints and memorabilia on the walls and jam-packed tables, is the one that set the style for those that followed and the one where the food remains the most succulent and inspired. (Later clones are the lackluster Trastevere on 84th Street, the uncomfortably cramped Erminia, which brings out my incipient claustrophobia, and the very good Lattanzi on Restaurant Row in the Theater District, also in this book.)

Dishes created by Paul Lattanzi and his mother, Erminia (brothers Maurizio and Vittorio manage dining rooms and business matters), are perhaps best described as larger than life and might be considered nuova cucina were they not so copious and lavish. I suppose casalinga, home-style, is the safest description, but you have to be lucky to have it come from a home like this. Consider the antipasti di vegetali, to be shared by two—assorted vegetables, each cooked in a different way and gently slippery with good olive oil; zucchini or eggplant might be grilled or stewed with tomatoes, broccoli may be steamed and dressed with olive oil and garlic, peppers might be fried and sparked with capers, and more. Some are cool, others warm or hot. If not those, have the sandless, briny mussels heaped in a bowl and underlined with an authoritative, garlic-scented tomato broth or the perfect spiedino alla Romana, the chunks of mozzarella melting between crisp-toasted bread slices with slivers of prosciutto and a golden anchovy sauce. Crisp salad of greens and radicchio and an inspired vegetable soup that is especially good when it is broccoli cooked with tomato and a very fine pasta are other irresistible first courses.

As for pasta, the four at Trastevere create only one problem, and that is choosing. Feeling delicate, I might have the fine capellini primavera tossed with cream and vegetables. Other times it might be fettuccine Trastevere with peas, mushrooms, prosciutto and cream, or the thick, hard-to-wind, marvelous-to-eat bucatini with an amatriciana sauce of tomato, onion and pancetta bacon. My single favorite pasta dish, linguine with white clam sauce (con vongole), is nowhere better, with clams always as fresh as a sea breeze and plenty of garlic bravely cooked to a golden brown patina. At times there are gnocchi that get a frothy marinara sauce, further complicating the delicious dilemma.

The management is not always willing to do different half orders of pasta for members of the same party, a complaint I have had from unknown guests. They will, of course, permit sharing, but with so many enticements, a party of four understandably might want to have different pastas before moving on to the main course, and at about $16 per portion, an accommodation seems in order.

Among main courses I have always been happy with are pollo alla Romana, the sautéed chicken fleshed out with green peppers and onion and seasoned with white wine, garlic and rosemary, or the chunky, tender bits of chicken browned with garlic, wine and mushrooms—pollo alla Gaetano. Skipping the overly sweet pollo alla Elvira, made with Marsala wine, which I dislike, there is veal to be considered, and here we come to a house classic now being copied (badly) all over town. It is the huge, flat, crisp and golden breaded veal Trastevere, a cutlet topped with a room-temperature, basil-scented tomato salad. The tomato's juices lend a sense of sauce to the veal without making it soggy, and the contrasting temperature of meat and salad has a tactile appeal that is almost Oriental in its sensibility. However, that is the only veal dish I really like here, the piccante and Anna being perfectly decent but short on character.

Two seafood dishes are spectacular, both based on similar garlic and herb tomato-broth sauces: calamari Trastevere, the rings and tentacles of squid tender but full of flavor, and the fish and shellfish soup-stew zuppa di pesce. Both are brightened with hot pepper and are served with thick croutons, much in order for blotting up the sauce. Scampi sautéed with garlic and white wine is fine as is the sole with mushrooms, but with so many other more breathtaking choices, I usually pass them by.

Wonderful desserts are the homemade napoleon, a miracle of flaky puff pastry with a custardy whipped-cream filling, or the equally ethereal cream puffs, or tartufo, that chocolate-glazed ice cream puff that is better here than in most places because it is homemade.

The wine list is short but includes a few high-quality choices that are a bit overpriced; I usually have the modest Sicilian red Segesta that goes well with the richness of the food.

Trastevere is crowded and the staff is at times pushy about hustling diners out; stand your ground and they will subside.

TIDBITS, ALL' ITALIANA

Also see *Bleecker Luncheonette*, under Luncheonettes, Café Il Nido under Cafés and *Sant Ambroeus*, under Patisseries.

Although billed primarily as French, *Le Cirque* dishes up some extraordinary Italian specialties, for which see Le Cirque, under French.

Heroes

Hero sandwiches filled with eggs and peppers, eggplant parmigiana, meatballs and peppers, and potato omelet are still what one wants them to be at *Manganaro's Hero Boy*, 492 Ninth Avenue, between 37th and 38th Streets, 947-7325. I skip veal, doubting its quality at these prices.

Pizza

Despite a few above-average versions of thin-crusted "new" pizza, I prefer the chewier old pizza, and currently my favorite spot for that is *Arturo's Pizzeria and Restaurant*, 106 West Houston Street, corner of Thompson Street, 475-9828. Now that John's on Bleecker Street has gone commercial, Arturo's coal oven heats up the most delectable char-blistered crust, thick with creamy mozzarella and spicy tomato sauce. It's usually jammed with young people digging into the inexpensive, luscious pies (I'm a margherita fan myself and rarely have pizza with other toppings, but the full range is offered) and the live music—guitar, jazz or whatever—that goes on most nights.

If I am with adventurous friends and in a car, I might go for another classic Neapolitan pizza to *Patsy's Pizzeria*, 2287 First Avenue, between 117th and 118th Streets in East Harlem, 534-9783. It's said to be Frank Sinatra's New York favorite, and in this case, his way is also mine. The broccoli salad with lemon, oil and garlic is a classic.

Among the few new, thin haute pizzas I have liked were those at *Mezzaluna*, the tiny, crowded, kindergarten-like café at 1295 Third Avenue, between 74th and 75th streets (535-9600). But considering the icy, rude service I was treated to at a recent lunch, when the café was almost completely empty and a friend and I were told that we could not sit at one of the "better tables," this place could hardly be a favorite. The house specialty should be pizza strafottenza—pizza dished up with impudence and arrogance.

Japanese

CHIKUBU

12 East 44th Street, between Fifth and Madison Avenues.
Telephone: 818-0715

Favorite meals:
    At counter, I just order omakase, the chef's choice, and
      have never been sorry.
    At tables:
    Pickles
    Sashimi
    Grilled eel (kabayaki)
    Flounder in broth (sasagare no oroshimi) or Yosenabe (cas-
      serole of fish and seafood in broth)
    Fruit
    OR
    SHARED BY TWO
    Cold noodles in soy sauce (soba)
    Grilled fatty tuna
    Pork cutlet with pickles (tonkatsu)
    Shrimp with rice (kamemeshi)

OTHER FAVORITE DISHES: At the counter anything the chef
    serves; at tables steamed custard (chawan-mushi), fried
    flounder (kara-age), chicken and egg steamed on rice (oyako
    domburi), shrimp tempura, fresh fruit. Scotch or Sapporo
    beer are good with all of this, as is green tea for a windup.

SETTING: Stunning Japanese modern dining room, counter and
    tatami rooms with gray tile and blond wood; casual and fairly
    noisy at peak hours; parties put in tatami room.

Service: Polite but often slow at tables; slow but exceptional at counter.
Dress Code: None.
Smoking regulations: No special policy.
Facilities for private parties: Tatami rooms for up to eight people.
Hours: Lunch, Monday through Friday, noon to 2:30 P.M.; dinner, Monday through Saturday, 5:30 to 10:30 P.M. Closed Sunday. Open for dinner on major holidays.
Reservations: Necessary.
Prices: Moderate at tables; expensive at counter.
Credit cards: AE, D.

Chikubu is perhaps the most unusual Japanese restaurant in New York; it is in fact two restaurants—the four-star counter, where owner-chef Hironobu Kishimoto presides and where the food is spectacular, and the one-star dining room, where menu choices are more ordinary and preparations are good but less than breathtaking. That is why the rating averages two stars. For years Chikubu was on 62nd Street just off Lexington Avenue, where it had a loyal Japanese following but discouraged others from coming in. The setting was tacky and uncomfortable, and it was virtually impossible for a non-Japanese to get a seat at the counter. But now Mr. Kishimoto has installed himself in this more central location and has a larger establishment, which is handsomely modern with stone gray tiles and blond cypress wood setting the scheme. Serving dishes were always beautiful, and there is a special shape and motif for each dish. The much longer counter-kitchen inside is still reserved far in advance, and if anyone calls who is obviously not Japanese, it may take some insistence to get a seat at that counter. That is not just snobbery or orneriness but has to do with the way meals are served there. Almost everyone who sits there quickly says "Omakase" to the lean, muscular chef, who then thinks a bit and begins to turn out, one by one, a series of exquisite dishes. I have gone as often as three nights in a row without having a dish repeated. Nor do all people at the counter get the same meal. But because of this method, the chef has to be sure that anyone sitting there will eat whatever is served.

It is not even considered good form to ask for a dish you see being served to someone else once your own meal is under way. Ask the name, and then next time, announce that you'd like it and the chef will work it into a harmonious meal. Watch Kishimoto as he wields his samurai steel knife—one costs $1,500—and you will understand what true deftness means, as well as the effect texture has on flavor. Following are some

229

of the stunning dishes my husband and I have had in our happy years of omakase-ing at Chikubu: sashimi of all sorts but best with fluke, snapper and tuna; cool custard squares in a winy sauce; soft-shell crabs in a sunny, yellow sauce sparkled with scallions; grated taro root with raw egg yolk; whole grilled pickled eggplant; shrimp or scallop and cucumbers; seared green chili peppers; squid nutta with a soybean and sake dressing; clams in a bracing salt-air broth; fiddleheads with toasted sesame seeds; marinated baby conch put back in its shell; squid wrapped around seaweed; fried bean curd in mirin broth with scallions; fried flounder with radish in broth (sasagare no oroshimi); and lobster in a spicy bouillon.

It is possible to have all of the above if you are at a table, but you would have to know how to ask for them, as few appear on the menu. But at both tables and counter I have had excellent grilled eel (kabayaki) served in small lacquer boxes, good steamed kamemeshi rice with chicken or shrimp, perfectly fried kara-age (flounder), delicate chawan-mushi (custard steamed with vegetables and shrimp) and creditable yosenabe (fish and shellfish steamed in broth) and oyako domburi (rice with egg, chicken and onions). The fried pork cutlet, tonkatsu, has a good crunch and a thick, seductive sweet and pungent sauce. But other dishes are lackluster and in general all food is better at dinner than at lunch.

Because the chef prepares and arranges each dish himself and can be serving twelve to fifteen people at a time, there may be a long time between courses, but sipping drinks and talking are part of the ritual. Meals at tables run between $15 and $30 a person, while I have usually spent about $50 a person at the counter, including two Scotches. But for a really adventurous eater, it is worth the price. So if you get a seat at the counter, say "Omakase" and lay back and let it happen to you.

INAGIKU

111 East 49th Street, between Park and Lexington Avenues, in the Waldorf-Astoria Hotel.
Telephone: 355-0440.

Favorite meal and favorite dishes:
At the tempura bar only!!
Tempura assortment ending with mixed fritter of fish, shrimp and vegetables (kakiage), shared by two.

230

SETTING: Tempura bar is simple, modern, somewhat crowded and in disarray.

SERVICE: Friendly, helpful and efficient; tempura chefs are especially obliging and informative.

DRESS CODE: Jacket required for men.

SMOKING REGULATIONS: No special policy.

FACILITIES FOR PRIVATE PARTIES: Two tatami rooms that take five to eight; one Western-style dining room that takes fifteen to twenty. Outside catering is done.

HOURS: Lunch, Monday through Friday, noon to 2:30 P.M.; dinner, seven days, 5:30 to 10:00 P.M. Closed major holidays and from January 1-5.

RESERVATIONS: Recommended for tempura bar.

PRICES: Moderately expensive.

CREDIT CARDS: AE, CB, D, MC, V.

Although this sprawling, confused, modern restaurant in the Waldorf has a full menu of Japanese dishes, the only thing that lures me is the tempura bar. By all odds this is consistently the very best tempura in the city, done piece-by-piece by chefs in high black-mesh hats who are masters of this frying technique. Using what is described as a blend of olive, sesame and camellia oils and constantly skimming off fried bits of batter so they do not burn, the chefs fry, and present at intervals, shrimp, fillets, whole tiny fish, squid wrapped with seaweed, zucchini, asparagus, green peppers, onion slices, lotus root, sweet potatoes and eggplant. Preceded by the lovely miso bean soup, here given an extra zesty salt-sea belt with tiny clams and refreshed with intermittent nibbles of the wilted spinach salad oshitashi, the tempura meal is nothing short of exquisite. The batter is always lacy and crunchy, and with dips of radish-flavored soy sauce or lemon juice with salt, it achieves a magical brightness. Kakiage, the traditional tempura windup in Japan, must be ordered a la carte. It is a solid, sustaining fritter formed of minced squid, shrimp, fish and vegetables, fried as a sort of croquette, which is meant to use up the bits and pieces left from making the main tempura items. One kakiage is enough for two, and it can be ordered as a main course in itself instead of other fish choices.

Better ventilation and more orderly housekeeping at the tempura bar would be welcome, but the slight discomfort is worth experiencing for the extraordinary food. Not so the disorganized staff, the high prices and the uneven preparations of other Japanese specialties in the rest of the dining rooms. If it made sense to rate one category of food, or one part of a restaurant, the tempura department at Inagiku would get four stars.

KITCHO

22 West 46th Street, between Fifth and Sixth Avenues.
Telephone: 575-8880.

Favorite meals:
SHARED BY TWO
Salmon caviar with grated radish (suzuko)
Miso bean soup
Fried pork cutlet (tonkatsu)
Pickles
Seafood and rice (seafood Kamemeshi)
Green tea ice cream
OR
SHARED BY TWO
Fatty tuna (toro)
Crabmeat and cucumber salad (sunomono)
Steak grilled on a stone (ishiyaki)
Spinach salad (oshitashi)
Steamed custard with shrimp and vegetables (chawan-mu-shi)
Fruit

OTHER FAVORITE DISHES: Grilled clams (yaki-hama), all sashimi (sliced raw fish), all soups, breaded fried pork (kushikatsu), teriyaki grilled beef or chicken, chef's special dinners. Scotch and sake are the best drinks with this food; beer is also good.

SETTING: Simple, pleasant, modern dining room downstairs that is informal and usually crowded; private tatami rooms upstairs must be reserved; no sushi bar.

SERVICE: Friendly, helpful and professional.

DRESS CODE: None.

SMOKING REGULATIONS: No special policy.

FACILITIES FOR PRIVATE PARTIES: One large tatami dining room that accommodates between ten and fourteen; three small tatami rooms that take parties of five or six.

HOURS: Lunch, Monday through Friday, noon to 2:30 P.M.; dinner, Monday through Friday, 6 to 10:30 P.M.; Sunday, 5 to 10:30 P.M. Closed Saturday and major holidays.

RESERVATIONS: Necessary.

PRICES: Moderately expensive.

CREDIT CARDS: AE, D.

Considering the enormous scope of the menu, the serious (and seriously priced) dishes that are available and the immaculate perfection with which most are prepared, Kitcho is a surprisingly casual restaurant. Although pleasant and brightly modern, the downstairs dining room has a café informality, with closely set tables that make for a fairly high noise level at peak hours. There are more atmospheric tatami rooms that can be reserved upstairs, but groups of dark-suited Japanese businessmen seem equally fond of both settings. As in so many Asian restaurants, some of the more esoteric dishes do not appear in English on the menu, so it is a good idea to ask for what you want, whether from the descriptions here or by spotting enticing-looking choices at other tables. That way I found that the kitchen turned out a fine, creamy nuta (the small salad of tuna, squid or fluke), that in autumn there were the golden matsutake mushrooms to be had grilled or steeped in a fragrant broth, and that at all times ishiyaki (tender fillet of beef sliced and grilled on a hot stone at the table) was on hand. Do not be embarrassed to ask about dishes you see, even if that means pointing, never mind what Miss Manners thinks.

No Japanese restaurant in this city performs as consistently as this one, and almost everything on the menu is first-rate. Through the years only sushi (not served at a counter) and tempura (deep-fried seafood and vegetable assortments) have been disappointing compared with other examples around town. But that leaves dozens of exceptional alternatives, all nicely presented by an interestingly diverse staff—male waiters in trim, conventional white jackets, women gracefully dressed in kimonos, and a waitress or two in a starchy white uniform suggesting a very efficient nurse. All seem intent upon being of service; if there is a hierarchy, it is not imposed on customers, or at least not on non-Japanese.

The current American dining phenomenon, grazing or eating small amounts of several appetizer-size dishes, comes naturally to the Japanese, who have been doing exactly that for centuries. Not only is it a diverting way to eat, but it makes it possible to maintain a varied diet nutritionally, as one eats through a tempting progression of fish, vegetable, bean curd, rice or noodles, small amounts of meat and finally fruit. The raw, transparently thin slices of saltwater fish that make up the sashimi selections are glowingly fresh at Kitcho, whether you choose the delicate fluke, the zesty yellowtail, the marinated mackerel or the favorite tuna, sliced in thicker strips as the lean, beefy makura or the prized fatty belly portion, toro. Dipped into soy sauce spiked with the fiery green horseradish, wasabi, sashimi can be an appetizer or a complete meal. Yakihama (broiled clams that are reminiscent of the Italian clams casino) are savory and satisfying, and other tiny enticements include the refreshing salad of crabmeat and wilted cucumbers (sunomono); warm grilled seaweed with wasabi (yakinori); and cool wilted spinach accented by sesame seeds (shitashi).

Cold buckwheat noodles (soba), sprightly with minced scallions and mellowed by soy sauce, are as delicious as they are restorative, and for an elegant touch, there is pale golden salmon roe caviar nestled against pungent grated Japanese radish. Clear or miso soups, salty crisp pickles and tiny nuggets of marinated chicken grilled on skewers (yakitori) are other delectable choices. More substantial dishes that would be considered main courses to Westerners are the breaded chicken or pork, crisp and greaselessly deep-fried in vegetable oil, and all of the teriyaki meats, poultry and fish. Salt-broiled salmon with a crackling edge of silvery skin and a sort of Japanese risotto—seafood kamemeshi—served in a handsome, rustic wooden steamer are favorites. I can almost never leave without having chawan-mushi, a winy custard flecked with ginkgo nuts, bright greens, bits of shrimp and fish and grated lemon rind, steamed in a pretty porcelain cup. It ranks among the world's great soul foods.

Ripe melon or pineapple, a nashi (Oriental pear-apple) and green ice cream are the best desserts. I prefer Scotch with this food as do most of the Japanese, judging by the bottles of "Pinch" and Black Label that stand on their tables. Sapporo beer is a second choice, and warm sake seems to be an obligatory, ritualistic starter before Scotch. Wonderful banquets can be ordered here for either the tatami rooms or the tables. They are best for groups of six to eight.

OMEN

113 Thompson Street, between Prince and Spring Streets.
Telephone: 925-8923.

Favorite meal:
  SHARED BY TWO
  Spinach, scallops and peanuts (peanut-ae)
  Nuta with clams
  Marinated chicken (sansho)
  Broth with noodles and vegetables (omen)
  Ice cream
  OTHER FAVORITE DISHES: Spinach and mushrooms with sesame (goma-ae), spinach salad (oshitashi), cold tofu (hiya-

yakko), clams steamed with sake, miso bean soup, chicken with radish (mizor), broiled salmon (yaki-jake), tofu with carrots and spinach (sira-ae), fluke sashimi (hirame), shrimp, octopus or clams with soybean sauce and scallions (nuta), pickles (tsukemono).

SETTING: Trim, rustic Japanese country café; informal and a bit noisy when full.

SERVICE: Generally good but slow and, with new waiters, often confused.

DRESS CODE: None.

SMOKING REGULATIONS: No special policy.

FACILITIES FOR PRIVATE PARTIES: None.

HOURS: Dinner, Tuesday through Sunday, 5:30 to 11:30 P.M.; brunch, Saturday & Sunday, 11:30 A.M. to 4:30 P.M. Closed Monday.

RESERVATIONS: Recommended.

PRICES: Moderate.

CREDIT CARDS: AE, D.

Men is one Japanese word for noodles, a derivation of the Chinese *mein*. (Larmen Dosanko, which we think of as a Japanese-style fast-food chain featuring noodle soups, is to the Japanese a Chinese restaurant specializing in lo mein, pronounced larmen.) Starting then with *men* for noodles and affixing the Japanese honorific *o* we get Omen, a three-hundred-year-old traditional soup enriched with burdock root, spinach, scallions, noodles and sometimes bean curd. Ribbons of the seaweed kelp add a salty tang as well as minerals, as do the dried flakes of bonito. Ginger, hot pepper powder and roasted sesame seeds make Omen as sustaining to the palate as it is to the body.

Although that is the specialty of this casual, rustic SoHo eating place, it is not the only unusual and pleasant offering. Small dishes to be had before or, in a progression, instead of Omen include coolly marinated sansho chicken or another cold chicken and cucumber salad, tori-tosazu. Tuna sashimi is not as fresh as it should be; for some strange reason the fluke (hirame) is more dependable. Maybe that is what they mean by a fluke. Small salads of shrimp and avocado with miso sauce (kimizu-ae), spinach with scallops and peanut sauce (peanut-ae) and nuta of clams or octopus are other tantalizing appetizers. Clams are sometimes on hand, steamed in sake, a subtle blend of the winy and the briny, but too substantial if Omen is to be had. Another sustaining main course alternative is yaki-jake, carefully broiled salmon that remains moist and tender. Skip tempura, chawan-mushi and the soybean salad natto that are not as well prepared as the other choices. Good brown rice provides a solid underpinning for most of these dishes, and fresh fruit or ice cream is a refreshing finish. There is a smart little bar-counter where singles can eat or meet; both beer and wine are available.

The young staff members at Omen are sweetly good natured and, as they say, mean well but too often slow down or just plain forget whole dishes or condiments. However, a brief word to a managerial type straightens things out quickly. Small, closely set tables make for a convivial din that no one seems to mind. Those who want quiet can ask for the back alcove-balcony, which has a curious out-of-it feeling. But take your choice between quiet and being part of the entertaining scene.

SERYNA

11 East 53rd Street, between Fifth and Madison Avenues. Telephone: 980-9393, 980-9394.

Favorite meals:
LUNCH
Stuffed fried crab (kohra age)
Steamed whole red snapper
Fruit
DINNER
Assorted sashimi
Sirloin steak, grilled on a stone (ishiyaki)
Pickles
Fruit

OTHER FAVORITE DISHES: Salt-broiled scallops; beef cooked in broth at table (shabu-shabu).

SETTING: Inviting, stylish dining room that somewhat suggests a tropical cocktail lounge in an international hotel; large tables are generally widely spaced; seating and noise level are comfortable.

SERVICE: Polite, professional and efficient.

DRESS CODE: Jacket required for men.

SMOKING REGULATIONS: No special policy.

FACILITIES FOR PRIVATE PARTIES: Four rooms, each accommodating up to twenty.

HOURS: Lunch, Monday through Friday, noon to 2 P.M.; dinner, Monday through Friday, 5 P.M. to midnight; Saturday, 6 P.M. to midnight. Closed Sunday and major holidays.

RESERVATIONS: Necessary.

PRICES: Moderately expensive.

CREDIT CARDS: AE, CB, D, MC, V.

Every restaurant critic is asked if there is a restaurant he or she does not write about so that it will remain an undiscovered private retreat. I have rarely been tempted to do that, always wanting credit for a good find. Seryna is one of the few exceptions, not because the food is extraordinary (just very good) or because it is a bargain (it is fairly expensive), but because it is a perfect place in which to talk. Being relatively invisible, it offers large tables, widely set apart from one another, comfortable upholstered lounge chair seats, a noise level that is usually benign, a charming and efficient staff and diverting food that is not too heavy. Also, although Japanese, it is not unremittingly so; that means even the least adventurous palate can be satisfied.

Apparently, there is no cause for worry. For though it does a nice brisk business, Seryna remains more or less undiscovered, apparently not dramatic enough to be the focus of the restaurant-madness set. In addition, it is very hard to find, laid out as it is in a set-back building with no name at the street line and only the most discreet lettering at the entrance. If the management wanted to keep it a secret, they could not do it better. As I understand it, Seryna is a chain in Tokyo and Yokohama (there is also a branch in Los Angeles) and exemplifies the Japanese idea of a Western restaurant. Here they take one more turn and make it the Japanese idea of a Western notion of a Japanese restaurant. Hence the conventional seating, the forks and knives offered right along with chopsticks, the tropical-cocktail-lounge look and the simple Japanese grill menu.

There are entertaining Western accents on that menu. The Japanese ishiyaki, steak sliced and grilled on a hot stone at the table, is accompanied here by excellent crisp french fries that have a fine potato flavor. Both filet and sirloin are available; the filet is easier to bite when held with chopsticks, but the sirloin has a better flavor, as usual. With the steak (best blood-rare) there are two dipping sauces—one aromatic with chili, the other gentled with garlic. Very Japanese and very good is the shabu-shabu, the boil-at-the-table combination of paper-thin sliced beef, noodles and vegetables, all to be dipped into ponzu—a soy and lime sauce. That is better than the bland kani shabu-shabu made with fish.

Skip crabmeat steak and stuffed Dover sole among the fish entries, and opt instead for the steamed whole red snapper, seasoned with exotic herbs and garnished with steamed vegetables. Sushi leave much to be desired, but the sliced raw fish sashimi is fresh and flavorful, although at times too cold. Salt(shio)-broiled scallops and the stuffed, greaseless fried crab in a shell are good starters. Not so the soups, the salads and the too-liquid version of the steamed custard, chawan-mushi. Teriyaki broiled scallops are decent, and the salt pickles make a refreshing contrast to the steak. Tempura could be crisper, and the oil used for frying it should be fresher.

The green tea ice cream has been unusually good, and fruit is always ripe.

SUSHI AND SASHIMI

Because all Japanese restaurants serving these raw fish specialties do most of the same classic combinations, it seemed a better idea to describe the basics without repeating them for each of the favorites below. Both raw fish forms are best when eaten at the counters behind which they are prepared. Master sushi chefs are few and far between in this country, where novices who are often completely untrained perform for unknowing audiences. Japanese sushi connoisseurs look for important telltale signs of quality even before they bite into a single slice of raw fish (sashimi) or one of the rice and seafood packets (sushi). Very short hair, clipped fingernails and clean shaves are considered essential for sushi makers, and the real purists do not even condone eyeglasses. The sushi master's work surface should be scrubbable wood. The flat sheets of seaweed (nori) used to enfold maki or rolled sushi should be crisp, golden-green and lightly heated for a second so their flavor freshens and becomes toasty. That slight warming also provides temperature contrast to the room-temperature rice that has been flavored with rice vinegar and the slightly cooler-than-skin-temperature fish.

Nigiri or squeezed sushi are simply pressed into packets— fish on top, rice on bottom. They are sometimes bound with a strip of seaweed to keep fish in place. Gunkan-maki are wrapped with sidebands of seaweed for loose toppings such as salmon caviar (ikura) or the beautiful orange sea urchins (uni) that taste like very intense lobster coral.

Temakisushi or handrolls are often called Japanese ice cream cones, and they mark the finish to the sushi meal for many aficionados. They are cone shapes of folded seaweed filled with rice and such ingredients as tuna, cucumber, grilled salmon skin or warm, glazed grilled eel. The customer or the sushi master makes the choice. As with all sushi, there is a touch of pungent green horseradish (wasabi) added, and soy sauce is used as a dip. Sushi may be handled with chopsticks, but fingers are preferable, and it is best to invert the sushi so that the fish, rather than the rice, is dipped into the soy sauce. It is also considered preferable to have the fish touch the tongue before the rice. Chirashi or scattered sushi combines the elements of sushi in loose fashion—slices of typical sushi fish, sweet omelet and pickles over vinegar rice in square lacquer boxes or bowls.

Fish for the plain sashimi slices or the sushi are generally raw. A few types are served cooked or marinated, among them squid, mackerel, most shrimp, octopus and salmon, which is smoked. Saltwater fish are the only kind served raw, although in Japan some buffs risk the parasites common to freshwater fish and eat those raw. When fresh river shrimp are available, they are served raw. One sushi-sashimi ingredient that has become common despite its inferiority is known either as surimi or kameboko—fish formed and colored to imitate a fish cake or Alaskan king crab, which itself seems an imitation of something anyway. There is also a tendency to use a very salty and unpleasant red fish roe for assorted sushi, rather than the fine salmon roe caviar used for a la carte orders. That rule prevails, by the way. It is always better to sit at the counter and order a la carte. Why that is so is a mystery, as the same chefs make sushi for counters and tables.

Besides, sitting at the counter, one sees a floor show as the sushi masters work their magic with knives, hands and rice. Ask what is especially fresh and good for the day, then order gradually. My own favorites among nigiri-sushi are fluke, snapper, yellowtail, the meaty clam muscle called geoduck, mackerel, shrimp and grilled eel. I like all the rolled sushi except futo-maki—a big, rather gross checkerboard mix of fish, plums and pickles. So-called California roll, an inside-out sushi with rice on the outside and with a filling of Alaskan king crab and avocado, is to me skippable. I always finish with a handroll and begin with a few slices of tuna sashimi, preferably the fatty pink toro. Miso soup and pickles (tsukemono) and spinach salad with sesame seeds (oshitashi) are also good accompaniments. Scotch is the drink I favor, with sake as a second choice.

Small dishes that we would consider appetizers are often served in sushi parlors, but the best do not have large main courses such as tempura, sukiyaki and so on. Full-fledged Japanese restaurants rarely produce great sushi. I know of none that does in New York. One sure sign of a good sushi restaurant is the crowd that gathers. If it is not absolutely full, with a waiting line by 12:15 at lunchtime or by 5:45 in the evening, mediocre sushi are the best you can expect. If there are vacant seats at 12:30 or 6:30, forget it. An early crowd is the best assurance of top quality.

Most of the places that follow do the above dishes, with a few variations as noted.

HATSUHANA

17 East 48th Street, between Fifth and Madison Avenues.
Telephone: 355-3345.

Favorite meal:
  Miso soup
  Sashimi of toro
  Squid nuta
  Assorted sushi
  Pickles

OTHER FAVORITE DISHES: Nuta, natto, broiled scallops, salt-broiled squid, pickles, and all sushi except futomaki, kameboko and California roll.

SETTING: Simple, brightly attractive modern dining rooms; table space is more comfortable upstairs; counter is livelier downstairs; crowded and noisy.

SERVICE: Generally good, but when rushed staff seems to fall back on a language barrier that at other times does not exist.

DRESS CODE: None.

SMOKING REGULATIONS: No special policy.

FACILITIES FOR PRIVATE PARTIES: One room, seats four to six.

HOURS: Lunch, Monday through Saturday, 11:45 A.M. to 2:30 P.M.; dinner, Monday through Sunday, 5 to 9:30 P.M. Closed New Year's Day.

RESERVATIONS: Necessary for both counter and tables.

PRICES: Expensive.

CREDIT CARDS: AE, CB, D, MC, V.

To be very clear, the Hatsuhana I like is the original on East 48th Street. The later clone on East 45th Street is neither as comfortable nor as dependable. Even here there is not quite the glow that prevailed six or seven years ago, but the quality and workmanship are still exceptional, and a seat at the street-level counter provides one of the best floor shows. Sashimi slices are presented on glossy ti leaves, sushi are pressed perfectly so the textures feel right against the teeth, and rice is firm but tender. Miso soup has an almost lemony edge to it and is one of the best in the city, rivaled only by the clam-enriched version at Inagiku.

This is one place where sushi at the table match those at the counter, and if four people order a deluxe array, they can be prepared for a huge round black lacquer box filled with a bright mosaic of delectables.

Small dishes are also nicely turned out in the upstairs dining room, where we sometimes plan a menu that includes scallops broiled in salt, the custard chawan mushi, squid nuta and the fermented soybean salad, natto, broiled clams and squid that have a smoky burnish about them and pickles. It is a costly but delightful way to eat unless, of course, there is a rush of business and waiters feign a language barrier.

NADA-SUSHI

135 East 50th Street, between Lexington and Third Avenues.
Telephone: 838-2537.

Favorite meals:
SHARED BY TWO
Miso bean soup
Osaka sushi of mackerel layered in rice (battera)
Osaka sushi of marinated crabmeat on rice (kanisushi)
Spinach salad (oshitashi)
OR
Cold buckwheat noodles in soy sauce (soba)
Cold bean curd (tofu)
Fried pork cutlet (tonkatsu)
OR
FOR AN INEXPENSIVE LIGHT LUNCH
Hot or cold soup or a casserole of rice with chicken and egg (nabe).
OTHER FAVORITE DISHES: Wheat vermicelli with soy sauce and wasabi horseradish (suomen); salad of fluke, shrimp or tuna (nuta); Japanese omelet (dashi maki).
SETTING: Japanese bric-a-brac tells you where you are, but otherwise this is a crowded, noisy, plain pipe-racks dining room.
SERVICE: Hectic at times but polite and fairly efficient.
DRESS CODE: None.
SMOKING REGULATIONS: No special policy.
FACILITIES FOR PRIVATE PARTIES: One room, accommodating up to eight.
HOURS: Lunch, Monday through Friday, noon to 2:15 P.M.; dinner, Monday through Friday, 5 to 10:15 P.M.; Sunday, 5 to 10

P.M. Closed Saturday. Open for dinner on all major holidays except Christmas.
RESERVATIONS: Usually not necessary.
PRICES: Moderate.
CREDIT CARDS: AE, D, MC, V.

This small, crowded and disorderly luncheonette is one of the few decent, moderately priced sources of good if not exceptional sushi, including a few versions not found elsewhere in the city. Osaka-style sushi are made with layers of vinegared seaweed, fish (mackerel for battera and crab for kanisushi) and rice, pressed into a pan and then cut in rectangles, much like a cake. They too are seasoned with the green horseradish, wasabi, and then with soy sauce and are milder in flavor and more filling than the better-known sushi. Both are well-turned-out at Nada-Sushi, a name that has always suggested to me a Spanish-Japanese hybrid. There are blessedly inexpensive lunch and dinner main courses, such as the delicious broths adrift with noodles, bean curd and bits of fish or chicken. Also satisfying and inexpensive are the nabe casseroles in which rice is steamed with bits of chicken and beaten egg—somewhat like a cross between fried rice and risotto. It would be soothing to eat this with a spoon rather than with chopsticks, but who wants to be branded a philistine? Frying and broiling are not nearly as careful as they used to be; only the crumbed fried pork cutlet, tonkatsu, is up to standards, and even this is inundated with a stupid green salad, probably as a concession to the Western blue-plate mentality. Like Inagiku, this place is a special favorite when I am alone and want a good, relatively fast lunch, and, in this case, an inexpensive one.

TAKESUSHI

71 Vanderbilt Avenue (230 Park Avenue), at 45th Street.
Telephone: 867-5120.

Favorite meals and favorite dishes:
SHARED BY TWO AT A TABLE
Spinach salad (oshitashi)
Deluxe "omakase" sushi and sashimi combination
OR
Clam soup
Grated radish with salmon caviar

Nuta with tuna fish
Chicken grilled on skewers (yakitori)
Grilled squid
Sunomono salad of tuna
Custard steamed with shrimp and vegetables (chawan-mushi)
Pineapple
OR
Alone at the sushi bar
Any sushi or sashimi

SETTING: Attractive modern dining room with blond wood and grass-green carpet; sushi bar and booths are the most comfortable locations; ventilation could be improved.

SERVICE: Polite and well meaning but very slow at peak hours.

DRESS CODE: None.

SMOKING REGULATIONS: No special policy.

FACILITIES FOR PRIVATE PARTIES: One tatami room accommodates four or five; another tatami room accommodates four to eight. Outside catering is available.

HOURS: Lunch, Monday through Friday, noon to 2:30 P.M.; dinner, Monday through Saturday, 5:30 to 10 P.M. Closed Sundays and major holidays.

RESERVATIONS: Necessary for tables and sushi bar.

PRICES: Moderately expensive.

CREDIT CARDS: AE, CB, D, MC, V.

Beautifully cool, fresh, well-crafted sushi and delicate, flavorful slices of sashimi are the main attractions of Takesushi, tucked away on Vanderbilt Avenue, and humming with activity day and night. It is also the most attractive of the sushi restaurants, with its blond wood trim, grass-green carpet and partitioned alcoves, which allow for more privacy and protection from noise than do the open tables. Otherwise, this is a hectic place with unfortunately slow if courteous service. When the management is aware that things have bogged down, complimentary dishes are sent to the table—a nice touch if it doesn't go on too long. On one such evening, we had oshitashi, the refreshing wilted spinach salad, set off with flakes of dried bonito fish, and baked scallops in a shell—good but uncharacteristically greasy.

The real action is at the sushi bar, where efficient, helpful sushi masters deftly turn out trim versions of all the standard specialties. They also do artful platters of sushi and/or sashimi assortments to be shared by two or more at the bar or at tables. Order the "omakase" version of either, meaning that the choice is left up to the sushi master. I like to finish up with a satisfying handroll, the best being yellowtail with scallions.

Both the golden miso bean soup and the invigorating clam broth with clams are good before sushi or a progression of small dishes.

Among such, my favorites are the snowy mound of grated white radish crested with red salmon caviar (sushi restaurants traditionally buy the best available specimens of that caviar); the grilled squid (tender but with a nutty bite); nuta, which is raw fish stirred through a velvety golden sauce; sunomono (any salad that has a clear vinegar dressing) made with octopus, tuna, squid or yellowtail, accented by cucumbers and marinated seaweed; and yakitori, the nuggets of boneless chicken glazed with teriyaki sauce and grilled on skewers. Tempura is hopelessly awash in grease, and it's pretty stale grease at that. I therefore avoid anything fried here. Salt-grilled salmon steak is fresh and cooked to moist, just-set perfection.

Chawan-mushi, the steamed custard with bits of fish, shrimp, vegetables and ginkgo nuts, is a lovely finish. Fresh pineapple has always proved a better dessert than the underripe melon.

At lunchtime only sushi, sashimi and soups are served downstairs, with all other dishes offered upstairs. At dinner the upstairs is closed, and the full assortment is served downstairs. Reservations are essential at both meals.

Jewish and Kosher, Restaurants and Delicatessens

Considering the size of New York's Jewish population, it is hard to understand why there is no really fine and attractive kosher restaurant and so few serve excellent Jewish food even if it is not kosher. Thirty or forty years ago, there were a number of savory options in this category, including full-fledged white-tablecloth restaurants, dairy restaurants and far more great delicatessens than we have now.

The best of the sparse possibilities follow.

CARNEGIE DELICATESSEN & RESTAURANT

 ★★★

854 Seventh Avenue, between 54th and 55th Streets. Telephone: 757-2245.

Favorite meals:
BREAKFAST
Fresh orange juice
Cheese blintzes with sour cream
Coffee
LUNCH OR DINNER
Hot pastrami or corned beef sandwich
Cold sauerkraut
Tea
OR
Chicken or boiled beef in the pot
Cheesecake
Coffee
OTHER FAVORITE DISHES: All smoked fish with or without bagels and especially smoked whitefish plate, oatmeal, French toast,

chicken soup with matzo balls, cabbage soup, hamburger, jumbo all-beef frankfurters with sauerkraut, salami or tongue and eggs, Nova Scotia salmon and onions with scrambled eggs, all meat sandwiches except rolled beef, Danish.

SETTING: Typical, huge, sprawling and crowded New York deli decor.

SERVICE: Quick, humorous, helpful and efficient.

DRESS CODE: None.

SMOKING REGULATIONS: No special policy.

FACILITIES FOR PRIVATE PARTIES: None, but they do outside catering.

HOURS: Food of all sorts, seven days, from 6:30 A.M. to 4 A.M. Closed the first day of Rosh Hashanah and Yom Kippur Eve and Day, opening after 6 P.M. on Yom Kippur night.

RESERVATIONS: Not accepted.

PRICES: Inexpensive to moderate.

CREDIT CARDS: None.

If the Carnegie Deli were to close, I have a feeling that real estate values in New York would plummet. Certainly this landmark Jewish (but not kosher) deli is one of the best reasons for living in the city, as its homemade, smoky, peppery beef pastrami and mellow, spiced corned beef are unmatched anywhere in the country. So is its method of layering up the half pounds of thinly sliced meat piled into every sandwich (on rye bread, of course), to be eaten along with wonderfully firm and succulently sour garlic-dill pickles and cool, saline pickled green tomatoes.

With so much talk about people giving up animal fats and salt, it's a wonder that the Carnegie does not resemble a deserted mining town in Colorado. But the lines that form before lunch, dinner and late supper almost every day indicate that the dedication to diet is less than complete. Never has this place been more jammed with out-of-towners and natives, and never has the management been more careful or attentive to food and service. Leo Steiner watches over the curing of meats, the expansion of the menu through research into matters such as baking the perfect cheesecake and general business tummeling, while Milton Parker runs between kitchen and dining room and Freddie the K (as in Klein), primarily a behind-the-scenes financial partner, helps in the dining room now and then to maintain his grasp on reality. All are needed to spell one another, as they must, given the many hours of operation. Then too, Steiner has a theatrical career to consider, now stopping to do a TV commercial for rye bread ("It makes a nice sandwich, a nice sandwich...") or doing a voice-over in the movie *Broadway Danny Rose*, much of which Woody Allen set in this restaurant. Woody Allen is also a loyal customer, ordering take-out food for location shooting and appearing intermittently for a midmorning bowl of oatmeal.

Local kibitzers gather around pieces of cheesecake and cups of coffee, while serious eaters try to open mouths wide enough to bite into one of the towering sandwiches. Many share (for a $2 surcharge) or take home uneaten halves to be consumed at a later meal. Most eat all and then some, getting a cholesterol and salt fix that should see them through the week.

In rating the Carnegie three stars, I must point out that there is a whole category of dishes I ignore. They are far less than wonderful and to me are out of keeping with the spirit of the place. They include cooked food such as goulash, short ribs, etc., not specifically recommended here and salad platters of tuna, egg or chicken, piled high with iceberg lettuce. Chicken in the pot and boiled beef, both with noodles, matzo balls and vegetables, are juicy and flavorful.

That still leaves more marvelous food than most people can eat in a month, all so superbly prepared it brings up the restaurant's average. My favorite times at the Carnegie are between meals, when the peak crushes are not in force. That means midmorning breakfast, at which I might have freshly squeezed orange juice, expertly cooked eggs (three is the standard portion), or smoked salmon with cream cheese on a bagel, or a slab of nice fatty woodsy smoked whitefish with a toasted bialy, or homemade cheese blintzes with sour cream.

For early or late lunch or dinner, I might start with the matzo ball soup that is the city's second best (the first is up at the Green Tree Hungarian Restaurant, for which, see Hungarian) or the cabbage soup when it is the du jour. Usually I have a half portion of soup, something the house willingly serves, and follow it with a pancake omelet of tongue and eggs, always asking that the tongue be center slices for which there is an added charge, but worth it. Or one of the spectacular sandwiches, not only pastrami or corned beef (not too lean), but rare roast beef, pot-roasted beef brisket, salami that has been allowed to dry and age (ask for it that way if that's how you like it), center slices of tongue and so on. Meats can be combined in sandwiches, although I do not like them that way. Rather, my husband and I order two different sandwiches and switch halves, for variety. I also like to order those meats on a plate if I am not in the mood for a super-sandwich; their flavor and texture is even better appreciated that way.

Salami and eggs is another of my preferred dishes, and though I do not often have one here, the Carnegie broils a terrific hamburger. Big thick jumbo beef frankfurters are served either boiled or, as I like them, split and grilled, and I choose sauerkraut rather than canned baked beans as an accompaniment. Cold sauerkraut, by the way, is the side dish I prefer to coleslaw with deli sandwiches. I can't remember when coleslaw first reared its mayonnaisey head as the accompaniment to these lusty meats, but it's an aesthetic gaffe.

Pickles are either entirely cured or doctored on these premises and get an extra belt of garlic and spicing, which gives them a special luster, my favorites being the full sours: but all stages of pickling are available. So is good, chewy rye bread with black onion seeds.

Dishes I avoid at the Carnegie, in addition to those mentioned, are chopped liver (not chicken liver and too pasty), potato pancakes, which are heavy, and gefilte fish, which is commercial.

"Beer is the wine of the great deli," the menu advises, to which I must add, so is hot tea. That, along with the firm but slightly custardy cheesecake is all the finish a meal requires.

Carnegie does a huge takeout, send-out business and caters for all sorts of parties and business meetings, all with the same flourish. As the Carnegie is opening outposts in other parts of the country and around the New York area, I want to make it clear that anything I write refers only to the original; I have not been to others.

SAMMY'S FAMOUS ROUMANIAN RESTAURANT

157 Chrystie Street, near Delancey Street.
Telephone: 673-5526, 673-0330, 475-9131.

Favorite meals:
SHARED BY TWO
Stuffed derma (kishka)
Eggplant salad, Sammy's style
One order of Rumanian tenderloin steak, large size
Silver-dollar potatoes
OR
SHARED BY SIX
Sliced brains
Broiled chicken livers and unborn eggs
Grated radish with onions and chicken fat
Rumanian beef sausages (karnatzlach)
Grilled rib steak
Stuffed cabbage
Breaded veal cutlet

Mashed potatoes with chicken fat

OR

Potato pancakes

OTHER FAVORITE DISHES: Calf's foot jelly (patcha), chopped eggs and onions, fried kreplach, chicken soup with noodles, mushroom-barley soup, eye of the rib steak (mush steak), broiled veal chops, broiled chicken, boiled beef flanken with mushroom-barley gravy, kasha varnishkes with onions and dried mushrooms, seltzer, lots of hot tea, Alka-Seltzer.

SETTING: No-frills dining room bursting with conviviality; jam-packed, noisy and with live music every night.

SERVICE: Cheerful, patient and efficient.

DRESS CODE: The management says, "Comfortable," which means no tight belts.

SMOKING REGULATIONS: No special policy.

FACILITIES FOR PRIVATE PARTIES: Separate dining room accommodates forty to one hundred.

HOURS: Dinner, Sunday through Friday, 3:30 P.M. to midnight; Saturday, 3:30 P.M. to 1:30 A.M. Closed Yom Kippur Eve, Day and night. There are special Seder dinners with songs and services on the first two nights of Passover with one seating only, beginning at 6:30 P.M.

RESERVATIONS: Necessary.

PRICES: Moderate.

CREDIT CARDS: AE, CB, D.

About twice a year—perhaps when the first cold snap of autumn arrives and when there has been a damp, wet snow in late February or early March—I get a yen for Sammy's. That longing builds slowly, but I know what's coming when I begin to dream about the garlic-zapped roasted green peppers always on the table and find that in the midst of serious business conversations my thoughts are on a big bowl of creamy gray mushroom soup fluffy with barley, and my teeth almost ache for a bite of that rare and bloody, sublimely tender and beefy Rumanian tenderloin, the skirt steak so impeccably grilled in the best Rumanian-Jewish tradition. Then my husband and I round up about four friends (six is my favorite number for this knock-down-drag-out evening of food and song) and make reservations. The rest becomes history, written in yet another inch on my waistline.

Everything about Sammy's needs an explanation, beginning with its name. Stated fully, it is "Sammy's Famous Roumanian Jewish Steak House Restaurant." Variations on that abound, including whether "famous" goes before or after "Sammy's" and the correct spelling of Roumanian-Rumanian-Romanian— take your pick. What also needs explaining is how a restaurant in this disaster of a Lower East Side neighborhood can pack people in, night after night, year after year, as big fancy cars pull up to the curb and the waiting line spills out of the three-steps-down doorway on weekends.

And how does this kitchen manage to maintain such high levels of excellence, turning out voluminous portions of hot, steaming and savory food at a rapid pace while the dining-room staff moving through the jam-packed room full of demanding, food-crazed customers maintains an air of cheerful goodwill and efficiency throughout? It should also be explained that though the food is Rumanian-Jewish, it is not kosher, witness the containers of milk on every table to be mixed with Fox's U-Bet chocolate syrup and seltzer to make egg creams. That milk with a menu featuring meat is all the tip-off one needs to the non-kosherness of Sammy's.

Finally, how is it possible for people to eat so much food and still walk out under their own power? Perhaps Alan King said it best: "When I go Sammy's, I make two reservations—one at the restaurant and another for a private room at Lenox Hill Hospital." But he goes and I go, as do young people in jeans or *Miami Vice* regalia and loyal middle-class devotees from Manhattan and the suburbs, and the local pols, theater folk, judges, writers and painters. It is that kind of place. The only people who do not go, because they have been and have not liked it, are those who are tone-deaf to New York. This is, in fact, the restaurant that separates true New Yorkers from lily-livered poseurs, those who are reluctant to mix it up with an essential element in the city's makeup.

Even to use the word "decor" in relation to Sammy's is stretching a point. It has none. It is just a room full of tables and chairs and people, clanging with voices of staff and customers against a backdrop of live singing and piano playing of a Jewish, Israeli and Eastern European repertory that sometimes includes a wild card number from a Broadway show, or even a French-inspired ballad. When the professionals take five, it is not unusual for a customer to get up and perform, often to be shouted down by fellow diners. There are a lot of memorabilia on the walls—photographs, newspaper clippings and signatures of happy eaters—but in general, this nonstop Jewish wedding takes place in a no-frills room. Through all the din and dining, the guiding light behind this establishment, owner Stan Zimmerman, circulates, schmoozing here, taking a sip from someone's drink there, being a little too insulting once or twice during the evening, but always keeping things moving.

It is, of course, unnecessary to eat oneself into stupefaction to appreciate the spirit of the place. I suspect that almost all Sammy-goers stuff themselves because they go infrequently

250

and so each time they order everything. But there is no house rule requiring such gorging, and my husband and I have enjoyed a number of dinners when we have shared an order of the frothy light eggplant salad that gets textural contrast from chunks of tomato, green pepper and onion, then shared a grilled Rumanian tenderloin steak, some crisply fried silver-dollar potatoes and hot tea. That is in no way an outrageous meal, even if we indulge in the garlicky peppers and pickles before other food arrives.

If desserts are short on appeal, the wonderful appetizers more than make up for that shortcoming. There is the city's best stuffed derma, the natural casing filled with a spicy meal of flour, chicken fat, onions and paprika, sliced and grilled. That final grilling makes the difference at Sammy's, giving a lean crispness to what can otherwise be soft and fatty. Unborn eggs, really yolks of unformed eggs taken from spring chickens, are lightly browned and served with sautéed chicken livers, or by themselves, or in the rich chicken soup that is also garnished with noodles. The chopped onions with hard-boiled eggs is light and refreshing. Black radish, grated and tossed with onions and chicken fat (a supply is on every table in syrup pitchers), stuffed cabbage in a gentle sweet and sour tomato sauce, and fresh, cool poached brains dressed with lemon and a little oil and minced onion are all among my favored openers. Hefty but delectable grilled beef sausage that are the garlic- and pepper-accented karnatzlach are wonderful as first or main course. Although I am not usually fond of calf's foot jelly (patcha), Sammy's is a meaty, flavorful exception. Only the very wet chopped liver and the greasy chicken fricassee have been disappointing. Soups never are, whether the rich mushroom-barley brew or the chicken soup with any of its garnishes, which can also include meat-filled kreplach.

Rumanian broiling is a tradition as it is in all Balkan countries and is the forerunner of the Jewish steak house that existed in New York years ago. At Sammy's those expertly broiled cuts include the tender eye of the rib steak known as "mush," the whole rib steaks (or what the French call entrecôte) here served with the bone for maximum flavor, veal chops that do not dry out, Rumanian tenderloin and moist, well-charred chicken. Sweetbreads and calves' liver fare less well, and can be very dry and dense, so I avoid them. All of the broiled meats are served in portions huge enough to share.

"Jewish veal cutlet breaded" is another larger-than-plate-size wonder, which is based on a big floppy veal rib chop, thickly breaded and crisply fried. Perhaps it is necessary to have grown up with that powerful dish to appreciate it, but as I did, I do. I especially like to chew the bone, which has bits

251

of the breading clinging to it, but my Italian husband, used to thinner cuts of breaded veal, cannot even contemplate it with equanimity.

Boiled beef flanken is meltingly tender and succulent at Sammy's, and I like it with a thick mushroom-barley gravy spooned over it.

A choice of vegetables at Sammy's means the following: boiled potatoes that can be topped with chicken fat and sautéed onions, the sliced rounds that are fried to become silver dollars, mashed potatoes with chicken fat and cracklings (greeven, on this menu), crisp, oniony potato pancakes, fried onions, kreplach, the stuffed derma, or kasha (buckwheat groats) varnishkes (pasta bow ties) tossed with sautéed onion and dried Eastern European mushrooms. Not exactly what vegetarians might have in mind, but then Sammy's is not really their glass of tea anyway.

There is a full bar here and that includes wine, but beer and the seltzer on every table are more suitable. The egg creams that are stirred up and enjoyed all over the room leave me cold. As much as I like that drink, I cannot understand drinking it with this food, and it is the one custom here that I regard as a bizarre aberration.

After all that food it is probably just as well that Stan Zimmerman has not come up with good desserts. The strudel is more like candy, with its heavy clogging of candied fruits, the chocolate pudding is the most banal packaged product, and rugelach are dry and tasteless. That still leaves applesauce and stewed prunes, but leave them is what I do.

To give you an idea of how low prices are, there has to be a $5 minimum charge per person, and there is a $1.95 cover charge on weekend and holiday nights after 5 P.M. Monday and Tuesday the entertainment is a violinist and a joke teller; piano and singing takes over from Wednesday through Sunday.

KOSHER DELIS

Though not in the same league with the Carnegie, a few kosher delis do have several very good choices on their menus.

At **Bernstein-on-Essex Street**, 135 Essex Street, between Delancey and East Houston streets (473-3900), they have

Rumanian pastrami—a leaner, narrower cut of meat that has a strong smoke-pepper flavor, making it much like Jewish barbecue. That and the bay-leaf-flavored corned beef are excellent. Other food leaves much to be desired. I have not tried the kosher-Chinese menu in years, so you're on your own. Bernstein is glatt kosher and so is closed from 3 P.M. Friday until Sunday morning.

Fine & Schapiro, 138 West 72nd Street, between Broadway and Columbus Avenue (877-2874), has very good corned beef and pot roasted brisket. Soups, including the famed chicken in the pot, and other meats are not what they once were. This is kosher but not glatt.

2nd Avenue Kosher Delicatessen and Restaurant, 156 Second Avenue, corner 10th Street (677-0606), is kosher but not glatt. Corned beef is delicious, but pastrami is sinewy and waxen. Soups, however, are wonderful, including the city's third-best matzo ball chicken soup and a smoky, earthy mushroom-barley masterpiece.

Katz's Delicatessen, *see* Hot Dogs

DAIRY RESTAURANTS

Meat is out at these kosher restaurants for obvious reasons, and what that leaves is a whole array of salads such as tuna, egg with peppers, egg with mushrooms, egg with onions, vegetarian liver (mushrooms, beans, onions, etc.), a variety of hot and cold fish and herrings, soups, blintzes, French toast, pirogen dumplings filled with cheese or potatoes that can be had boiled or fried with sour cream, and coffee cakes. Here too, present options are pale shadows of former marvels such as Hammer's, Rappaport's and the Garden in its heyday. Most now are sloppy in both housekeeping and cooking, but if I am in the mood, I go to one of the following:

R. Gross Dairy and Vegetarian Restaurant, 1372 Broadway, between 37th and 38th streets (921-1969), is my current favorite. I skip hot fish, pasta and vegetable dishes but choose the cold schav (sorrel), mushroom-barley or split pea soup, or fish chowder, eggs with smoked salmon and onions, fried pirogen, the good cheese blintzes and, for breakfast, excellent French toast made with challah bread. Recently under new ownership, the freshly painted dining room with white tablecloths, an art exhibit on the walls and even a trendy cactus is an encouraging development. It is super kosher, closes from sundown Friday to Saturday night.

Ratner's Dairy Restaraunt, 138 Delancey Street, between Norfolk and Suffolk Streets (677-5588), is fine for soups, eggs dishes, fried potato pirogen, and cheese blintzes. There are some cakes satisfying in this genre—the marble cake, the Russian coffee cake, poppy seed cake, rugelach and the crisp, bubbly sugared egg boards, chremslach.

Korean

Few ethnic cuisines have made such instant and far-reaching inroads as this one. For many years the only place where New Yorkers could try Korean food was at Arirang, and a banal and sorry representation it was. Then a few more outposts were added in the theater district but still none with outstanding food. Now my two favorites below give interesting and varied interpretations of this country's specialties. In addition, there are literally dozens of tiny Korean eating places in the mid-'30s, mostly between Fifth Avenue and Broadway. Few such places are intended for non-Koreans, as a glance at the wholly non-English menu will indicate. Rather, they serve the many Koreans in the fabric, gift and related businesses in that area. At last count there were nine such places on 36th Street between Fifth and Sixth avenues alone. Someday I mean to venture into those pocket-size eateries to see what they are like and how far a non-Korean can get.

Korean food has elements of the Japanese and Chinese in it. Specialties are Mongolian-style meats grilled at the table, and soups, even if by other names. Cold in summer, hot in winter, these rich broths laden with noodles or dumplings, vegetables and bean curd, and often fish, meat and innards are the mainstays of a diet that is generally lean, if high in sodium. Kimchee, the hot and salty pickled cabbage, is a refreshing eye-opener.

Like other Asian cuisines, Korean is most fun when shared by four to eight eaters.

WOO LAE OAK OF SEOUL

77 West 46th Street, between Fifth and Sixth Avenues.
Telephone: 869-9958

255

Favorite meal:
  SHARED BY TWO
  Grilled marinated beef (bool koki)
  Pickled cabbage (kimchee)
  Pickled radish (kaktoogi)
  Egg-rolled fish (koo jul pan)
  Stir-fried vermicelli, beef and vegetables (chap chae)
  Fresh fruit
  SHARED BY FOUR
  All of the above plus fish casserole (me-oon tang)
OTHER FAVORITE DISHES: Grilled chicken leg (dak gui); grilled beef tongue (hemmit gui); egg-rolled meatballs (goki jun); grilled beef heart (yumtong gui); grilled marinated pork (daeji gui); meatball, fish and vegetable casserole (shin sul lo); raw beef in sesame oil (yook hwe bibim bap); mixed plate dinner (jung sik); mixed cold noodles (bibim naeng myun); dumpling soup (mandu kuk); deep-fried fish and vegetables (twikim). Beer and whiskey are the best with this food.
SETTING: Big modern dining room with large, well-spaced tables that allow for private conversations; ventilation could be better; pleasant bar and cocktail area.
SERVICE: Only a language barrier stands in the way of totally helpful service; staff is otherwise polite, patient and prompt.
DRESS CODE: None.
SMOKING REGULATIONS: No special policy.
FACILITIES FOR PRIVATE PARTIES: Three private dining rooms accommodate between twelve and fifty.
HOURS: Lunch and dinner, seven days, 11:30 A.M. to 10 P.M. Closed New Year's Day.
RESERVATIONS: Necessary for four or more.
PRICES: Inexpensive to moderate.
CREDIT CARDS: AE, D, MC, V.

Large and spacious, informal and friendly, Woo Lae Oak is a branch of a Korean chain that is also represented in Seoul, Los Angeles and Jakarta. Charming and polite waitresses in romantic costumes are as helpful as they can be given the language barrier, but any customer who is really stymied can ask for a hostess or a manager who will translate graciously. Menu items are explained in English that is often confusing, and I always point at anything that looks interesting at a neighboring table. Never mind Emily Post on pointing; when gourmandise is the goal, manners bend.

Because Mongolian-style meats grilled at the table are featured, each table is set under a ventilating hood, which rarely seems to work. Nevertheless, it does provide a sort of divider that suggests privacy. Such grilled meats can be ordered as first or main courses. The best at Woo Lae Oak include strips of marinated beef served with scallions (bool koki), nuggets of chicken leg (dak gui), soft, gentle beef tongue (hemmit gui), meaty beef heart (yumtong gui) and pork (daeji gui), all sparked with a vinegar and soy sauce that is best when fired with a dab of hot chili paste. Diners cook these meats themselves, using chopsticks for turning and cooking to the desired degree of doneness. (Except for the chicken and pork, I prefer these meats rare.) Sesame-flavored raw beef (yook hwe bibim bap) is an intriguing variation on steak tartare.

Delicious morsels such as fish fillet or tiny meatballs are dipped in a frothy egg batter and lightly fried, again edible as appetizer or main course. For parties of four or more, a special appetizer assortment (koo jul pan) can be preordered, and it is an enticing array of abalone, octopus, squid, fried or salt-cured fish, cold egg preparations and crisp vegetables.

Pickled in salt with fiercely hot chili peppers, kimchee (made of cabbage) is standard with any Korean course, and variations on it include radish, cucumber, turnip, spinach and bean sprouts. Here, as in most Korean restaurants, if you order kimchee, the whole assortment arrives.

Whether they are so-called or not, many dishes turn out by our standards to be soup. At Woo Lae Oak one extraordinary example is the fish casserole (maewoon tang) that appears seethingly hot, both in temperature and flavor. Fish, slippery bean thread noodles, vegetables and bean curd make this a fine one-dish meal, but order some rice on the side as beer or tea will not assuage the effect of the chili oil. Another soupy casserole (koong joong jungol) combines tripe, intestines, meat, noodles, vegetables and hard-boiled eggs in an aromatic broth. Shin sul lo, cooked on a brazier at the table, has many of the same ingredients, usually minus the intestines. In midsummer the hefty noodles and greens in cold broth (bibim naeng myun) is sustaining and restorative. More conventionally, there is a broth with large meat-filled dumplings (mandu kuk). To all of these add hot sauce, coriander or soy sauce to taste, as recipe writers like to say.

For beginners, there is an assorted plate dinner (jung sik), a good idea that includes dishes described above, a winy bean soup, and the soothing traditional filler, jap chae, a stir-fried blend of noodles, meat and vegetables.

Japanese specialties such as sushi and sashimi are available, but I always skip them, having found them far from fresh and ineptly crafted. Twikim, the Korean version of tempura, is preferable, if not the most diverting dish here.

Other dishes I avoid on this menu are the jungol, a sort of sukiyaki based on ropy beef, and any grilled meats other than those mentioned, as they tend to be greasy and stringy.

After so many complex flavors, fresh fruit and ice cream

are the most welcome desserts. Ginseng tea is available, but its publicized palliative effects are lost on me. Scotch and beer have more to offer.

Because of all the table cookery and the less-than-perfect ventilation, I avoid wearing clothes that have just come from the cleaners as I find they always have to go right back. Washables are preferable.

YOUNG BIN KWAN

10 East 38th Street, between Fifth and Madison Avenues. Telephone: 683-9031.

Favorite meal:
SHARED BY TWO
Egg-rolled fish fillet (saeng sun jun)
Assorted pickled vegetables (kimchee)
Grilled skirt steak (bank ja)
Stir-fried vermicelli, beef and vegetables (chap chae)
Fresh fruit
SHARED BY FOUR
All of the above plus yellowtail fish casserole (jogi mea-wuntang) and fried dumplings (mandoo tui gim).

OTHER FAVORITE DISHES: Assorted appetizers of pickled vegetables; grilled marinated pork (je yook gui); grilled marinated chicken (dak gui); brazier with tripe, beef, chicken, mushrooms and vegetables (shin sul lo); egg-rolled stuffed green pepper (go chu pa jun); roast whole red snapper (domi gui); whole snapper with sweet and pungent sauce (hong cho); dumpling soup (mandu kug); raw marinated beef (yook hwe bibim bab); plain buckwheat noodles (naeng myun sari). Beer or Scotch go best with this food.

SETTING: Attractive, two-story dining room with buffet upstairs; large and lively bar scene; ventilation is poor in back portion of downstairs dining room.

SERVICE: Polite, efficient but limited because of language barrier.

DRESS CODE: None.

SMOKING REGULATIONS: No special policy.

FACILITIES FOR PRIVATE PARTIES: Two rooms hold between twenty and fifty.

HOURS: Lunch, Monday through Friday, 11:30 A.M. to 3:00 P.M.; Saturday and Sunday, noon to 3 P.M.; dinner, Monday through

258

Friday, 5 to 10:30 P.M.; Saturday and Sunday, 6 to 10:30 P.M.;
buffet lunch and dinner, Monday through Friday.
RESERVATIONS: Recommended.
PRICES: Inexpensive to moderate. Buffet is $7.95 for lunch,
$10.50 for dinner.
CREDIT CARDS: AE, CB, D, MC, V.

Newer than Woo Lae Oak, Young Bin Kwan is slightly more modern and attractive, with a polished bar and cocktail lounge and a big upstairs for private parties. Nevertheless, the low ceiling in the back portion of the main dining room can be intolerably smoky as meats are grilled on table braziers, so when making reservations, I always ask for the front of that room. Although I do not think I have ever been recognized there, I have always been given the requested part of the room. Even so, I wear something washable or that needs dry cleaning anyway.

The menu here is larger than that of Woo Lae Oak, which is a plus, but the dishes are seasoned slightly less authentically, perhaps to please the American palate.

Here too there are charming, colorfully costumed waitresses with little understanding of English and again a manager or a waitress who will come over to help with ordering. Skirt steak, being a juicy, meaty cut, is especially good when marinated and grilled (bang ja) and, along with the flavorful grilled pork (je yook gui) and the moist leg of chicken (dak gui) dipped in the pungent soy-chili sauce, becomes an intriguing appetizer. Guests do the cooking on grills set in tabletops, and long chopsticks facilitate turning. Rare is the way to cook beef, with well done being more suited to chicken and pork. I like to nibble on the sharp Korean vegetable pickles stung with chili oil, most especially the cabbage (kimchee) and the cucumber (oi kimchee).

Other wilted, salt-cured vegetables such as spinach and bean sprouts, gentled with sesame oil are refreshing foils for egg-dipped fish fillet (saeng sun jun) and the similarly prepared stuffed green pepper (go chu pa jun). That same fragrant oil adds subtlety to raw beef tartare (yook hwe bibim bap). Shin sul lo, the casserole of tripe, beef, eggs, noodles and vegetables, is good here, if smaller and less sprightly than at Woo Lae Oak.

Chap chae, the lovely sauté of delicate, silky noodles, slivered beef and vegetables, is to the Korean meal what fried rice is to the Chinese. I like to have it after something like the roast snapper, the more sophisticated whole snapper in sweet and pungent sauce, or the casserole of yellowtail in a paprika-bright sauce. Another soother for this aromatic food is naeng myun sari, cold buckwheat noodles with a belt of soy sauce.

Broiled meats other than those mentioned are disappointing, but the meat-filled dumplings are satisfying fried (mandoo tui gim) or in soup (mandu kug). Portions tend to be smaller than those at Woo Lae Oak, and it may take more dishes to satisfy lusty appetites. Fresh fruit is the best choice for dessert.

At both lunch and dinner there is a generous eat-all-you-want steam table buffet of Korean dishes in the balcony dining room. At $7.95 for lunch and $10.50 for dinner, it is a bargain, especially early in the meal hour when the food is firm and fresh. Later on, vegetables grow limp, and anything fried in batter is to be avoided.

Raw fish for Japanese sushi and sashimi looks awful here, especially on Sundays when specimens at the sushi bar seem well past their prime.

Mexican and Tex-Mex

Most of what passes for Mexican food in New York ought to be illegal. From Cinco de Mayo in SoHo to Juanita's on the Upper East Side, including the madhouse single scene that is El Rio Grande and the bland disappointments at Rosa Mexicano and Rosa's Place, to name only a few, I have been served the typical, mushy messes that apparently are beguiling yuppie palates. My husband, who has never been to Mexico, doubts me when I try to convince him that food there is exciting, varied, fresh and at best exudes a palate-tingling progression of seasonings. Try telling that to anyone who sticks a fork into a plateful of tostadas, enchiladas and burritos all melded together with melted cheese, so that if the fork goes in exactly right, the whole mess can be picked up in one piece. And then there is the cumin madness, a spice I find appeals to vegetarian palates that apparently crave substance and so take to this flavoring, which should be used with discretion. Whatever the reasons for this culinary wasteland, the best that I found appears below, with apologies to the Mexican people, who might well have their government break off relations with ours for the food that is ruining their culinary reputation.

THE BEACH HOUSE

399 Greenwich Street, corner Beach Street.
Telephone: 226-7800

Favorite meals:
Nachos with chorizo and jalapeños, SHARED BY TWO
Guacamole, SHARED BY TWO
Shrimp with green sauce

261

Buñuelos with ice cream, cinnamon and maple syrup
OR
Ceviche of fish, SHARED BY TWO
Chicken wings in spicy sauce (mixiotes), SHARED BY TWO
Grilled beef in sauce with wheat tortillas (fajitas)
Kahlúa flan

OTHER FAVORITE DISHES: Tostadas with beans, cheese and pico de gallo sauce (tostadas Jalisco); fried chorizo; grilled wheat-flour tortilla with cheese (quesadillas); soup of chicken, rice and vegetables (sopa de pollo); beef burritos; beef tacos; deep-fried tortillas with beef guacamole and sour cream (chimichangas); chicken in mole sauce (pollo mole poblano); chicken fajitas; stew of shellfish, fish, vegetables and potatoes (guisado de mariscos Vera Cruz); plain flan.

SETTING: Charming, easygoing brick-walled bar and grill with many booths, which are relatively quiet, and some closely set tables midroom; Mexican artifacts add atmospheric but not corny touches.

SERVICE: As friendly, helpful and accommodating as can be, with only occasional slowdowns at the busiest times.

DRESS CODE: None.

SMOKING REGULATIONS: No cigars or pipes are permitted.

FACILITIES FOR PRIVATE PARTIES: None.

HOURS: Lunch, Tuesday through Saturday, noon to 4 P.M.; dinner, Tuesday through Thursday and Sunday, 4 P.M. to midnight; Friday and Saturday, 4 P.M. to 1 A.M.. Closed Monday and major holidays.

RESERVATIONS: Required for parties of eight or more, but no reservations are accepted on Friday or Saturday.

PRICES: Inexpensive to moderate.

CREDIT CARDS: AE, CB, D, MC, V.

In the land of the blind, the one-eyed man is king. In New York, The Beach House is the best Mexican restaurant I know, all of which is not meant as a left-handed compliment but rather as a reminder that two stars means very good, not consistently excellent. But the food is so fresh and freshly cooked, so cleanly presented and brightly seasoned, it is way ahead of its competition. The chef here is said to be from Mexico City and the cooks from Oaxaca, Puebla and Guadalajara, and it is too bad that a tiny kitchen prevents them from exhibiting more of their regional specialties. Owner Judith Socolov, who operates this with her sons, hopes to remedy that in a new and larger outpost on the Upper West Side. I hope that the additional place will not draw their attention away from this already felicitous restaurant.

The Beach House avoids the cornier, more overpowering Mexican decor accents. It is set in what was obviously a corner bar and grill, and that atmosphere still prevails, with brick walls, big ceiling fans, Mexican masks and wood carvings, and assorted old and antique accessories, giving the restaurant a laid-back, all-bets-off casualness. But there is nothing lackadaisical about the young staff, with waitresses and busboys operating efficiently and good naturedly. Only at the very busiest weekend dinners does the kitchen slow, thereby causing a lag, but with the good Tecate or Dos Equis beer, the crunchy, hot pico de gallo sauce, with its diced avocado, peppers, tomatoes, onions and coriander, and the nice lumpy guacamole that the sauce can be stirred into, there is much to while away the minutes with.

Appetizers are intriguing and neatly done. Mixiotes—peppery, chili-spiced chicken wings steamed in parchment—are unusual in these parts and great to chew on with one of the tart margaritas, which are cold even if not frozen, as I prefer them. Grilled slices of chorizo sausage, ceviche of fish (better than the crabmeat because it is frozen Alaskan king crab) with a cool, verdant marinade, and the pile of nachos bolstered with chorizo and jalapeño peppers are all diverting and rich. So is the golden, slightly salty chicken soup full of chicken meat and vegetables and rice, a better choice than the stodgy, puddinglike black bean soup, although a spoonful of pico de gallo sauce improved that a bit.

But black refried beans, for which there is an extra $1 charge on main course plates, are superb—firm, smoky and pungent. Flour tortillas filled with beef and gentled in tomato sauce (burritos) are at once crisp but mellow and better than those with pasty chicken filling. A beef filling much like chili or picadillo is excellent in tacos, topped with shredded lettuce to which I add guacamole and pico de gallo. Enchiladas tend to be too mushy and the deep-fried, filled corn tortillas (flautas) are too stiff and tasteless. But chimichangas, deep-fried wheat tortillas with shredded beef, get their crispness modified by guacamole and sour cream, for happier results. I keep missing chili rellenos at The Beach House—but I hope to correct that soon as it is a favorite and critical dish.

There is also what I think of as "real food on plates" here, differentiated from the tortilla-held fare. A smooth red-brown mole sauce with hints of bitter chocolate and sesame is hefty and flavorful and fine on chicken, though it would be better if the chicken had truly been simmered in it rather than just covered with the sauce. That way, all the flavors would be absorbed by the meat. The grilled strips of beef or chicken, fajitas, here come with a moistening Creole-type sauce that I like, and they are good rolled into wheat-flour tortillas along with a special salsa that is extra fiery.

Pollo Alicia is perfectly decent marinated broiled chicken,

if somewhat non-Mexican, and much the same can be said for the steak (carne Tampiqueña). Shrimp and mussels on rice are dull compared with the firm, fresh shrimp in salsa verde or with the stew of shrimp, mussels, fish, potatoes, peas and tomatoes, which can be sparked with jalapeño peppers on request. I request them and recommend you do the same.

Regular refried beans (frijoles) are acceptable, and rice has always been fresh without the stiff glassiness it takes on in too many other Mexican restaurants.

There are delicious desserts, in the bargain. The custard flan is soothing plain or with a splash of the coffee liqueur Kahlúa, and the real winner is the fried beignet or buñuelo topped with vanilla ice cream, cinnamon and maple syrup. Mousses are thin and watery, much like baby food, but then, you can't have everything.

There can be a slight unevenness in the kitchen's performance, which means, in my experience, one out of four meals can be lackluster.

EL CHARRO

4 Charles Street, between Greenwich and Seventh Avenues. Telephone: 242-9547

Favorite meal:
  Black bean soup
  Fried chicken with garlic (a la Charro)
  Ice cream or fresh fruit, somewhere else

OTHER FAVORITE DISHES: Shrimp with garlic (gambas a la plancha), guacamole with added hot sauce, beef tacos, chicken mole poblano, chopped meat Creole-style (picadillo) with fried plantains.

SETTING: Old-style Village bohemian, with the expected tiles, wrought iron and genuine oil paintings of bullfight scenes and such; tiny bar is a neighborhood meeting place.

SERVICE: Generally good if at times inept; polite and friendly, and the owner watches over all with dedication.

DRESS CODE: None.

SMOKING REGULATIONS: No special policy.

FACILITIES FOR PRIVATE PARTIES: None.

HOURS: Monday through Thursday, 11:30 A.M. to midnight; Friday and Saturday, 11:30 A.M. to 1 A.M.; Sunday, 1 P.M. to midnight. Open all major holidays.

RESERVATIONS: Recommended; not accepted on Sunday.

264

PRICES: Inexpensive to moderate.
CREDIT CARDS: AE, CB, D, MC, V.

El Charro has been a Village landmark for about thirty-five years, the sort of Mexican place that was typical in that neighborhood and that still is a meeting place for locals who gather at the tiny, tiled bar. If the cooking is not up to former standards, most especially with dishes on the Spanish side of the menu (hence its inclusion under Mexican), there are at least some good and interesting choices that still prevail, at remarkably low prices. I have never had a better Latin-style black bean soup in New York than the one made here. Whole tender beans in a velvety broth have exactly the right smoky overtones, and sprinklings of lemon juice and raw onions take me back to what I remember as the world's very best bean soup at the Floridita in Havana. Appetizers are disappointing at El Charro, and I include all except the guacamole with a dash of hot sauce and the Spanish grilled shrimp with garlic. Good chewy beef hash, picadillo, is soothing and satisfying, with its Creole sauce and crunchy slices of fried plantains; that same filling makes lusty beef tacos. Mole sauce may lack the finesse one finds in Mexico, but it has a nice balance of chocolate, sesame and spices and the chicken is fresh. Unfortunately, that sauce cooks down too much once in a while and emerges gooey, in which case send it back. What has never failed is fried chicken a la Charro, nuggets of bone-in chicken steamed to tenderness, then browned with onions and nutmeats of garlic, a New York classic that is unmatched.

Desserts can be matched almost anywhere. I skip the tough, fabriclike flan and the cloying vanilla custard, natilla, and buy some ice cream or fruit elsewhere.

Beer is the best drink with food here, although margaritas are decent, excepting only the touch of bar foam. Too bad paella has become so dry and listless and the Spanish green sauce so dark and characterless.

There is also an El Charro on East 34th Street, but I have never been there, so this applies to the Charles Street restaurant only.

TIDBITS

There are a few good Mexican dishes here and there around town, as follows, but none of these places has enough dependable food to rate as a favorite restaurant—just a spot for a preferred dish.

Café Marimba, 1115 Third Avenue, with entrance just off the corner on 65th Street, 935-1161, was touted as New York's great white hope of Mexican dining. Not quite. The downstairs room of what used to be David Keh's Chinese restaurant—still owned by Mr. Keh—is done up in corny, obvious Mexican cheap shots, including phony shadows and studied arrangements of third-rate pottery. But the worst of it is the nauseating noise which seems to circulate and recirculate like stale air. If I can get there early before the din becomes head-cracking, I might have a meal made up of appetizers and desserts, the best courses, but I would drink beer, not the stagnant pools of margaritas. I suspect the mix is meant to be frozen, but since I like unfrozen drinks, I am at a loss there.

But one can have a diverting meal by sticking to guacamole, after bolstering it with hot sauce; the tiny flautas, for which the rolled tortillas are filled with chicken and fried, to be topped with guacamole; the mesquite-grilled salmon; and the grilled beef fajitas, though they occasionally dry out and become tough. Queso fundido, a sort of cheese meltdown that is good with chorizo and/or jalapeños, has to be dipped into quickly before it all congeals, but it is worth the effort.

Red snapper hash, a seemingly non-Mexican mix of fish and cinnamon served warm, is fine, and the chili relleno, in its golden batter and hot tomato sauce, is the best I have had in New York, unless my friend Gail George decides to make them at home, when they are spectacular.

If I had to have a main course at Marimba it would be either the pollito Yucatan, spicy roast chicken (or roast pork) that is marinated to tenderness, the shrimp in green sauce, or duck with pumpkin-seed sauce. Seafood in coconut is awful, and beef fillets are dry.

Things pick up with desserts. There are nice crisp tortillas and ice cream sprinkled with cinnamon and apple, a chocolate brownie with cinnamon ice cream, and a fair chocolate cake.

Juanita's, 1309 Third Avenue, corner 75th Street, 517-3800, is an attractive tavern-type restaurant, with a glassed-in café and a trendy following that includes yuppie singles and the sort of decent but innocuous food found at Mortimer's and Harry Cipriani. Even so, staff members are sweet, accommodating and efficient, and there are a few above-average dishes. Guacamole is fine and appropriately lumpy but needs the addition of a spicy pico de gallo, for which there is an extra charge. Nachos are the kind I like—each individually topped with refried beans, then glossed with cheese and a slice of jalapeño pepper before being baked. Fajitas, the strips of beef served still sizzling on an iron griddle, are tender and juicy and are fleshed out with sautéed new potatoes and onions. Folded into a wheat tortilla with hot sauce, they are better than most. Similarly, tacos al carbon, beef rolled in a soft grilled-marked taco, is satisfying and better than the mushy enchilada, tamale and burrito combinations. The fried beignet sopaipillas with honey and cinnamon and the fried tortilla filled with apples and edged with ice cream are almost meals in themselves, and pretty good ones at that.

Mexican Gardens, 54 West 13th Street, between Fifth and Sixth Avenues, 245-9878. A Village outpost since 1929, this has always been dependable for two dishes that they do better than anyone else in the city: the neatly made, delicious nachos for which each tostada chip is spread with refried beans, then topped with cheese and a slice or two of jalapeño chili and baked; and the large, crisp flautas made of rolled wheat-flour tortillas filled with beef, all topped with guacamole and sour cream. Those dishes, plus decent beef tacos and burritos, are the only things I have there but they are above average.

This is a new address for this old-timer, but it has already taken on a convincing raunchiness. It is open for lunch and dinner, seven days and serves until about midnight.

Middle Eastern, North African and Armenian

These sensuous, unctuous cuisines are badly represented in New York, a pity because they are so good on their home ground, most especially as they are in Turkey and used to be in Lebanon. We did have a much better representation, and perhaps with luck we will again. Meanwhile, whenever I am in the mood for the shish kebob, vine leaves, couscous and moussaka repertory, I go to one of the restaurants below and pick my way carefully through the menus, much as though I were picking daisies in a briar patch. Or I go to the Greek Xenia. Not that all those national cuisines are the same, but they do satisfy the same longing in me, given the limitation of choice.

DARDANELLES EAST ARARAT

1076 First Avenue, between 58th and 59th Streets.
Telephone: 752-2828

Favorite meals:
    Mixed appetizers, SHARED BY TWO
    Chicken Dardanelles, pan-fried with garlic
    Yogurt with walnuts in syrup
    OR
    Hot yogurt soup with mint
    Lamb shish kebob
    Rice pudding (gatnabour)
  OTHER FAVORITE DISHES: Lamb tartar steak (chi kufta), bulgur and parsley salad (tabbouleh), feta cheese salad with black olives, borscht, vine leaves stuffed with meat (yaprak sarma), moussaka of eggplant filled with lamb and pine nuts, lamb chops or steak, ground lamb on skewers (lulu shish kebob),

268

yogurt kebob, ground lamb and wheat balls in broth (harpoot kufta), swordfish shish kebob, rolled pastry dough with pistachios and syrup (bourma).

SETTING: Grandiose, corny details add up to a bright and festive dining room; avoid airless tables against the walls.

SERVICE: Friendly but lackadaisical and unprofessional; can be forgetful and slow.

DRESS CODE: None.

SMOKING REGULATIONS: No special policy.

FACILITIES FOR PRIVATE PARTIES: None.

HOURS: Lunch, Monday through Saturday, noon to 4 P.M.; dinner, Monday through Saturday, 4 P.M. to midnight; Sunday, 2 P.M. to midnight. Singer and piano player at dinner Wednesday through Sunday, emphasizing Armenian songs Thursday, Friday and Sunday.

RESERVATIONS: Suggested for all dinners but essential on Friday and Saturday nights.

PRICES: Inexpensive to moderate.

CREDIT CARDS: AE, CB, D, MC, V.

Fame and fortune aside, Dardanelles East Ararat, a mouthful in more ways than one, may be my biggest reward for writing this book. A lover of the rich and seductive Armenian cuisine, I gave up on it when Sayat Nova closed its door in Greenwich Village too many years ago. There Arshag Tarpinian and his mother turned out food so cleanly delicate and bright that nothing else in town came close. But in my search for the Armenian and Middle Eastern flavors (not the same, but related) to include here, I tried every restaurant I could find that purported to offer the vine leaf-shish kebob-pilaf trinity. Eventually, I came to this East Side establishment, a reincarnation, I learned, of Dardanelles, formerly on University Place, and Ararat, which used to be on East 36th Street. Bedros Jevikian, the chef-owner of Ararat, now operates this outpost. That complex genealogy has nothing to do with my liking for the food, but at least it indicates there are some roots attached to it.

During my first few minutes in the restaurant, I was convinced it would be awful, a sharp judgment drawn from the stale lavash, the crisp wafer bread sprinkled with sesame seeds—in this case rancid. Repeated requests to the waiter brought forth more of the same. Fortunately, much that came after was delicious, and after several visits, and more stale lavash, I realized it was simply a matter of the management selling its kitchen short. The cooking is so good it deserves first-class trimmings. So I stick to the pita bread (limp but acceptable) and enjoy just about everything else.

Armenia is divided between Russia and Turkey, and each has its culinary specialties. Add to that the large number of

Armenians throughout the Middle East, and you grasp the reason for the menu mix here. Among the subtly oily, lemony dishes of Turkish Armenia are such irresistible appetizers (mezeler) as the bright, almost crisp grapevine leaves rolled around an herbed rice filling; eggplant that is either stewed or baked with onions and tomatoes and is delicious both ways; and white beans with chopped onions and parsley in a near vinaigrette dressing. Middle Eastern elements among appetizers include the Greek fish roe caviar that is tarama, the Lebanese parsley and bulgur salad tabbouleh, puree of chick-peas and sesame oil (homos tahini) and a fresh, crunchy spread of farmer cheese, walnuts, dill, parsley and garlic creamed with a little yogurt. The cured meat pasterma adds a saline tang, as do chunks of feta cheese, and there is also chi kufta, which, I suppose, is how you say kibbe in Armenian. It is raw lamb tartar, combining meat, bulgur, onion and parsley. Less satisfactory are stale, fishy stuffed mussels, the woebegone smoked fish, and limp tasteless artichokes, and the cheese beoreg. That last has a succulent filling of farmer and Muenster cheese, butter and dill, but the phyllo pastry has a white heaviness instead of the desirable golden brown flakiness. That same flaw mars almost all phyllo-based desserts, so perhaps the chef should consider changing his brand. Although available in an appetizer assortment, which is the best solution when two people are dining, each element is more attractive and retains its own flavor when ordered separately so each arrives on an individual dish.

Both the Armenian hot yogurt soup with crunches of whole wheat grains and the hefty cabbage borscht are fine choices if you skip the appetizers; the egg-lemon chicken soup is bland and starchy.

Broiling is an Armenian specialty, and there is a full array of kebobs here, the best being the lamb chops and steak and shish kebob—big chunks of meat that are properly rare inside and alternate on skewers—and ground lamb lulu kebob, a personal favorite because I like the oniony, peppery overtones. The swordfish shish kebob was amazingly moist and flavorful. Beef is skippable, but the chicken is delectably moist and mellow either as shish kebob or, even better, in the Caucasian manner, pan grilled under a brick weight. Called chicken tabaka in Soviet Georgia but Chicken Dardanelles here, the small bird is flattened and seasoned with salt and a generous perfuming of garlic. Meat remains moist while skin turns to goldleaf crispness to make one of the house's best dishes.

A rare specialty in New York is yogurt kebob, a dish I fell in love with in Istanbul and have never before seen here. Grilled lamb is sliced and laid over bread along with pan drippings, onions and yogurt. At Dardanelles the whole is then baked until brown and bubbling on top. It is very good but would be even better if the meat were rare. Nevertheless, it is worth trying.

There are other things I like at Dardanelles that are not broiled, among them the savory moussaka, with its layerings of ground meat and pine nuts, eggplant and a soufflélike topping of béchamel sauce. There are a variety of vegetable dolmas (zucchini, green pepper and tomato) stuffed with meat and served with a warm yogurt sauce that is fine if not overcooked, as it often is, and baked eggplant stuffed with bits of lamb. Harpoot kufta may sound like an Armenian movie star but is, in fact, another version of kibbe. For this, balls of the ground lamb and bulgur are simmered in broth for a very special taste, which I find soothing. Less enjoyable is the greasy, overly reheated lamb shank and the stiff, greasy chicken cutlet Kiev.

Pilafs of both bulgur and rice accompany virtually all dishes and so do impossibly dull and overcooked boardinghouse-style vegetables. Pass on those vegetables as well as the awful mixed salad. Instead, nibble on the salt-pickled fresh vegetables placed on every table when guests arrive, and hope that the mix includes cabbage, which is wonderful.

Baked desserts are disappointing, first because of the poor-quality phyllo already mentioned and second because the nut fillings of the baklava and the shredded wheat (tell kadayif) are at times rancid. Bourma, a little round twist of phyllo with pistachio nuts and syrup, seems better, but the nicest choices are the rich rice pudding with cinnamon and the refreshing yogurt topped with preserved walnuts in syrup. Never mind the maraschino cherry; you can extricate it before digging into the rest.

There is a modest, adequate wine list with Greek reds the best choices for this food. And for a windup have the thick and sugary Armenian coffee.

La Metairie

189 West 10th Street, between Bleecker and West 4th Streets.
Telephone: 989-0343.

Favorite and only meal:
　Mixed green salad
　Couscous royale
　Crème brûlée or orange givrée

Setting: Tiny storefront dining room with charming French country decor; cramped, uncomfortable and stuffy.

Service: Friendly and helpful; too many off-menu dishes are described and no prices are given.

Dress code: None.

Smoking regulations: No special policy.

Facilities for private parties: Will close and can accommodate parties up to twenty-four.

Hours: Dinner, Monday through Saturday, 6 to 11:30 P.M.; Sunday, 5 to 11 P.M. Closed Christmas and New Year's Day.

Reservations: Recommended.

Prices: Moderately expensive.

Credit cards: MC, V.

La Metairie is a nouvelle French restaurant that offers only one North African dish. But as a French restaurant, it would not be in this book. It is the couscous, the city's best, that makes it a favorite. Although the French food ranges from acceptable to good, nothing about it would lure me to pay these very high prices in such uncomfortable surroundings. For couscous, it is worth it.

This was the original La Petite Ferme, begun by Charles Chevillot. It was the forerunner of the simple, small French country restaurant, with plaster white walls, farm implements, hanging garlands of garlic and dried flowers, cotton dish towels as napkins and, in this case, caged mourning doves cooing over the heads of diners. That decor still prevails and is as charming as ever, but it looks a lot better than it works.

The room is small and airless, and diners are wedged in elbow-to-elbow. Tables are so small they can barely hold two of the large dinner plates without having them hang over the edge, and ventilation is an added problem, especially since the management does not curtail smoking.

You can imagine how much I like the couscous to put up with all this, but it is remarkably well done (at least one of the owners is said to be Tunisian) and is not too expensive when you consider the size of the serving. The plain couscous, with chicken, lamb and beef meatballs, is $19, and the royale, to which the peppery lamb sausages, merguez, are added, is $24.

The couscous is served on one side of a deep, oval, glazed earthenware baking dish, with chick-peas, carrots, celery, pumpkin squash and so on heaped on the coarse-grained semolina. The meats take up the other side, and a separate bowl of broth to be poured over all is set on the table. Harissa, the red-hot chili pepper paste, is also on hand, and it is best added by being beaten into a spoonful of the broth that is poured over vegetables and grain. That way it can be evenly distributed.

Hints of cumin emanate from this hefty dish, and it is al-

272

together delicious, if less bristling with authenticity than versions I have had in Morocco and Paris.

A crisp green salad with a sharp vinaigrette dressing is more than enough as a starter, and it is worth ordering just to fill in the time. At one dinner I had a cooling orange givrée—orange sherbet frozen into a hollowed-out orange shell—and it was perfect after the couscous. But crème brûlée, baked and caramelized in a wide, flat dish, is also lovely. House red wine by the glass is good enough with this powerfully flavored food. I would prefer beer, but none is available.

SIDO ABU SALIM

174 Lexington Avenue, between 30th and 31st Streets.
Telephone: 686-2031.

Favorite meal:
  Sido mezze FOR TWO, as follows:
    Chick-pea and sesame puree (hommus)
    Eggplant puree (baba ghannouj)
    Sesame puree (tahini)
    Bean and vegetable croquettes (felafel)
    Homemade yogurt cheese (labanee) with yogurt and cucumbers
    Rice-stuffed grape leaves
    Fried ground lamb croquettes with bulgur (kibbee)
    Stewed fava beans (foul moudammas)
    Halawa
    Mint tea

OTHER FAVORITE DISHES: Broiled kafta kebob, shish kebob, raw lamb tartare (kibbee naya), meat-stuffed grape leaves.

SETTING: Fairly pleasant, simple modern decor halfway between a luncheonette and a café.

SERVICE: Good natured, helpful and prompt.

DRESS CODE: None.

SMOKING REGULATIONS: No special policy.

FACILITIES FOR PRIVATE PARTIES: None, but it does outside catering.

HOURS: Lunch and dinner, Monday through Friday, noon to 11 P.M.; Saturday and Sunday, 1 P.M. to 11 P.M.

RESERVATIONS: Accepted for dinner.

PRICES: Inexpensive to moderate.

CREDIT CARDS: AE, D, MC, V.

Run by Palestinians formerly of Haifa, this small, pleasant and lively restaurant has had several branches through the years. A newer offspring, Sido, on Sixth Avenue near Bleecker Street, was unfortunately short-lived, but this one is far more successful with neighborhood people, Israelis and various Middle Eastern rug and antique dealers in the area. Dark walls, simple furnishings and an open service bar combine to create an effect somewhere between a luncheonette and a dining room.

The food is Israeli-Egyptian-Lebanese in inspiration. What really sparkles, and what regulars rely on, is the copious, excellent meze, the varied appetizers that make up a satisfying meal for two at $12.95. Good warm pita bread, and a little dish of briny green and black olives along with pickled hot green chili peppers, whet your appetite for the array to come. In that selection is the eggplant puree baba ghannouj, for which the eggplants are grilled over flame so they develop the characteristic smoky flavor. Beaten with oil and lemon, it is a delectable jade-green dip for the pita. That is the way other meze are scooped up as well, including the chick-pea and sesame spread, hommus, and the parsley, mint and scallion salad that is tabbouleh. I like more bulgur in that salad than they use here, but it is sprightly and tantalizing nonetheless. Tahini is a velvety dip of sesame seeds, somewhat like a gorgeous liquid halvah, and enough oil is drizzled over it to make it easy to swallow. Felafel, the croquettes of mashed beans, onions and subtle Middle Eastern spices such as cumin, is golden and greaseless, as are the croquettes of ground lamb (kibbee) filled with bulgur. Yogurt drained until curds form the cheese called labanee is pungent and creamy and is served with added yogurt and icy slices of cucumber. Grape leaves stuffed with herbed rice are also good, if slightly less so than the meat-filled variety served as a main course. Foul moudammas, the fava beans that are the mainstay of the Egyptian diet, are stewed to softness, then dressed with oil and lemon to round out the meze. This is a course much like Spanish tapas in spirit. You drink (ouzo or arack or beer), talk, dip, nibble and drink again.

One specialty I like to add to the standard assortment is raw kibbee, much like a lamb tartare. One has to wait while the lamb is ground and is mixed with bulgur and served with slivers of raw onion. Gentle hints of cinnamon and allspice mellow this mix.

Broiled meats, such as lamb shish kebob or the marinated ground beef, kafta kebob, and the meat-stuffed grape leaves are the best main courses. Stewed and braised meats are overcooked and greasy, and couscous is washed out. A good buy is the main course combining the baked kibbee, hommus, baba ghannouj, felafel and a salad at $7.50.

274

Baklava is heavy going here, but the moist, fresh sesame halvah, one of my more enduring addictions, is perfect and well complemented by hot mint tea.

The appetizers can be ordered singly, and two or three will suffice if any of the main courses are to be ordered.

Seafood

Always among the most popular restaurants in New York, the institution known as the seafood house has undergone an enormous change. Until about thirty years ago, almost all seafood restaurants looked alike. The theme was Cape Cod nautical, with fishnets, cork floats, anchors and ships' wheels as the main motifs. Tabletops were usually scrubbed oak, walls were pine, and the menu consisted of Manhattan and New England clam chowders, steamed clams, oysters and clams that could be had fried, stewed or raw on the half shell, broiled or fried fish, boiled or broiled lobster and a few fancy preparations such as curries, creoles, gratins and Newburgs of shellfish, deviled crabs and a few salads. Hot biscuits, pilot crackers, coleslaw and french fries were standards, as were pies for dessert. When well prepared, as the food often was, it was superb and a true fish lover's joy. Outstanding examples were The Lobster near Times Square, Lundy's in Brooklyn, the original Sea Fare in Greenwich Village and both Sloppy Louie's and Sweets in the Fulton Fish Market.

Gradually in the '50s and '60s, such restaurants began to disappear. Sloppy Louie's and Sweets still exist but, like the South Street Seaport around them, are sorry imitations of their former, genuine selves. Gloucester House (37 East 50th Street) follows the old formula and does serve some excellent broiled and fried fish, fluffy homemade biscuits and, at times, first-rate french fries. But anything cooked, including soup, sauces and other kinds of potatoes, is dismal. Considering the sky-high prices, that batting average is not high enough. Le Bernardin, the newly opened branch of the Paris restaurant, in the Equitable Building, still seems too inconsistent at the price to be classified as a favorite, and the service will have to be far more gracious than it has been during my early visits.

New Yorkers have finally learned that excellent fish can be had at many places not specializing in that alone—French, Italian, Chinese and Japanese restaurants being the most delectable examples. And fish is also important on the menus of "new American" restaurants, even though there is a tendency to undercook it, as much a mistake as the old crime of over-

276

cooking used to be. Cool raw fish, as in sushi and sashimi, is delicious. Warm raw-to-rare fish is disgusting. Properly cooked, fish will be moist and pearly, much like set custard. It should separate easily from the bone and not show any traces of blood.

A new style in seafood has been evolving in the past few years and is best realized at the four favorites below. Among them, the Jane Street Seafood Café and the re-created Oyster Bar in Grand Central Station combine American and Continental classics with their own inventions. The most serious fish eaters should find what they love at The Captain's Table. That's where I go when I want to see and consider a dazzling array of whole fish before making my choice. When I am in the mood for richer, gussied-up seafood inventions and a trendy, romantically decorated setting, I go to Pesca, risking the noise for the intricate culinary rewards.

THE CAPTAIN'S TABLE

860 Second Avenue, corner 46th Street.
Telephone: 697-9538.

Favorite meals:
   Mussels marinière or calamari salad
   Broiled whole fish (especially pompano) with Provençal herbs
   Arugula, radicchio and endive salad (SHARED BY TWO)
   Crème caramel
   OR
   Artichoke vinaigrette or spinach and bacon salad (SHARED BY TWO)
   Red snapper en papillote
   Fresh fruit salad
OTHER FAVORITE DISHES: Langoustine, baked clams casino, oysters and clams on the half shell, New England clam chowder, all broiled fish and shellfish, poached salmon, steak au poivre, all fresh fruit desserts.
SETTING: Fanciful café-garden atmosphere, with flowery fabrics, colored lamp shades and amusing bric-a-brac; some tables are cramped; moderately noisy when full.
SERVICE: Generally prompt and polite but slows at peak hours; unknown customers may be treated summarily.
DRESS CODE: None.
SMOKING REGULATIONS: No special policy.

FACILITIES FOR PRIVATE PARTIES: None.
HOURS: Lunch, Monday through Friday, noon to 3 P.M.; dinner, Monday through Friday, 5 to 11 P.M.; Saturday, 5 P.M. to midnight. Closed Sunday and major holidays.
RESERVATIONS: Necessary for lunch; recommended for dinner.
PRICES: Moderately expensive.
CREDIT CARDS: AE, MC, V.

The Captain's Table has a long history in New York. Originally, in its Greenwich Village location, it followed the standard Cape Cod format, borrowing some of the more distinctive dishes created at the first Sea Fare restaurant nearby. (It was, in fact, the place to go when it was impossible to get into Sea Fare.) Then in 1971 it was purchased by Gino Musso, a dedicated, colorful Italian who dresses in a casual style suggesting that he has just come from a marina, and his French wife who added engaging Mediterranean overtones to basic broiled, fried and steamed fish. It is Mrs. Musso, I was told, who is responsible for the best vinaigrette dressing in the city, equally subtle and effective on green salad, on cold artichoke or asparagus, on the sparkling fresh arugula, radicchio and endive salad, or on the combination of spinach, bacon and raw mushrooms.

Somewhere along the line, Musso hired Thai waiters and kitchen help, and another dimension was added, mostly by way of exotic herbs, occasionally too liberally applied. There is something vaguely Thai too about the flowery, almost musical comedy setting, with its lavish bouquets, garden print fabrics and colorful lamp shades and bric-a-brac around the room.

If the setting is amusing, the fish cookery here is wholly serious. What true seafood buffs will appreciate is the huge plank with the day's catch that is passed to every table. There is something about examining the bright eyes and firm flesh of a fish that whets a fish lover's appetite and suggests which specimen looks best and how it might be prepared. Noble and humble fish share this plank: steaks of mako shark and swordfish, halibut and tilefish, blowfish and pompano, flounder and gray sole, salmon and white or red snapper and, in season, shad roe. Flown-in imports include French rouget and Italian spigola. Some choices are excellent poached (salmon or halibut, for example), and all can be immaculately broiled. Whole fish profit from a sprinkling of the aromatic herbs of Provence, only occasionally too liberally applied and so overwhelming the fish.

Frying is also crisply, greaselessly accomplished on flounder or sole, or at times for squid and an hors d'oeuvre giveaway, tiny whitebait. Sea urchins may be on hand as appetizers, as is a variety of oysters and clams. The usual seafood cocktails

278

are well prepared, as are sautéed wild mushrooms, and the mussels marinière in a heady white wine and garlic broth are perfection. So are the salads of calamari or octopus and the baked clams casino, smoky with curls of bacon. Snails have been disappointing at times because of a herbal overdose that makes them musty. New England clam chowder can be fine if it has not cooked down too much and so become overly thick.

Two classic house specialties worth trying are the red snapper en papillote and the brochette of mixed seafood, which includes lobster tail, shrimp, mussels and scallops on rice. The papillote, a big puff of shiny foil, seethes with its bubbling garlic-herb-tomato broth, which flavors the snowy snapper along with shrimp, scallops and mussels. This is virtually a bouillabaisse in a bag and is similar to the papillote fish dish featured in many Thai restaurants. The same is true of the grilled brochette of seafood, altogether lovely when it is not overcooked; a bit of forewarning can prevent that.

Steak, plain or au poivre, is provided for non-fish eaters. The au poivre is preferable, for though a bit tough, it has the right peppery belt. French fries would be more appropriate with that steak than the baked potato. Well-cooked rice and firm, fresh vegetables accompany other dishes.

Baked desserts are disappointing, including an overly rich, uninspired Black Forest cherry-chocolate cake and a Sara Lee-type cream cheese cake. Crème caramel and anything made with fresh fruit are better endings. In the past oranges flambéed with cognac and bananas baked in rum have been winners.

There is a very carefully and well-chosen wine list featuring French, Italian and Californian selections at fair prices. Among reds, however there is a shortage of choices in the mid-$20 range.

Service is generally good, but there is the unfortunate habit of giving away the poor tables first, even if the room is empty. Things also get a bit slow at peak meal times. Menus, by the way, with their hand-painted flourishes, are especially beautiful.

JANE STREET SEAFOOD CAFÉ

31 Eighth Avenue, corner Jane Street.
Telephone: 243-9237 or 242-0003.

Favorite meals:
 Mussels with linguine (SHARED BY TWO)

Fried fillet of sole with vegetable
Key lime pie
OR
Fried squid or mussels baked in snail butter (SHARED BY
    TWO)
Poached king salmon with dill
Strawberry-rhubarb pie

OTHER FAVORITE DISHES: Mussels steamed in white wine with
    garlic, oysters and clams on the half shell, lobster bisque,
    swordfish with wine and herbs, steamed snapper with ginger
    and scallions, all poached or fried fish, broiled fish if not
    underdone.

SETTING: Casual tavern with New England overtones; mod-
    erately noisy but with a convivial charm; stuffy in back room,
    especially in warm weather.

SERVICE: Polite and helpful if sometimes slow.

DRESS CODE: None.

SMOKING REGULATIONS: No special policy.

FACILITIES FOR PRIVATE PARTIES: None.

HOURS: Dinner, Monday through Thursday, 5:30 to 11 P.M.;
    Friday and Saturday, 5:30 P.M. to midnight; Sunday, 4 to 10
    P.M.

RESERVATIONS: Not accepted.

PRICES: Inexpensive to moderate. There is a $9.75 minimum.

CREDIT CARDS: AE, MC, V accepted for checks over $25.

Every good neighborhood deserves a pleasant, friendly, competent and moderately priced seafood restaurant such as this one. If it is the one I visit most often, it is because it is close to my home and provides cheerful, delicious food in a very casual tavern setting. The drawback is the no-reservation policy, understandable at prices as low as these, but even so the line that usually forms at around 7:30 can be discouraging. Jane Street is an excellent choice for anyone who is downtown and wants to eat early before theater. There is no wait, service is prompt when there is no crowd, and it is easy to get a taxi that goes straight up Eighth Avenue.

This trim, lively restaurant has flourished despite its apparent attempt to hide its light under a bushel. The only sign marking it is small and practically invisible. But with walls of brick and pine, a handsome service bar, interesting seashell collages and its Cape Cod charm, it has become justifiably popular. Tables are small but adequate and the staff is good natured.

It is possible to skip an appetizer here because the complimentary coleslaw is so extraordinary and refills are rapidly forthcoming; it is a refreshing first course for those with small appetites or budgets. Made with coarsely shredded cabbage tossed with a sour cream and mayonnaise dressing, it is a lovely contrast in textures, and sesame breadsticks enhance the effect.

But loving appetizers as I do, I usually share one, such as any of the fried specialties—zucchini, clams, oysters or squid; or the mussels baked on the half shell with snail butter or steamed in white wine with garlic butter. Clams or oysters on the half shell are clear and cold, but steamed littlenecks are too rubbery. Baked clams oreganate are properly fragrant with garlic and hot without being tough.

Manhattan clam chowder here used to be wonderful. Lately, however, it has alternated between its old self and a pallid imitator. Not so the seductive, faintly garlicked linguine with a cream and mussel sauce. It is a first-rate appetizer when shared, or a thoroughly satisfying main course.

All frying is a wonder of greaseless crunchiness, and the fillet of sole, prepared that way, and served with an herbaceous tartar sauce, is perhaps my favorite dish here. Second choice is the thick cut of king salmon (all portions are large) that is poached and glossed with dill butter. If you do not want fish rare, say so when ordering the salmon. The same warning is true of broiled fish, not the kitchen's strong point. At times fish is broiled with water, a sort of combination steaming and broiling that results in a wet whiteness I find unattractive.

Among better complex dishes, try the swordfish glazed with wine and herbs, the steamed snapper with ginger and scallions and the baked, breaded bluefish. Some inventions are heavy-handed and obscure the delicacy of the fish. Among such are the red snapper with onions and potatoes and the stir-fried vegetables with shrimp. Vegetables and brown rice, alternatives with most main courses, are cooked to perfection but minus all salt, giving a meal depressing health-food connotations. Baked potatoes are easier to doctor with butter and seasonings. One important omission is any sort of cold seafood salad, missed particularly in summer. The kitchen will prepare one to order but usually of freshly cooked shrimp or salmon, which remains warm. Iced tea also needs improvement; it is so weak it is a dead ringer for water.

Simple desserts are adequate, with Key lime pie or strawberry-rhubarb pie providing pleasantly astringent finishes.

Wines are moderately priced with daily specials, and several are available by the glass. It is possible to have a good dinner with some sharing, or by having two of the substantial appetizers, for about $20; it is also possible to spend twice that or a little more for a larger meal of expensive fish or lobster.

Oyster Bar & Restaurant

42nd Street, corner Vanderbilt Avenue; Grand Central Station,
lower level.
Telephone: 490-6650.

Favorite meals:

Oyster pan roast for a quick, satisfying lunch at the counter
OR
A variety of clams or oysters on the half shell
Poached fillet of salmon with hollandaise sauce
Green salad
Old-fashioned apple tart
OR
New England clam chowder
Halibut flakes on fresh spinach with lemon-mustard dress-
ing
Rice pudding (PREFERABLY SHARED BY TWO)

OTHER FAVORITE DISHES: Smoked salmon, smoked trout,
oyster stew, squid salad with avocado, crab cakes without
sauce, fresh salmon salad, all broiled fish, fried oysters,
broiled or steamed lobster, chocolate nougat dome, pear
caramel torte, cheesecake.

SETTING: Wonderful old landmark with huge cavernous tile and
wood-paneled walls and counters for full meals in addition
to back dining room and front bar-grill; noise seems appropriate here.

SERVICE: Always excellent at the counters; generally good at
tables but can be perfunctory in main dining room, especially
at dinner.

DRESS CODE: None.

SMOKING REGULATIONS: No special policy.

FACILITIES FOR PRIVATE PARTIES: None.

HOURS: Lunch and dinner, Monday through Friday, 11:30 A.M.
to 9:30 P.M. Closed Saturday, Sunday and major holidays.

RESERVATIONS: Necessary for lunch except at counter; recommended for dinner, especially for bar-grill.

PRICES: Moderately expensive.

CREDIT CARDS: AE, CB, D, MC, V.

In a city where so many great architectural landmarks have
disappeared, the Oyster Bar is a treasure. Opened almost sev-

enty years ago, it has always been famous for clams and oysters on the half shell—opened as ordered at a stand-up bar or sit-down counter (or at tables, of course)—and most especially for its oyster stew and pan roast. Those marvels of creamy, peppery salinity are still bubbled up in their original chafing dishes, which pivot over the flame to be poured into deep bowls and dusted with paprika. I usually add a shot or two of Tabasco as well. That, with plenty of oyster crackers, makes one of my favorite quick, solitary lunches. And as I often like to have early brunch-lunch and the Oyster Bar opens at 11:30, we seem to be made for each other. At times, the stew or pan roast can be disappointing if stray bits of cracked shell find their way into the soup. Otherwise, all is as expected.

So is the general action in this restored setting, with a cross-roads hustle and bustle, a masculine air of hearty, turn-of-the-century-style eating, combined with new, fashionable dishes and a huge variety of fish, which varies on a daily basis. The management tries hard for such unusual specimens as wall-eyed pike, channel bass, Virginia spots, wolffish, Lake Winnipeg goldeye, sand dabs, and so on. There are also many types of oysters on hand—Apalachicola, Belons, box, Wellfleet, Malpeques, Marennes, Chincoteague and more. Like the varieties of clams, they are priced singly, as in Europe, so a sampler assortment can be ordered. A dozen oysters of mixed origins is the quick lunch I favor most as an alternative to pan roast. I prefer oysters and clams with only lemon juice and, for variety, a drop of Tabasco or two. Those who like a more sophisticated touch get it with the shallot- and tarragon-scented mignonette sauce.

Broiling and poaching are the most dependable cooking techniques here. The cold fish salads, such as the salmon and fresh tuna, are fine. The most exceptional is billed as flakes of halibut (more like snowy chunks) on spinach salad. Frying can be properly crisp or limp, the reason behind the difference being a mystery, and complex preparations show the same inconsistency. Soup is the prime example. It may be New England or Manhattan clam chowder at their best, or either can be overly thick. Recently the New England has outclassed the overly thick Manhattan, but that has not always been true. She-crab soup tasted like pure starch, and a floury film formed as it cooled. Broiled giant freshwater prawns, though delicious, were so difficult to extricate from shells that there was virtually nothing to eat. On the other hand, crab cakes have been good right from the start *if* you forego the sauce. Potatoes, coleslaw and salads are fine, and though the homemade biscuits are still strong on baking soda, they are good when hot. If yours are cold, send them back.

Home-baked cakes and pies are by and large excellent, the

flaw being a few that are too sweet—blueberry almond pie being a case in point. But the lofty cheesecake, apple pie in whole-wheat crust, and pear caramel torte will make you glad you had nonfattening fish so you can splurge at the end. Ditto the fluff of cool rice pudding adrift with whipped cream.

Considering the enormous menu and the gigantic seating capacity, the Oyster Bar does a remarkable job of turning out very good dishes.

White wines make up about nine-tenths of the list, and all are American. There are only eight reds, again California, and of these only the two Jordan cabarnets are decent, and those carry $30 and $32 price tags. Similarly, the good whites, such as Acacia Chardonnay, are pricey. But there are plenty of inexpensive whites for those who have a taste for the West Coast products, which I do not.

The best service is at the oyster bar itself and at the low comfortable counter. It also tends to be fine in the bar-grill but can range from indifferent to downright rude in the dining room, where waiters grunt and food is thrown onto tables.

PESCA

23 East 22nd Street, between Broadway and Park Avenue South.
Telephone: 533-2293.

Favorite meals:
Mussels cataplana
Deep-fried catfish or broiled salmon
Lemon tart
OR
Deep-fried calamari or zucchini
Cioppino (San Francisco bouillabaisse)
Apple crisp
OR
Valencia seafood chowder
Oven-roasted lobster
Chocolate-walnut pie or sherbet

OTHER FAVORITE DISHES: Oysters on the half shell, gravlax, smoked fish, seafood lasagne, poached salmon and scallops with buckwheat blini, grouper milanese, broiled red snapper with tomato coulis, chocolate-nut torte.

SETTING: Romantically glowing, spacious café setting with dramatic lighting; moderately noisy.

284

SERVICE: Preppie staff is concerned, accommodating and polite; slowness at peak hours seems due to poor kitchen organization.

DRESS CODE: None.

SMOKING REGULATIONS: No cigars or pipes are permitted.

FACILITIES FOR PRIVATE PARTIES: None.

HOURS: Lunch, Monday through Friday, noon to 3 P.M.; dinner, Monday through Saturday, 6 to 11 P.M.; Sunday, 6 to 10 P.M. Closed major holidays.

RESERVATIONS: Necessary for lunch; recommended for dinner, especially after 7:30.

PRICES: Moderate to moderately expensive.

CREDIT CARDS: AE.

When I want some rich, lushly creative seafood in a soignée setting, I go to Pesca. It has improved markedly since it opened in 1979, when it played to SRO crowds nightly. Although it is still very popular at lunch and almost full for at least one seating at dinner, the rush has abated. So has the noise, somewhat, because of the elimination of live piano music, which created acoustical havoc. Pesca has settled into becoming one of the city's best seafood restaurants. Let's hope it won't be forgotten in the yuppie rush to the new and the trendy.

This was one of the first of the theatrical restaurant settings and a pioneer in the Park Avenue South area. The decor has held up well, with enameled walls of peach to mauve-pink (stage lights with colored filters account for the impressionistic color variation) and shiny cream-colored stamped metal ceilings; the huge bouquets of persimmon gladioli give the room an air of silken luxury. Light shining through from the faux courtyard beyond the dining-room windows heightens the effect, as do silk shades on wall sconces and the attractive prints, photographs and paintings of fish and sea themes.

The same sort of distinguished stylishness is reflected in the menu, as it was from the start, but the kitchen is more consistently excellent now, offering plain or gussied-up choices. Portuguese cataplana (authentically a combination of clams and sausage cooked in the hinged, rounded casserole that gives the dish its name) is rendered here with mussels and paprika-bright sausage in a light, garlic-scented tomato essence and is equally delicious as appetizer or main course. Another trademark dish is the Bermuda fish chowder dark and heady with chili peppers; if it is not too fishy, Valencia seafood chowder with fish, shrimp, orzo, tomato, and saffron is even better and, in honor of its place of origin, a hint of orange peel, gives the soup a sunny spark. Here too there is a light needling of chili.

That sort of spiciness adds a raffish touch to many dishes, most especially the peppery, vinegar-based sauce for the im-

285

peccable fried calamari and the cioppino, the California soup-stew of fish, lobster, mussels, clams and scallops in a winy, herbed tomato soup.

Another ethnic adaptation, seafood lasagne, is a delicate layering of pasta with fish, shrimp and scallops in a pink tomato-cream sauce that makes a soothing main course or subtle appetizer when shared by two. When in the mood for less elaborate dishes, I begin with the fried zucchini, oysters on the half shell, the cured salmon, gravlax, or smoked trout. There are seafood terrines here, always decent but uninterestingly bland. The only really awful first course I have had in recent visits is the carpaccio of tuna—a lot of thick, warm raw fish I found impossible to get down after the second bite.

Whole lobster, baked and beautifully presented on seaweed, could not be better. Frying and broiling are carefully accomplished. Fried catfish, though a bit mild in flavor, is firm and crackling crisp, and broiled salmon emerges as moist and done as it should be. Sautéed grouper milanese, in a light breading, is simple yet given interest by the fresh lemons and slivers of anchovies. The same is true of the broiled red snapper glossed with a chiffon-light tomato puree and garnished with red onion marmalade that has just enough burnishing to keep it from being cloyingly sweet. Lightly poached salmon and scallops, frothed with a gossamer cream sauce and underlined with buckwheat blini, is another ethnic variation that works beautifully.

Not all inventions do as well, with overcomplication being the reason. Examples are the buckwheat pasta, pizzoccheri, tossed with salmon, scallops, squash and root vegetables; a timbale of salmon trout with eggplant, basil and garlic; and a shellfish salad combining rosemary dressing, a gratin of root vegetables and, of all things, gravlax. One suspects the problem lies with a menu writer who loves food words, forgetting that someone has to eat those words in a single mouthful.

Coleslaw is crunchy and refreshing, and potatoes and vegetables are freshly, firmly cooked. Too bad they are unsalted, a common failing in seafood restaurants these days, probably because so many customers are health- and sodium-conscious. Many, that is, but not all. Why not offer a choice? Another flaw on the coldest days is a chill in the dining room, which in turn chills the food.

Tempting homemade desserts remain a Pesca feature and also are now better than ever, whether it is the astringent lemon tart, the creamy, deep chocolate-walnut pie or the thin, moist nut and chocolate torte. Whipped cream accompanies these desserts as it does the homespun apple crisp. Lighter desserts include good sherbets, ice cream and fruit. Strawberries, however, are often unripe and hollow.

There is a thoughtful wine list of moderately priced domestic, French and Italian choices, all at reasonable prices and with several half bottles available. Whites predominate, but there are also five good reds.

The dining-room staff adds to the pleasure of Pesca and could not be more polite, interested and helpful. Too bad they are sometimes undercut by a kitchen that slows between appetizers and main courses.

Spanish

THE BALLROOM

253 West 28th Street, between Seventh and Eighth Avenues.
Telephone: 244-3005

Favorite meal:
    An assortment of tapas, as described below
    An assortment of desserts, as described below

OTHER FAVORITE DISHES: Boar stew with spaetzle, grilled duck with figs, grilled rack of lamb.

SETTING: Attractive modern café—dining room with beautiful bar hung with hams, sausages, cheeses, dried peppers, etc.; the renowned mural of the SoHo art set that hung in the West Broadway original is now here; noisy but convivially so.

SERVICE: Sometimes slow but polite and accommodating.

DRESS CODE: None.

SMOKING REGULATIONS: No special policy.

FACILITIES FOR PRIVATE PARTIES: Part of the restaurant can accommodate up to eighty; part of the cabaret can accommodate eighty to ninety.

HOURS: Lunch, Tuesday through Friday, noon to 3 P.M.; dinner, Tuesday through Saturday, 5 P.M. to midnight. Closed Sunday, Monday, and all major holidays but open for Thanksgiving.

RESERVATIONS: Recommended for lunch, necessary for dinner.

PRICES: Moderate to moderately expensive. Those tapas can add up.

CREDIT CARDS: AE, CB, D, MC, V.

One of my favorite dining places since it opened in its original SoHo location in 1973, the Ballroom now specializes in tapas, the progression of small dishes that in Spain are nibbled at bars as customers talk, drink and get in the mood for dinner. Prepared by Felipe Rojas-Lombardi, the Peruvian chef who has worked with James Beard and in a number of catering enterprises, the tapas here are so rich, brightly fresh and satisfying that they become dinner for most Americans into the grazing habit—eating small amounts of many dishes to make a meal. That may not be the Spanish way with tapas, but it is clearly becoming ours, even though there are main courses to be had at The Ballroom.

Those tapas are virtually the only dishes that designate this restaurant as Spanish, but they are the overwhelming feature of its format. Always a cabaret-restaurant, the Ballroom now has a separate theater for acts that range from Blossom Dearie to Larry Adler, and here too tapas can be served. The dining room has a bright, modern café aura, and if the noise and closely set chairs are not conducive to formal dining, they are much in the café spirit. The focal point of that room is the famed Marion Pinto mural of the SoHo art set, created for the original Ballroom and still as bright and stunning as ever. In fact, it casts its own spell over the room, making Larry Rivers & Company seem a living part of the scene.

The most colorful point of the room is the huge bar from a 1922 Bronx speakeasy (Bronx provincial would probably be the decorator's appellation), turned Spanish by the proliferation of air-dried hams, winged slabs of dried salt codfish, ropes of dried peppers and garlic and pale mahogany to dark, blood-red sausages, all hanging over it like an edible mobile. The tapas assortment is laid out in sections on that bar, with a whole suckling pig often part of the choice as are red beans with snails, fusilli in pesto, little white squid chubby with their filling of pork, nuts and raisins, curried scallops, a light and yet chewy potato and onion omelet (tortilla española), fresh anchovies in grape leaves, mussels vinaigrette, escabeches of various sorts, grilled eggplant slices, and more.

It is a good idea to shop this array if you plan to sit at a table, because though waiters bring many choices for perusal, they do not bring all, All, by the way, adds up to the very best tapas in this city, so much better than the tepid, greasy and tasteless repertory at El Internacional in SoHo and the bland home-economist tapas at Café San Martin, it's impossible to guess why anyone chooses either of those places over this. Among cold tapas I especially like are, in addition to those mentioned above, pepper salad with eggplant, nuggets of suckling pig with cracklings, mussel and potato salad crunchy with flecks of vegetables, escabeche of chicken, ceviche of scallops tinted with turmeric, mushrooms à la grecque, pasta with coriander sauce, white beans vinaigrette, and Serrano-style ham.

Among hot tapas, only veal on skewers is lackluster. More savory choices include crunchy fried whitebait, squid in a garlicky pepper sauce, grilled shrimp with garlic and bulgur, and fried plantains. With the tapas, one can choose from a variety of sherries or good strong Spanish wines and nibble on chewy, hard-crusted French bread.

Then comes the main-course menu, and things pale somewhat but not entirely. The choice is more Continental-new American, with the only Spanish choice being a seafood cazuela, which was greasy when I had it and included shrimp marred by the telltale trace of iodine, indicating they were past peak freshness. However, a boar stew in a slightly sharp sauce was tender and fragrant with spicing. The spaetzle with it seemed dry at first, but the dark, rich gravy they absorbed worked like magic in improving them. Grilled duck with figs that were plumped in red wine could not have been better, and a broiled rack of lamb though a little too rare was nonetheless delicious.

There is a tantalizing display of desserts, and these too can be had tapas-style, a concession to the American sweet tooth. My favorites in that assortment are the orange pound cake, the Linzer torte, with its tawny hazelnut crust, an ethereal custard with a burnt-sugar glaze, pears in red wine and the chocolate Rigo Janci torte. Cheesecake is unpleasantly gummy.

If the spirit of tapas eating is virtually lost in America, at least the pleasures are not, and The Ballroom, with its friendly service, festive white globe lamps and lively crowd, adds much to that pleasure.

EL RINCÓN DE ESPAÑA

226 Thompson Street, between Bleecker and 3rd Streets.
Telephone: 260-4950.

Favorite meal:
Grilled chorizo sausage, SHARED BY TWO
Octopus à la Carlos
Vanilla custard (natilla)
OTHER FAVORITE DISHES: Grilled shrimp with garlic (gambas à la plancha); mussels in hot red sauce (mejillones à la Carlos); all soups; any shellfish except king crab with green, garlic

or egg sauce; codfish with potatoes and onions (bacalao à la Gallega); all paellas, flan.

SETTING: Jam-packed, noisy and predictably corny Spanish decor but with a lively, friendly informality.

SERVICE: Good natured and helpful but drags between courses on busy weekend nights.

DRESS CODE: None.

SMOKING REGULATIONS: No special policy.

FACILITIES FOR PRIVATE PARTIES: None.

HOURS: Dinner, seven days, 5 to 11 P.M.

RESERVATIONS: Necessary, especially from Wednesday through Sunday.

PRICES: Inexpensive.

CREDIT CARDS: AE, CB, D, MC, V.

With such a paucity of really great Spanish food in New York, El Rincón has in recent years represented one of the better options. (Years ago—say 30 or 40—places like Jai-Alai and the old Granados in the Village and Fornos in the Theater District were nothing short of wonderful.) Although not as consistently expert as it used to be, the kitchen still turns out the most dependable version of sauced shellfish dishes, paellas and so on in town. Having learned the hard way, I never eat meat dishes here, but that leaves a number of fragrant, hot and richly flavored choices.

It is difficult to plan a meal at El Rincon because the main courses I like are more or less shellfish stews, and shellfish dishes are also the best appetizers. The only option is the oily, peppery grilled chorizo sausages, which I often have. Then too, I like the soups—the cool, crunchy gazpacho, the lentil with ham (if it is fresh) and caldo Gallego, a mix of kale, pork and potato. But soups do not work well before those sauced shellfish, so I usually try one when I am having the gently salty, antique-tasting dried salt codfish bacalao, stewed with potatoes and onions in a paprika-burnished sauce that has a mild chili sting, all garnished with a hard-boiled egg.

Mariscados—the mix of shellfish that includes mussels, clams, shrimp, scallops and sometimes lobster—can be had in big potfuls, graced with one of three delectable sauces—the parsley and garlic green sauce, the lightly garlicked, sunny egg sauce, and the frankly garlicked garlic sauce. There is also a tingling hot red sauce, superb with tender octopus simmered with herbs, spices and, of course, garlic. For zarzuela de mariscada, shellfish are bedded down on rice and topped with egg sauce, a little lighter and easier to negotiate than paella. For that Spanish classic, big pots of moist rice flecked with peppers, olives and onions are baked with seafood (paella marinera), chicken and seafood (paella Valenciana) or with lobster

291

(paella Valenciana con langosta), my favorites being the first and the third. As in all dishes, mussels here are remarkably sweet and free of that sewer taste those mollusks so often take on, shrimp never hint of iodine staleness, and lobster is tender though apparently precooked. Chicken is not always fresh, however, and is the weak point in the mix as is the occasional tendency to let the rice dry out. Not all the ingredients seem to have been cooked from scratch for each order of paella, but at least they are together long enough to trade flavors a little.

Because of the chancy chicken, I never have arroz con pollo, which eliminates all nonfish dishes. Tough, sinewy meats and careless cooking make them unpleasant. Flan is hefty and cooling and the vanilla custard, natilla with cinnamon and creme de cocoa is restoring.

Guitar music every night adds to the already intense din, but because food is less good on slow, nonguitar nights, I brave the noise.

El Rincón de España has a downtown branch on Beaver Street, which used to equal this one. No longer, as a recent meal of stale, greasy food indicated.

TIDBITS

Café San Martin, 1458 First Avenue, at 76th Street, 288-0470, has a seven-day and Sunday brunch loyal following of Spanish food lovers for reasons that generally escape me. Attractive though it is, with enameled white brick walls, hanging plants, a skylight and a sort of enclosed garden atmosphere, it is cramped, noisy and uncomfortable. I could forgive those failings if the food were spectacular, and I do occasionally for the few dishes they do well. Those are the appetizer of baby eel as fine as angel's hair pasta, sizzling in a skillet full of hot oil and garlic sauce, and the paella, which is made to order for two and contains moist, flavorful rice, good sausage, olives, peppers, onions and the classic shellfish mix of which only mussels tend to be disappointing—often gritty and half rank. Eliminate those and you have a very good paella. Whole oranges Orientale with caramelized orange peel, a nice cool though slightly spongy flan and a custardy bread pudding flavored with orange and garnished with fruit sauce are fine finishes. Now if only they would prepare better tapas, not overcook seafood and get rid of that piano...

Steak

CHRIST CELLA

160 East 46th Street, between Lexington and Third Avenues.
Telephone: 697-2479.

Favorite meal:
  Spinach and bacon salad
  Sirloin steak or sautéed calves' liver with baked potato
  Napoleon
OTHER FAVORITE DISHES: Shrimp or crabmeat cocktails without
  sauce, lamb chops, veal chop, broiled chicken, Caesar salad,
  cheesecake.
SETTING: Clean and orderly dining rooms that are character-
  less; lighting is depressing; moderately noisy.
SERVICE: Very professional and polished, if sometimes dis-
  tracted.
DRESS CODE: Jackets and ties required for men.
SMOKING REGULATIONS: No special policy.
FACILITIES FOR PRIVATE PARTIES: Three private rooms; two ac-
  commodating up to ten; one accommodating up to twenty-
  four.
HOURS: Lunch and dinner, Monday through Thursday, noon to
  10 P.M.; Friday, noon to 10:45 P.M.; dinner, Saturday, 5 to
  10:45 P.M. Closed Sunday.
RESERVATIONS: Necessary.
PRICES: Expensive. Ask prices of choices waiter describes.
CREDIT CARDS: AE, CB, D, MC, V.

In a way, I am surprised to find Christ Cella among my
favorite restaurants, and it is a delightful surprise at that. For

though I have never liked the drab and characterless setting of this traditional steak house, for years I thought the food was, as the house ads stated, "quite simply, perfect food." Then a few years ago things went awry. Steaks were so-so, fish was not always fresh and almost always overcooked, salads went limp, and the service grew perfunctory. But a few recent visits indicate that the kitchen is back in form, especially with the dishes recommended. Now if we could get rid of those packaged saltines, add some really substantive bread, teach the broiler man not to ruin fish and to scrap the bitter broiled mushrooms that top filet mignon, we would be getting somewhere.

Still, great steak is hard to find these days, and now that the sirloins here are almost as good as the Palm's, it is worth going to Christ Cella just for a change, and because you can make dinner reservations. When ordering the always fresh and bright shrimp or crabmeat cocktails, ask to have cocktail sauce on the side, if you want it at all. Warm bacon lends smoky overtones to a sprightly spinach salad. Sirloin steak, cooked exactly as ordered, is immaculately served by smoothly professional white-coated waiters, as are the sautéed calves' liver, lamb and veal chops and broiled chicken. Soft-shell crabs can be excellent when crisply fried, but they are sometimes too large and tough. Roast beef varies with the time of night, and lobsters ($39 for three pounds), though nicely cooked, are less exciting than those at the Palm. Hash brown potatoes are sometimes burned black beyond tasting, so a fresh, flaky baked potato is preferable. Cheesecake is excellent, being the same S & S brand most steak houses favor, but the creamy custard-filled napoleon is unique to these premises and so a better choice.

Waiters can be friendly and helpful, but as in other steak houses they too call off choices rapidly here, where no menu is offered. They can also be pushy and lax, so bring them up short early on. Again, because there is no menu, ask prices.

Why the management persists in keeping the light level so lugubrious is beyond me, and why the upstairs is so dreary is hard to explain. Make reservations for the downstairs whenever possible. There is a strictly observed dress code, meaning jackets and ties for men, and in a sense it reflects the slightly square tone of Christ Cella. But at times, what I feel like eating is exactly what they do well.

PALM

837 Second Avenue, between 44th and 45th Streets.
Telephone: 687-2953.

Favorite meals
> SHARED BY TWO HUNGRY EATERS
> Chopped tomato and onion salad
> Shared lobster followed by shared sirloin steak, with half
>   orders of cottage fries and onion rings
> One portion of cheesecake and two forks
> OR
> Clams Posillipo or linguine with white clam sauce
> Lamb chops with hash brown potatoes
> Shared cheesecake

OTHER FAVORITE DISHES: Minestrone when available, steak tartare, roast beef, veal chop, steak à la Stone, corned beef and cabbage, and roast beef or corned beef hash when available for lunch.

SETTING: Wildly noisy and convivial, colorful, old New York atmosphere, with celebrity cartoons on the wall and sawdust on the floor.

SERVICE: Superprofessional and adept, although the house style of brusqueness can put off the timid. If you do not want steak, chops or lobster, insist that the waiter tell you about other dishes, as no menu is offered.

DRESS CODE: None.

SMOKING REGULATIONS: No special policy.

FACILITIES FOR PRIVATE PARTIES: None.

HOURS: Lunch and dinner, Monday through Friday, noon to 11:30 P.M.; dinner, Saturday, 5 to 11:30 P.M. Closed Sunday and major holidays.

RESERVATIONS: Necessary for lunch; not accepted for dinner.

PRICES: Expensive. Ask prices of choices waiter describes.

CREDIT CARDS: AE, CB, D, MC, V.

Few restaurants in New York are as controversial as this sixty-year-old steak house begun by the newly arrived Bozzi and Ganzi families, who named it after their native Parma. It took a city licensing clerk to write down Palm, thereby giving the restaurant its unlikely tropical name. Half the people I know detest the Palm for its noise, the huge quantities of food served and eaten, and an overall style they regard as vulgar. Imagine! The other half adore it as I do, finding the noise convivial, the plain setting a signal that all is genuine, and the frankly macho esprit, well, sort of sexy. In many ways the Palm is the spiritual cousin of my world-favorite restaurant, Chez l'Ami Louis in Paris.

Not that the Palm is what it was ten years ago, which is why it gets three stars instead of four. Somehow, the cleaning of the cartoons on the wall signaled a subtle change in the consistency of the cooking, although that is probably more traceable to the management's spreading itself too thin with Palm clones across the street (Palm Too, which I advise you to forget) as well as across the country. Then too, with new beef-grading regulations, a lot of what used to be top choice is now passing for prime, so at times the extra edge of beefy flavor is lacking. And if this steak house takes itself seriously, it should offer steak on the bone and, the best cut of all, a porterhouse. Such cavils aside, I think the Palm still does what it does better than any other restaurant in town, and it is my choice for sirloin steak, for the sensational chubby and pink double-rib lamb chops with their burnishing of charred fat, and for the gigantic broiled lobsters ($44 for 4½ pounds) that are miraculously sweet and tender (only the claw meat sticks to the claw at times, from being overcooked).

Right from the start, the Palm provides a feast. The firmest, crispest kosher-style pickles and pickled green tomatoes are on the table with icy red radishes. All are fine with the rough-textured Italian bread. Waiters hurriedly call off "steaks-chops-lobsters" in hopes of pushing an order through quickly, but it is worth pressing on to learn what variety there is. That way you get a chance to start with the clams Posillipo with or without shrimp in a garlicky tomato broth, or with the linguine with red or white clam sauce. You might prefer the thick minestrone or a tomato and onion salad, which is much better chopped than sliced. Grilled veal chop, always pink and moist, is juicy and delicious as is the roast prime rib of beef, the broiled chicken and the steak tartare. At lunch on certain days there is mildly saline, tender corned beef with cabbage or crusty-outside-gently-oniony-within roast beef or corned beef hash. Hash brown potatoes are done in a firm pancake-style, and the famed cottage fries are tender but crisp and, with the greaseless, crackling onion rings, are good foils for the rich meats.

Other cooked dishes are not as good as they used to be, but steak à la Stone—sliced beef on toast given the cool, satin contrast of roasted peppers and sautéed onions—is again satisfying. Skip vegetables. The only dessert worth saving room for is the S & S cheesecake, a matchless blend of the creamy and the solid. There is a very basic Italian wine list here, but somehow Scotch, followed by beer, seems more appropriate.

PETER LUGER STEAKHOUSE

178 Broadway at Driggs Avenue, Brooklyn.
Telephone: (718)387-7400.

Favorite and only meal
  Sliced tomato and onion salad
  T-bone or porterhouse steak and baked potato.
SETTING: Basically handsome old German brauhaus tavern,
  which is raucous, unkempt and cramped.
SERVICE: Slam-bang, often contentious and wise-guy in tone
  but can be professional.
DRESS CODE: None.
SMOKING REGULATIONS: No special policy.
FACILITIES FOR PRIVATE PARTIES: Upstairs dining room accom-
  modates thirty to forty-five.
HOURS: Lunch and dinner, Monday through Friday, 11:45 A.M.
  to 10:45 P.M.; Saturday, noon to 11:15 P.M.; Sunday, 1 to
  9:45 P.M.
RESERVATIONS: Necessary for dinner and taken only for fifteen
  minutes before the hour.
PRICES: Moderately expensive.
CREDIT CARDS: None.

I have always felt that if Peter Luger were in Manhattan, no
one would go there. Somehow, its bizarre location in the disaster area known as Williamsburg gives it a sort of chic. It is
a handsome old place of course, dating back to 1876, and is
one of the city's oldest restaurants extant.

Too bad the tone is rude from the first phone call for reservations ("You gotta be here a quarter of, or else..." I was told
recently), and no one bothers to say that no credit cards are
accepted. There you are in the wilds of Brooklyn with no cash
and what do you do? After giving us a hard time, they took a
check, but who needs the punishment?

Then why is Luger's in this book of favorites? For two reasons only—the superb T-bone steaks for three and four, and
the lusty porterhouse for two. Also worth noting is the sirloin
for one, served on the bone. If anyone needs proof that bones
add flavor, it is here. So does fat, and the prime steaks have
plenty. Would that waiters pour off the greasy pan drippings,
however; such fattiness is overkill at its most cloying. Ask to
have steaks drained, and you will enjoy beef that sets a stan-

297

dard for all others, and a flavor few people under forty can remember. Nothing else on the menu lives up to the steaks— not the burned potatoes, tasteless lamb chops or overcooked spinach. Shun the metallic-tasting house steak sauce too. Tomatoes are usually good in summer as are the sweet Bermuda onions. Prices are somewhat lower than in Manhattan. Noise is rampant here, as at most steak houses, and don't attempt to go to Luger's without a car. There is a parking lot and valet of sorts who keeps an eye on things and who seems to expect to be tipped when you arrive *and* when you depart.

TIDBITS

Not all great steaks are in steak houses. Beef lovers who want to sample the full range in New York should note several other exceptional candidates. At *Sammy's Famous Roumanian Restaurant* (*see* Jewish and Kosher), broiled rib steaks and the puffy, juicy skirt steak known as Romanian tenderloin are always available. If you like the flavor of beef, pass on the garlic. At *Texarkana* (*see* American) there is a thick, luscious barbecued rib steak that looks as though a whole steer were plopped on your plate, and a more delicate and succulent barbecued beef tenderloin. Both can be had with some of the best french fries in town.

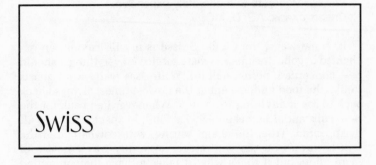

Swiss

CHALET SUISSE

6 East 48th Street, between Fifth and Madison Avenues.
Telephone: 355-0855.

Favorite meals:
Cheese and onion pie
Sautéed calves' liver with bacon
Coupe au chocolate
OR
Ramequin
Bratwurst with onion sauce, sauerkraut and rösti potatoes
Surprise Valaisanne
OR
For a one-course pre-theater meal, Fondue Neuchâteloise

OTHER FAVORITE DISHES: Herring, air-cured beef (Bündnerfleisch), air-cured ham (Bündnerschinken), cervelat salad, medallions of veal with morels, kidneys and liver, rack of lamb, Zuger Kirschtorte, chocolate fondue.

SETTING: Travel-poster Swiss chalet; you can almost hear the yodel; comfortable and cheerful.

SERVICE: There are still people who care and here they are; waitresses are polite, concerned, efficient and helpful.

DRESS CODE: Jacket required for men.

SMOKING REGULATIONS: No cigars or pipes are permitted.

FACILITIES FOR PRIVATE PARTIES: None.

HOURS: Lunch, Monday through Friday, noon to 2:30 P.M.; dinner, Monday through Friday, 5 to 9:30 P.M. Closed Saturday, Sunday, major holidays and for the month of August.

RESERVATIONS: Necessary.

299

PRICES: Moderate to moderately expensive.
CREDIT CARDS: AE, D, MC, V.

In some ways, the Chalet Suisse is my Brigadoon, an enchanted bygone dreamland where service is everything it should be—concerned, polite, helpful. Waitresses really want guests to like the food and, except at the busiest times, always check back to see if anything is needed. Whenever I go back for the rich, substantial homespun Swiss food, I expect it to have all disappeared. True, the chalet setting, with cowbells and the folk costumes on the waitresses, is cornily travel poster in inspiration, but if that's what it takes to have the committed staff, the glowingly spotless table settings and the comfortable food, I'll pass on a more stylish come-on.

For obvious reasons, fall and winter are my favorite seasons for the Chalet Suisse. Everything about the place and its food seems suited to crisp weather, Christmas, and snowfall, and it provides a glowing cheerfulness to gray midwinter days. Simple products are always perfect. The air-cured beef and ham from the Grison Alps (Bündnerfleisch and Bündnerschinken, respectively) have the right saline meatiness, the appropriate sheen and chewiness, much like good prosciutto. With sweet butter and the yeasty bread, either makes a fine first course. So does the herring, its saltiness gentled by the sour cream and onion topping. Sliced wurst (cervelat) in a pungent vinaigrette dressing is a refreshing appetizer as are the mushrooms Ascona, really à la grecque with tomato and onion.

Hot appetizers include two famous specialties of the Swiss kitchen, both based on cheese, not too surprisingly. Onion and cheese tart, a sort of quiche, is served bubbling hot, and the ramequin, a frothy cross between a soufflé and pudding, requires a twenty-minute wait—one I have never regretted. Snails and ravioli glazed with cheese are also good, if not quite up to other choices. Soups vary, from flavorful to stodgy.

Main courses range from humble offerings such as bratwurst in a golden onion sauce on sauerkraut to an elegant rack of lamb crunchy with a breadcrumb veneer. Calves' liver is remarkably fresh and is as delicious sautéed with bacon as it is combined with veal kidneys. Tender, moist veal medallions with cream and morels is a more savory choice than one of Switzerland's favorite dishes, Geschnetzeltes Kalbfleisch—slivered veal in cream sauce, a special taste and perhaps soothing when one has had a bad day. In the past daily specials such as roast pork and grilled chicken have been fine, as has poached salmon with dill sauce.

Spätzli, the flecks of pasta dumplings, and rösti, the crisp-crusted Swiss potato pancake, are the right foils for most of the dishes. Vegetables, like soups, are likely to be institutionally bland. Get your vitamins someplace else and save room here for desert. Of the two Swiss fondues—Neuchâteloise, made with cheese, and Bourguignonne, consisting of beef cooked at the table in hot oil—I much prefer the former and consider it a satisfying yet uncomplicated pretheater meal.

Chocolate is, of course, another Swiss triumph, so the excellent desserts made with it are worth trying. Fondue (melted chocolate into which fresh fruit is dipped) and the coupe au chocolat (a hot bittersweet chocolate fudge sundae of sorts) are cases in point. Layers of whipped cream, meringue and strawberries form Surprise Valaisanne, while kirsch is the operative flavor sharpening the butter cream that is layered between meringue and genoise cake in the Zuger Kirschtorte.

Beer or Dole de Sion, one of the better Swiss red wines, is the right accompaniment to the food. With fondue, a white wine is preferable. There is a complete dinner that includes appetizer, soup, main course, dessert and coffee for $30. It is an exceptional bargain. Lunch is more crowded than dinner, at which time Chalet Suisse is a real find.

Thai

The little country that we used to know as Siam has a diverting and herbaceous cuisine that combines Chinese stir-fry dishes, Indian curries of the most incendiary sort and Malaysian grilled satays and meats. More strongly flavored and less intricately wrought than similar food of Vietnam and Cambodia, Thai dishes depend on larger dosings of much the same spices those countries use. The fermented fish sauce, nam pla, adds an anchovylike flavor which, if properly cooked off, leaves no overpowering fishiness. Chili peppers, coriander, lemon grass, a mustily aromatic basil, garlic, scallions, ginger and onions, along with mint, Kaffir limes, lemon and parsley, spark the palate. There are certain standard dishes prepared in all the Thai restaurants that I favor, and it seems pointless to repeat descriptions. Among appetizers, grilled beef satays dipped in a peanut chili sauce and fried patties of minced kingfish are to be found, usually with egg rolls or spring rolls. Some cold salads also lend themselves to first courses, among them squid, beef, shrimp or sliced Chinese sausage with a vinegary tang and a topping of minced green chilies and slivers of raw onion. Soups are heady with ginger and, usually, lemon grass; among such are the shrimp or chicken in a clear broth astringent with lime, and a combined chicken and coconut cream soup, also with the Thai ginger, galanga, and chilies. Curries, red and green, range from mild to fiery if you can get the management to believe you about wanting them really hot. Chicken, beef, pork, scallops, shrimp and frogs' legs are among foods most frequently served curry-style. Steamed or fried fish, with a chili or pepper and garlic sauce, are usually on the menu as are many foods sautéed either with garlic and pepper or with basil and chili. Mee krob is a tantalizing noodle dish—very thin rice noodles fried to a glassy crispness and tossed with shrimp, bits of pork and vegetables; the result is a slightly sweet, hotly crunchy side dish that complements almost all main courses. Pad thai, fried rice stick noodles that are soft and tossed with bean sprouts, shrimp and egg, is another national dish that alternates with mee krob, as does kow pad, fried rice, Thai-style. Thai desserts tend to be cloyingly sweet, but if coconut custard, sankhaya, is offered, try it. Beer and Scotch and soda are the drinks I prefer with this food.

The conventional Thai eating implements are a fork and spoon; knives do not appear at the table nor do chopsticks, although Americans seem to think they are correct here. Thai restaurant owners wisely comply.

The traditional Thai seating arrangement is on the floor, leaning or reclining against triangular bolsters. A variation of that, in a very atmospheric setting, is at Baan Thai on Upper Broadway. Unfortunately, the staff service has been brusque and inhospitable and the food mediocre. It's a pity for it is my favorite Thai setting. Maybe I should order out food from one of the restaurants below, then eat it at Bann Thai. Like other Asian cuisines, a Thai meal is more fun when served to a large group—four to eight—so many shared dishes can be tried.

SIAM GRILL

585 Ninth Avenue, between 42nd and 43rd Streets.
Telephone: 307-1363

Favorite meals:
  SHARED BY TWO TO FOUR
  Kingfish patties (tod mun pla)
  Chinese sausage with chili and onion
  Grilled chicken gai yang
  Fried flounder with chili sauce or garlic and pepper
  Mee krob (fried crisp rice noodles)
  Fresh fruit, if any, or ice cream
  OR
  SHARED BY FOUR
  Beef satays
  Shrimp soup with lime juice (tom yam koong) and/or chicken
    soup with coconut cream (gai tom ka)
  Frogs' legs with basil and chili (gob pad bai gra prou)
  Minced pork with lime juice and peanuts (nam sod)
  Chicken or beef with Thai hot curry (gai or neau padped)
  Rice stick noodles (pad Thai)
  Fresh fruit, if any, or ice cream
  OTHER FAVORITE DISHES: Marinated baby ribs; frogs' legs with
    garlic and black pepper; steamed flounder with vegetables;

303

shrimp, squid or beef salad with onion and chilies; ba me noodles with chicken curry.

SETTING: Small, informal but attractive with Thai decorative touches; tables are close and small for four.

SERVICE: Polite, accommodating but slow at peak hours because of kitchen limitations.

DRESS CODE: None.

SMOKING REGULATIONS: No special policy.

FACILITIES FOR PRIVATE PARTIES: None.

HOURS: Lunch and dinner, Monday through Friday, 11:30 A.M. to 11:30 P.M.; dinner, Saturday and Sunday, 5 to 11:30 P.M. Closed major holidays.

RESERVATIONS: Not accepted; go early if planning a visit to theaters on West 42nd and 43rd streets.

PRICES: Inexpensive.

CREDIT CARDS: AE, CB, D, MC, V.

What first seemed to me merely a convenience in an otherwise gastronomically barren area has grown to be a favorite even without that consideration. Small, trim and pretty, with a cheerful and obliging staff, Siam Grill now turns out some of the better versions of standard Thai dishes, and does so at amazingly low prices. It has a fairly good lunch following, and early dinner is crowded with customers going to off-Broadway theaters on 42nd and 43rd Streets, in the Manhattan Plaza area.

Grilling is especially well done here, both for the tender, juicy beef satays and the barbecued chicken gai yang, which has a zesty glaze of garlic, curry spices and lemon and gets added spark from a pungent sauce. Spareribs are not usually meaty enough; marinated baby ribs, when available, are far better. Minced kingfish patties (tod mun pla) are tender and accented by vinegared cucumber slices, and the soups described above are delicate and bracing; the dry strawlike strands of lemon grass can be annoying in these Thai soups as they are meant to be avoided, not eaten. Crab soup is the only disappointment—a watery, characterless brew. Mee krob, the Thai fried rice-noodles, is not too sweet and remains crisp throughout the eating.

Fried flounder, with a thick, hot, sweet and sour chili sauce, is perhaps the most exceptional dish and one I rarely resist. For a lighter sauce, the same fish, moistly, carefully cooked, can be had with a veneer of brown garlic and black pepper, the same combination that distinguishes frogs' legs and shrimp. Minced pork brightened with lime juice and peanuts is delicious rolled in lettuce leaves and eaten out of hand. Salads of onion and green chilies with sausage, shrimp, beef or squid are equally good as shared appetizers or as a light lunch for

304

one. Curries of all meats and fish, mild-to-hot, are nicely done, if not quite up to other dishes. A slight unevenness mars the kitchen's batting average, as does a reluctance to flavor food with enough chili, even when a fervent plea is made. Noodle dishes, described above, are good, but fried rice is sometimes greasy and cold.

Siam Inn

916 Eighth Avenue, between 54th and 55th Streets.
Telephone: 489-5237.

Favorite meals:
SHARED BY TWO
Steamed mussels in white wine
Beef curry with coconut milk
Sauté chicken with basil leaves and chili
Mee krob
Coconut ice cream
OR
SHARED BY FOUR
Kingfish patties (tod man pla)
Beef or squid with cucumber, onion and chili
Shrimp soup or chicken soup with coconut milk
Bangkok duck
Whole fried fish with chili and garlic sauce (pla lad prig)
Pad Thai or white rice
Mango or coconut ice cream

OTHER FAVORITE DISHES: Seafood combination (shellfish, squid and fish in garlicky tomato sauce, steamed in foil packet); frogs' legs any-style; deep-fried whole fish with ground pork, mushrooms and ginger (pla jearn); all shrimp dishes; chicken, beef or pork with basil and chili or with garlic and pepper; poached whole fish

SETTING: Pleasant café-dining room with long, attractive bar; back of dining room is a bit roomier than the narrow front.

SERVICE: Excellent.

DRESS CODE: None.

SMOKING REGULATIONS: No special policy.

FACILITIES FOR PRIVATE PARTIES: None.

HOURS: Lunch, Monday through Friday, noon to 3 P.M.; dinner, Monday through Saturday, 5 to 11:30 P.M.; Sunday, 5 to 11 P.M.

RESERVATIONS: Recommended.
PRICES: Moderate.
CREDIT CARDS: AE, CB, D.

Every now and then I hear of a new Thai restaurant that is supposed to be sensational, and of course, I invariably go and eat for myself. So far none has matched this one for consistent excellence at dinner. Lunch, unfortunately, is far less even. The one enduring flaw is the refusal to spice food enough even when requested; at times it is impossible to tell a three-asterisk curry (the hottest) from one that has none.

Having gotten that cavil out of the way, I can be more positive. Though functionally designed with glass tops over tablecloths, this dining room is pleasantly trimmed. Tables in back have a bit more space around them than those in front but are somewhat small for four people and all the dishes they might order. What the efficient and polite staff serves forth is a palate-tingling assortment of beautifully cooked dishes, foremost among them being plump, sweet mussels, always sand-free and steamed in white wine and garlic, much like the French marinière version. I like to share that as a first course. It is a mild-flavored, aromatic opener and a good forerunner to beef curry with coconut milk, bamboo shoots and chili—marked with three asterisks and actually hot if you insist. Fork-size pieces of chicken sautéed with chili and Thai basil, which is stronger and more mentholated than our own, adds a soothing, satisfying note, as does the mee krob—crisply fried thin rice noodles.

Sharing food between four (or even six), as when eating Chinese food, is the most fun here. It allows for other excellent dishes, such as the fried minced kingfish patties dipped in vinegar sauce, the satays or a crisp cool salad of thin slices of beef or tenderized squid sprinkled with green chilies, sliced onion and slightly lemony fish sauce. Egg rolls and spring rolls are skippable, but when available, Thai steamed dumplings make good hors d'oeuvres with drinks. Soups, both the shrimp and lemon (tom yom koong) and the chicken with coconut milk (tom ka kai), are bracing introductions to heartier dishes. Bangkok duck, braised in a chili and tamarind juice curry, has mild overtones of anise, and the meat is lean, greaseless and meltingly tender. By contrast, the big crisp fried fish with a thick sauce of chili and garlic (pla lad prig) is piercingly hot. In another version the fish is sauced with ginger and mushrooms (pla jearn). Frogs' legs are a Thai specialty, and at the Siam Inn they are equally delicious whether seasoned with coconut milk and basil or with garlic sauce. One very ambitious dish that requires a very ambitious eater is the combination of crabmeat, shrimp, squid and sometimes scallops steamed with fish in an almost Provençale tomato-garlic sauce, zapped with chili and arriving at the table as bubbling hot as an active volcano. Modest appetites might better choose poached whole fish.

The food at Siam Inn has a distinctly Chinese bent, for I-know-not-what-reasons in the kitchen. Why ask when the results are so delectable and the prices are so moderate? As in other Thai restaurants, avoid dishes that include pineapple and stick to ice creams for desserts, the mango being a velvety alternative to the coconut.

The problem at lunch may be the short shrift the kitchen gives the less expensive dishes featured at that time of day.

TOONS

417 Bleecker Street, corner of Bank Street.
Telephone: 924-6420 or 243-9211.

Favorite meal:
SHARED BY TWO
Sausage salad
Frogs' legs with basil and chili pepper sauce
Whole deep-fried fish with hot chili and garlic sauce (pla muk pad tua)
Soft sautéed rice noodles with shrimp (pad Thai)
Pumpkin custard or orange crème caramel

OTHER FAVORITE DISHES: Sautéed squid with chili paste and herbs (pla muk), steamed red snapper with ginger and scallions (pla bae sa), "special honor to the king" (boneless fried chicken breasts with red curry sauce), eggplant in soybean, garlic and chili sauce (ma-kuur pad), marinated and grilled chicken (kai yung), fried rice-noodles (mee krob).

SETTING: Theatrical café setting with huge windows, flowers and candlelight; tables are cramped, and there is no provision for checking coats.

SERVICE: Helpful, well meaning and prompt.

DRESS CODE: None.

SMOKING REGULATIONS: No special policy.

FACILITIES FOR PRIVATE PARTIES: Back room accommodates up to forty.

HOURS: Dinner, Monday through Thursday, 5 to 11:30 P.M.; Friday and Saturday, 5 P.M. to midnight; Sunday, 4 to 11 P.M.

RESERVATIONS: Recommended, especially for parties larger than two and for peak dinner hours.

307

PRICES: Moderate.
CREDIT CARDS: AE, MC, V.

With its dramatic spotlighting, sprays of purple orchids, plants and decorative artifacts, Toons is as pretty as a movie set. Big windows give it a café atmosphere, spoiled only at a few tables as oncoming automobile headlights flash into the eyes of diners. It's too bad that the tables are touchingly close and that there are no provisions for checking, or at least hanging up, coats; as it is, winter outer clothing must be stuffed onto vacant chairs, adding to the crowded feeling at the height of busy dinner hours.

Earlier, or on slower nights, Toons is a delightful option for Thai food in Greenwich Village. Since it is close to my home, I go fairly often and have learned that about one-third of the menu is dependable. Even so, what is good is very, very good, hence its inclusion here.

What is not good is the appetizer assortment; fried choices are greasy, including a shrimp fritter that many regulars seem to favor. A sprightly sausage salad (more salad than sausage) is a refreshing alternative when it is on the menu as is the frogs' legs with basil and chili pepper, meant as a main course but fine shared by two as a starter.

Fish is generally well prepared at Toons, most especially the big, moistly meaty, crisp-coated fried bass or snapper that is enriched by a hefty, chili-sparked sauce. Lighter, but no less appealing, is the steamed red snapper with ginger and scallions, a dish that owes much to the Chinese kitchen. "Special honor to the king," boneless chicken fried and topped with a red curry sauce accented by cool, vinegar-marinated cucumbers, is far better than "special honor to the queen," a mishmash fish combination overcomplicated with bean curd and pineapple. (Could there be overtones of sexism in the kitchen?)

Chicken kai yung, marinated and grilled, as juicy and tender inside as the menu promises, is good as well as blissfully dietetic. (So is that steamed snapper, by the way.) Sautéed squid either with chili paste or with string beans is satiny and delicate, and sautéed eggplant with soybeans and the heady array of traditional Thai herbs is soothing. Mee krob, the crisp, fine fried rice-noodles, and pad Thai, softer fried noodles, are better than the greasy, often cold fried rice.

Desserts are unusually good for a Thai restaurant; a version of the coconut custard sankhaya is steamed in acorn squash (it is referred to as pumpkin custard) and the crème caramel has a sunny orange accent.

Tibetan

TIBETAN KITCHEN

444 Third Avenue, between 30th and 31st Streets.
Telephone: 679-6286

Favorite meals:
SHARED BY TWO
Steamed beef dumplings (momo)
Spicy mixed cabbage (tang tsel)
Chinese cabbage sautéed with chicken (patsel)
Tibetan lamb curry (shamdeh)
Rice with yogurt and raisins (deysee)
OR
SHARED BY FOUR
Mixed-vegetable dumplings (tsel momo)
Fried beef dumplings (fried momo)
Spicy mixed cabbage (tang tsel)
Sautéed sliced steak with hot Asian bread (shapta)
Sautéed noodles with vegetables (tsel gyathuk ngopa)
Tibetan chicken curry (chashah shamdeh)
Mixed fresh fruits with yogurt
OTHER FAVORITE DISHES: Sautéed noodles and vegetable with
beef, peas with beef and egg, peas sautéed with shredded
beef and egg, spicy hot potato dish. Beer and white wine
go best with this food. No liquor license, take your own.
SETTING: Simple, crowded storefront dining room with a few
Tibetan artifacts; noisy and cramped, especially when there
is a line waiting at the door.
SERVICE: Concerned, naive and polite; slow at peak hours because of kitchen limitations.

309

DRESS CODE: None.

SMOKING REGULATIONS: No special policy.

FACILITIES FOR PRIVATE PARTIES: Claustrophobic downstairs room accommodates up to twenty-five.

HOURS: Lunch, Monday through Friday, noon to 3 P.M.; dinner, Monday through Saturday, 5 to 10:30 P.M., Closed Sunday and holidays.

RESERVATIONS: Necessary for more than four people; suggested even for two (though there may be a wait anyway) on Friday and Saturday nights.

PRICE: Inexpensive.

CREDIT CARDS: None.

It is not only the pleasant and unusually diverting food that makes this inexpensive little restaurant one of my favorites. Add to that the endearing staff, as polite, gracious and genuinely concerned as can be despite a sometimes language barrier that makes explanations of the food virtually impossible. Fortunately, the small menu describes dishes in detail so no one need fly blind, gastronomically.

Professionalism is not the word to use here; this is more like a cottage-industry effort. The long, narrow storefront setting has a few decorative Tibetan motifs, and at peak hours—Friday and Saturday nights—it is cramped and noisy.

But at other times it is less hectic and, therefore, more enjoyable. Tibetan food combines elements of the Chinese kitchen (stir-fried dishes and meat or vegetable dumplings, or momo, that are steamed or fried) with Indian-style foods such as curries and filled flat breads such as the chapati-like shapta and shaphali that accompany sliced beef. A hot chili paste, sephan, lends fire to other seasonings, such as garlic, onions, coriander and soy sauce, in dips and sauces.

Among stir-fried dishes are the Chinese cabbage with chicken (patsel), a variety of noodles combined with vegetables and beef, and curries (shamdeh) of lamb or chicken.

A hot and spicy cabbage salad with carrots (tang tsel) provides coolness and crunch with either appetizers or main courses such as the gentle, chewy combination of peas sautéed with shredded beef and egg threads. Soups and vegetarian dishes tend to be uninteresting in flavor, but there is a spicy potato salad (shogog khatsa) with hot bread that is especially good as is spicy cauliflower with bean curd (Himalayan khatsa).

Deysee, a dessert described as being served at all religious ceremonies in Tibet, is indeed soul food and a lovely surprise, much like rice pudding. The firm white rice is served hot, studded with raisins and topped with cold yogurt. Mixed fresh fruits, also with yogurt, is the acceptable second choice. Thara,

310

a yogurt shake, should make you feel as though you could conquer the world. Bocha, tea that is buttered and salted, may make you feel as though you'd like to retire from it. Tibetan black tea is a far more viable alternative, as they say.

Vietnamese

SAIGON RESTAURANT

60 Mulberry Street, near Bayard Street.
Telephone: 227-8825.

Favorite meals:
SHARED BY FOUR
Barbecued shrimp on sugarcane (chao tom)
Barbecued pork ball (nem nuong)
Chicken salad (ga xe phay)
Crab cooked in beer (cua lave)
Saigon special beef (thit bo vi)
Chicken with lemon grass (ga xao xa)
Red bean ice cream (dau do nuoc dua)
OR
For a quick one-dish lunch when alone, raw and cooked
 beef noodle soup (pho tai chin)
OTHER FAVORITE DISHES: Spring roll (cha gio), steamed pork
roll (banh cuon), pork and shrimp salad (goi tom sua), Vi-
etnamese salami (cha lua gio heo), shrimp or lobster steamed
in beer or fried in salt and pepper, beef in vinegar (thit bo
nhung giam), pork chops with lemon grass (thit suon),
steamed pork with crab and egg (cha chung), curried eel
(luon xao xa), shrimp in satay sauce (tom satay), chicken
curry rice (com ga cari), steamed chicken rice (com ga tay
cam), all rice noodle soups and rice vermicelli dishes.
SETTING: Clean, bright downstairs, luncheonette.
SERVICE: Charming and helpful, if occasionally forgetful.
DRESS CODE: None.
SMOKING REGULATIONS: No special policy.

FACILITIES FOR PRIVATE PARTIES: None.

HOURS: Lunch and dinner, Monday through Thursday, 11:30 A.M. to 10:30 P.M.; Friday and Saturday, 11 A.M. to 11 P.M.; Sunday, 11 A.M. to 10:30 P.M.

RESERVATIONS: Necessary for more than five.

PRICES: Inexpensive.

CREDIT CARDS: AE, MC, V.

If I have always enjoyed jury duty, it is not only because I have been on interesting cases and feel jurors are treated with consideration and respect in New York. It is also because I can have many lunches at Saigon, a cheerful, very good and inexpensive Vietnamese restaurant in Chinatown. It is a short walk from the various courts. I simply go through the Criminal Courts Building, then cross the little park behind it, and there is the downstairs restaurant, a neat, shining sort of luncheonette with a young, polite and accommodating staff.

The food of Vietnam is beyond doubt the most beguiling in Southeast Asia. Having first tried it in 1960, both in Saigon and then in Cambodia, where there were several Vietnamese restaurants, I hoped for years that it would become available in New York. The flavor contrasts of lemon grass, garlic, coriander, chili, ginger and peanuts, combined with the textural counterpoints of the soft and silken and the crackling crisp, make it an unusually diverting cuisine. There are elements of both the Chinese and Thai kitchens, with many Malaysian accents, such as satays and the use of peanuts as a soothing base for the fiery chili oil. Paris has had excellent Vietnamese restaurants for many years—far better, in fact, than the Chinese eating places in that city—but they have been a long time coming here. In the mid-'60s there was one small outpost called Vietnam up near Columbia University, but the war put an end to it, sadly and abruptly.

Now New York has several restaurants featuring this food, and of them, Saigon is far and away the best. Why anyone would eat the tepid, bland and greasy offerings at the trendy Indochine on Lafayette Street or the even worse interpretations at Cuisine de Saigon in Greenwich Village is hard to understand. New Vietnam (11 Doyers Street) is better than the other two but runs a distinct second to Saigon, because of the lackluster performance of both kitchen and dining-room staffs.

If I am alone at Saigon for lunch, I have one of the marvelous soups adrift with rice or noodles, vegetables and beef, chicken and shrimp. The raw and cooked beef noodle soup is a particular favorite, with a steaming hot soup that slowly, gradually cooks carpaccio-thin slices of raw beef, so that they're eaten half-raw-to-rare and flavor the broth. Soft egg noodles are satisfying as are the bean sprouts meant to be added to the soup

313

as the eating progresses. The effect is sustaining and yet not deadening and, at $2.95, probably the biggest bargain in town. Despite the hot pineapple in them, which I dislike, the sweet and sour soups, most especially the shrimp, are also good, assuming you can avoid the pineapple as you go along.

Appetizers are intriguing, not only the meaty beef satays with their peanut-chili dip but also barbecued pork balls, the ground shrimp grilled on sugarcane skewers and the pungent chicken salad. Fried spring rolls tend to be greasy, but both the steamed and shredded pork roll and the shrimp and pork roll are expertly prepared. The most spectacular main course is the crab or lobster fried in beer—really steamed to a kind of eggy, puffy near-soufflé. Extracting the meat from the shell is a bit difficult, but the effort is worthwhile as the warm yeasty beer mellows the shellfish. Shrimp can also be had that way and are easier to handle, if less breathtaking to taste. Saigon special beef (thit bo vi) is fried at the table in ginger- and lemon grass-flavored oil, and thit bo nhung giam is similar, thinly sliced beef cooked at the table in vinegar-flavored beef broth. The latter method produces a lovely scallion-scented soup, which is served last. Chicken stir-fried with lemon grass is pleasant if a bit mild in flavor; it provides a soothing foil to other dishes. Hot chili in many forms is a staple of the Vietnamese kitchen, and it does well by the casseroles of eel or frog in a curry sauce, the barbecued fish and the chicken curry rice.

Pork and seafood are combined with delectable results throughout—in appetizers such as the spiced pork and shrimp crackers and the rock shrimp with pork and in main courses such as the steamed pork with crab and egg.

Desserts tend to be stickily sweet, the red bean ice cream being a notable exception. French filtre coffee is disappointingly weak; better to opt for tea. There is full bar service, and beer lends itself best to the food.

The View, the Setting and the Scene

Only occasionally is food the secondary reason for my going to a restaurant, but there are a few instances where some other aspect draws me. It might be a view I want to show out-of-town friends or to take another look at for myself, or an interior I find beautiful and uplifting, or a scene that is amusing or exciting, or a particular time of day or season that appeals to me.

Some of these restaurants have better food than others, but none are consistently good enough to attract me for that alone. That, in short, is the test that determined which restaurants go into this category, and I have developed a strategy for eating, choosing those dishes that have proved the most likely to succeed. **The ratings represent an averaging of food and setting, in this case with emphasis on the latter.**

AMERICA

9-13 East 18th Street, between Fifth Avenue and Broadway. Telephone: 505-2110.

Favorite meals:
SHARED BY FOUR
New Orleans Cajun popcorn
Buffalo chicken wings
Albuquerque blue corn tostadas with sour cream, guacamole, salmon caviar and scallions
Traditional pizza with cheese, tomato and basil
OR
New Mexican black bean cakes with sour cream, chilies and salsa, SHARED BY TWO

315

Grilled whole chicken with garlic and herbs
Brownie with vanilla ice cream
OTHER FAVORITE DISHES: None.
SETTING: More a town square than a room, with airy murals and deafening noise level.
SERVICE: Friendly and good natured but also forgetful, laid-back and mindless.
DRESS CODE: The crazier the better, but anything goes.
SMOKING REGULATIONS: No special policy.
FACILITIES FOR PRIVATE PARTIES: One large room can accommodate as many as thirty.
HOURS: Lunch and dinner, seven days, 11:30 A.M. to 1 A.M.
RESERVATIONS: Recommended, especially at peak meal hours.
PRICES: The range is enormous, from inexpensive to moderately expensive.
CREDIT CARDS: AE, CB, D, MC, V.

I never expected to love a terrible restaurant, but here I am crazy about America. The food and service are lunatic, the noise deafening, the 350 or so seats create a rush-hour crush, and the 200 plus-item menu makes me feel full just reading it. But the saving grace at America is that it is *funny*, surely meant as a parody of today's "in" restaurants, a put-on I regard as social commentary on our fevered eating scene.

It is (of course) in the trendiest new lower Fifth Avenue neighborhood, and (also of course) its sign is invisible until you are on the top step leading to the doorway. There, embedded in concrete, is the restaurant name in brass. And brass is what it took to put this together, to dare to try a 10,000-square-foot space and to offer a cookbook index of a menu that reflects every hot food trend, from the Southwest and Louisiana to New England, Buffalo and Rochester, by way of France, Italy and Japan. There are down-home culinary memorabilia such as meat loaf with onion gravy (awful), baby food such as a fluffernutter sandwich (marshmallow whip with peanut butter and disgusting), sushi, alligator sausages (dry), nuova pastas and green eggs and ham, for Dr. Seuss fans in the audience. Most of the kitchen's efforts are dismal, and the service is a perfect match. But the young staff is so good natured and unpretentious that though they approach with trays, asking not "Who gets what?" but "Does this table get this food?" I am inclined to forgive them. An order may take so long in arriving that when a waiter finally brings anything, I am tempted to take it even if I did not order it. "Let the next table worry" is the philosophy here.

There is a three-deep bar scene at night and a constant promenade of people looking for friends to join, so they can mix-match shared choices from the menu. It might be a salad, a pizza or pasta and some Cajun popcorn, the fried, breaded crawfish tails.

But the chairs are comfortable, the action is diverting, and the pastel, wide-horizon abstract murals are fresh and bright, and so I rely solely on the dishes recommended above for favorite meals. Friends from out-of-town or out-of-country get as much of a kick out of this as I do. After all, there are lots of places to get good food, but only one America. Also, prices can be low, with sandwiches and burgers (fair) at $2.95 and $5.95, or as high as $15 for grilled steak or lamb chops (just edible). Oversize bowls and coffee cups and larger-than-life portions indicate food is merely a prop in this theatrical production, but there is no minimum, so kids have a wonderful time. America is great for large groups and small children. An assortment of appetizers, as indicated, should keep you from starving.

But what do you suppose they had in mind with Salade Mimi, a combination of hearts of that dreadful iceberg lettuce and 1000 Island or Maytag blue dressing? And does Maytag imply that the dressing was made in a washing machine?

America is brought to us by the same wonderful restaurant group that gave us The Saloon and Ernie's, among others, but those places are no laughing matters. America is.

CAFÉ DES ARTISTES

1 West 67th Street, between Central Park West and Columbus Avenue.
Telephone: 877-3500.

Favorite meals:
  BRUNCH OR LUNCH
  Asparagus vinaigrette
  Grilled swordfish
  Key lime pie
  OR
  Cauliflower salad
  Boiled beef with vegetables in broth (pot au feu)
  Strawberry sherbet
  OTHER FAVORITE DISHES: Assorted pâtés and sausages (charcuterie), asparagus with hollandaise sauce, assorted cured salmons, Chef André's pâté, duck liver terrine, clams on the

317

half shell with Mexican relish, eggs Benedict with smoked salmon, mocha dacquoise, orange savarin, chocolate Ilona cake, sour cream apple walnut pie.

SETTING: One of New York's most beautiful; a romantic Continental café with flowery murals and a wonderful glow of daylight coming through plant-trimmed windows; tables are close and noise level can be a bit high.

SERVICE: Friendly, helpful and efficient.

DRESS CODE: Jackets required for men.

SMOKING REGULATIONS: No cigars or pipes are permitted.

FACILITIES FOR PRIVATE PARTIES: None.

HOURS: Lunch, Monday through Friday, noon to 3 P.M.; dinner, Monday through Saturday, 5:30 P.M. to 12:30 A.M.; Sunday, 5 to 11 P.M.; brunch, Saturday, noon to 3 P.M.; Sunday, 10 A.M. to 4 P.M.

RESERVATIONS: Necessary.

PRICES: Moderate to moderately expensive.

CREDIT CARDS: AE, CB, D, MC, V.

As romantic and sentimental as a Viennese waltz, Café des Artistes is a beautiful Continental café that I prefer for brunch or lunch. The effect of daylight (with luck, sunshine) pouring through the small windowpanes reflecting greens, pinks and reds of plants and fruits seems a continuation of the lush sylvan murals painted by Howard Chandler Christy for the café's opening in 1917.

Magnificently well maintained, this could have become a lady's restaurant were it not for the touches of dark wood, the clubby bar and the solid food served there. Through the years the kitchen's performance has been uneven, but the same sort of dishes that have always been good for brunch and lunch still are. And since that is the time of day I prefer, it raises no problems.

The buffet of appetizers and desserts in the center of the front room is a tip-off to the kitchen's strong points. There is always a nice, coarse saucisson to be had warm in a crust (en croûte) and assorted pâtés and terrines that may be ordered singly or in combination. Recently, Chef André's pâté, a meaty and subtly fat loaf, had the pleasant crunch of big, crisp dark walnut meats while a more sophisticated and elegant terrine of duck livers had a mousselike texture and rich flavor. Too bad better breads are not served with these, the pumpernickel and rye on the table looking far better than they taste. There was, however, nice hot Dijon-style mustard.

Much is made of asparagus in season, when they are listed on a separate card as in Germany. They are as good cold in vinaigrette dressing as in hollandaise sauce. The only mild disappointment was an asparagus omelet, for while the vege-

318

table was firm and verdant, the omelet was the pale, spongy kind that suggests having been cooked in a Teflon pan. I prefer the golden brown, runny and ruffled French variety or the near-crisp Italian frittata, browned on both sides. But the omelets here are an American phenomenon and, though not bad, are boring.

In the mood for an egg dish, I would rather have the poached eggs Benedict Café des Artistes, which means smoked salmon is substituted for ham. But next time I'll remember to remind the waiter about toasting both sides of the English muffin and bringing the eggs steaming hot. That lovely tarragon-flecked hollandaise and the nicely cooked eggs and asparagus deserve that extra attention.

Pastas have always seemed too rich and complex, witness such combinations as tortellini with porcini and seafood (those earthy, meaty mushrooms and sea-fresh fish are a misguided combination), or fettuccine with scallops and leeks in creamed sauce with Parmesan, again because that cheese is a mistake with seafood. A far better choice is the house pot au feu, that fragrant boiled beef, tender in its golden broth and garnished with leeks, carrots, potatoes, coarse salt and gently sharp horseradish sauce. A cut of the marrow bone is presented along with a proper marrow spoon so the soft fatty substance can be extracted gracefully, to be spread on the rounds of croutons.

That dish, by the way, is also in the dinner menu and makes Café des Artistes a convenient option for a before- or after-Lincoln Center meal. Cold raw clams topped with a spicy Mexican pepper and onion relish and cold poached salmon are dishes I have enjoyed in the past, and there are some attractive cold plates (buffet platters) I mean to try on future visits. I also mean to repeat the excellent grilled swordfish steak, one of the dewiest I have ever had.

If the dazzlement of desserts makes choosing impossible, then share with a friend the Grand Dessert, a killer of a finish unless it is divided and unless it follows a light main course. Then on future visits you will know if you want to restrict yourself to the cool, creamy and airy Key lime pie, the moist orange-accented savarin pound cake, the thick apple pie made with sour cream and walnuts, or the creamy and seductive layered chocolate Ilona cake. Mocha dacquoise with rosettes of butter cream hiding between layers of crisp meringue is also delicious and preferable to the cloying marzipan torte or a thinner, cocoa-dusted chocolate torte with a name I don't remember. Cake is not quite all, as there have always been refreshing fruit sherbets, my current favorite being the strawberry.

The bar shakes up a perfect Bloody Mary, cold but without ice if ordered that way, and with lemon juice instead of lime, all my preferences and beautifully executed.

THE FOUR SEASONS

99 East 52nd Street, between Park and Lexington Avenues.
Telephone: 754-9494.

Favorite meals:
  IN THE BAR ROOM GRILL FOR LUNCH
  Seviche of scallops
  Pappardelle with game sauce
  Fruit sherbet
  OR
  IN THE POOL ROOM FOR LUNCH
  Crabmeat gumbo or seasonal vegetable soup
  Breast of pheasant with Gorgonzola polenta
  OR
  Grilled breast of pigeon with wild rice and spinach
  Fresh or poached fruit

OTHER FAVORITE DISHES: Smoked or marinated salmon, game pâtés, calf's brains with capers, calves' liver with shallots or avocado, crisp shrimp with mustard fruits, grilled scampi, risotto with squid ink, buckwheat noodles with crabmeat, rack of lamb, côte de boeuf, chocolate velvet cake, chocolate soufflé.

SETTING: Perhaps the world's most beautiful modern restaurant, with a tailored, clublike Bar Room grill, which I like for the lunchtime scene, and the large, flowery Pool Room, which I like for the setting.

SERVICE: Excellent.

DRESS CODE: Jacket and tie required for men.

SMOKING REGULATIONS: No special policy.

FACILITIES FOR PRIVATE PARTIES: Three rooms of varying sizes that can accommodate from about twelve to one hundred twenty-five.

HOURS: Bar Room grill: Lunch, Monday through Saturday, noon to 2 P.M.; dinner, Monday through Friday, 7:30 to 11:30 P.M. Pool Room: Lunch, Monday through Friday, noon to 2:30 P.M.; dinner, Monday through Saturday, 5 to 11:30 P.M. Closed Sunday and all major holidays.

RESERVATIONS: Necessary.

PRICES: Expensive. Spa menu and pre- and post-theater dinners are moderately expensive.

CREDIT CARDS: AE, CB, D, MC, V.

When The Four Seasons opened in the summer of 1959, its interior by Philip Johnson and William Pahlmann became an instant design landmark, perhaps the first modern restaurant to be formal and substantial. Until that time it was assumed that any restaurant offering serious food at very serious prices had to be traditional. But following the lines established by Mies van der Rohe, the architect of the Seagram Building, which houses The Four Seasons, the interior designers came up with a result as distinguished as the exterior. The proof of its excellence is in the classic quality it has taken on. The Bar Room grill, with its dark "leather" and wood and the glittering brass rod sculptures by Richard Lippold that hang over bar and balcony dining area, is crisp and handsome. The Pool Room, with its white marble reflecting pool and hanging plants, presents a less tailored, more glamorous aspect, and in both rooms, swags of metal chains curtain windows.

My favorite meal at The Four Seasons is lunch, when daylight filters through those chains, making them sheer and translucent. At night when the chains become opaque, they are less magical, and their upward movement (an illusion caused by ripples of rising air currents) makes me feel as though I am going under.

What actually can go under at almost any time of day is my bank account, for this is probably New York's most exorbitantly expensive restaurant, which is why I have relegated it to this category. For as good as dishes can be here, there is simply not enough culinary consistency to justify the price. There are a few special dinners (pre- and post-theater and a diet Spa menu) that are $35 prix fixe, but that means eating lean and dull, or too early or too late.

Yet I go for other reasons. Lunch in the Bar Room grill is a special kind of delight, being a meeting place for movers and shakers in the publishing world, and I see many people I know and like and so have a good time. The lunch menu in that room is trim and easygoing with simple dishes that get diverting flourishes and that are somewhat less costly than those in the Pool Room. But sitting on comfortable banquettes or chairs and watching the action is something I enjoy now and then, especially if someone else is paying the check. When I am feeling more festive, or having lunch with someone from out of town or the suburbs (usually a woman) who prefers a little saucing of glamour, I go to the Pool Room, where roomy tables and chairs rim the watery center and everyone gets bowls of tiny, flaky croissants.

Even though I am recognized here (though rarely expected in advance), I get food that may be good, indifferent and even, at times, bad. Bad would be the rating for crab cakes I shared with a Condé Nast editor one day, when both of our palates went numb from the oversalting. And I have had meat paillards both dry and succulent and scampi grilled perfectly or dried out. What has never failed for lunch in the grill is pasta, whether the wide pappardelle with game sauce or porcini, or ravioli with shellfish, or the risotto with a dark sauce of squid ink, as dense and rich as caviar. Seviche, whether of scallops or red snapper, has a nice limy edge that is sparked with red peppers, and both game and charcoal-grilled fish dishes have been fine. This menu is cleverly devised to be entertaining but not intrusive. No dish requires tableside service to distract the big-dealers in their manipulations nor is any complicated to eat.

The Pool Room menu is far more ambitious and includes one of the house's original dishes that I love—crisp shrimp breaded and fried and garnished with the sweet-sour preserved mustard fruits of Cremona. Clams or oysters on the half shell with grated fresh horseradish and a wine-vinegar mignonette dip are sparkling and clear, and nice things happen to medallions of calf's brains dotted with sautéed capers. Smoked Scottish salmon has the right drypoint finish, and marinated salmon, gravlax, is silky and airy with dill. Chef Seppi Renggli is Swiss and so has a special talent for game, in pâtés or with main-course birds and meats. I especially like grilled pheasant or pigeon breast (the latter part of the contrived, overpriced Spa cuisine that has had so much press) with Gorgonzola-zapped polenta or wild rice. Buckwheat noodles with crabmeat and watercress is the only other really good Spa dish I tried and is worth having, diet or no. What is not worth having is trout smothered in acidic eggplant, or sea bass at roughly $33 a throw, à la carte. Rack of lamb and the ultimate beefsteak, côte de boeuf, are dinner main courses I always mean to try again, but other options interfere.

Most fruit tarts and cakes are not what they were when baked by master pastry chef Albert Kumin, but the dense, chocolaty velvet cake has held up well as have soufflés, fruit sherbets (the grapefruit is beautiful) and poached fruit compotes.

Originated by Restaurant Associates, The Four Seasons is now operated by Tom Margittai and Paul Kovi, and the difference between such personal management and an absentee restaurant corporation should be a lesson to anyone planning to go into this precarious business. They are wonderful hosts, consummate pros, and they have given the restaurant a stability it lacked before.

MAXWELL'S PLUM

1181 First Avenue, corner 64th Street.
Telephone: 628-2100.

Favorite meal:
Steamed mussels marinière
Roast free range chicken
Blueberry buckle

OTHER FAVORITE DISHES: Mozzarella with sun-dried tomatoes and olive tapenade; lentil and ham soup; angel's hair pasta with tomato, prosciutto and basil; sautéed salmon with white peppercorns; grilled calves' liver with onion marmalade; rack of lamb; ginger almond pound cake; individual bread pudding; warm chocolate cake when it's warm; chocolate walnut tart; pecan tartlet with banana ice cream.

SETTING: Think larger-than-life Gigi, Art Nouveau, gaslight era opulent, and you'll be on the right track. Some tables are cramped, all are noisy. Glassed-in sidewalk café is nice for brunch or lunch.

SERVICE: Erratic, slow and often confused. As always.

DRESS CODE: None.

SMOKING REGULATIONS: Separate smoking and nonsmoking sections.

FACILITIES FOR PRIVATE PARTIES: Can close back dining room to accommodate between fifty and one hundred or more.

HOURS: Lunch, Monday through Friday, noon to 3 P.M.; dinner, Sunday through Thursday, 5 P.M. to 12:30 A.M.; Friday and Saturday, 5 P.M. to 1:30 A.M.; brunch, Saturday, noon to 5 P.M.; Sunday, 11 A.M. to 5 P.M.

RESERVATIONS: Recommended.

PRICES: Moderate to moderately expensive. Pre-theater menu from 5:30 to 7 P.M., Monday through Friday, is $13.50.

CREDIT CARDS: AE, CB, D, MC, V.

Who would have thought that Maxwell's Plum would become a classic? The stagy decor, with its kaleidoscopic array of stained glass, real and fake brass, gaslight era touches and an infinity of glitter, reminds me of a line from the movie version of Truman Capote's *Breakfast at Tiffany's*. Speaking of Holly Golightly, the character played by Martin Balsam says to a friend, "This one's a real phony!"

Maxwell's Plum is in every way a real phony and fun be-

323

cause of that. It would be hard not to feel festive and up for almost anything in this setting created by Warner LeRoy, the owner whose Hollywood childhood is evident in this extravaganza that has been copied but never equaled. In fact, the new Maxim's in New York looks like a fake Maxwell's Plum, so solid and seriously is LeRoy's fantasy installed. There are balloons given to children of any age, big tables for large groups, as many families as swinging singles, and both a bright glassed-in café for informal eating and a huge dining room for a more luxurious feeling.

Throughout its history, Maxwell's Plum has been uneven both in service and in the performance of its kitchen, no matter who does the cooking. Perhaps the ghosts-of-chefs-past have put a whammy on the kitchen, for unevenness remains the menu theme. One night I had a dinner so good I thought perhaps this restaurant should be listed under "American." The very next night I had a dinner that was mediocre at best, and I wondered if I could even suggest a menu strategy, given the confused and drawn-out service in which a waiter offered specials only to find one was not available. There also was an agonizing lapse between courses while the staff stared off into space.

Still, some dishes prove dependable, which is good news, because I enjoy this place once in a while. Absolutely sand-free, saline mussels steamed marinière-style in white wine become even more pungent when dipped into their garlic and oil aioli sauce (called on the menu rouille but with no trace of the cayenne that makes the difference).

Free range chicken (it walks around and eats bugs and worms in addition to feed) is more tender than usual and yet has all the depth of flavor that species is prized for. Roasted with herbs, it makes a savory main course along with crisp shoestring potatoes and a shallot vinaigrette sauce. Blueberry buckle, a sort of deep-dish crumb-topped cobbler, has a nice homey sweetness.

Pizzas are disappointingly bland, but simple first courses are much better, including sun-dried tomatoes contrasted with fresh mozzarella spread with a dark and pungent olive tapenade puree, and lentil and ham soup, especially good in cold weather. Not all pastas work, but the angel's hair with tomato, prosciutto and basil does just fine. Another version called black pepper fettuccine is inadequately drained and so the sauce is more like a watery broth. (That same flaw marred a simple dish of buttered spaghetti that I ordered many years ago for a young child at Tavern on the Green. That is another LeRoy enterprise, and I wonder if perhaps he likes his pasta that way.) Though lean and meaty, spareribs are a near miss because they look as though they had been steamed.

Crunches of white peppercorns give a needly spiciness to sautéed salmon that is mellowed with a sweet red pepper puree and a white wine sauce, and thin, moist, grilled calves' liver with a satiny bittersweet onion marmalade is delicious. Rack of lamb seems to be another foolproof dish here, and I usually have it when it is a special.

Desserts have always been the house strong point. Ginger sharpens a smooth, fragrant pound cake with a creamy, vanilla flavored sauce and individual bread puddings with caramelized applesauce and a froth of crème fraîche are, like the blueberry dessert, fundamental and sustaining. There is a richly chocolated walnut tart confection and a pecan tart that gets a knob of banana ice cream, a bit small for the size of the tart, but pleasant nonetheless. One night the waiter touted the warm chocolate cake special, then brought it ice cold. But it was very good, much like a super-brownie.

Fortunately many of these dinner dishes appear also on lunch and brunch menus. What is listed on the lunch and dinner menus as "Special bread for two" at $1 is merely another way of saying cover charge. The bread is automatically placed on the table, and there is nothing very special about it, except the charge.

ROXANNE'S

158 Eighth Avenue, between 17th and 18th Streets.
Telephone: 741-2455.

Favorite meal:
   Ravioli filled with crabmeat and ricotta in court bouillon
   Rack of lamb with Moroccan spiced couscous
   Lemon curd tart with strawberries and whipped cream

OTHER FAVORITE DISHES: Pizzette, marinated chèvre salad, mixed green salad, wild mushroom sauté in croustade, assorted smoked fish, grilled salmon with mustard glaze, strudel with seafood, herbed chicken breasts. Long Island bouillabaisse, lobster salad on pasta with tomato and basil, tournedos with Margaux or zinfandel sauce, chocolate cake Rennie, cheese with fruit and walnut bread, pear in red wine with white and dark chocolate sauce.

SETTING: Small, stylish and romantic duplex café with wonderful open garden for eating in warm weather; upstairs balcony is the least comfortable area; downstairs is moderately noisy.

SERVICE: Excellent.

DRESS CODE: Says the management, "Casual chic." That translates as none.

SMOKING REGULATIONS: No special policy.

FACILITIES FOR PRIVATE PARTIES: The entire restaurant or only the lower level can accommodate between twenty and forty.

HOURS: Lunch, Monday through Friday, noon to 2:30 P.M.; dinner, Monday through Saturday, 6 to 11:30 P.M. Closed Sunday and major holidays. May close for lunch in winter, so check carefully.

RESERVATIONS: Necessary, especially before performances at the Joyce Theater, across the street.

PRICES: Moderate to moderately expensive.

CREDIT CARDS: MC, V.

As good as the nouvelle-American-Continental food can be at Roxanne's, given the frequent menu changes and, therefore, the frequent absence of dishes I like, I go when I am in the mood for a romantic setting. Also, because it is small and popular, it is difficult to get reservations for peak dinner hours, another deterrent that is my problem, not the restaurant's. But it is always a pleasure to be there, as long as I am not seated on the street-level balcony that is too cramped and noisy with the action at the small polished bar. Downstairs is preferable, with its garnet red-brick walls, the candlelight and flowers, and the big glass wall that opens onto the city's most beautiful restaurant garden. Lights twinkle through green-black foliage, high walls add a sense of privacy, and the small bar and tables make this one of New York's prettiest summer lunch and dinner opportunities, all in a smartly urbane way.

The food is light, innovative and somehow feminine. That last attribute works less well with pâtés and sausages that should be lusty but here are bland and usually too airy than with some of the more naturally delicate creations such as the sheer ravioli puffed with crabmeat and ricotta served in a clear tomato bouillon that takes on a Southeast Asian finesse with coriander and chili pepper. Pizzette, one of the earliest appetizers, is a cross between pizza and the Nice pissaladière, and has the added zest of goat cheese, one of the rare times that strong cheese works when warm. Lighter but no less delicious are the wild mushrooms sautéed and topping a croustade, mixed green salads with or without chèvre, and an assortment of smoked fish that includes a snowy mousse of smoked whitefish, crème fraîche adding a lighter note than sour cream.

Long Island bouillabaisse is a bit awkward to maneuver in its big bowl at such small tables, but it is worth the effort, combining as it does shrimp, mussels, clams, squid, salmon

326

and flounder in tomato-saffron broth that is fired with a garlicky rouille. Grilled salmon glazed with mustard is remarkably moist, and in summer there is a wonderful cold lobster salad bedded down on room-temperature pasta tossed with chopped fresh tomato and basil. Herbed chicken breast and strudel with shellfish are diverting summer lunch dishes.

Spicy cumin-mellowed couscous with rare-roasted rack of lamb is a favorite I hope will be on the menu when I go to Roxanne's and if it is not and I feel like having meat, I rely on one of the tournedos-in-red-wine variations. Whether made with a Margaux or a zinfandel, that sauce has none of the overcondensed sweetness that is a common failing (as on calves' liver or sweetbreads, for example) here. Crisp rösti potatoes and firm asparagus or green beans accompany the beef and are as carefully cooked as the meat itself.

Unless I have had a heavy main course, the dessert I prefer is the cheese with fresh fruit and walnut bread. But as alternates, I choose the properly sour and astringent lemon curd tart or the thin, light chocolate cake Rennie, more like a torte and deeply chocolated. Pear poached in red wine and set in a swirled lake of white and dark chocolate sauce is another refreshing choice after a meat or pasta. The management thoughtfully includes a couple of white and red wines in half bottles as part of a varied, fairly priced list.

THE "21" CLUB

21 West 52nd Street, between Fifth and Sixth Avenues.
Telephone: 582-7200.

Favorite meals:
Smoked salmon
The "21" burger (without sauce)
Rice pudding
OR
LATE NIGHT
Steak tartare with vodka-on-the-rocks
OTHER FAVORITE DISHES: Lump crabmeat cocktail, smoked trout, matjes herring, sunset salad, calves' liver, sautéed bay scallops, grilled paillard of chicken, rack and saddle of lamb with sauce on the side.

SETTING: Downstairs bar and grill, with toys hanging from ceiling and handsome macho action, is my favorite room; upstairs dining rooms lack character even though the west end of the room attracts celebrities; the east side is strictly bridge-and-tunnel.

SERVICE: Unparalleled if one is known; polite-to-indifferent if one is not.

DRESS CODE: Jacket and tie required for men.

SMOKING REGULATIONS: No special policy .

FACILITIES FOR PRIVATE PARTIES: Six attractive rooms that suggest a very traditional private club; can accommodate between twenty and two hundred.

HOURS: Lunch, Monday through Saturday, noon to 5 P.M.; dinner, Monday through Saturday, 5 to 10 P.M.; supper, Monday through Saturday, 10 P.M. to midnight. Closed Sunday, all major holidays and Saturday from the first weekend in May until after Labor Day.

RESERVATIONS: Necessary.

PRICES: Expensive, with a heavy 50 percent penalty for sharing dishes and a $1.50 cover charge.

CREDIT CARDS: AE, CB, D, MC, V.

This New York landmark, now almost sixty-five years old, is so much a part of the local scene that I get intermittent longings for it, although I confess those longings are in force only since I have been known there. It is hard to understand why unknowns go at all, banished as they most surely will be to the noncelebrity upstairs wing, where the service ranges from very good to very indifferent. To me, being at "21" means sitting in the downstairs bar, where the low ceiling is hung with toy symbols of the various businesses whose executives are regulars and the macho bar scene is frankly sexy. Or at least sexy to a woman brought up in the olden days and still susceptible to masculine power as an aphrodisiac. And power is the name of the game here, whether played by pols or theatrical agents and producers, by denizens of the publishing world or sports figures, department store bigwigs and Seventh Avenue big spenders, white ties and pinky rings firmly in place. The tone is Broadway in the classy, old-time sense, and I guess that is the scene I miss.

And so when my husband and I are taking a night off or feel like a festive lunch before a holiday weekend, "21" might well be our choice. The scene is what we go for despite the kitchen. This may all change, for between the writing and the publication of this book "21" will be closed for six weeks while the kitchen is redone. Menu changes, with more Italian dishes, are to be added. If the results are good, "21" may be ruined, as I have long felt that restaurants such as this thrive because their food is decent in quality but totally lackluster and will not break the tone of a business negotiation.

Products are all first-rate, and I tend to have them as un-cooked as possible. Beautiful smoked salmon, nicely sliced, and smoked trout are two such favorites as are all shellfish cocktails, but without cocktail sauce. Not even Russian dressing is a good idea as it is sweet and knocks out the saline brightness of the lump crabmeat. Not long ago, I noticed that the new menu listed the price of the famed "21" burger, a big chopped steak glossed with a misguided brown sauce, but otherwise juicy and beefy. The lunch menu listed it as $18.50 and the dinner at $21.25 (not exactly a round number that). Realizing that the printed price was an innovation on that item, I pointed it out to "21" owner-partner Sheldon Tannen, who expressed astonishment at its presence and said it would be off the next week's menu, the non-price on the burger being a house tradition.

Herring is firm, icily chilled and succulent, and sunset salad, a dish I may share as a first course, is, I suppose, a personal aberration. To make it, I suggest you start with a bacon, lettuce and tomato sandwich on toast but with Russian dressing instead of mayonnaise and hard-boiled egg layered in. Then put the whole thing in a food processor and let it rip. When finely minced, turn out on a plate and serve. "I can't believe you really ordered this," a good friend said at a recent lunch, as he proceeded to eat every last crumb. It's that kind of soothing baby taste, perfect for the toothless.

Less babyish are the pink fresh thin calves' liver served with bacon and the only really moist and flavorful chicken paillard I have ever had. Usually that meat dries in the grilling. Here woodsy herbs finish it nicely. Soft-shell crabs can be crisp and moist or completely overdone, but tiny sweet bay scallops always take on a sweet butter-nuttiness when sautéed.

Steak tartare is masterfully mixed at the table, so the captain can add what the customer wants, and for a change, ask to have it pan-broiled medium rare. Roast rack and saddle of lamb has been one of the more dependable dinner main courses, but with this, as with all other dishes, I ask for sauce on the side. A good saucier would be a welcome addition to that new kitchen.

I would love to love one of the five chicken hash variations, but all have been soupy and bland. I'll keep trying, though, in the hope that I will find what I miss from the luncheon menu of the old Ritz-Carlton Hotel.

Recent samplings of homemade napoleon and strawberry tart indicate that rice pudding is still the best dessert. It is creamy, eggy and topped with cinnamon. Baby food again, but with class. A $1.50 cover charge is one dated element on the menu, and a 50 percent additional charge for sharing a dish is punitive. C'mon fellas—at these prices do you have to be so chintzy? And that goes for the "suggested tip" slip handed to guests with their checks. The management explains that the many Europeans who come in think service is included and so unwittingly stiff the help. But other restaurants around town manage to overcome that without this inhospitable, totally bush league presentation.

WINDOWS ON THE WORLD

1 World Trade Center, 107th floor of the North Tower. Telephone: 938-1111.

Favorite meal:
    Clams or oysters on the half shell or mussel bisque
    Rack of lamb James Beard (but if it is not rare, back it goes)
    Hazelnut dacquoise

OTHER AESTHETICALLY SAFE CHOICES: Asparagus with walnut oil, seafood sausage when available, whole roast baby chicken without sauce, roast tenderloin of beef with morel sauce on the side, figs or pear in red wine with walnut ice cream, golden lemon tart, or cold amaretto soufflé when available.

SETTING: Glowing, theatrical dining room with the world's most spectacular view; two can rarely get a window table so try going with four, but some views can be glimpsed from other points in the room.

SERVICE: Friendly, well meaning but often slow and forgetful.

DRESS CODE: Jacket and tie required for men. Ridiculously, no denim is permitted. Not even if by Ralph Lauren or Karl Lagerfeld?

SMOKING REGULATIONS: No special rules.

FACILITIES FOR PRIVATE PARTIES: Sixteen handsome private rooms and four ballrooms can accommodate between six and one thousand.

HOURS: For main restaurant only: Lunch, Monday through Friday, is a private club, charging a $7.50 surcharge to each nonmember and serving from noon to 2:30 P.M.; dinner, Monday through Saturday, from 5 to 10 P.M.; grand buffet, Saturday, noon to 3 P.M.; Sunday, noon to 7 P.M.

RESERVATIONS: Necessary, but available on short notice if weather is bad; unknowns have a hard time getting 7 to 8:30 reservations for dinner.

PRICES: Moderate to moderately expensive. Prix fixe dinner is $29.95. Grand buffet is $19.95.

CREDIT CARDS: AE, CB, D, MC, V.

Take away the magnificent view of New York and the city lights, and what you're left with is a lousy restaurant, one that seems to have declined in the past two or three years. But as only God takes away the view now and then with curtains of fog, rain or snow, that generally leaves a breathtaking experience. It's one I like to introduce to young people from out of town and to foreign visitors who have not seen it before. It's also one I like to experience again and so am always tempted to go back, especially if I'm not too hungry.

Why this kitchen can't dish up more dependable offerings is beyond me. The rack of lamb James Beard served with what was a herb-scented sauté of Provençale-style tomatoes arrived on a recent visit overdone and muffled by what can only be called brown gravy. Were the meat rare and the gravy on the side, where it could be ignored, the dinner would have been much better even if the huge chunks of tomato are not in the spirit of the original presentation. Still, it was wholly edible. That much too can be said for the roasted chicken and the roast tenderloin of beef if cooked rare, if its morel sauce is on the side and if the gratin of potatoes is not gray and mushy. Not even the duck pâté at a recent dinner was acceptable, but tortellini with cream and sun-dried tomatoes almost were. The pasta appeared to have been cooked in advance and held so long that it turned stiff and dark. Better to have oysters or clams on the half shell, asparagus in a walnut oil vinaigette dressing, or the seafood sausage if it is on the menu. Creamy mussel bisque, once salted, has an enticing edge. Many of the original spectacular desserts are left off the menu from time to time, but the hazelnut dacquoise, with its alternate layers of meringue and mocha cream, and the sharp, fresh lemon tart are reliable. Poached pear or figs in red wine are nicely complemented by walnut ice cream.

There is an eat-all-you-want grand buffet on Saturday and Sunday that enables guests to enjoy the daytime view of the city. Because it is a big buffet, there are usually some more-than-merely passable choices. It seems simpler to have a drink at the bar or brunch in the Hors D'Oeuvrerie, but then you see only the Statue of Liberty or New Jersey, which is the lesser view. The restaurant affords the real dazzler, looking over Manhattan north to the Empire State Building and south to Brooklyn and Queens, all linked by necklaces of lights on bridges, rivaling the sparkle of a Van Cleef and Arpels window. The rose-gold lushness of the dining room, designed in ocean-liner tiers by Warren Platner, has held up remarkably well and is as sparkling and felicitous as ever. Too bad I can't say the same for the kitchen.

Alphabetical Index

333

R.S.V.P.

Your answers to the following questions would help make the next edition of this guide even more practical and useful. All answers and information will be appreciated and kept confidential.

Name _____

Address _____

City, State and Zip Code _____

Occupation _____ Age ____ Married ____ Single ____

1. How did you acquire this guide: Purchase ____ Gift ____

2. Are there any New York City restaurants not included in this edition that you think should be considered for the next?
    Please write name and address. _____
    _____
    _____

3. How many times a week do you eat in restaurants? ____ How many of those are for business? _____ How many for purely social occasions? _____ How many are strictly utilitarian, that is, a quick lunch on a workday? _____

4. Do you agree with the price designations (expensive, moderately high, moderate and inexpensive) in this book? _____ If not, what prices would justify those classifications? Expensive _____ Moderately high

337

_____ Moderate _____ Inexpensive _____

Do your prices include drink and tip, or food only?

_____

5. What matters most to you when dining in a restaurant?

   Food _____ Setting _____ Service _____

6. What annoys you most in a restaurant? _____

   _____

   _____

7. How do you choose a restaurant? Past experience _____

   Reviews _____ Recommendations from friends _____

   Advertisements _____

8. What is your favorite type of food? _____

9. Do you subscribe to any restaurant newsletters? _____

   If so, which? _____

10. What features would you most like to see added to the
    next edition of this book? _____

Please feel free to make additional comments on the blank side
of this page or on a separate page.

Please send this to: Mimi Sheraton
                     P.O. Box 1396
                     Old Chelsea Station
                     New York, NY 10011

To receive a free sample issue of a New York restaurant
newsletter by Mimi Sheraton, be sure to include your
name and full address in the space provided on p. 337.
The sample issue will be completed early in 1987.